THE CANALS OF THE
WEST MIDLANDS

THE CANALS OF THE BRITISH ISLES

Edited by Charles Hadfield

Vol 1   *British Canals. An illustrated history.* By Charles Hadfield
Vol 2   *The Canals of South and South East England.* By Charles Hadfield
Vol 3   *The Canals of South West England.* By Charles Hadfield
Vol 4   *The Canals of South Wales and the Border.* By Charles Hadfield
Vol 5   *The Canals of the West Midlands.* By Charles Hadfield
Vol 6   *The Canals of the East Midlands (including part of London).* By Charles Hadfield
Vol 7   *The Canals of Eastern England.* By John Boyes and Ronald Russell
Vol 8   *The Canals of North West England Part I.* By Charles Hadfield and Gordon Biddle
Vol 9   *The Canals of North West England Part II.* By Charles Hadfield and Gordon Biddle
Vol 10 *The Canals of Yorkshire and North East England Part I.* By Charles Hadfield
Vol 11 *The Canals of Yorkshire and North East England Part II.* By Charles Hadfield
Vol 12 *The Canals of Scotland.* By Jean Lindsay
Vol 13 *The Canals of the North of Ireland.* By W. A. McCutcheon
Vol 14 *The Canals of the South of Ireland.* By V. T. H. and D. R. Delany

THE CANALS OF THE WEST MIDLANDS

by
Charles Hadfield

WITH PLATES AND MAPS

The Canals of the British Isles: Vol 5

DAVID & CHARLES
NEWTON ABBOT   LONDON   NORTH POMFRET (VT)

THIS BOOK
IS RESPECTFULLY DEDICATED
TO THE MEMORY OF
WILLIAM CUBITT
AND EDWARD LEADER WILLIAMS
ENGINEERS OF THE SEVERN NAVIGATION
AND OF
WILLIAM AND RICHARD REYNOLDS
IRONMASTERS AND CANAL BUILDERS

British Library Cataloguing in Publication Data
Hadfield, Charles
　　The canals of the West Midlands.——3rd ed.
　　——(The Canals of the British Isles; v. 5)
　　1. Canals——England——Midlands——History
　　I. Title　　II. Series
　　386'.48'09424　　HE436.Z4M5
　　ISBN 0-7153-8644-1

© Charles Hadfield 1966, 1969, 1985

First published 1966
Second edition 1969
Second impression of second edition 1977
Third edition 1985

All rights reserved. No part of this
publication may be reproduced, stored in
a retrieval system, or transmitted, in
any form or by any means, electronic,
mechanical, photocopying, recording or
otherwise, without the prior permission
of David & Charles (Publishers) Limited

Printed in Great Britain
by Redwood Burn Limited, Trowbridge, Wiltshire
for David & Charles (Publishers) Limited
Brunel House　Newton Abbot　Devon

Published in the United States of America
by David & Charles Inc
North Pomfret　Vermont 04053　USA

CONTENTS

Preface to the Third Edition   7

PART ONE—TO 1790

Chapter		Page
I	Three Rivers	15
II	The Grand Trunk	29
III	The Line to Bristol	49
IV	Beginnings round Birmingham	63

PART TWO—1790–1845

V	The Birmingham Canals	83
VI	The Black Country Canals	100
VII	The River Severn	115
VIII	The Tributaries of the Severn	128
IX	The Canals of East Shropshire	150
X	The Ellesmere and its Connections	166
XI	The Grand Trunk and the Macclesfield	197

PART THREE—1845–1947

XII	The Grand Trunk Continues	217
XIII	The Shropshire Union	231
XIV	Birmingham and Stourbridge	252
XV	The Lines to the South	269
	Conclusion	291
	Author's Notes and Acknowledgements	295
	Notes	297

APPENDICES

Chapter		Page
I	Summary of Facts about the Canals and Navigations of the West Midlands	314
II	Principal Engineering Works	333
	Index	337

PREFACE TO THE THIRD EDITION

Demand suggests that this old favourite of mine be put back in print. With its companion, *The Canals of the East Midlands*, it gives an historical account of the navigations between and near the Thames and the Trent. On the west, however, this book excludes the River Weaver as linked more intimately with the Mersey than with the Trent & Mersey Canal.

The Midlands saw the rise and fall of a busy and extensive commercial canal system. I found it impossible satisfactorily to arrange the text so that the reader could simultaneously read the complete history of a waterway in one place, and understand how that history was being affected by what was happening elsewhere. I therefore compromised by dividing it into three parts, the first telling of the building of the earlier canals, the success of which led men greatly to expand the system; the second of the period when waterways flourished; and the third of competition with railways and, later, road transport, and of their decline. He who wishes to read the story of a single canal straight through can do so by using the page references given in the text, or the bold figures of the index.

I have amended a few misprints and errors. Otherwise the text wears reasonably well, though in some respects it has been supplemented by such books as S. R. Broadbridge's *The Birmingham Canal Navigations, 1768–1846*, Jean Lindsay's *The Trent & Mersey Canal*, and for the Lower and unrestored Upper Avon, my own and John Norris's *Waterways to Stratford*. *William Jessop, Engineer*, by myself and Professor A. W. Skempton, gives a good deal of new information about the early history of the Ellesmere Canal, including the genesis and construction of Pontcysyllte aqueduct. As well, several excellent books of early canal photographs have now been published.

There is very little in the text about the years since nationalisation in 1948. I hope that these pages of preface will give a little of the feel of the near-forty exciting years between. A fuller general account will be found in the last chapter of my *British Canals*,

7th edition, 1984.

I have told of the past commercial importance of the Severn and the Gloucester & Sharpness Canal. From the 1960s, however, demand continued to fall, and in 1969 the BWB relinquished their Bristol Channel carrying fleet. The G & S, however, was enabled to take 1,000-ton tankers, and new business was sought not in obsolete Gloucester docks, but below on the canal at Monk Meadow. Meanwhile, Sharpness modernised its facilities to become the busy port it now is.

It has been becoming clear that canal and river dimensions are too small for modern needs so, in 1983, BWB approved the Severn Corridor concept as a basis for discussion with the many interests involved. The concept envisages the G & S's enlargement to take 2,500dwt craft and, by way of a new lock at Gloucester, that of the Severn for 1,500dwt craft to Worcester. Dimensions would enable modern low-profile coasters, container-carrying barges, and the largest ship-carried barges to use the route. As I write, preliminary discussions are going on.

Within the West Midlands the waterways scene has been transformed. Before 1963, the future of many of the navigations described in this book was seriously in doubt, except for a few like the Llangollen line, formally abandoned but far too useful as a navigable water channel to be lost, or the Lower Avon, reborn under its Trust. In that year the British Waterways Board took over from the former British Transport Commission. No longer were the smaller waterways tied to a transport purpose, or financed with transport money. Instead, a specialist Board was now empowered to develop pleasure cruising; in other words, deliberately to give a very old transport system a second creative life as a major national amenity. No longer, too, were commercial waterways to be part of a formally integrated transport organisation, but would henceforth be managed and developed single-mindedly.

Five years later the Transport Act of 1968 listed commercial waterways, cruiseways to be maintained for pleasure use, and remainder waterways to be kept as they were until their future became clearer. In our area the Severn from Gloucester to Stourport was named a commercial line, and as cruiseways the Trent & Mersey main line and Hall Green branch; Macclesfield; Shropshire Union from Ellesmere Port to Autherley, with its Dee, Llangollen and Middlewich branches; Staffs & Worcs; Stourbridge thence to Black Delph; the Birmingham Canal Navigations main line from Farmer's Bridge or Worcester Bar to the S & W, along with the branch through Netherton tunnel to Black Delph; the Birmingham & Fazeley; and the Worcester & Birmingham.

Thirteen years before the Act, in April 1955, our family took out *Venturer* from the Wyatts' yard at Stone on the Trent & Mersey for a fortnight. My wife keeping a diary, we climbed to Etruria top lock (covered then), and passed on our left Josiah Wedgwood's original Etruria pottery building, an old canal branch, disused through subsidence, behind it. Through Harecastle tunnel with its broken towpath and subsidence-sunken roof, and up the Macclesfield to Marple. Back again to Kidsgrove, and down the Cheshire locks to the Middlewich branch. Along it to Barbridge, and left on to the Shropshire Union—Barbridge then still had its warehouse roof spanning the canal. On to the S & W and up the Wolverhampton flight, factory workers leaning out of windows to cheer us on. Along the BCN main line to the Newhall branch, where we moored for the night by the Dirt Boat and listened to rats running over the cabin—the Long Boat pub now stands thereabouts. Down Farmer's Bridge locks, and back to Stone by way of Fazeley and Fradley; 189 miles in all.

We met quite a number of narrow boats, many worked by British Transport Waterways (ie the Transport Commission), including one in Coseley tunnel when we were on the wrong side (I had forgotten that it then had its own rule of keeping to the left, and learned some new words in consequence). There was a fair amount of Potteries traffic, but only round Wolverhampton power station were craft queueing to unload. Beyond, I had difficulty in passing a tug towing four coal boats on long lines.

The past predominated. Sunken boats at wharves, and a faded notice: 'Good Accommodation Moderate for Boat Horses Straw Provided'; the beautifully painted and kept craft of 'John Walley, Flint Merchant', who was bow-hauling his butty *Margaret* into a narrow lock, but also two boats crewed, the diary says, by 'man and wife, grandmother, three kids and dog, all dirty beyond all ordinary dirtiness'.

Pubs had lost their old trade but not their old feel. My wife noted of the Blue Bell at Kidsgrove: 'Snug; big fires; piano; white haired highly scrubbed pair kept it; put us in a polished room and opened piano and invited me rather insistently to play'. And of the tavern at Goldstone wharf: 'Completely primitive except for looped flexes of electric light. Door opened into back of settle in tiny dark room with wooden benches, panelling, tables, beams and brick floor'.

The then-shadowy future was represented by two or three small pleasure boatyards. In our fortnight we encountered about eight cruisers, two only in the whole distance from Kidsgrove to Curdworth on the Birmingham & Fazeley. It was a time when people stopped work to watch and wave at us going by, and children yelled, 'Give us a ride, guv'nor, go on, do!'

In 1955 the canals were waiting, their ancient traffics, some nearly two centuries old like that of clay to the Potteries disappearing, the new hardly yet noticeable. Meanwhile, their future was being debated. The Rusholme Board of Survey had just reported; the Bowes Committee was soon to begin sittings. That was only thirty years ago.

'But 'tis the talent of our English nation,
Still to be plotting some new reformation.'
And so we did. To find it out, the reader needs no words of mine. He has only to take out a cruiser and repeat our voyage.

Without the Transport Act, 1968, I should probably be recording here the closure of several West Midland canals, for the system's very age has meant that many of its structures have needed major repairs. The old canal companies could not have afforded them, the British Transport Commission would have given preference to commercial waterways. As it is, government grants to the British Waterways Board have enabled such major tunnels as Harecastle, Wast (West) Hill, Netherton, Saltersford and Preston Brook, and aqueducts as Pontcysyllte and Alvechurch, all on cruiseways, to be made safe and re-opened. New tunnels have been built on the Birmingham Canal Navigations Main Line near Galton bridge, and its companion higher up on the 473ft contour, and a new one is planned into the limestone cavern under Dudley as part of the Black Country Museum project.

Long before the 1968 Act the waterway restoration movement had been initiated, when the Lower Avon Navigation Trust was set up in 1950 to acquire the navigation from the old company and restore it by raising money from a steadily widening membership, seeking help from the skills of the Royal Engineers, the co-operation of the River Board, and the assistance of volunteers.

This, like the later restoration of the Stratford-upon-Avon Canal, outside our area, was an unofficial effort. The British Waterways Board's establishment at the beginning of 1963 soon led to restoration work done jointly by the Board and local canal societies or groups. The pioneer scheme was carried out by the Board and the Staffordshire & Worcestershire Canal Society to restore the sixteen locks at Wordsley, and so re-connect the Stourbridge Canal leading off the S & W with the Dudley No 1 line of the BCN. Soon afterwards talks began between the Board and what was then called the Caldon Canal Committee, with the aim of restoration from the Trent & Mersey at Etruria through to Froghall. The whole canal, much of it through lovely cruising scenery, was reopened in 1974; since then, along with the remaining portion of the Leek arm, it has become a cruiseway. A third reopening, initiated later but completed in 1973, put Parkhead locks back into use, and so re-joined the Dudley No 1 line to the BCN by way of Dudley tunnel. A fourth, this time carried out by a trust on non-BWB water, was that of the Upper Avon in 1974, which re-connected that river to the Stratford-upon-Avon Canal. The Droitwich Canal restoration is now making solid progress while the Upper Severn scheme is under brisk discussion.

The re-opening of the line that runs from the Llangollen Canal at Frankton by way of Llanymynech to Welshpool and on to Newtown is a much bigger project. It seemed impossible, but when local authorities and other bodies such as the Prince of Wales Committee and the Welsh Development Agency joined in, hope arose. A start was made in the 1970s on two sections, one between Arddleen and Welshpool, the other through Welshpool itself, and also upon Frankton locks. Then in 1983 a consultants' report recommended the restoration of the whole 33-mile line through to Newtown, along with the Guilsfield branch. As a remainder waterway, outside finance is necessary. Meanwhile, volunteer work takes place at Frankton and Carreghofa, and an engineering study is being made of the difficult four miles between Frankton and Queen's Head.

The great increase in public enjoyment and awareness of canals has thrown up a difficulty and offered a valuable new development. The very first restoration, the Lower Avon, exhibited the problem one faces when converting an old commercial to a modern cruising waterway—the inevitable destruction of much that was interestingly historical. The two old watergates at Pershore and Cropthorne had to go. Sometimes, as with a canalside building, one can compromise by finding a new use for it; sometimes old work can be embodied in new; occasionally a replica, or something in a similar style, can be provided. But often one cannot compromise. In the end life is to be chosen rather than death; a well-used and efficient cruising waterway is preferable to venerable but impracticable structures.

The growth of waterway museums has been a compromise solution that has gained extraordinary support. For in them boats especially, but also buildings, artifacts, tools and methods of working can not only be seen as once they were, but then explained.

Outstanding within the scope of this book is the North Western Museum of Inland Navigation, usually called the Ellesmere Port Boat Museum. It was started in 1970 by five enthusiasts, soon settled down at the junction of the Ellesmere Canal with the Manchester Ship Canal, and opened in 1976. Then it had nine boats, now it has sixty. Round these, restored buildings house exhibitions and displays, craft workshops, steam engines (those of the former hydraulic power system), archives, teaching rooms and equipment, plus refreshments for the near 100,000 visitors each year.

Two among several other museums must be noted specially: the canal section of the Black Country Museum at the end of Dudley tunnel nearest Tipton, with its BCN day-boats and reconstructed working boatyard, and the Ironbridge Gorge Museum Trust. The latter has restored the Hay inclined plane with its 207ft vertical rise as it was in the twenty years before disuse in 1894, and at its head a short length of tub-boat canal complete with boat.

One can also study history enjoyably by walking canal lines, whether open or long disused. Ronald Russell's *Walking Canals* offers West Midlands towpath walks in the Potteries and along the Staffs & Worcs, while the contents page alone of his *Lost Canals and Waterways of Britain* raises real nostalgia in me—the days I spent with the late W. Howard Williams exploring the inclined planes and works of the Shropshire and the Donnington Wood; those in which my wife and I traced the Newcastle-under-Lyme Canal from the Trent & Mersey to the Boat and Horses in Newcastle, then past an inclined plane that was never built to the Junction Canal right through Newcastle to Gresley's, and so to Apedale colliery, or that other time when I first discovered the level crossing over the Churnet on the old Uttoxeter branch.

We who love waterways have a world of interest and enjoyment open to us in what our predecessors did. In turn we have to ensure that we do better than they, so that our children will in their time come to study our achievements—and find them both good and enjoyable.

CHARLES HADFIELD

PART ONE—TO 1790

CHAPTER I

Three Rivers

About February 1765 we may imagine a meeting between Doctor Erasmus Darwin[1] of Lichfield, physician, scientist and poet, then a man of thirty-three, and Josiah Wedgwood,[2] potter of Burslem, then thirty-four, and for the last six years the master of his own business. Wedgwood probably talked on his favourite subject of the transport difficulties of himself and his fellow-potters. The growing industry round Burslem and Stoke-on-Trent obtained its china and stone clay from Cornwall, Devon and Dorset, by coasting vessels to Chester on the Dee, or to the Mersey where, together with the salt used for glazing, they were transhipped to flats to be taken up the Weaver to Winsford and thence by packhorses and waggons, which then took back pots for Liverpool. From Willington on the Trent (Burton) Navigation flint-stones brought from the south coast round to Hull and Gainsborough were carried by road to the Potteries, wares being taken back to be shipped for London and export. Pots also went to Bewdley and Bridgnorth by packhorse and waggon to be sent down the Severn to Bristol, the same transport returning with white clay, groceries and iron.[3]

Neither the Trent, the Severn or the Weaver were first-class navigations, but to one struggling to expand his already considerable business,[4] they were better than land carriage.

The Trent

The Trent was a natural river, with no navigation authority or works below Wilden Ferry.* It carried coal from the Derbyshire and Nottinghamshire mines, iron products from south Staffordshire, lead from Derbyshire, cheese from Cheshire, timber and

---

* Where Cavendish Bridge at Shardlow now stands, rather over one mile east of the present end of the Trent & Mersey Canal at Derwent Mouth.

pottery. Some was for local use, some for transhipment at Gainsborough into coastal craft, the barges then loading corn or merchandise for upriver. From Gainsborough vessels traded to Hull, London, places on the Aire & Calder, and ports on the east and south coasts.

Some of the craft working upwards from Gainsborough could carry 40-50 tons, but whether they did so depended upon the amount of water in the river; often they were limited to as little as 10 tons. In 1761 John Smeaton had said: 'the present navigation is much obstructed by shoals and scours, insomuch that in several places, in the common state of the river in dry seasons, there is not above 8 inches depth of water, and that at such times, without the aid of flashes[5] from King's Mills upon the Trent, and the lowest mills upon the Derwent, the navigation would then be impracticable'.[6] There was no horse towing path, and though horse towing had been tried, it had caused so much trouble with landowners that boats were now dragged by men when they could not be sailed, sometimes with 10 men to drag 10 tons. The river had three navigable branches: the Derwent to Derby, the Idle to Bawtry, and the Fossdyke to Lincoln and by the Witham to Boston and the sea.

Above Wilden Ferry the Trent had been made navigable to Fleetstones Bridge, Burton, under an Act of 1699,[7] the main promoter being William, Lord Paget, a local coal and landowner, who had obtained it against Nottingham opposition. This enabled Commissioners to make the river navigable and to take 3d a ton toll, and also forbade the building of any wharf or warehouse between Nottingham Bridge and Burton without Lord Paget's consent.

Apart from £600 that could be assessed on the inhabitants of Burton, Lord Paget seems to have found the money to build locks at King's Mills and Burton Mills and the necessary cuts and basin. He then leased the navigation and Burton wharf to a man called Hayne, whose partner, Leonard Fosbrooke, held the ferry at Wilden and leased the wharf and warehouses there. These two, holding the navigation's only wharves, refused to allow goods to be landed except from their boats, and therefore got monopoly freight rates. About 1748 some Nottingham merchants tried to evade Hayne and Fosbrooke by landing goods on the banks where their boats could be met with carts, whereupon Fosbrooke first blocked the river at Wilden with his ferry rope, and then made a bridge of boats and hired men to defend it, while Hayne in 1749 sank a barge in King's Mills lock that forced transhipment round it for eight years. Chancery granted an injunction to open the river, but the two men took no notice, though a bill they introduced to legalize their operations failed to pass.⁸

The lease ran out in 1762, and the Earl of Uxbridge* then renewed it to a new concern, the Burton Boat Company, one of the partners in which was Sampson Lloyd II of Birmingham, who also owned a forge and mills below the warehouses at Burton.⁹ But the river's reputation lingered: in early 1766 the Staffordshire merchants were to say that they had

'suffered greatly in their Trade, for many Years, by the Badness of the Navigation ... from Burton ... to Wilden Ferry ... and that the said Navigation is greatly obstructed by Floods in Winter, and by the Shallows in Summer, so as to render the Carriage of Goods upon it uncertain and precarious ... also a Monopoly in the Hands of a few Persons, who have greatly injured Trade by their Carelessness, and oppressed it by their Exactions'.¹⁰

(*To continue the history of the Trent, see Ch. II of 'The Canals of the East Midlands'.*)

The Severn

By the time of our imaginary conversation, the Severn was a well-used and natural river navigation which extended to Shrewsbury and, in times of flood, to Welshpool. Below Gloucester the navigation was estuarial: thence to Tewkesbury and Upton boats were helped by the fortnightly spring tides. Its biggest traffic was the soft clod coal, of which in 1752 about 100,000 tons had been carried from the collieries round Madeley and Broseley to the saltworks at Droitwich and for household use at Shrewsbury, Bridgnorth, Worcester, Tewkesbury (and up the Avon, navigable to Stratford), Gloucester, Bristol and elsewhere.¹¹ In the early eighteenth century the upwards iron trade had been added, pig-iron being carried from the furnaces of the Forest of Dean to the forges of Shropshire, Worcester, Warwick, Stafford and Chester till shortage of fuel and ore caused this trade to be replaced as the century advanced by the import of Swedish, American and other overseas ores unloaded at Bristol and brought to Bridgnorth or Wribbenhall near Bewdley to be carried thence by land. In return,

* Lord Paget who obtained the 1699 Act died in 1713. His heir was created Earl of Uxbridge in 1714.

B

'from Manchester, Stourbridge, Dudley, and the iron works of the Stour, innumerable pack horses come laden with the manufactures of those places to be put on board the barges . . . at a spring tide I have been told 400 pack horses have been for several nights together quartered in this neighbourhood, and in consequence Bewdley was a rich and very trading town'.[12] As the century moved on, however, the centre of the iron trade shifted towards Birmingham and the importance of Bewdley declined.[13] The river also carried salt sent by land to Worcester from the brine springs of Droitwich and then shipped to Gloucester and Bristol, corn from Tewkesbury and the vale of Evesham, cheese from Cheshire and Warwickshire, fruit, cloth and wool from the Midlands.[14] The main market and export point for this produce was Bristol, whence came in return Bristol's own products and those imported from abroad. As an example of a perhaps exceptional movement of this period, we may take the goods that left Birmingham by road waggon at 6 p.m. on 8 May 1762 and arrived by trow at Bristol at 8 p.m. on 11 May, transhipment having taken place at Bewdley.[15]

The bigger trading craft were either barges or trows. The former were from 20 to 50 tons burthen, and mainly worked above Gloucester in the coal trade. What they could actually carry much depended on the current and the depth of water available. Trows were larger, carrying from 40 to 80 tons or more, and mainly working downstream from Upton or Gloucester to Bristol, transhipment taking place there if necessary. A writer in the *Gentlemen's Magazine* for 1756 took a census of the craft on the river. Out of 376, 304 were owned at places from Bewdley upwards, of which 47 were at Bewdley, 75 at Bridgnorth, 87 at Broseley and 39 at Madeley. When possible the river boats were sailed, but sometimes they had to be towed by gangs of six, eight or more men, and a rough towing path therefore existed. The first effort to substitute horse towing, and to provide a better path for horses than that which men had been accustomed to use, was made in the autumn of 1761, when meetings of merchants were held,[16] and there was talk of a bill. (*To continue the history of the Severn, turn to p. 53*.)

The Weaver

The making navigable of the Weaver from Frodsham Bridge near its junction with the Mersey to Winsford, and of its tributary the Witton Brook to Witton bridge, by undertakers, had been authorized in 1721.[17] Work did not start till 1730, and the navigation was opened at the beginning of 1732, by which time eleven mainly wooden locks had been built, and a towing path for haulage by men.[18] The minimum depth was 4 ft. The river carried a considerable trade, mainly in coal and salt, but the undertakers did not maintain it properly, and complaints increased, especially from the merchants of Liverpool. In 1758, therefore, the Commissioners appointed under the original Act bought out the undertakers for £17,000. They made some improvements, and in 1760, after a great struggle with the Liverpool merchants, obtained an amending Act.[19] This set up a new body of 105 trustees, who replaced the former Commissioners and undertakers. They were to build larger brick locks, on the pattern of one already constructed at Pickerings by Henry Berry, and to get a depth of 4½ ft. By the time of our conversation two new locks had been built at Northwich and Saltersford, other repairs had been made, and the making navigable of the Witton Brook was actually in progress. For the year to 5 April 1763 the river had carried 76,952 tons, mostly coal and salt.[20]

Erasmus Darwin, having listened to Wedgwood's complaints, may then have reminded him that in 1758[21] James Brindley had at the instance of Earl Gower, Lord Anson and Thomas Broade surveyed a line from Stoke-on-Trent to Wilden Ferry and proposed a canal 'with Locks to pound the water and make it dead as in Holland',[22] and in the same year Henry Bradford had proposed to make the rivers Trent and Tame navigable to Tamworth; and that John Smeaton, reviewing Brindley's proposals in 1761, had suggested that they might be extended 'to join the navigable river* that falls into the west sea',[23] the possibility of which Brindley himself had seen.

Finally, Darwin might have added, that same Brindley, then comparatively unknown, with John Gilbert had by 1761 built the Duke of Bridgewater's Canal from his mines at Worsley to Stretford. While they were talking, he was finishing the extensive engineering works of the canal's Castlefield terminal at Manchester,[24] and building the Duke's extension from Stretford to the banks of the Mersey at the Hempstones, which had been authorized in 1762, and which was reaching beyond Sale Moor towards Altrincham.[25] He was therefore the obvious man to consult.

I have assumed that Erasmus Darwin fired Wedgwood's imagi-

* He probably meant the Weaver.

nation, for soon afterwards Wedgwood wrote to him as 'you, who have public spirit enough to be Generalissimo in this affair' and 'we shall be governed by your advice'.[26] It was not long, however, before Wedgwood's drive and organizing ability had left Darwin as 'our ingenious and poetical friend'.[27] Darwin may not have heard of Smeaton's rider of 1761, for it was Brindley's original idea to which Josiah referred when he next wrote: 'On Friday last I dined with Mr. Brindley the Duke of Bridgewater's engineer, after which we had a meeting at the Leopard on the subject of a Navigation from Hull, or Wilden Ferry, to Burslem agreeable to a survey plan before taken. Our Gent^n seem very warm in seting this matter on foot again, and I could scarcely withstand the pressing solicitations I had from all present, to undertake a journey or two for that purpose; we are to have another meeting at Hanley tomorrow.'[28]

Fourteen months of organization followed. Wedgwood's main ally was Thomas Bentley, a cultivated and influential merchant friend at Liverpool who was probably instrumental in making him a scientific potter.[29] Interests there were sounded; the Mayor of Newcastle-under-Lyme agreed to call a corporation meeting to petition Lord Gower (the Duke of Bridgewater's brother-in-law) to become the patron of the scheme, and Darwin used his contacts in Birmingham. Two of these were John Taylor and Samuel Garbett. Taylor had in this same year of 1765 joined Sampson Lloyd II in the partnership that was to become Lloyds Bank,[30] and because Lloyd was one of the proprietors of the Burton Boat Company, lessees of the Trent (Burton) Navigation, which would be injured by the new canal, Wedgwood proposed to carry it to Wilden Ferry just outside that concern's navigation rights, 'in order to keep clear of their Locks and Shallows'.[31] Samuel Garbett was a wealthy Birmingham manufacturer, an old friend of Matthew Boulton (later to be a promoter of the Birmingham Canal), a partner with John Roebuck in a sulphuric acid works in Scotland and soon to be one of the founders of Carron Company.[32] In two months the scheme was clear in outline: a 3 ft deep canal (2 ft 6 in. at the fords) 15 ft wide at bottom with narrow locks to run for 76 miles from Wilden to the River Weaver at Frodsham bridge, just below the jurisdiction of the Weaver trustees, with a branch 28 miles long to Lichfield, Tamworth and Birmingham, and another 3 miles long from Stoke to Newcastle. The tunnel at Harecastle was to be 'above a mile' long, its purpose being to save lockage and provide canal water from the mines there. The canal and vessels were to be constructed on the plan found most eligible from various experiments made on the Duke of Bridgewater's navigation by 'his excellent engineer, Mr. Brindley', who had estimated the eastern section at £700 a mile, the western at £1,000 a mile, and the tunnel at £10,000 exclusive of the cost of the Act. The craft were to measure 70 ft by 6 ft, draw 2 ft 6 in. and carry 15–20 tons. These dimensions were probably derived from the mines craft used at Worsley, for Wedgwood goes on: 'a Cut and Vessels on the above Plan have been found to be the most practicable from various Experiments on the Navigations of his Grace the Duke of Bridgewater'.[33] Except that it was subsequently widened to 6 ft 10 in. and given greater draught, we have here the narrow canal boat as it afterwards developed.

During April the plan was written down and circulated, and we now find in it[34] the suggestion that a canal could be made to the Severn, and another thence to the Thames at Lechlade. The two got busy. Darwin drafted material for the newspaper, upon which Josiah commented: 'Your scheme for instilling the knowledge of Navigation into the Public by degrees and by stealth as it were, is certainly the best that could be hit upon, for if the individuals of this Public sho^d once perceive that instruction is offered them, *without their asking for it*, they are sure to be refractory.'[35] These early examples of public relations, which first welcomed generally the idea of inland navigation, and then gave news of what was being proposed, duly appeared in *Aris's Birmingham Gazette*.[36] Wedgwood met people, held meetings and rushed about to such an extent that his brother John expostulated, and received the reply: 'I will promise you not to ride my Hobby horse out of sight of my private affairs'.[37]

Then, in mid-April, a significant meeting took place. 'We met Mr. Gilbert* in[38] our way to Trentham† & stop^t here long enough to shew him our plan and explain the scheme a little to him. He immediately ask'd if it could not join the Duke's Canal which wo' be allmost as near a way to Liverpool, & much nearer to Manchester and save our locking down into the River,‡ for which we might afford to give his G^e a small Tonnage.' He added that he would do what he could to make the scheme agreeable to the Duke, 'consistent with Public utility'.[39] At Trentham Lord Gower was favourable, and Thomas Gilbert, his agent, suggested getting

---

* John Gilbert, the Duke of Bridgewater's agent.
† The home of Lord Gower.
‡ The Weaver.

'a Pamphlet well wrote upon the subject'. Wedgwood then wrote to Bentley to ask him to 'draw his quill for the service of his Country',[40] and the result was the pamphlet, *A View of the Advantages of Inland Navigation, with a plan of a Navigable Canal intended for a Communication between the Ports of Liverpool and Hull*.

About this time a rival scheme appeared, promoted by Sir Richard Whitworth who also wrote a pamphlet. Josiah Wedgwood wrote: 'I do not know anything of the merits of the latter or its Author, but assure you he bears no great Character among the Gent^n here, but rather a laughable one.'[41] Sir Richard Whitworth of Batchacre Grange, who later became M.P. for Stafford and High Sheriff of the county, was a clever and vigorous man, who ended poor, having spent his assets on experiments and improvements to his estates.[42] His pamphlet, *The Advantages of Inland Navigation*, suggested a canal with locks 60 ft by 13 ft to take 30-ton barges drawing 3½ ft 'much after the manner and form of those made at Bridgnorth', from the Severn at Atcham below Shrewsbury to Great Bridgeford, and then past Stafford to Great Haywood and Burton or Wilden Ferry on a rather different line from that proposed by Wedgwood. From Great Bridgeford there was to be a connecting canal by Standon, Whitmore, Madeley and Nantwich to the Weaver at Winsford bridge. His Weaver–Trent line was 75¾ miles long to Wilden, estimated at £73,231,[43] and that from Atcham to Great Bridgeford 31¼ miles estimated at £26,572. There was much sense in his ideas, for his canals could have taken barges capable of navigating any of the three rivers, so making transhipment unnecessary, and he proposed also to improve the Severn between Shrewsbury and Worcester, and build horse towing paths. His scheme got some support, but against the shortness and cheapness of its lines had to be set the disadvantages of not running through the Potteries or near Birmingham, entering the Severn too high up for reliable navigation, and connecting with the Weaver.

On 2 May Josiah and Richard Wedgwood attended a Weaver trustees' meeting held to suggest that their canal should end at Frodsham bridge. As this was below their jurisdiction, the trustees tried to alter the Wedgwoods' ideas by engaging Hugh Henshall and their own engineer Robert Pownall to survey alternative lines from Winsford to Lawton near Harecastle by Middlewich or Nantwich, and from the lower Weaver below Saltersford to the nearest part of the Bridgewater Canal, and offering attractive tolls upon them.

The rest of the year was given to controversy upon whether the Trent & Mersey should be run by a trust or a company, and to a struggle between the Weaver trustees and the Duke for possession of its western end. That the canal should be 'free as a Turnpike road and conducted by commissioners chose out of the Gent^n in the country along which the canal shall be made'[44] was proposed at a meeting at Newcastle at the end of June, and for a time Wedgwood was inclined to support it. If it had come about, other canals might have followed the pattern, and our canal system would have been built by trusts equivalent to those for turnpike roads. If this had happened, the eventual abolition of the trusts would have left them toll-free waterways analogous to the roads, maintained by the state or the local authorities on the Continental pattern.

However, there was precedent in the Sankey Brook (St Helen's) Canal Act of 1755 for organization by a company, whose proceedings were to some extent inspected by Commissioners drawn from local people. The merchants of Liverpool pressed this plan strongly upon Wedgwood, the Sankey 'hav^g given universal satisfaction'.[45] He felt on the one hand that 'the very term *Private Property* is obnoxious'; on the other hand, it would be difficult to find enough trustees to 'bestow so much of their time & attention Pro Bono Publico as the carrying into execution & conducting the design will require'.[46] It may have been John Sparrow the solicitor of Newcastle, the hard-headed man who became the Trent & Mersey's first clerk, who settled the matter; certainly by 24 June he was writing as if it were settled, as indeed it was.[47]

The promoters found the struggle between the Weaver trustees and the Duke for the western end of their canal more difficult, because they could not decide upon the Duke's real motives. In early July the Duke played a useful move when Wedgwood and Sparrow met him with their plans. Josiah 'had all the assurances of his concurrence with our designs that we could wish;—His G—— gave me an ord^r for the completest Table service of Cream colour that I could make. . . . After His G—— had dismissed us we had the honour, & pleasure too of sailing in his Gondola nine miles along his Canal, thro' a most delightful vale to Manchester'.[48] Considering that the Duke was saving every penny to put into the construction of his Runcorn line, that order for a complete table service must demonstrate his anxiety to get the connection.

It did not convince Wedgwood, however, who three weeks later was writing about 'our design to unite the Trent & Weaver'.[49]

The summer was spent in getting out Bentley's pamphlet, which appeared in November, was sent to landowners and sold to the public at 1s, and in resisting the blandishments of the Weaver trustees. They now went so far as to offer a maximum toll of 6d a ton for all Trent & Mersey traffic, and to make the river navigable to Northwich for 120-ton craft.[50] They went on to flirt with Richard Whitworth's scheme, now gaining some support, by proposing early in December to build a canal themselves from the river at Winsford to Wrinehill near Madeley, a strategic point from which other promoters could continue to either the Trent or the Severn. This was on Whitworth's line, but they hoped it would be 'an alluring charm to the Weilden schemers to come into us there, and save cutting through Harecastle at a great expence'.[51]

Their other fling was to give support to a plan which had been put forward in the previous May for a branch from the Duke's canal to Macclesfield[52] by a Mr Roe of that town. They announced that they would support a canal from Witton bridge on the Witton brook by Knutsford, Mottram St Andrew and Stockport to Manchester, with a branch from Mottram St Andrew to Macclesfield, hoping that this would 'surround his grace's navigation' and make difficult a junction between it and the Trent & Mersey.[53] Wedgwood thought that 'this bustling affair . . . is done in order to bring us to a compromise',[54] but the Whitworth scheme with its allies in the Weaver trustees, was building up, 'though I believe . . . that they meant it at first merely as a *Bug Bear* to us I do not think we should treat at alltogether as a chimerical scheme'.[55]

A matter of great interest to Thomas Bentley and the Trent & Mersey's supporters in Liverpool was still doubtful: whether the Duke intended to carry his canal past Runcorn and over the Mersey by an aqueduct to Liverpool. No one could find out, probably because the Duke did not himself know. The best Wedgwood could write was 'I have now learn'd all I can from the Duke, both Mr. Gilbert and Mr. Brindley, and the whole amounts to this, that his Grace intended to bring you a Canal to L'pool *some way* and *some time*, neither of which Circs were determin'd . . .'.[56] Bentley was doubtful of the Duke, and replied that he feared they might all be humbugged. Wedgwood then wrote his decisive letter: 'I believe that we are in very little danger, we have fixed upon an expedient to avoid it, & that is to insist as much as decency will permit us of Ld Gowers comeing down into Staffordshire & PUBLICLY at a meeting of the Gentlemen of this Country . . . to put himself at the head of our design & take it under

WHEREAS at a General Meeting of the Trustees of the RIVER WEAVER, held at *Northwich*, in the County of *Chester*, on *Thursday* the 5th of *December* 1765, a Plan was produced for extending the Navigation of the said River from WINSFORD BRIDGE, in the said County, to the RIVER TRENT, in the County of STAFFORD; and it was then ordered, that further Surveys should be made, and Plans taken, to promote a COMMUNICATION from the TRENT to the RIVER SEVERNE.

AND WHEREAS it appears by Surveys since taken, that the most proper Method to carry the same into Execution, is by making a CANAL from WINSFORD BRIDGE (which is near the Center of the said County of *Chester*) to CHECKLEY BROOK, near WRINE-HILL, upon the Borders of the County of *Stafford*; from whence it is practicable to Join the SEVERNE and TRENT by CANALS, and thereby open an INLAND COMMUNICATION between the three great Ports of LIVERPOOL, BRISTOL, and HULL, which is a much more Extensive Plan for the Benefit of Trade, than any other that has yet been proposed. And it is Computed that the Tonnage necessary to be imposed upon all Goods passing on the said new Navigation, from *Checkley Brook*, to *Winsford Bridge*, (which is Twenty-one Miles or thereabouts) will not exceed One Shilling per Ton, so that including Freight and Tonnage, all heavy Goods may be carried from the Termination of the said Navigation at *Checkley Brook*, to *Liverpool* (which is Sixty Miles) for Six Shillings per Ton at most.

It is therefore hoped, that any Gentlemen or Tradesmen of the Trading Towns in *Lancashire* and *Staffordshire*, or others who may be affected by such Undertaking, or have any Method to propose of rendering the above Scheme more effectual for the Service of the Public, will be so obliging as to give their Attendance at the Adjournment of the General Meeting of the Trustees of the *River Weaver*, on *Wednesday* the 15th of *January* next, at the *Angel*, in *Northwich*, when a Petition to Parliament, for Leave to bring in a Bill for carrying the said Scheme to *Checkley Brook* into Execution, will be offered to be signed by the Gentlemen present, if then approved of,

By Order of the Trustees,

JONA. BRAYNE, Clerk.

his patronage ... if L^d G sho^d publicly espouse our cause & take the lead in it, & afterwards desert us when the D^s purposes were served, the County wo^d never forgive him.'[57]

Brindley said that a junction with the Duke's canal was practicable, and 'Ld Gower comes into Staffs to put himself at our head on Monday 30th inst'.[58] At once landowners' consents began to come in. The meeting at Wolseley bridge* was attended by many landowners and influential men of Staffordshire. 'Earl Gower ... opened the meeting with a very sensible and elegant Speech, in which he expressed his Determination to support (the canal) with all his Interest, both Provincial and Political.'[59] James Brindley was there, and presented his plan and estimate of £100,000 for a canal 3 ft deep, which was adopted. One is amazed that the estimate was accepted by such men as the Gilberts, for in 1761 Smeaton had put £77,939 as needed for a canal from Wilden to the Potteries only. Though it still left open the western termination, the Liverpool representatives present were clear that the canal would not join the Weaver, and that there would be no Mersey aqueduct.[60] The Duke had won. An application to Parliament was authorized, and so enthusiastic had been the meeting that when the masterpotters got back to Burslem they lit a bonfire in the market-place, and toasted the leaders, including Wedgwood, Anson, Gilbert and Lord Gower. When subscriptions were opened, other prominent men, such as Matthew Boulton of Birmingham and Samuel Crompton of Derby were shown to be supporters. This meeting was decisive. Though a petition in favour of Whitworth's scheme was presented to Parliament on 13 February 1766, nothing more was heard of it.

The branches from the Trent & Mersey that had been projected earlier were dropped, that to Birmingham mainly because of apathy there, and the organization of a line to the Severn left to separate promoters. On 18 February 1766 the bill for the Trent & Mersey Canal was presented, and after second reading was referred to a committee of which Thomas Gilbert, Lord Gower's agent, was Chairman. On 12 March the Duke of Bridgewater petitioned for power to alter the line of his own canal so that it should run through Preston Brook to Runcorn Gap, 2,500 yd from its original termination at the Hempstones, with the proposed Trent & Mersey joining it at Preston Brook.

The Act[61] was passed on 14 May for the Trent & Mersey

---

* Near Colwich, where the main London road from Stafford crosses the Trent. The bridge was blown up in 1795 to release the flood-water.

Canal,* authorizing a line from the River Trent near Wilden bridge to Runcorn Gap. In it the Duke, who was described as having 'made great Progress in the Execution' of the Hempstones line, engaged to join the Trent & Mersey with his own canal at Preston Brook, and to build the line thence to Runcorn at his own expense, such portion to be his property; he could take toll on it up to the amounts he was authorized to levy on his own canal. If he had not completed the line to Runcorn Gap in four years, the Trent & Mersey company were empowered to do so.

'It is impossible to express the Joy that appeared throughout the Potteries, in the Neighbourhood of Newcastle, on Receipt of this important News—For nothing but an Inland Navigation can ever put their Manufactory on an Equality with their Foreign Competitors,'[62] wrote *Aris's Birmingham Gazette*, referring to the passage of the bill through the House of Commons.

The authorized capital was £130,000 in £200 shares, no one person to hold more than twenty, and £20,000 more if necessary, payment of 5 per cent interest on calls being allowed. Tolls were to be a maximum of 1½d per ton per mile, with limestone and lime at one-third of other tolls, and manure and road-making materials free between locks or when water was running over them.

Among the shareholders were the Duke, Lord Gower, Thomas Gilbert, John Brindley of Burslem (James's brother) and James Brindley himself, with ten each, and the canal's old rival, Sir Richard Whitworth of Batchacre, with five. A meeting on 3 May elected John Sparrow of Newcastle Clerk at £100 p.a. and Josiah Wedgwood Treasurer. James Brindley was appointed Surveyor-General at £200 p.a. and Hugh Henshall, his brother-in-law, and an engineer in his own right, Clerk of Works at £150 p.a. to include the cost of a clerk. Work was ordered to be begun at once on either side of Harecastle and at Wilden, and the first sod was cut on 26 July.[63] The great design was launched.

The Duke had, incidentally, tied up a loose end. Faced with possible difficulties from the Weaver, he had quickly moved to obtain an Act[64] in March 1766 for a branch from his canal to Stockport. Roe's scheme, shortened to an extension from Stockport to Macclesfield, failed in the Lords after having passed the Commons in January 1766, however, and therefore the Duke never built his branch, and Macclesfield had to wait some sixty

* The official title was 'The Navigation from the Trent to the Mersey', and that of 'Trent & Mersey Canal' was only a convenient abbreviation. Contemporaries often called it the 'Grand Trunk' or the 'Staffordshire Canal'.

years for a canal. (*To continue the history of the Trent & Mersey Canal, turn to Ch. II.*)

The Wolseley bridge meeting made it clear that a connecting canal to the Severn would not be built by the Trent & Mersey promoters. After it, a separate and less well-known group of men, led by James Perry and others mainly based on Wolverhampton, quickly made plans for such a line, which were reported in *Aris* on 20 January 1766. The Whitworth supporters held rival meetings at Wolverhampton at the end of January and at Shrewsbury early in February, but on 19 March Perry's group at Wolverhampton[65] decided to promote a bill. Hugh Henshall and Samuel Simcock did the survey, and the Act[66] was obtained on the same day as that for the Trent & Mersey. It authorized a line from that canal at Great Haywood to the Severn at 'some Place between Bewdley and Titton Brook',* and a capital of £70,000, with £30,000 more if necessary. Brindley was made Surveyor and James Perry Treasurer. (*To continue the history of the Staffordshire & Worcestershire Canal, turn to Ch. III.*)

* Below Stourport.

CHAPTER II

The Grand Trunk

✦

ALTHOUGH the authorized capital of the Trent & Mersey company was £130,000 in 650 shares of £200, only £86,900 had been subscribed in 434½ shares. Most was local money, but the surprisingly high total of £10,900 came from London. Curiously enough, Josiah Wedgwood, Bentley and Darwin were not original shareholders, perhaps to emphasize that their efforts had been disinterested, and that the motto chosen for the company's seal, *Pro Patriam Populumque Fluat,** meant what it said.

The first committee was solidly based on the Potteries, with Samuel Garbett from Birmingham, James Falconer and Edward Sneyd to represent Lichfield, and, surprisingly, Sir Richard Whitworth, who had presumably been given his seat in recognition of his canal enthusiasm. He must have been somewhat of a trial, for Josiah Wedgwood soon wrote to Bentley: 'I wish you could make one of our Ctee sometimes if it was only to hear & edify by some of Mr. W——hs wise speeches.'[1] One would have expected to find one of the Gilberts, but perhaps their various enterprises kept them too busy.

As the canal was cut upwards from Derwent Mouth and work proceeded on Harecastle tunnel, the committee had to struggle to keep their engineer fit and on the job, and to cope with the inventors, writers and visitors who came to view the astonishing new works. Of Brindley, Wedgwood said in 1767:

'I am afraid he will do too much, & leave us before his vast designs are executed; he is so incessantly harrassed on every side, that he hath no rest, either for his mind, or Body, & will not be prevailed upon to have proper care for his health . . . I think Mr. Brindley—the *Great,* the *fortunate, money-geting* Brindley, an object of Pity! . . . He may get a few thousands, but what does he give in exchange? His *Health,* & I fear his *Life* too.'[2]

* May it flow for fatherland and people.

So others were to say later of Brunel and Robert Stephenson. Not long afterwards Wedgwood wrote again:

> 'Poor Mr. Brindley was not well enough to attend the Committee and General Assembly . . . his ailments proceed from a too intense, & constant application to business.'[3]

The spread of Brindley's interests meant inevitably that he had not always done his homework. One feels this to have been the case when in September 1767 he assured the committee 'that he could complete the whole in five years from Xmass next' and, when some of the members doubted it, offered to bet £200. All the same, T & M shares remained at par.[4]

Among inventors there was Randal, whose 'scheme for executing our Canal with ploughs proved abortive';[5] among visitors, George Merchant: 'he is a Navigator . . . in short a Gimcrackarian & is come all the way from Twickenham Common to view our Harecastles, our Tunnels, Grand Trunks, & Navigat[ns].'.[6] As for the writers, they were continuously astonished, especially by the tunnelling:

> 'Gentlemen come to view our Eight Wonder of the world—the subterraneous Navigation which is cutting by the great Mr. Brindley who handles Rocks as easily as you would Plumb Pyes and makes the four elements subservient to his will . . . he has cut . . . about a Quarter of a Mile into the hill . . ., on the side of which he has a pump, which is worked by Water, and a Stove, the Fire of which sucks through a Pipe that Damps that would annoy the Men who are cutting towards the Centre of the Hill.'[7]

On 24 June 1770 the canal was opened from Derwent Mouth as far as Shugborough,[8] and on 12 November 1771 to Stone. The celebrations here proved over-exuberant, for owing to the repeated firing of a cannon, a bridge and lock collapsed, which cost £1,000 to repair.[9] Meanwhile the waterway was earning its title of the Grand Trunk, for branches were appearing. The Coventry Canal was authorized in January 1768: 'the foundation is now laid for extending it to the *Tide way of the R. Thames*', wrote Wedgwood, 'which extension must double, at least, the value of our stock'.[10] At the end of 1768 a party from Chester were discussing the project that became the Chester Canal, and in 1769 the Oxford company got its Act to continue the Coventry to that city. 'We shall be very anxious to have the Coventry and Oxford Canals finish'd,' Josiah wrote, 'that Land Carr[e] may be totally abolish'd betwixt us and London.'[11]

Wedgwood had always hoped that the Mersey aqueduct would be built, if not by the Duke, then by Liverpool; 'this Canal is pointing at your Harbour', he wrote to Liverpool, 'and was at first intended to terminate in it'.[12] He saw the Mersey as an obstacle, and feared to be 'drowned in the Tideway at Runkhorn'.[13] In November 1768 he wrote that he considered it practicable, that it seemed to him 'the Tonnage furnish'd from other navigations will be . . . vast, and increasing every year' and suggested that roads should be built on each side of the waterway, and tolls taken for carriages and passengers.[14] Later in the month Liverpool corporation[15] asked Brindley to survey the proposed canal route from the northern end of the aqueduct (also to carry a path or road) to Liverpool, and to estimate for the whole, but probably the Duke's opposition defeated it. The broad canal that was in fact built from the junction with the Duke's canal as far as Middlewich seems to have originated in connection with the aqueduct, for Wedgwood wrote to Bentley at the end of 1769: 'The advocates for a wide Tunnel* say that salt cannot be transhipped if the labour of doing it could be got for nothing, therefore we must either have a wide Tunnel, a Bridge at Runcorn, or carry no Salt to L'pool. The wide Tunnel therefore is continued till we see the probability of a bridge, as we cannot think of giving up the salt trade.'[16] He was right, for without the aqueduct the canal only got a small share of the salt business in which the Weaver remained predominant.

In 1769 the proprietors subscribed for the remaining unissued shares,[17] and in 1770 a new Act[18] authorized £70,000 more, 'by reason of the great Increase in the Value of Land, and Wages of Artists and Labourers, and from other unforeseen Expences and Circumstances'. Wedgwood's letters show unvarying confidence, but this was not always outside opinion. In July 1771, for instance, the Derby newspaper said: 'Many of the most experienced Navigators† and Traders are of opinion that there is no possibility of the Trent and Mersey Canal paying Interest.'[19]

On 27 September 1772 Brindley died, being succeeded as engineer by his brother-in-law Hugh Henshall, and a few days later the canal was opened to a temporary wharf at Stoke, so fulfilling his original project of 1758.[20] In April 1775 the canal was open through Harecastle to Sandbach,[21] and on 26 September to Middlewich,[22] while at the other end Preston Brook tunnel had been completed in February 1775[23] and the canal was open to Acton,[24]

* At Preston Brook.
† The word is used here of the boatmen on the Trent and the Derwent.

though at the junction craft could only travel towards Manchester, as the Duke's extension to Runcorn was not completed till 21 March 1776 by the finishing of the last section at Norton Priory.

The gap between Middlewich and Acton involved Henshall in some difficult engineering. Wedgwood wrote in September 1774: 'On Wednesday we proceed to view the course our Canal is to take by Middlewich, to Northwich, & from thence to Preston in the Hill, which track I am told in some places approaches as near to impracticability as anything can do which is really to be executed, as our Canal is, you know.'[25]

Afterwards he wrote again:

'Mr. Henshall deeming it impracticable to make the Canal along the high sloping banks on the side of the Weaver, has cut out these new Tunnels,* & very happy it is for us that the ground has been found capable of admitting this alternative, or I verily believe we must have given up this part of our Canal, & even now we have some tremendous Gullies & sidelong banks to pass over, but none I hope impracticable.'[26]

At last, in May 1777,[27] the canal was completed, seemingly without any ceremony. Brindley would have lost his bet, but would have had no cause to be ashamed of Henshall's[28] work. Before the opening, however, a further Act in 1775[29] had stated that of the previously authorized £70,000, £68,550 had been borrowed (and that no interest on calls had been paid for four years), and authorized £70,000 more. The main line, therefore, cost about £300,000. The length was 93⅜ miles, with a rise of 326 ft by 35 locks[30] from Preston Brook to Harecastle, and then a fall of 316 ft by 40 locks to Derwent Mouth. The dimensions had been increased from Brindley's original plans. From the junction to Middlewich on the west, and from Derwent Mouth to Horninglow (Burton) on the east, the waterway was built 31 ft wide at surface and 5½ ft deep to take the Duke's 60-ton barges at one end and 40-ton Trent craft at the other. There were one broad lock at Middlewich and six on the eastern section. The rest of the canal was built narrow to take boats of 70 ft by 7 ft, 29 ft wide at surface and 4½ ft deep. Harecastle tunnel was 2,880 yd long,[31] and had several branch tunnels leading to collieries in the hill. There were also tunnels at Preston Brook (1,239 yd), Saltersford (424 yd), and Barnton (572 yd) on the western side, all of which were built broad, and the narrow Armitage (130 yd) on the east. The principal aqueducts were those of 23 arches over the Dove, six

* Saltersford and Barnton.

I. Some canal seals

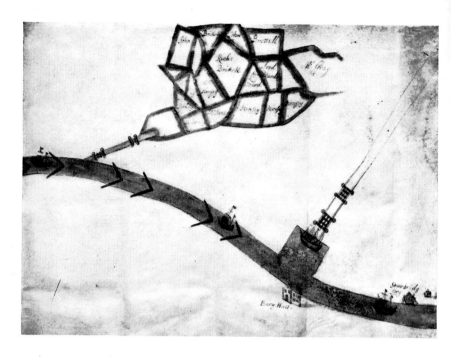

II. (*above*) A plan of suggested locks and wharf on the River Stour near Stourbridge in *c.* 1662. This plan shows two very early representations of railways. (*below*) Tub-boats in use on the Shrewsbury Canal

arches over the Trent near Rugeley, and three arches over the Dane; there was also a level crossing of the Trent at Alrewas.

To build the canal broad from Preston Brook to Middlewich cost an extra £20,000, and up to 1785 it had not been used for barges. The Duke said it was too narrow for his craft; 'the engineer, on the contrary, said it was of the dimensions agreed upon, and that the boats were built too wide for the tunnels *after those tunnels had been made*',[32] in order to compel transhipment to take place at Preston Brook. Whatever the truth, the transhipment point between broad boats and narrow for goods to and from Liverpool became Preston Brook, where extensive wharves and warehouses grew up, and not Middlewich as the company had hoped.

As early as January 1773 a branch from the summit level to Leek was being considered, 'the Locks of which are to be *inclin'd planes*.[33] The Canal 12 ft wide only and the boats to carry five Tons burthen; Coales & Lime & Stone for our Roads are the main objects'.[34] This was not proceeded with, but instead negotiations were opened with the Earl of Stamford, owner of limestone works at Breedon (later to be served by a tramroad from the Ashby Canal) for 'a junction between Harecastle & Breden—Coals & Lime'.[35] This idea of a connection between the Trent & Mersey near Burton and the Breedon works, often to be brought up, came to nothing, and in September 1775 a third plan was brought forward. Josiah Wedgwood wrote to Thomas Bentley: 'they have enlisted me here in another Navigation scheme, to effect a junction between Calden Lime Quarries & our Canal & Collieries. You know the Plan, I only mean that we are begun upon it in earnest'.[36] A second main purpose was to make additional reservoirs to supply the summit of the main line. By November the branch had been surveyed and an estimate prepared.

At this time there was apparently talk also of a canal to Leek by an independent company; a survey was made and subscriptions entered into, but the Trent & Mersey seems to have prevented the scheme being carried out.[37]

The canal company made contracts with the owners of the various limestone quarries at Caldon Low. These were in four groups: the Earl of Shrewsbury (who had leased to John Gilbert, Richard Hill, George Smith and Sampson Whieldon); Thomas Gilbert; Henry Copestake; Robert Bill, Sampson Whieldon and William Woolliscroft; most of whom were connected with the company in any case. The Trent & Mersey agreed with them to supply limestone ready broken at the quarries in the proportions of two-fifths from the first group and one-fifth from each of the others at an agreed price, giving the company the right to operate the quarries themselves if limestone were not delivered in adequate quantities. Limestone was to pay full toll unless the water was running over the weirs, and the company was to build branch railways to the quarries.

In May 1776 an Act[38] authorized a branch canal 17¼ miles long, originally with sixteen locks from the main canal just above Etruria top lock at Stoke to Froghall by way of Hanley and Cheddleton, which for 1½ miles made use of the bed of the river Churnet at Consall. The Act authorized the borrowing of £25,000 for construction, and the canal was probably opened during 1779.[39] Originally there were eight locks up (a two-lock staircase at Etruria, one at Engine, and five at Stockton) and eight down, three from the end of the original summit at Park Lane, two at Cheddleton, and three beyond.

The first tramroad* to the quarries from Froghall was also opened about 1779.[40] It started from Froghall by the original kilns on the north side and ran up Shirley Hollow along the Shirley Brook to Shirley Common. It then crossed the Garston-Foxt lane obliquely and ran towards Shirley House farm, beyond which it cannot now be traced. There seems to have been early trouble upon it, for in January 1780 a letter says: 'The Railway has been repaired, but in Frost the waggons slide so much, that it is almost Impossible to carry any thing upon it.'[41] A new tramroad was authorized by an Act of 1783,[42] the preamble of which said that £23,660 had been raised under the earlier Act, but that the tramroad 'has been found to be laid and placed in a very inconvenient Course and Direction and has not answered all the good Ends and Purposes thereby intended'. The new Act also authorized an extension of the canal for 530 yd on the level, so making it clear that the original end of the canal was beside the road, and that the 76 yd tunnel and the canal beyond it were built under this Act. The new railway ran up Harston Wood, and then turned right beyond the Harston Rock to emerge above Whiston; it then ran past Garston and over Cotton Common to the quarries. It was 3⅛ miles long.[43] As the Act did not authorize any capital, presumably the new line was paid for out of income.

* As in former books, I use the word 'tramroad' to mean a horse-drawn railway, whatever the type of rail laid, to simplify indexing and avoid confusion with later locomotive lines.

Soon after the Trent & Mersey was opened, the great traveller Thomas Pennant described the benefits it had brought in terms which, though fanciful to our ears, yet expressed a real revolution:
'The cottage, instead of being covered with miserable thatch, is now secured with a substantial covering of tiles or slates, brought from the distant hills of Wales or Cumberland. The fields, which before were barren, are now drained, and, by the assistance of manure, conveyed on the canal toll-free, are cloathed with a beautiful verdure. Places which rarely knew the use of coal, are plentifully supplied with that essential article upon reasonable terms: and, what is still of greater public utility, the monopolizers of corn are prevented from exercising their infamous trade.'[44]

Another traveller gave a similar impression:
'In a few years after it was finished, I saw . . . the value of manufactures arise in the most unthought of places; new buildings and new streets spring up in many parts of Staffordshire, where it passes; the poor are no longer starving . . . and the rich grow steadily richer. The market town of Stone . . . from a poor insignificant place is now grown neat and handsome in its buildings, and from its wharfs and busy traffic, wears the lively aspect of a little sea port.'[45]

As for the great tunnel, pleasure-boat trips were run into it:
'The procession was solemn; some enlivened this scene with a band of musick, but we had none; as we entered far, the light of candles was necessary, and about half-way, the view back upon the mouth, was like the glimmering of a star, very beautiful. The various voices of the workmen from the mines, etc., were rude and awful. . . .'[46]

The opening of the canal had an immediate effect on the trade of the Weaver at Winsford, which fell from 13,917 tons in 1776–7 to 5,284 tons in 1779–80, and meant that raw materials for the Potteries and crates of outgoing pottery were now going by canal instead of by the Weaver and land carriage. The Middlewich trade also went to the canal. On the other hand, the bulk of the Northwich trade remained on the river, coal coming up and salt going down.

The river trustees set about improving the river and also seeking a connection with the canal. The latter was first suggested in 1778, when a meeting of the trustees decided that 'if proper quays with communications and other conveniencys were erected and made at Anderton or Barnton for reshipping of goods and merchandizes into the river Weaver from the Staffordshire canal it would be a more eligible plan for the benefit of trade on the Weaver than a reduction of the tonnage'.[47] The first step was to build an improved road from the river at Northwich and later Witton to the canal at Broken Cross, where a warehouse was built. This work was finished about the beginning of 1780. The trustees then became carriers on the canal between Longport, where they had a wharf, and Liverpool, via Broken Cross, in crateware one way and clay the other, but lost money, and gave up the business in 1784. They then set to repairing the road connecting the two waterways.

In November 1788 the Middlewich salt proprietors suggested to the committee that if proper quays and communications were made at Barnton or Anderton, it would be convenient for shipping goods from the canal on to the Weaver. The trustees agreed in March 1789, and in August 1790 put two schemes to the Trent & Mersey, one for cutting a sluice across the towing path, the other for wheeling goods over it. The canal company refused the former, which may have been a proposal for a boat incline, but agreed to the latter scheme, which went ahead at Anderton, where a basin was built on the river. Transhipping of salt to the Weaver probably began about 1796. In September 1799 a 'railed way' was ordered to be built, and was in existence in the following year. These facilities were expanded in 1801 and 1802 into what was described in 1813 as an inclined plane,[48] though not one carrying boats, but trucks to and from which goods had to be transhipped. Later a boat plane may have been contemplated, for Telford sent drawings to Count von Platen, when the Göta Canal project was beginning, entitled 'A Machine for raising vessels out of the River Weaver at Northwich'.[49]

The opening of the Trent & Mersey greatly reduced the rates of carriage, and so encouraged the growth of industry. For instance, the rate for merchandise from Manchester to Lichfield is said to have come down from £4 to £1 per ton.[50] Additional wharves and warehouses were quickly built by private carriers, such as those at Shardlow constructed between 1774 and 1780 by the Cavendish Bridge Boat Co, who in the latter year had 20 boats on the canal.[51] The company also were carriers. At first the carrying business of Hugh Henshall & Co, which existed by mid-1770 between Shardlow and Great Haywood,[52] was a separate concern run by a group of proprietors to bring business to the canal, but later it was taken over by the company itself, and brought a great deal of business. There were three reasons behind this carrying

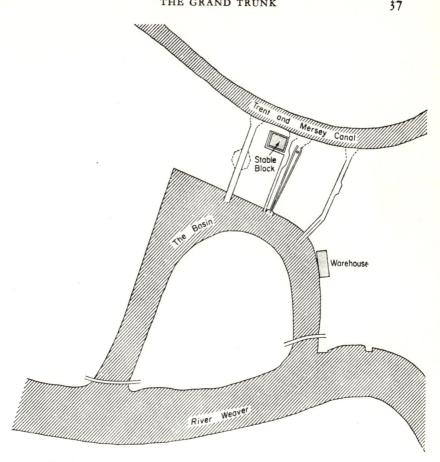

2. Plan showing tramroad and other connections between the Trent & Mersey Canal and the Weaver Trustees' basin at Anderton in 1831, just after the second (downstream) entrance to the basin had been built

enterprise. Two were straightforward enough; to get business for the canal, especially in its early days, even though some of it was uneconomic in terms of carrying alone; and to prevent any combination among the independent carriers to raise rates. The third was more complicated. All canal Acts prohibited the companies from varying their tolls as between one customer and another, or one part of their line as against another. But freight rates could be adjusted as necessary, and Hugh Henshall & Co enabled the company, for instance, to offer cheaper rates at either end of their canal, where they were in competition with the Trent (Burton) Navigation and the Weaver.[53] In the year ending midsummer 1778 Hugh Henshall & Co had a turnover of £19,671; by 1784 this had risen to £54,579, and by 1790 they seem to have carried almost all the traffic passing from the canal down the Trent,[54] probably working with contractors who operated services onwards to Hull.[55] In 1795 65 boats of the company's were recorded in the barge register.

It was, however, a policy that had its dangers, as the company found in 1782 when John Gilbert, the Duke of Bridgewater's agent but also a member of the canal committee, took as his partner a road carrier, Worthington, and set up the new canal-carrying firm of Worthington & Gilbert in competition with Hugh Henshall & Co on the Manchester and Stourport run. Not unnaturally, the Duke's traffic went to Gilbert, and 'His Grace's people are all very partial to Worthington; his boats can be discharged in two hours, while ours must lie a day or more under their cargo for want of proper assistance to discharge them'.[56] It was all very awkward, and precipitated a row which broke the committee into two groups, one led by Josiah Wedgwood supported by the potters, the other by the Duke, the two Gilberts, the two Bills, brothers-in-law to John Gilbert, and Richard Hill, associated with the Gilberts in the Caldon quarries. In March Thomas Gilbert circulated shareholders about the committee, 'representing their Affairs as totally derang'd ... when, he says, Misconduct, Misrepresentations, & constant Quarreling have brought them almost to Ruin'.[57] Two shareholders who received the circular were alarmed: 'we fear from it, that what is already subscrib'd is far from Safe, as well as our Mony lent to it'. Pamphlets flew back and forth, and the potters intervened to protest about accommodation on the Duke's and their own canals. This protest seems to have made the Duke realize that he had gone too far in treating the Trent & Mersey as a branch of his own canal: he took steps to meet the potters' wishes, and the dust slowly settled.

For the last four years before opening throughout, the company had not been able to pay the usual 5 per cent interest on the calls made on its shares. Its early years were penurious, and would have been more so had it not been for its carrying business. In January 1779, for instance, the Staffs & Worcs company sent them a notice to pay what they owed in tolls for their carrying craft promptly

THE GRAND TRUNK

each half year, or they would be given no credit.[58] However, by June 1781 they were in a position to start paying a 5 per cent dividend,[59] and in 1783 to arrange the funding by bonds of £45 per share of the unpaid interest on calls.[60]

In this year a three-months account (mid-June to mid-September) shows a wide variety of traffics, the most important being:

Traffic	Tolls £
Crates of earthenware	587
Clay	541
Lime and limestone (Caldon branch)	515
Grain, meal, flour	456
Salt	326
Harecastle coal	296
Timber	259
Flint	249
Iron	184
Groceries	158

Tolls, and the profit on carrying, rose satisfactorily, especially after the through connection with the Coventry Canal was made in 1790:

Year ending Midsummer	Tolls £	Carrying profit £	Total £
1784	23,152	1,272	24,424
1785	26,054	3,859	29,913
1786	26,964	1,522	28,486
1787	28,459	2,780	31,239
1788	30,362	2,995	33,357
1789	33,861	3,079	36,940
1790	36,950	5,108	42,058
1791	40,773	5,084	45,857
1792	42,505	3,681	46,186

The dividend for 1787 was 5 per cent; for 1788, 5½; for 1789, 6; and for 1790, 6½; the concern was prosperous, and was clearly destined to be still more so. (*To continue the history of the Trent & Mersey Canal, turn to Ch. XI.*)

The principal branches from the Grand Trunk, those towards the Thames and the Severn, will be described elsewhere. Three other canals were, however, in some way associated with it during this period: Sir Nigel Gresley's, the Donnington Wood, and the Chester Canal. A few other minor canals can also conveniently be described here.

Gresley's (later Heathcote's) Canal

A branch to Newcastle-under-Lyme formed part of the original Trent & Mersey scheme. Newcastle had to wait some forty years for its branch, but in the meantime was provided with coal by a canal from the opposite direction.

In 1775 an Act[61] authorized Sir Nigel Gresley, Bt. and his son Nigel Bowyer Gresley to build a canal from their mines at Apedale to Newcastle, it being stated that they already owned much of the necessary land, and would make it at their own expense. The Act provided that the price of coal from the canal sold in Newcastle should be controlled for 42 years.

The canal was 3 miles long, and ran on the level from Apedale collieries to a basin beside the Liverpool Road leading into Newcastle. It was probably built soon after the Act was obtained, for it was from the Gresleys that the Chester Canal obtained supplies, presumably carried from the Liverpool Road canal wharf by road.[62] (*To continue the history of Gresley's Canal, turn to p. 206.*)

The Speedwell Level

With John Gilbert in charge, and probably using experience gained at Worsley, an underground level to carry lead ore and waste rock, was built at the Speedwell mine at Castleton, Derbyshire. Tunnelling began in 1774 and was completed about 1778, the navigable length being about half a mile. The boats were 12 ft long and 3 ft wide, and were hauled by men pulling on pegs fixed in the tunnel walls. The ore content proved insufficient, however, and mining only lasted a few years.[63] Farey[64] mentions two other such levels, Hillcarr near Darley and Meerbrook near Wirksworth.

Donnington Wood Canal

Lord Gower, the Duke's brother-in-law, was familiar with his canal that ran right into the collieries at Worsley, so that small canal craft could be loaded near the face.[65] With John and Thomas Gilbert, therefore, he formed Earl Gower & Company in 1764, and decided to build a small canal for 3-ton tub-boats from the coal deposits on his estate at Donnington Wood to run south of Muxton and past Lilleshall Abbey for 5½ miles to Pave Lane on the Wolverhampton road two miles from Newport, where a coal wharf was built for its sale.[66] At Donnington Wood the canal appears to have connected with one or more navigable levels in the mine there, themselves perhaps linked by an underground inclined plane as at Worsley.[67] This main line was being built in February 1765,[68] and was completed before July 1768.[69]

Later a branch canal was built from Hugh's Bridge a little east of Lilleshall Abbey to limestone quarries by Lilleshall village, and from this branch again at Willmore Bridge another (itself with two small branches) ran through seven small descending locks with a total fall of 35 ft to Lilleshall limeworks, a coal wharf, and a stone pit at Pitchcroft. Coal was therefore carried in one direction to burn limestone into lime, and limestone in the other to burn in the iron furnaces of Donnington.

The branch at Hugh's Bridge was 42 ft 8 in. below the main line. Originally there was no physical connection, but a tunnel at the end of the branch, which ran underneath two vertical shafts. Goods in crates were then lifted by cranes at the top of the shafts from one boat below to another above, and others lowered, the cranes being connected together so that the weight of the coal descending would raise a smaller weight of lime or limestone. This method was used by Brindley to raise goods from the Duke's canal at Castlefield to the Manchester wharves,[70] and later on the Coalbrookdale branch of the Shropshire Canal. At some time before 1797 an inclined plane 123 yd long was substituted. John Farey, writing for Rees's *Cyclopaedia* in 1805, describes it as follows: 'boxes of lime-stone descend and draw up empty boxes by means of ropes passing over a large drum, to which a brake-wheel is adapted to regulate the motion'. Such a description implies that boats were not themselves carried on the plane, but boxes were hauled up and down on trucks, as for a time at Combe Hay on the Somersetshire Coal Canal.[71] On the other hand, there is evidence on the ground, and from personal memory[72] that the plane carried boats. This may mean that Farey was wrong, or that the plane was originally as he described it, and was later converted.

In 1786 Lord Gower was created Marquess of Stafford, his son, the second Marquess, becoming Duke of Sutherland in 1833. The Donnington Wood was therefore often referred to later as the Marquess of Stafford's or the Duke of Sutherland's Tub-boat Canal. (*For the later history of the Donnington Wood Canal, turn to p. 150.*)

Chester Canal

In March 1771 the following paragraph appeared in the Press: 'The Navigation of the Dee up to Chester, is, by some late Improvements, become so much more safe and commodious than the Navigation of the Liverpool Channel, that the City of Chester is now applying for leave to cut a Canal from their City to Middlewich, to communicate with the great Canal from the Trent to the Mersey. Should they succeed, Salt, Cheese, Earthen-Ware, and other Commodities, which Used to be conveyed to Liverpool by the River Weaver, will with more speed be conveyed to Chester, and exported from thence to foreign Parts.'[73]

The Trent & Mersey Act of 1766 had been a blow to Chester, for, should the canal be built, it would divert inland trade towards the Mersey and Liverpool. By 1771 the threat was becoming real. The River Dee Company had spent £80,000 on improving the main channel of the river, and if Chester were not given an inland communication of its own, the future of the port and river alike were unpromising. James Folliott, a Chester merchant, put the position well to the Parliamentary committee: 'when Goods are Water-borne upon . . . the Mersey, they will not come to Chester, but would go to Liverpool . . . and if the Runcorn Gap Navigation were made . . . the Witness thinks the Trade of Chester will be totally ruined, because the new Canals will carry the Goods of all the Kingdom'.[74]

This hopeful but belated idea of making Chester an alternative to Liverpool was first put to the Trent & Mersey proprietors in late 1768 in the form of a canal from their line to near Runcorn. Liverpool decided not to object;[75] the canal company avoided giving an answer. In 1770 and 1771 the promoters again pressed for a line to Middlewich to join the Trent & Mersey there, with a branch to Nantwich. Chester Corporation subscribed £100 and the Societies and Clubs of Chester £2,000, but neither the Weaver, whose trade from the Northwich area was threatened, nor the Trent & Mersey, who might lose traffic from the lower part of their canal, were enthusiastic. Nor, indeed, was anyone; the atmosphere was that of a forlorn hope. The Duke of Bridgewater was applied to, and replied briskly that if the Chester promoters undertook not to make a physical connection at Middlewich, he would not oppose the bill.[76] The canal company's clerk, in his most obsequious prose, reported it to be

'the opinion of this Meeting, that His Grace be requested to

accept the most humble Thanks of the Subscribers for this great
Act of kindness and condescension, and that he will be pleased
to pardon their presumption in begging that His Grace will
vouchsafe still further to countenance their Undertaking, by
using his Interest . . . to induce the Proprietors of the Grand
Trunk to allow by their free consent, that Junction, which . . .
they have weighty reasons for not submitting to by Parliamentary compulsion'.[77]

Mr Chancellor Peploe of the Cathedral was also asked to get the
Bishop of Peterborough to approach the Duke and to assure him
'that the Effect of this Compromise cannot fail to render him dear
to the Citizens of Chester and his Memory equally so to their
latest Posterity'.[78]

Both the Duke and the Trent & Mersey company showed themselves impervious alike to flattery and the affections of the posterity of the citizens of Chester, and insisted that the canals should
be kept a hundred yards apart at Middlewich. To this the Chester
company had to agree, while hoping for a change of heart. It was
a bad start.

With this restriction, they got their Act[79] by a small majority on
1 April 1772, the authorized capital being £42,000 in £100 shares,
and £20,000 more if necessary, though only £28,000 had been
subscribed when the application was made. They decided, however, to build a barge canal with locks 80 ft by 14 ft 9 in. Samuel
Weston, whose experience had so far been only in surveying and
as a contractor for cutting, was appointed engineer with John
Lawton to assist him, the Mayor of Chester cut the first sod about
the end of the month,[80] and cutting began in and near Chester.
Almost at once an unusual engineering problem arose, for in July
a deputation was sent to the Sheriffs to discuss 'a proper method
of securing the Prisoners confined in the Northgate Gaol from
making their Escape during such time as the work shall be carried
on, in or under the Northgate Garden'.[81] Later, the company had
to give a bond against them doing so.

The concern ran into early difficulties. There was a long argument with the River Dee company about the river lock at Chester.
They had inserted a clause into the canal Act limiting its width to
7 ft, and it seems that such a lock was indeed built, and a few boats
constructed to pass through it. Later, after much argument, they
agreed in 1776 to a new entrance 15 ft wide, apparently a single
pair of gates 15 ft apart leading to a basin, from whence the
canal then rose to the Northgate level. As the basin stood on the

Dee company's land, tolls had to be paid on goods passing through it. There was also bad engineering, for in 1774 it was resolved 'That the Parts of the Aqueduct Bridge that have given way be immediately taken down and repaired in the best manner possible'.[82] Weston now left, and Thomas Morris, who had worked with Brindley on the Bridgewater extension to Runcorn and had then gone to Ireland, was fetched back to take over.

On 16 January 1775[83] the first section of canal, from Chester to the aqueduct near Huxley below Beeston, was ready, and a 70-ton barge went up with coal. By June the line was open to Beeston, and a passenger boat to Chester was put on, the fare being 6d single or 9d day return, common cabin, or double fares in the grand cabin. By September Morris also had been dismissed. Josiah Clowes, then apparently a carrier on the Trent & Mersey, succeeded him, and was in turn dismissed for inattention to duty, in spite of which bad start he later became a competent canal engineer. Morris's assistant Moon followed him, and finally Joseph Taylor. The connection with the Dee was made in September 1776; by the end of 1777 £42,000, the whole of the share capital, had been spent, as well as £19,000 raised on loan under the guarantee of Samuel Egerton of Tatton, a shareholder and relation of the Duke. A new Act[84] of 1777 authorized another £25,200 to be raised by a call of 60 per cent on the existing shareholders, and also £30,000 by mortgage; under this an additional £6,000 was raised on calls, and, surprisingly, Richard Reynolds of Ketley lent £4,000. It was enough to complete the canal to Nantwich about August 1779 and build a reservoir at Bunbury Heath. The line was $19\frac{1}{4}$ miles long, with 16 locks, not counting the entrance gates to the Dee.

The company at first hoped to raise enough money to complete their line to Middlewich with narrow locks, so saving £20,000, but the shareholders had had enough canal building; instead they tried to perform the impossible, in order to get some traffic on the line they had. First, they started rock salt workings at Nantwich, but found no salt. Then they put two of their own boats on the Trent & Mersey, and tried to compete with Liverpool for the Potteries and Birmingham trade by carrying once weekly by boat to Wheelock, transferring the goods there to road waggon for Nantwich to be put on the canal to Chester and then to be again transhipped into one of the company's four flats for the voyage to Liverpool. On the Chester Canal itself they ran 'regular Stage Boats of Sixty Tons Burthen, decked over, and perfectly dry. . . .

Likewise Passage Boats, with comfortable Accommodation for Passengers, and for the carriage of small packages and parcels.'[85]

It was all uneconomic. In May 1780 boring for salt was stopped; in August it was decided to take off the boats trading on the Trent & Mersey, and in October to lay up the flats. Over one-third of the shares had been forfeited for non-payment of calls; there was no money, and loan interest could not be found. The canal was a failure, and by 1781 the company had had enough. They resolved in December:

> 'That Mr. Turner be requested to wait upon Mr. Egerton and acquaint him, that they are ready and desirous to do him all the Justice in their Power, by delivering up the immediate possession of the Navigation and Appurtenances, and all the Boats, Vessels, Goods, Chattels and other property and Effects belonging thereto, provided he will undertake the payment of the Simple Contract Debts due from the Compy of Proprietors.'[86]

Egerton did not move, and in March 1782 landowners who had not been paid let off the water from Bunbury reservoir. The Committee notified Egerton wearily that the canal 'will be totally destitute of Water the next Summer if their Demands are not paid'.[87] However, by selling a flat here and a piece of land there, the loyal committee just managed to keep the canal open, till in November 1787 Beeston lock, with which there had been constant trouble because of the running sand beneath it, collapsed. For a time traffic above it then ceased, because there was no money for repairs. In April 1788 they had only £21 7s 5½d in hand.

A year later there was the first breath of hope, though it was long to be deferred, when 'The Chairman . . . informed the Meeting, that some favourable Circumstances appear from the Execution of other Canals, and that there is great probability of a Junction taking place'.[88] Encouraged, the meeting resolved to try to raise £200 from the shareholders for necessary repairs, in order, as was said a few months later, 'to prevent the little Business there is on the Canal being wholly lost'.[89] By November 1790 a little money had been found, 'the Canal is now nearly filled with Water and Business begins to stir'.[90] The project that became the Ellesmere Canal was just over the horizon. (*To continue the history of the Chester Canal, turn to Ch. X.*)

To end this chapter, let us look briefly at three enterprises in north Wales.

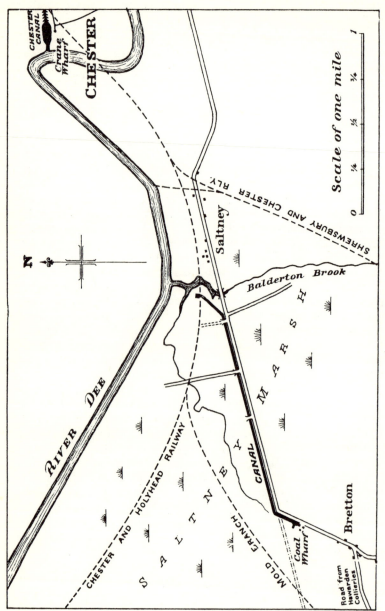

3. Sir John Glynne's Canal

Sir John Glynne's (Saltney or Hawarden) Canal

Sir John Glynne built a small canal in 1768 to carry coal from the Sandycroft colliery near Bretton to Saltney. It is said that it ceased to be used in 1775, but a minute of the Chester Canal company of 1779 about coal at Bretton says: 'Putting the same on Boats and deliv^g them at the East End of Sir J^{no} Glynne's Canal, 2½d.'[91]

Vale of Clywd Canal

In the seventies Fitzmaurice of Llewenni tried to interest some Liverpool merchants in a canal from the collieries near Whitford to a shipping place at Foryd near Rhyl, and a branch up the vale of Clywd. This was to run to Rhuddlan, then cross the river by an aqueduct, and continue upwards past St Asaph and Denbigh to Ruthin, which was seen as a distribution centre for north Wales. By its means coal would be carried up the Vale, and agricultural produce downwards.[92] The idea was revived in 1807.

Flint Coal Canal

A group of industrialists founded the Flint Coal Canal company about 1784, among them being John Wilkinson of Bersham, the Rev Edward Lloyd of Kinmel Park, one of the founders of the Parys Mine Co, Thomas Williams of Llanidan, Anglesey, managing director of the Parys company, Edward Jones, a lead-mine owner of Wepre, Flintshire, and Thomas Harrison of Wolverton, Bucks, agent to Lord Uxbridge, copper-mine owner at Parys, and probably grandfather of the contractor for the Wolverton aqueduct on the Grand Junction. The project was therefore connected with the Greenfield Copper and Brass Co, set up in 1785 as the manufacturing subsidiary of the Mona Mine Co, which, like the Parys mine, was controlled by Thomas Williams. He, Wilkinson and Harrison were shareholders in the Greenfield works.

William Jessop surveyed the proposed line in 1785, and in 1788 an Act[93] was obtained. The preamble referred to 'great and extensive Copper and Brass Works, and Mines, and Works of Lead and Calamine, and Coal Mines, and Manufactories of Cotton' which were carried on at or near Greenfield and Holywell, and the text authorized a canal, said to have been intended for 100-ton craft, from a safe and sufficiently deep anchorage on the Dee at

Pentre Rock over the salt marshes to Greenfield, with power to coalowners to make branches. The authorized capital was £20,000, and £10,000 more if necessary.

Curiously enough, the only work recorded in the canal company's name is a bridge begun in 1788 over the Wepre brook between Connah's Quay and Shotton, nowhere near the canal line, that was seemingly built as a toll-bridge.[94]

III. Stourport in 1776

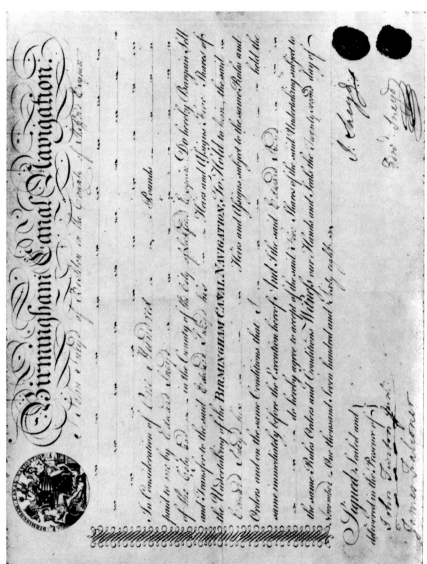

IV. A Birmingham Canal share transfer certificate of 1768

CHAPTER III

The Line to Bristol

✦

As built, the Staffordshire & Worcestershire Canal had a main line 46⅛ miles long from Great Haywood on the Trent & Mersey by way of Penkridge, Autherley* near Wolverhampton and Kidderminster to Stourport on the Severn, then called Lower Mitton. There was a rise from Great Haywood through 12 locks to the summit at Gailey, and then a fall from Compton through 31 locks to Stourport. The last two, connecting the basin at Stourport with the river, were barge locks, which were later paralleled by two pairs of narrow staircase locks opened in 1781; the other locks were all narrow. There were two short tunnels of 65 yd at Cookley and 22 yd at Stourton. James Brindley seems to have set out the line and given general superintendence, while the actual engineering was done by his assistants Samuel Simcock and Thomas Dadford, senior, assisted by John Baker, Clerk of Works, Simcock being also engaged on the Birmingham and the Oxford Canals for much of the time.

An advertisement of June 1766 in the Birmingham newspaper mentioned a canal digging machine whereby eight men could do the work of twelve with wheelbarrows. The two inventors offered to dig the Staffs & Worcs in two years for the price of doing it manually in three.[1] They were asked to attend a meeting of the canal committee on 25 July to contract for doing so, but nothing more was heard of them. The managing committee were efficient, and construction went steadily on. In November 1770 the canal was reported 'finished and completely navigable'[2] from Compton near Wolverhampton to the Severn, though a newspaper notice of its being open did not appear till 1 April of the following year.[3]

---

* At this time the names Autherley and Aldersley were interchangeable. Later Autherley was used of the junction between the Staffs & Worcs and the Birmingham & Liverpool Junction (Shropshire Union), and Aldersley of that between the Staffs & Worcs and the Birmingham.

D　　　　　　　　　49

The basin at Stourport was begun about 1768, and was in use in 1771.[4] In 1772 the head office was established in Wolverhampton at the address where it was to remain all its life. In the same year, on 28 May, the whole canal was open,[5] and on 21 September it acquired its first branch, when it was joined at Aldersley to the Birmingham Canal, after the Staffs & Worcs company had taken action against that company to compel them to complete it. At once a profitable trade began. There does not appear to have been any connection between the supporters of the Staffs & Worcs and the Birmingham. Only two names appear prominently in both companies, one of them being the energetic James Perry, who, though concerned with promoting the Birmingham, did not take an active part in managing it afterwards.

One may speculate upon how far the efficiency with which the canal was built depended upon two resolutions passed by the committee early in its construction: the first, of 1766 said: 'that no Officer or other person employed or to be employed in this undertaking do make known or give Information to any person or persons, save only to the Members of this Committee, or of any Matter or Thing relating to the said Canal or the manner of working the same'.[6] The second, of 1768, said: 'That no Woman be employed in future in the immediate service of the Company of proprietors in or about any Business concerning this Undertaking.'[7] Was the second perhaps connected with the first?

The authorized capital was £70,000, and £30,000 more if necessary. A supplementary Act of 1770[8] authorized a further £10,000 to be raised by further calls on the original £100 shares. Apparently £135 was called on each £100 share [9](later raised to £140), and a debt may have been incurred as well, the cost of construction being probably rather over £100,000. Only eighteen months after completion the company was able to announce that in addition to paying the interest at 5 per cent due on calls on shares made before March 1768, it was declaring a maiden dividend of £4 per share. By 1775 this had risen to £12, and in 1783 the shares were worth £400 each.

A provision in the 1766 Act for this, as for the Trent & Mersey, was that all alterations of toll had to be approved by Commissioners, whose functions in most later canal Acts were limited to the settlement of land valuation disputes;[10] this safeguard was an echo of the controversy upon public versus private ownership that had taken place when the Trent & Mersey was being planned. In April 1785, after the Commissioners' powers had been reiterated in the 1770 Act, the company introduced a bill to get rid of them, but were naturally opposed by the Stourbridge and Dudley companies, who regarded them as a protection. However, in 1786 an amicable rates agreement between the three stipulated that changes should be made 'without the interference of Commissioners'.[11]

In August 1774 what was probably the first pleasure voyage on the canal was made by James Sharp's family of eight brothers and sisters, and a niece. The party had started from Braunston on the 15th, using a portable cabin that fitted a narrow boat. On the 21st, after having explored the unfinished Harecastle tunnel, they arrived at Great Haywood. Here is their itinerary for the next few days, as recorded by Elizabeth Prowse, one of the sisters:

22nd to tetnal entered the Wolverhampton Canal
23rd passed 3 Acquiducts & the Tunel 240 feet. Stewponey Mr. Hoggetts where the Gleeners were. Kidderminster Tunal under the Street 120 feet. Storeport a Basson that covers 3 Acres and locks down into the Severen. great Works done in 5 years by Mr. Datford, & within 12 M of Woster.
24th Returned to Wolverhampton Lord Dudley etc. came on board . . .
25th Brumagam Lay
26th See Mr. Bolton's works and Lay at Wolverhampton
27th Lay at Wolsley Bridge
28th Stay^d Sunday there, Drank Tea at Mr. Anson's Shugborough.

They finished at Cavendish bridge (Shardlow), having done 284 miles by water and 170 by land in 15 days.[12]

As early as 1775 the newspaper said of Stourport:
'This place is becoming the resort of people of fashion. The Beauty of the Country round about it, the fine navigable Canal now compleatly finished, the spacious Bason for the Vessels, the River Severn, and the New Bridge over it,* form altogether a pleasing Picture. Scarce a day passes but several Parties of Ladies and Gentlemen come there in their Carriages. Regattas (the fashionable Term for the Water Parties) are not unusual.'[13]
The opening of the Dudley and Stourbridge Canals (see Ch. IV) late in 1779, and the development of traffic off the Birmingham, soon made Stourport less Arcadian. It became the transhipment point for Staffordshire coal going downwards to compete with

* A bridge with brick abutments and a cast-iron centre dated 1774, designed by Thomas F. Pritchard, designer of the iron bridge at Coalbrookdale.

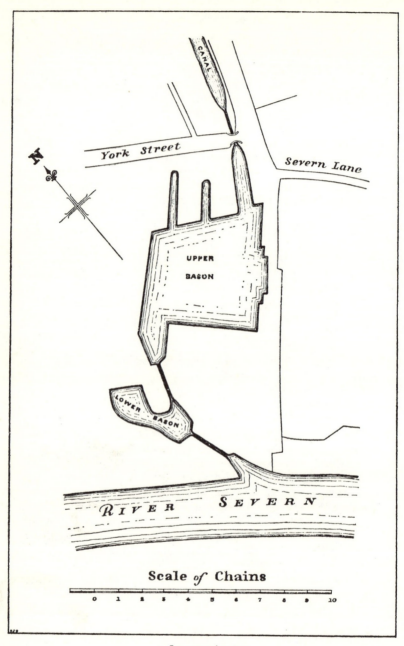

4. Stourport in 1804

and later to supersede that from the Shropshire collieries, and for manufactured goods such as ironware, glass, pottery and textiles from the Stourbridge, Dudley and Birmingham areas, the Potteries and Manchester, much of it going to Bristol for export. In return, goods imported at Bristol, agricultural produce of all kinds going to the towns, and the varied output of the Coalbrookdale area were landed on the wharves of Stourport on their way to the Midlands.

The old shipping places of Wribbenhall, Bewdley and Bridgnorth decayed before the newcomer, though for some time regular trow services to Gloucester and Bridgwater started from Bewdley and called at Stourport. Basins were constructed for transhipment and timber storage; gauging and graving docks, boat-building yards and warehouses were built.

'Houses, warehouses and inns . . . sprang up as if by magic, the magic which wealth-creating industry usually gives; and iron foundries, vinegar works, tan-yards, spinning mills, carpet manufactories, and boat-building establishments were added.'[14]

The canal company took a lively interest in the growing town, and the town in the canal, such as the occasion in 1812 when the inhabitants presented a clock to one of the warehouses, towards which the company subscribed £25.

The company was concerned with the navigation of the Severn, as we shall see. It was also anxious to develop connecting navigations. In 1774 they sent a representative to a meeting to promote the Stroudwater Navigation[15] from Framilode below Gloucester to Stroud; it was opened in 1779. In 1781 they began to take an interest in a canal from the Severn to the Thames. With the Stourbridge and Dudley companies, they sent representatives to a meeting on 22 December 1781 at Cirencester that decided to employ Robert Whitworth to survey a route from Tewkesbury to Lechlade,[16] and another to the gathering on 17 January 1783 that, having heard his report, decided instead upon an extension of the Stroudwater Navigation upwards and through a tunnel to Lechlade.[17] The Staffs & Worcs helped to pay Whitworth for his preliminary survey, as did the Dudley and Stourbridge companies, and many Staffs & Worcs shareholders subscribed to the resultant Thames & Severn Canal,[18] authorized in 1783. James Perry became a leader of the Thames & Severn as well as of his old company, and there were other connections between the personalities of the two concerns.

Unfortunately for the Staffs & Worcs, the line to London by

way of the Severn was only completed late in 1789, the route being 269¼ miles long from Farmer's Bridge, Birmingham, to Brentford. In the same year the Oxford line by way of Duke's Cut was completed, which shortened the route to 227¼ miles. Almost at once, therefore, Staffordshire coal lost any market it might have gained at Oxford or below, though it did win a certain sale along the Thames & Severn in competition with that from the Forest of Dean and later from the Somerset collieries. Down the Severn itself it competed with that from the Forest at Gloucester and Cheltenham, and hardly penetrated below Gloucester.

The increase in river traffic led to efforts to improve the river's channel and to build horse-towing paths, though little had resulted by 1790. During the winter there was usually enough water, but adequate summer freshes were scarce. Then the section above Worcester, with its many shallows of rock or gravel, could only be passed by very small boats, or, for nearly two months in an average year, by none at all.[19] In 1784 William Jessop, who already had experience of the Trent, was commissioned by the Staffs & Worcs company to estimate the cost of removing the shallows and improving the navigation, and also of making a horse towing path.[20] He reported to a public meeting in August, proposing to make the river navigable from Diglis below Worcester to Meadow Wharf, Coalbrookdale, at all seasons for vessels drawing 4 ft by building 13 or 14 locks and weirs, and below Diglis by dredging and altering the channel to counteract silting and the undermining of the banks.[21] Apparently also he proposed to collect floodwater in reservoirs.[22] Slightly altered after a re-survey by George Young to provide 15 locks, these plans, except for the last, were embodied in a bill of 1786 on which Robert Mylne also gave evidence;[23] to placate up-river interests Shrewsbury trade was exempted from toll.

The main opponents of the bill were those who, like Lord Dudley, were supporting a proposed canal from Stourbridge to Worcester (see p. 75) which would by-pass the Stourport–Worcester section; its backers therefore withdrew it after it had passed second reading in order to seek a compromise. A new plan was prepared that tried to meet objections. It proposed to set up Commissioners empowered to reduce tolls if they yielded more than an 8 per cent dividend, and to open subscription books along the whole river so that control would be widely spread.[24] In the meantime the canal company had itself done some dredging between Stourport and Diglis, but had been indicted at the Assizes for damaging the river,[25] and had had to stop.

In early 1790 Mylne was called in to re-survey the river, and then attended a committee on a new bill introduced in that year by the Staffs & Worcs company. This Act enabled them to raise £10,000 on mortgage to improve navigation between Stourport and Diglis by removing shoals, presumably by dredging and building training walls, for no locks were authorized. It seems that under Mylne's direction work was going on in May 1791, but he resigned in June. Much later it was said that this work was 'so obnoxious to the watermen on the River that they destroyed the works in the night';[26] legal action then seems to have been taken, and efforts at improvement came to an end.

In spite of many efforts, horse towing paths were also late in coming. In the early sixteenth century, landowners had tried to levy charges for men towing over their lands in the form of 'fynes and draughtes and botels of wyne', but these were forbidden by an Act of 1521-2.[27] A rough towpath suitable for use by gangs of bow-hauliers had therefore been created over the years. The first efforts to provide a path for horses were made in 1761 when the merchants of Bewdley, Stourbridge, Dudley and Kidderminster petitioned for a path from Bewdley to Worcester, and were supported by traders in Wolverhampton, Birmingham and Manchester.[28] Meetings were held at Digbeth and Wolverhampton, and in December there was talk of a bill.[29]

No action followed, but the opening of the canal in 1772 probably stimulated the Act[30] of the same year to authorize the Bewdley Bridge and Coalbrookdale Horse Towing Path Company to build a path for the short distance between those points. There had been considerable opposition to the Act, probably from those who were naturally allergic to paying tolls when they need not, and though the trustees appointed under it did meet several times at Bridgnorth, nothing further was done. In 1777, again, there was an abortive move for a path from Upton to Bewdley, to the bill for which the Staffs & Worcs agreed to subscribe £100.[31] The need for a path was growing, however, as traffic increased; a newspaper note in 1789 complained that there were now too few 'towing men', and that delays resulted.[32]

To complete this picture of the Severn before the big expansion of traffic began, let us look at the history of some efforts to make navigable branches from it. The oldest were all connected with the name of Andrew Yarranton, the seventeenth-century engineer and entrepreneur. (*To continue the history of the Staffordshire & Worcestershire Canal, turn to p.* 128); *of the Severn, to p.* 115.)

Warwickshire Avon

William Sandys of Fladbury began to make the Avon[33] navigable in 1636, and after three years and the expenditure of a large sum had made the river passable from Tewkesbury to Stratford for barges of 30 tons by building thirteen flash and pound-locks. During the Commonwealth William Say made further improvements, and then from 1664 onwards a syndicate which included Yarranton built six more flash or pound locks on the river above Evesham, and provided an adequate navigation.

The river was in the hands of owners who had leased sections of it to those who in turn had sub-leased it to others, and overcharging was common; in 1751, therefore, the borough of Evesham and others obtained an Act[34] to throw the river open to all, and to lay down a scale of tolls. Soon afterwards the Lower Avon, downwards from Evesham, was bought by George Perrott, who made some improvements between 1763 and 1768 which enabled 40-ton barges to use it. He died in 1780 and was succeeded by his nephew George. The upper river above Evesham remained in the possession of relations of the last Lord Windsor, who had died in 1758, and whose ancestor had been granted it in 1664. In 1790 the river downwards from Stratford was a passable but not good navigation, 'Subject to Floods & Drought which makes the Passage difficult and tedious',[35] and without a horse towing path. (*To continue the history of the Warwickshire Avon, turn to p. 146.*)

Dick Brook

In 1653 Andrew Yarranton, who had already interested himself in ironmaking, found Roman slag remains near the city wall at Worcester. He built a small charcoal blast furnace on a site west of Glasshampton bridge over the present B4196 road, operated by the power of the Nutnells stream. East of the bridge a leat was led from Dick Brook, three miles south of Stourport on the western bank of the Severn, to operate a forge downstream, a level cartway connecting the two works.

To bring the ore up the Brook[36] from the Severn, Yarranton built two flash locks in the first 300 yd, the remains of which are still visible. Each was about 70 ft by 10 ft 9 in., probably fitted with a single pair of gates. The forge was half a mile above the upper lock. Nothing is known about the boats used, but because

5. The Dick Brook

of the narrow and winding brook, they must have been small, two or three perhaps being joined together.

It is likely that the works only operated for a short period, but it is not known when they closed.

Worcestershire Stour

In 1662, after opposition from the Shropshire collieries, an Act[37] was passed to authorize the Earl of Bristol, Lord Windsor and Thomas Smyth of London* to make the Stour navigable from the Severn to the collieries round Stourbridge, so that coal could be carried downwards to such towns as Worcester and Gloucester.

The original plan had been to make the river navigable for craft of 6 tons, with 11 locks between the Severn and Stourbridge, and two branch tramroads.[38] It may be that a start was made on the three uppermost locks, for an account of 1667 includes the cost of 'taking up the bones of three Locks below Barge Hall'. However, the main work, on a bigger scale, was done between 1665 and 1667 by Andrew Yarranton. He built 12 locks and four turnpikes (presumably half-locks) between Stourbridge and Kidderminster to take 16-ton craft, and also a tramroad from near Stourbridge to a colliery, for a fee of £1,255. According to his own account, he 'fell on, and made it compleatly Navigable from Sturbridge to Kederminster; and carried down many hundred Tuns of Coales, . . . and there it was obstructed for want of money, which by Contract was to be paid'.[39]

There seems to have been local opposition to the navigation, for in November 1667 when seven barges came down, the lock at Kidderminster was chained and had to be broken. Robert Yarranton then started to complete the works, but ran into scarcity of money after a little more had been done. Soon afterwards, the works seem to have been destroyed by floods, and although efforts were made to revive the project in the 1670s and 1700, nothing was done until the original purpose of the schemes was fulfilled by the building of the Stourbridge and Staffs & Worcs Canals.[40]

River Teme

The same Order in Council which authorized William Sandys to make the Warwickshire Avon navigable allowed him also to do the same to the Teme towards Ludlow, 'whereby the counties . . .

---

* There were several subsequent changes among the undertakers.

may be better supplied with wood, iron, pit-coals, and other commodities which they now want'.[41] He does not seem to have carried out any work.

In 1750 Edmund Bury, a miller, advertised for sale at Stanford-on-Teme a large, flat-bottomed boat complete with mast, oars and cordage that would carry about ten tons. R. C. Gaut considers that such craft were probably used to serve mills and iron forges along short stretches of the unimproved river.[42] Apart from such use, there was, at any rate from the early part of the nineteenth century onwards, traffic on the first 1½ miles of the river to Powick Bridge, where there was a large coal wharf, the ownership of which included the right to use freely a towpath to the Severn.[43]

River Salwarpe

I do not know whether Richard II's grant in 1378 to the bailiffs of Droitwich of the right to levy tolls on the Salwarpe implies that the river was then passable. If so, it afterwards ceased to be so, for in 1655 Andrew Yarranton and Captain Wall offered to seek letters patent from the Lord Protector to make it navigable. Yarranton made an agreement with the corporation of Droitwich, which provided that certain lands should be allotted to him for twenty-one years in payment,[44] but the times were too unsettled, and nothing was done. Then in 1660 or 1661 Lord Windsor proposed a navigation scheme, and another agreement was made providing for payment as the work was done. Nash says that he had built five locks out of six before his scheme failed and was left unfinished.[45]

Authority was then given to the Earl of Bristol, Lord Windsor and Thomas Smyth in the same Act that authorized them also to make the Stour navigable. Dr Willan tells us[46] that Sir Timothy and Sir Samuel Baldwyn bought the Earl of Bristol's rights for £1,450, and Sir Samuel also bought some of Smyth's. In 1673 a half-share of Lord Windsor's was transferred to Sir Thomas Cookes.[47] Sir Timothy and Sir Samuel's son Charles then spent a further £4,000 on the river, as well as some thousands spent by others, including salt water valued at £2,000 provided by the Droitwich salt proprietors. Lord Windsor was presumably otherwise occupied, perhaps on the Avon.

The aim could not have been attained, for in 1693 a bill was introduced to improve the Salwarpe, the Earls of Shrewsbury and Coventry to be undertakers. Ten years later the Earl of Plymouth,

Lord Windsor's son, petitioned for another, but by now the salt works proprietors had become discouraged, and they opposed it. Still another failed, that promoted by Simon Wood of London in 1747; he wanted to buy a new brine pit and also make the river navigable. Finally in 1755 Mr Baker, a druggist of London, revived an old plan to carry brine by pipeline to the Severn at Hawford, but this failed also. Some such scheme must have been still active while the Droitwich Canal was being projected, however, for in 1846 the Droitwich Patent Salt Company alleged that the canal company had broken faith with them 'by not carrying out the arrangement by which the Canal Company induced the Salt Company to give up their intention of carrying their Brine by pipes to the Banks of the Severn'[48]

Droitwich Canal

The failure of these efforts to make the Salwarpe navigable, and the development of the salt trade from about 1725 onwards, made it necessary to build a canal, and in January 1768 an Act[49] was obtained for making a barge waterway beside the river from the town to the Severn at Hawford. The authorized capital was £13,400 in £100 shares, with power to raise £20,000 more. All the 134 shares had been subscribed by the date of the first shareholders' meeting in March 1768, 71 from Droitwich itself, 41 from the rest of Worcestershire, and 22 from elsewhere. It was therefore a very local effort.

The authorized tolls were substantial for a canal only 6¾ miles long, with eight locks, which took craft up to 64 ft by 14 ft 6 in., carrying 60 to 70 tons; 1s 6d per ton for salt, coal and stone for any distance. Therefore the enterprise offered good prospects. James Brindley, who is said in 1767 to have made alternative estimates for a narrow and a barge canal,[50] was appointed 'Inspector of the Works', which were to be carried on 'under his Care and Direction',[51] at a salary of £60 p.a. John Priddey was to be resident engineer at £90 p.a., and started by sending John Bushel, the contractor for the locks, to be instructed by Brindley on the Trent & Mersey. One result of his activity was that it appeared to the Birmingham Canal company, then building its main line, that 'some person concern'd in the Droitwich Navigation had enticed away Stone Cutters employ'd in this Undertaking'; they wrote a couple of stiffish letters to the Droitwich committee.[52]

Work began on 27 June 1768[53] and went ahead steadily, though not without friction, judging from this protest signed by twelve men:

'Com posol of the Bricklars at Lady Hood at the Lock to be all In one mine

'We af Bin yoused Very ill for Thy Will not pay for Wat we work for. If you dont pay for watt Time as Bind We Will not Work and wee will not Work under 11s a wick and to be yusde well.'[54]

By March 1770 the capital had all been spent, and it was decided to raise £6,600 more by issuing further £100 shares. Between March and October another £3,500 was borrowed, so that the cost of the canal was £23,500. A curious order of the time appoints three lock-keepers, orders watch houses to be built, and instructs them to conduct vessels up and down the canal from one to the next. A peculiarity of the canal itself was that its water was salt.

The canal had been built from Hawford to Droitwich on the south side of the river, though in order to do so Brindley had used the river's bed for a short distance from the lock to the west of Chapel Bridge to a little beyond the footbridge at the bottom of Rickett's Lane, a new river bed being cut fifty or so yards to the north. Rees's *Cyclopaedia* says: 'This canal was executed by Mr. James Brindley, and it is said to present a pattern to canal-makers by the neatness and regularity of its curves, and the stability and excellency of all its works.'[55] There was an exception to this regularity, the sharp bend at Salwarpe by the south side of the church which resulted from the prohibition contained in the Act against making the canal to the north of that building, and which made navigation difficult. Judging by the fewness of references to him in the records, I suspect that Brindley had little to do with building the canal, and that most of the credit should go to John Priddey.

The Worcester newspaper reported the canal open on 12 March 1771: 'There were great Rejoicings at Droitwich . . . on Account of two Vessels arriving at that Place, up the new Canal, loaded with Coals.'[56] In 1774 the company began wholesale and retail trading in coal at Droitwich, opening the wharf on Tuesdays and Fridays and charging 6d a ton wholesale and 1s retail more than the cost price. In this year shares were changing hands at £140 to £165. At the end of 1775 dividends began, and by 1777 the shares were up to £160. By 1780 trade was sufficiently established for the company to dispose of the coal trading business.

In March 1784 the company heard of the proposal (see p. 75) to extend the Stourbridge Canal southwards to Worcester, and offered £20 towards the cost of the survey on condition that it joined the topmost pound of their own waterway. When it was decided that it should end at Diglis, Droitwich shares fell to about £130. They then negotiated with the promoters for a branch from their canal to join the new one. A group of Droitwich shareholders strongly disagreed with this policy, holding that such a branch would seriously damage the Droitwich company. The result of the argument was an agreement between the canal company and the promoters for an amalgamation of the two concerns on the basis of the purchase of Droitwich shares for £140 cash or a perpetual 5 per cent dividend at the choice of the shareholder. The bill failed, and so the amalgamation, but an aftermath of the quarrel, which had evidently led to the packing of the shareholders' meeting that had decided on amalgamation, was that in future proxies had to be shareholders, because otherwise people attended who were 'unacquainted with the Real Interests of the Company, but who procure such Proxys from absent Members from a desire to promote some particular purposes'.[57]

So matters rested till in 1789 the idea of a waterway to Worcester was revived, this time not from the Stourbridge Canal, but from Birmingham, and with a proposed branch to Droitwich; in October the Droitwich company once again began negotiations with the promoters. Another stage in the development of lines to Bristol was about to start. (*To continue the history of the Droitwich Canal, turn to p. 133.*)

Eardington Forge Canal

The Upper Forge at Eardington on the Severn below Bridgnorth was erected between 1776 and 1781 by the ironmaster John Wheeler. At the same time he and William Wheeler built a canal* about 9 ft wide and 750 yards long, 600 yards of which was in tunnel, to provide transport to and from a river wharf. Later it also supplied water to Lower Forge, built between 1782 and 1789. The canal was probably not used for navigation after 1815, though it continued to supply water until 1889.

---

* This canal is not included in the Summary at Appendix I.

CHAPTER IV

Beginnings round Birmingham

THE promoters of the Trent & Mersey having dropped their projected branch to Birmingham, then a town of some 30,000 inhabitants, by way of Lichfield and Tamworth, its citizens had to look elsewhere for their canal connection. It was badly needed, for road transport was hard pressed. 'It was common', said Hutton, 'to see a train of carriages for miles, to the great destruction of the road, and the annoyance of travellers.'[1]

Even before the Acts had been passed for the Grand Trunk and the Staffs & Worcs, 'A Well-Wisher to Trade' had written to the newspaper to suggest a canal from Birmingham to the Staffs & Worcs that would pass through the coalfields; it would cost about £20,000, he said, and would pay 20 per cent. Early in 1767 he was followed by 'Well-wisher to the Town' with the same proposal, and

> 'whereas the Utility of a Navigable Cut or Canal from this Town (thro' the Coal Works) to Wolverhampton, setting forth the great Advantage the Inhabitants wou'd receive not only in reducing the price of the Carriage of Coals and other Commodities, but also the price of Provisions, Oats, Beans, etc. by reducing and rendering useless the great Number of Horses that are now kept and employed for such Purposes, having been made appear and offered to the Consideration of the Publick: an Advertizement was soon afterwards* inserted in the Publick Papers Solliciting the Attendance of the Inhabitants at the Swan Inn'.[2]

This meeting, on 28 January, opened a subscription and approved a survey, Brindley being asked to carry it out. At a further

* On 26 January 1767.

meeting on 4 June he put forward two possible lines, but 'gave it as his opinion that the best was from New-Hall, over Birmingham Heath, to or near ... Smethwick, Oldbury, Tipton Green, Bilston, and from thence to the Staffordshire and Worcestershire Canal, with Branches to different Coal Works'.[3] The cost should not exceed £50,000. The plan was agreed, and soon afterwards a Select Committee was chosen to carry it through. It contained some famous Birmingham names, among them Samuel Garbett, the original supporter of Darwin and Wedgwood, Dr William Small, Matthew Boulton and Samuel Galton. By July £35,400 had been subscribed, no one person being allowed to hold more than £1,000 worth of shares, and by August the full £50,000.

Two groups of people made their views known. In November the local coalowners, fearing that the canal might bring in cheap coal to compete with theirs, and wanting low internal tolls but a high charge on that coming up Wolverhampton locks, met Brindley. It was doubtless as a result that the general meeting on 13 November that decided to go forward for a bill stated clearly: 'That the Primary and Principal Object of this Undertaking was and is to obtain a Navigation from the Collieries to this Town.'[4]

A second group was concerned about the dangers of monopoly, and in the light of what happened their proposals are not without interest. They suggested that dividends should not exceed 10 per cent, and that any surplus should be used to buy shares, lower the tolls or perform other benefits. In their reply the promoters said that

'the Subscribers are not so sanguine as to expect a profit near so great, and ... they are quite convinced the quantity of Goods they can now realize as coming to Birm^m or passing thro' such a part of the Country as may be convenient for the Navigation, would not afford common Interest upon their Capital, and that the Supposition of a considerable encrease of Tonnage would pay them no more than 6 per cent'.

They added to this philanthropic statement an appeal to economics, saying that were the bill to be delayed a year,

'the Town of Birmingham alone ... cannot suffer so small a loss as £8,000, ... and will in course be most severely felt by the Poor'.[5]

However, the Committee was instructed to accept the restrictions rather than lose the bill, but this turned out not to be necessary.

The Act[6] was obtained on 24 February 1768, authorizing a line from Birmingham along Brindley's route to join the Staffs & Worcs at 'Autherley otherwise Aldersley', with branches to Wednesbury and Ocker Hill. The capital was £55,000 in £100 shares and £15,000 more if necessary (altered by an Act of 1769 to £50,000 and £20,000). The only unusual feature of the Act was the power given to the Staffs & Worcs company to make the canal themselves to join their own should the junction not be completed six months after the canal was open to Birmingham, the cost to be recovered from the Birmingham company.

A meeting on 2 March appointed officers. Brindley was made engineer at £200 p.a., and John Meredith clerk at £100. Presentations of plate were made to William Bentley and Joseph Wilkinson, who had greatly helped to get the Act, and a resolution was passed 'That the Navigation be immediately begun'.

The work seems to have been done mainly under the superintendence of two of Brindley's engineering assistants, Robert Whitworth and Samuel Simcock. The most important alteration made from the original plan was to avoid a tunnel at Smethwick after the discovery of 'running sand and other bad materials for such purpose'. On Brindley's recommendation it was thought 'less expensive and equally beneficial to carry the Canal over the Hill . . . and that the same will not be attended with more delay than Tunnelling'.[7] The first object of the Committee was to complete the canal from the Wednesbury mines to Birmingham, and as its value became apparent, the drive became faster. On 31 March 1769 the General Assembly ordered the Committee 'to execute the Locks and Bridges with all possible dispatch, without regard to any extra expence they may think necessary for that purpose'. Boats were built by the company so that the undertaking 'may be forwarded with all possible Dispatch',[8] and 'Mr. Bentley is requested not to regard Expence for the security of our Affairs for a few weeks'.[9] Brindley himself evidently preferred the works to the committee-room, for on 14 July 1769 the committee observed 'That Mr. Brindley hath frequently passed by, and sometimes come into Town, without giving them an opportunity of meeting to confer with him upon the progress of this undertaking' and 'expressing their dissatisfaction at not being able to see him at such times'.

The canal from the collieries at Wednesbury to Paradise Street, some ten miles long, was opened on 6 November 1769.[10]

> Then revel in gladness, let harmony flow
> From the district of Lordesley to Paradise Row,
> For true-feeling joy in each breast must be wrought
> When coals under fivepence per hundred are bought.

This was the retail price;[11] wholesale, coal that had before been

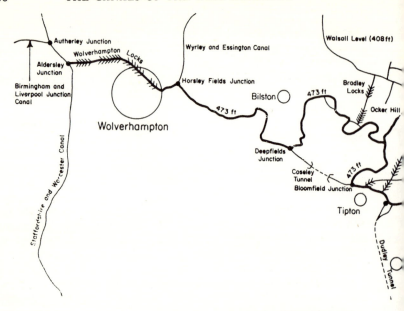

6. The Birmingham Canal and its branch

selling at from 15s to 18s a ton, by May 1770 fell to 4s,[12] though this price was not held. The authorized termination at Newhall was not opened till 25 March 1772. It was used for timber, stone and merchandise, coal being handled at Paradise Street.

The Company organized the coal trade tightly. It could not refuse facilities to other traders, but it built up its own system of buying coal at the pits, loading it, maintaining a steady round service of boats moving day and night to and from the collieries, landing it on Birmingham wharf, loading it into carts controlled by the company, and distributing it with company's men. The committee were instructed that 'they will take care to make profit thereon over and above every contingent Expence, and £5 per Cent Interest on the money employ'd. But that such Profit do not exceed one farthing per Hundred on the Coal'.[13] Later, order offices were set up (seven were announced in March 1770) to avoid the inconvenience of having to go to the wharves to place orders, and special arrangements were made to sell small quantities to the poor at almost as cheap rates as large. The supply of men, towing horses and carts all presented problems. The day after the canal was opened, an officer was sent 'to Broseley and Madeley

BEGINNINGS ROUND BIRMINGHAM 67

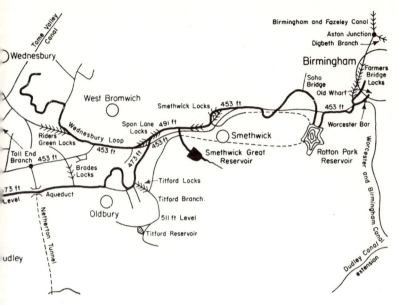

1771-3, are shown with a thick line

Wood to endeavour to procure two proper persons to steer, and three to stow, the Company's Boats',[14] presumably off the Severn craft, and a few days later Garbett was asked to write to Gilbert at the Duke of Bridgewater's 'to lend the Company a Boy or two to steer the Boats'.[15] Early in 1770 the company was advertising for towing horses that they could hire by the return trip;[16] carts and their horses also had to be hired to supplement those the company owned.[17] The demand now extended beyond the town; John Ash wrote on 3 February 1770: 'the Canal is full of Boats belonging to the Company and private owners ... & coals are daily hawked abt the streets for purchasers, the Town is fully stocked & the Country Teams increase on the Wharf, so that the Waggons are very few indeed.... Three Hundred Tons at least are brought daily by the Navigation, which is 100 Tons more than the Town has demand for'.[18]

Work on the extension now began, but not quickly enough for the Staffs & Worcs company, who in May 1770 had sought, but failed to get, a mandamus to compel a junction to be made, and had then in January 1771, brought in a bill to make it themselves: whereupon the Birmingham company agreed to pay their costs and hurry up completion. By May 1770 coal was being carried to Birmingham from Tipton, and by November from Bilston.

The flight of 20 locks* at Wolverhampton was then built, and the junction with the Staffs & Worcs was declared complete on 14 September 1772,[19] but actually opened to traffic on 21 September.[20] The length of the main line was 22⅝ miles, of the Wednesbury branch 4⅜ miles, of that to Ocker Hill ⅝ mile, and of the cut to Newhall ½ mile. It was built 28 ft wide at top, but by 1795 had been widened to an average of 40 ft. From Aldersley the original canal ran over the present course to Deepfields junction, where it followed the Wednesbury Oak loop line to rejoin the present course at Bloomfield Junction. It left it again 2½ furlongs farther on at Tipton Factory junction and rejoined it at Smethwick junction. Soon afterwards it curved, south by the Cape arm, north by the Soho branch, south again by the Icknield Port Road loop-line and also by the Oozell's Street branch, to end near Farmer's bridge.

The cost was £112,000 and a rent charge of £550 p.a.[21] Of this sum, £70,000 had been raised in shares, giving each share a value of £140, and the balance by loans. While the canal was under construction, the shareholders had been paid the usual 5 per cent on their calls, and this was continued until the first dividend of 5 per cent (£7 per £140 share) paid for the year ending 25 March 1774. It was thenceforward the policy of the company not to increase the share capital, but to finance improvements out of profits or by loan. Dividends and tolls rose as follows:

Years	Average tolls	Average dividends per £140 share			Average dividends per cent		
	£	£	s	d	£	s	d
1771–3	8,888						
1774–6	12,291	7	0	0	5	0	0
1777–9	13,743½*	16	6	8	11	5	0
1780–2	15,169	19	10	0	13	18	7
1783–5	16,290½†	16	16	0	12	0	0
1786–8	NK	18	18	0	13	10	0
1789–91	26,461‡	24	10	0	17	10	0

* 1778 and 1779 only.
† 1783 and 1784 only.
‡ 1791 only.

From the time of opening of the first section to Birmingham the

---

* The 10 ft lock at the bottom of the flight was later found to be wasteful of water, and was converted to one of 5 ft, another being built above it to make 21.

company was accused of high-handedness and monopoly; of illegal seizure of land, illegal entry to other people's premises, opposition to loading basins and branch canals not built by themselves, monopoly of wharves and weighing machines, as traders in coal ignoring their own by-laws,[22] and having built their canal with many windings to increase their tolls. The last accusation drew a denial from Brindley and Simcock in an advertisement of 14 January 1771; they said that many people would not have been served if the canal had not wound about. As for the rest, the tight organization of the coal trade, which presumably seemed businesslike and efficient to the committee, looked very different to the general public; it was just as well they had no access to such minutes as this: 'it is necessary that the Company shou'd exert such Powers as the Law hath given them to obtain the sole Possession of all convenient Landing places in order to establish the best and most distinct Rules possible for Public accommodation'.[23] The company got a bad reputation in this respect; on 15 September 1770 James Sharp, a member of the Common Council of the City of London and a believer in canals being built by public bodies, talked to George III about them. He said:

'subscribers are always looking after their private gain instead of the improvement of the Navigation; this is the Case att present upon the Birmingham Canal, for it is cramp'd in many particulars on account of the Expence, although att this time tho' only just finished, every £100 share* sells for £170. If this additional value had been expended upon the Canal instead of falling into private pocketts, it would have been much more noble than it is'.[24]

In addition to bearing such accusations, the Committee saw a quarrel between the Chairman, William Bentley and Samuel Garbett, who considered that he had been accused of seeking priority supplies of coal for his brass works. The trouble was patched up at the December 1769 General Assembly, but immediately afterwards Garbett resigned from the committee, sold most of his shares, and became the company's enemy, accusing it of favouring the coalmasters and ignoring the public interest by not supplying coal as cheaply as possible, and suggesting that it be taken over by Commissioners. In 1770 he promoted a rival canal, and in early 1771 threatening to go to Parliament with hostile petitions. Indeed, on 22 January 1771 Mr Aris had to stop controversy in the columns of the *Birmingham Gazette*, 'having received from my

* In reality, £140 share.

Friends a Variety of Complaints, that my Paper is filled with Disputes relative to the Birmingham Navigation'. Thenceforward controversy quietened down, and the canal became an essential means of Birmingham's growth by bringing in not only coal, but 'pig-iron for the founderies, lime-stone, articles for the manufacture of brass and steel, also stone, brick, slate, timber, etc.'.[25]

The company continued in the coal trade, but less hectically; prices were reduced, and boats no longer worked at night. Water was always a difficulty on such a high-level canal; in its early years any possible source was used, yet shortage was frequent. A reservoir was built at Smethwick and soon afterwards at Titford. In 1778 a Boulton & Watt engine started to pump water back up the three locks at Spon Lane, in 1779 another up the Smethwick flight of six locks, and in 1784 a third on the Ocker Hill branch, soon afterwards to be pumping 66 ft from the Willinsworth level below Riders Green locks, with the help of two other engines. After the Smethwick summit had been lowered in 1790 the Spon Lane engine was no longer needed, but that at Smethwick was supplemented by another for pumping back up the duplicate sets of three locks. Other engines were erected on the system, while the reservoir on the Wyrley & Essington Canal at Cannock, built in 1800, and that at Rotton Park in 1826, provided further supplies.

The great battle for the Birmingham & Fazeley Canal was one of the consequences of the quarrel with Garbett and the fear of monopoly by the Birmingham company. It began with a meeting at Lichfield on 18 August 1770 to consider a canal from Walsall, a coal-producing area which had been left untouched by the Birmingham Canal, by Lichfield to Fradley on the Trent & Mersey, at which Garbett was present.[26] After opposition from landowners and an effort to placate them with a more modest scheme, the project was wound up.[27] The Coventry, Oxford and Birmingham companies then from time to time discussed a number of plans, but a decisive moment was reached when a new independent group called a meeting at Warwick in August 1781 to consider a canal from Wednesbury by Fazeley to the then end of the Coventry Canal at Atherstone, and modified this in October to a line to end at Fazeley seemingly also adding a branch to Birmingham itself. The Birmingham shareholders at a special meeting recognized a serious threat. In January 1782 they referred to

'Several Publick Meetings having been held and Advertizements appeared ... indicating an intention in a set of people to apply ... for Powers to make another Navigable Canal from the Collierys to this Town and from thence to Fazeley, and it appearing to this Company not only unnecessary that any other Canal should be made to this Town but that the same if made would greatly prejudice the present Undertaking and that such Measure is not warranted in Equity or Justice.'[28]

They decided upon 'all possible Opposition', and at the same meeting also to extend their own canal from the Wednesbury branch to Walsall. Bills for this and for the rival project were presented in 1782, and each defeated the other.

Often suggested, and of some relevance at this time, were schemes to make the River Tame navigable to Tamworth. In early 1783 William Jessop was employed to survey the Trent from Burton, the Tame and the Anker, and apparently reported that they could be made navigable to Birmingham for wide boats at one-third the cost of the projected Birmingham & Fazeley Canal,[29] but the proposal was not taken up.

The Birmingham & Fazeley promoters now made contact with the Trent & Mersey, Coventry and Oxford companies, and concluded the Coleshill agreement on 20 June, announcing at the meeting that they had already had enough subscriptions to complete their canal.[30] In despair, the Birmingham shareholders decided to seek power for a new company controlled by them to build a canal from the Birmingham at Riders Green to Broadwaters, part-way to Walsall, with eight branches, and another from Farmer's Bridge near Newhall to Fazeley.

'Both parties beat up for volunteers in the town, to strengthen their forces; from words of acrimony, they came to those of virulence; then the powerful batteries of hand-bills, and newspapers were opened: every town within fifty miles, interested on either side, was moved to petition, and both prepared for the grand attack, confident of victory. . . . Each party possessed that activity for which Birmingham is famous, and seemed to divide between them the legislative strength of the nation; every corner of the two houses was ransacked for a vote: the throne was the only power unsolicited. Perhaps at the reading ... there was the fullest House of Commons ever remembered on a private bill. . . . As the old company were the first adventurers, the house gave them the option to perform this Herculean labour, which they accepted.'[31]

Immediately the Act[32] had been passed, an agreement was made with the subscribers to the rival company by which their shares were bought at the sums expended—except for one or two recalcitrants who were compensated—and in 1784 the two concerns were formally amalgamated[33] as the Birmingham & Birmingham & Fazeley Canal Company.

John Smeaton was employed as engineer of the new lines. The Broadwaters canals with 8 locks at Riders Green were finished in April 1786;[34] that to Fazeley with 38 was then undertaken, with the incompetent or perhaps unlucky John Pinkerton as contractor and was completed in August 1789,[35] though Pinkerton had been removed in February. The cost seems to have been about £110,000, which was raised by loan. Lichfield now found itself within two miles of a canal, and road transport developed from Streethay where the Birmingham & Fazeley met Ryknield Street.[36]

As soon as the Broadwaters extensions were finished they threw a big additional burden upon the flights of six locks up to and down from the mile-long summit level of the Birmingham's main line at Smethwick, and it was obvious that this would be further increased when the Fazeley line was open for traffic towards the Coventry and Trent & Mersey Canals. Therefore in 1787 the company decided to reduce the height of the 491-ft summit by 18 ft to that of the Wolverhampton pound, and remove three locks at each end by digging a new cutting that would be 46 ft deep at its lowest point. The contract was advertised in December, and the work was carried out in two stages. A new cut was first built south of the existing line and 12 ft below, the spoil from which was raised and boated away on the old line. This cut, which eliminated two locks at each end, was opened on 2 July 1789, just in time for the new traffic. The newspaper said of it: 'So vast and seemingly impractical an undertaking has, we believe, never before been attempted in this kingdom; mountains have been raised and levelled and a canal of a well's depth has been cut almost under the canal.'[37] The final level was then cut still farther to the south and the spoil boated away on the intermediate line. This, which cut out a third lock at each end, was opened on 6 April 1790 after navigation had been stopped for twenty-two days for the re-alignment of the ends and filling with water. At the same time the remaining three locks were duplicated.

The cost was between £30,000 and £40,000, and by 1793 a hundred boats a day were passing.[38] By standing at Smethwick anyone who doubted the value of canals to the modern world would soon be converted; by studying the profit and loss account of the Birmingham* company he would also appreciate the potentialities of canal shares as an investment. (*To continue the history of the Birmingham Canal, turn to p. 83.*)

Stourbridge Canal

The Stourbridge and the Dudley Canals were part of a single scheme to bring coal from the mines round Dudley to works near Stourbridge and also to the Severn towns by way of the Staffs & Worcs Canal, and carry ironstone and limestone for local use. In February 1775 a Stourbridge meeting approved a survey of Robert Whitworth's and subscribed the entire cost,[39] Lord Dudley being the leading promoter. Because of likely opposition from the coal-owners of Shropshire and Staffordshire, petitions were obtained from Worcester, Gloucester and other towns of the Severn valley as well as from Stratford-upon-Avon.

The first bill, for the Stourbridge and Dudley lines as a single unit, was introduced in the spring of 1775, but was opposed by the Birmingham company and withdrawn. With the proposed line unchanged, but now split into two, bills for the Stourbridge and Dudley Canals were introduced again in the autumn, and passed together on 2 April 1776 'notwithstanding the most effectual opposition possible' by the Birmingham company.[40] The Stourbridge Act[41] authorized a line from the Staffs & Worcs, which had been open for four years, at Stourton to Stourbridge, from which, at Wordsley junction, a branch ran to the Fens on Pensnett Chase, where the reservoir was to be. From this branch at Lays junction another line ran to Black Delph to meet the Dudley Canal. As built, the waterway was $3\frac{1}{4}$ miles long from Stourton to Stourbridge, with four rising locks near Stourton. On the first branch, 2 miles long, there were 16 rising locks;† the second, $1\frac{3}{8}$ miles long, was level. A 56-yd tunnel with a towpath was apparently built under Brettell Lane, but was subsequently opened out and a bridge substituted.

A capital of £30,000 was authorized, but perhaps by oversight no powers to raise additional money were included. The leading promoters were Lords Dudley & Ward, Stamford and Foley, together with local manufacturers such as John Foster and John

* I use this name throughout instead of the cumbersome 'Birmingham & Birmingham & Fazeley', which in 1794 was altered to the 'Birmingham Canal Navigations'.

† Originally there was a staircase lock which was replaced by two single locks, probably in 1827.

Pidcock. A number were glass-men, and clearly glassmakers' needs had influenced the route, since nearly all the glass-houses were within a quarter-mile of the canal.[42] Francis Homfray of Wollaston Hall, the ironmaster, held six shares and was made treasurer, and Thomas Dadford, junior, engineer at £120 p.a. and a house, with James Green* to help him, and made a prompt start on the aqueduct over the Stour.

By April 1778 the share capital had all been called, and the company started issuing bonds. By early 1779 trading was taking place, and two more reservoirs on Pensnett Chase were commissioned later in the year. The canal was probably open throughout on 3 December.[43] On Lady Day 1781 Dadford resigned, and was succeeded as engineer by Abraham Lees, who also acted as agent, till he in turn was replaced in 1800 by James Green, who was also the engineer to the Dudley company. A further Act[44] of 1782 regularized some unauthorized calls and borrowing by permitting additional calls up to £10,000, and recognizing calls of £3,000 already made. The company's capital therefore became £43,000, and the eventual nominal value of the shares £142 $\frac{8}{7}$.

The company was hampered by a clause in their original Act to which they had had to agree, that the Staffs & Worcs were allowed to charge 2d a ton per mile on coal from the Stourbridge Canal, against 1½d on other coal carried, so that the older sources of supply should not be penalized. They tried but failed to get the clause repealed and, being dissatisfied with the trade that was passing, began to look about for possibilities of increasing it. They had already started a coal business at Stourport to promote the sale of coal off their canal, which lasted till 1792, contributed to the cost of Robert Whitworth's survey of the Thames & Severn Canal, and supported its successful bill of 1783. Could not a worthwhile trade down the Severn and into the Thames be built up if access could be obtained to Staffordshire and if they had their own line to the Severn independent of the Staffs & Worcs? And did not the authorization of the Birmingham & Fazeley open a possible trade towards the north and east?

In 1784, therefore, the Stourbridge company joined with the Dudley in sending to the Birmingham proposals for a junction with that company's line that resulted in an Act of 1785 to authorize a connection by way of the Dudley tunnel, to be opened in 1792.

At the same time the company commissioned a survey for a

* Probably the father of the Westcountry canal engineer.

canal from near Stourbridge through Bromsgrove to Diglis below Worcester, which would have been 26 miles long with two tunnels and 128 locks.[45] A separate company was formed to promote it, strongly supported by Lord Dudley and the Stourbridge shareholders. The opposition of the Droitwich was changed into support, as we have seen, by agreeing to amalgamate, and a bill* was introduced in 1786. It was bitterly opposed by the Staffs & Worcs[46] and was defeated in the House of Lords, whereupon there were rejoicings and bellringings at Wolverhampton, Kidderminster, Stourport and elsewhere.[47] The failure had two results: in 1786 the Staffs & Worcs agreed to reduce their tolls on coal from Aldersley and from Stourton as soon as the Dudley tunnel was completed, and in fact did lower them from 2d to $1\frac{1}{2}$d on coal from the Stourbridge Canal and from $1\frac{1}{2}$d to 1d on that carried on their main line in March 1788, well before the tunnel was finished. As for a canal to Worcester, the idea was revived in 1789, but this time as a direct line from Birmingham, which was to be opposed by the Stourbridge company until they obtained a dividend guarantee as the price of acquiescence.

A first dividend of £3 10s 0d per £142 $\frac{8}{7}$ share (£2 9s 0d per cent) had been paid for 1785, and by 1789 this had reached £9 (£6 6s 8d per cent). Comfortably based on the local coal trade, and on their traffic in rod and bar iron, nails, ironstone and limestone, glass, clay, bricks and earthenware, the Stourbridge company reached 1790 in good order. This was far less the case with the Dudley. (*To continue the history of the Stourbridge Canal, turn to p. 100.*)

Dudley Canal

The company's Act[48] was passed on the same day in 1776 as that for the Stourbridge, and the first meeting was held on 6 June at the *Swan Inn* at Dudley. The principal shareholders were Lord Dudley & Ward, T. T. Foley and a group of businessmen from Dudley and its neighbourhood. Abiathar Hawkes, glassmaker of Dudley, was appointed treasurer, and Thomas Dadford, senior, engineer and surveyor, a post he held till 1783, being afterwards employed *ad hoc*.

It was soon afterwards agreed that the canal should have two ends in fields called the Great Ox Leasow and the Little Ox Leasow, both on Foley's land. After these had joined, the line then

* It is often referred to in newspapers as a canal from Bilston to Worcester.

ran through Lord Dudley's land at Brierley Hill at a rather higher level than had first been planned, and down to the nine locks* at Black Delph that led to the junction with the Stourbridge, being 2¼ miles long. By July 1778 the whole of the authorized capital of £7,000 had been raised, except for £400 from a forfeited share, and further calls were made till about £9,200 had come in, making the shares worth £128 each. In addition, £500 was borrowed. It was finished about 24 June 1779, except for a reservoir on Pensnett Chase, but there was probably little trade till the Stourbridge opened in December. Not till 1781 did the company provide themselves with a seal showing Hope and an anchor, though with no inscription. In the years to come, they were often to be in need of both.

In 1784, sharing the motives of the Stourbridge company, the Dudley joined in sending to the Birmingham proposals for a junction. Lord Dudley & Ward, who had been mining limestone from the Castle Mill and Wren's Nest areas, raising it to the surface for land carriage, about 1775 began a private cut (Lord Dudley & Ward's branch) from the Birmingham Canal at Tipton. This was carried by a tunnel, first into the Tipton colliery—this was reported complete in the newspaper of 1 June 1778[49]—and later to a basin at Castle Mill. The company planned to build five rising locks from near the end of their existing canal to Park Head, and then a tunnel to link with Lord Dudley's and so, through a stop-lock, with the Birmingham. Lord Dudley consented to sell on terms to be agreed,† but the Birmingham company, who were supported in their uneasiness by the Staffs & Worcs, took the opportunity to exact stiff terms. Compensation tolls were to be paid at the junction, on coal, coke and limestone varying from 9d to 1s 1d a ton, and for other commodities a higher rate, these being roughly based on the losses the Birmingham company might suffer if the goods no longer passed via Aldersley.‡ Also the stop-lock had to maintain the Dudley Canal's water 6 in. above that of the Birmingham, and to be controlled by that company's man.

James Watt helped the Birmingham company with engineering

---

* Rebuilt in 1858 as eight locks, the new flight utilizing the top and bottom locks of the old flight and having six new ones.

† They never were, and Lord Dudley was never paid, the canal company arguing that his favourable tolls and the convenience the Dudley Canal had been to him so benefited him that compensation should be waived. Apparently it was.

‡These were repealed in 1835, and a charge of 3d a ton on all goods that had not passed two miles on the Birmingham Canal substituted.

advice when the junction was being discussed. He had long been friendly with them, perhaps because Matthew Boulton was a committeeman, and on this occasion was presented with £200 as a 'compliment'. In 1804 he joined the Birmingham Canal committee, on which he sat for the rest of his life and his son after him.

The Act[50] was passed in July 1785, and Lord Dudley was thanked for his 'unremitted Attention to the Interests of this Company, and for his very powerfull and successfull Exertion in Parliament in support of the Extension of this Canal'.[51] It stated that the extension was to be made jointly by such old subscribers as wished to put up money, together with a new group named in the Act, amalgamation to take place when the line was finished.

John Snape and John Bull had originally surveyed the extension, and Dadford senior had checked it. He now became consulting engineer, with Abraham Lees as resident. Specifications for the tunnel were published in September 1785[52] and stated the dimensions to be: width 9 ft 3 in., depth of water 5 ft 6 in., headroom 7 ft. Completion was needed by 25 March 1788. John Pinkerton was given the contract under a bond of £4,000, with William Jessop as his surety, presumably because Jessop had worked with him on the Trent. A steam engine was built on the hill to drain the tunnel, a reservoir was planned at Castle Mill pool, above its north end, and Dadford was told to plan a commodious basin at Castle Mill where the company's tunnel would join Lord Dudley's. Prospects were good, and the shares stood at 5 guineas premium.

By the beginning of 1787 it was clear that the contractor's work was unsatisfactory. Payments to Pinkerton were stopped, two experienced members of the Committee were asked to superintend the work on the approach cutting, and in early February the company resolved to take over the works. A pause for argument followed, at the end of which, in July, it was agreed that Jessop should be released from his bond and that Pinkerton should pay £2,000 by instalments, these being guaranteed by Jessop and others. Dadford was paid off and Isaac Pratt, a prominent member of the Stourbridge and Dudley committees, was put in charge. Work re-started, with Abraham Lees still as resident.

In 1788 the company favoured an amalgamation with the Stourbridge and talks took place. They were unsuccessful, but the two companies thereafter worked closely together, and often shared the same officers. In 1789 they were perturbed to hear of the promotion of the Worcester & Birmingham Canal, which 'will be

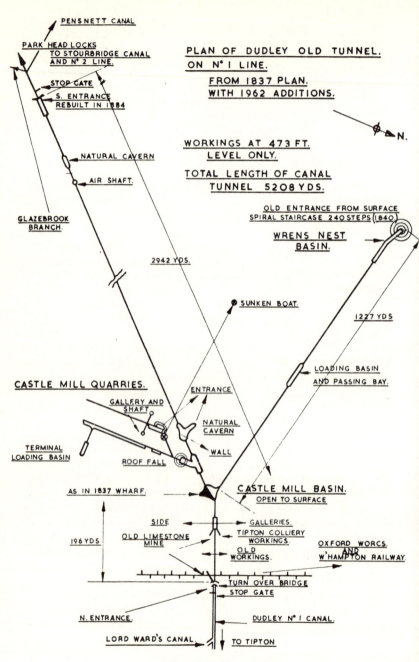

7. Plan of Dudley tunnel

destructive in its consequences to the Interests of this Company and Defeat the purposes for which this Canal was obtained'.[53] This was true enough, for their projected route to the lower Severn was longer and less convenient than that proposed. At the least they hoped for a repeal of the compensation tolls at the junction.

Meanwhile in May 1789 the committee learned that the tunnel 'hath been carried on out of the proper Line in several parts And that very little progress is making in the Execution thereof'.[54] After more delay, Isaac Pratt laid down his responsibility on 30 May 1790, and early in June Josiah Clowes, just free from helping Robert Whitworth on the almost completed Thames & Severn, was engaged at 1½ guineas a day and expenses, with John Gunnery under him. Though he had some contractor trouble, he went on to finish the tunnel, put a stop-lock* (accessible by a stair-case and guide rail) inside it 'contiguous to the new Lime Stone Quarry opened by Lord Dudley in the said Tunnel',[55] and build a reservoir at Gad's Green. A new and straighter junction with the Birmingham than Lord Ward's was provided at Tipton, and opened on 6 March 1792.

John Gunnery died at the end of 1791. A newspaper notice of 19 December[56] stated that the tunnel was complete. It was not, however, reported so till a special shareholders' meeting on 25 June 1792, while the opening was announced in *Aris* on 15 October. The tunnel was 3,172 yd† long, the fifth longest canal tunnel built in England, and with the new reservoirs and approach locks had cost about £50,000. The delays in completion, trouble made by the Birmingham company over the stop-lock,‡ and the incidence of the compensation tolls caused trade to start slowly, and on 29 August 1793 the committee ordered handbills to be printed to give public notice that the tunnel was open and completely navigable.

If we enter the tunnel from the Tipton end, we reach a small basin with workings leading left into limestone workings and right into the old Tipton colliery. Another short length of tunnel leads to Castle Mill basin. To the right the Earl of Dudley's old tunnel continues for 1,227 yd to Wren's Nest basin, past many subterranean workings and loading bays at canal level. This ex-

* This was removed in December 1795.
† 196 yd of Lord Dudley's old tunnel from Tipton to Castle Mill, 34 yd across the basin, and 2,942 yd in the Dudley company's tunnel.
‡ Resolved by an agreement of 25 June 1792.

tension was built privately by Lord Dudley after the opening of the main tunnel, probably in stages between 1805 and 1837. To the left the Dudley Canal tunnel leads to Park Head. A short way from Castle Mill a branch to the left leads off through the 'Cathedral Arch' to the Castle Mill quarries. Just beyond this junction the canal passes through a cavern that is open to the surface at two places, and then enters the rest of the tunnel.

Sixteen years had passed since the Dudley company had been formed, during most of which it had been raising money. Its shareholders could have rested, and looked for dividends. Instead, within a few months of having completed the Dudley tunnel they decided upon a further major expansion. (*To continue the history of the Dudley Canal, turn to p.* 106.)

PART TWO—1790-1845

CHAPTER V

The Birmingham Canals

In 1789, with the Birmingham & Fazeley almost finished, the work on lowering the summit at Smethwick going well, and heavy compensation tolls having been extracted from the Dudley company as the price of Dudley tunnel, the Birmingham Canal's shareholders were satisfied with their position. In that same year a project for a canal from Birmingham to Worcester had been put forward, which seems to have had their acquiescence, so long as there was no physical connection with their own at Birmingham, and all the water needed would be pumped from the Severn. When, however, the Dudley proprietors saw the resulting notice for a bill, they wrote to the Birmingham that this must have received the consent of their company, and that they therefore proposed to promote their own bill to get rid of the compensation tolls on the Dudley tunnel route, since the proposed canal would be exceedingly injurious to them by providing a shorter route to the Severn.[1]

The Birmingham committee made no concessions, and the bill was lost in 1790, then passed in 1791. A year later they were painfully shocked to learn that the Worcester & Birmingham and the Dudley, tired of the Birmingham's high-handed ways, had come to an agreement, whereby an extension of the Dudley Canal would be built to Selly Oak on the W & B, so giving coal from the Dudley and Stourbridge canals a market down the W & B to the Severn, and via the proposed Stratford-upon-Avon Canal and its Kingswood branch to the proposed Warwick canals and so towards London and Oxford. The Birmingham proprietors were furious. They issued a statement[2] which, in a year in which they had paid £31 10s 0d dividend on each of their £140 shares, described their financial situation as follows:

'Their capital Stock consists of five hundred Shares, of which one hundred and thirty-two only, are now in the Hands of original Proprietors or their Families; the remainder have been purchased by the Holders of them at large Premiums; the Dividends on several do not amount to Three per Cent Interest, and one hundred and fifty-two Shares are now held by, or in Trust for Widows and Children, or are in the Hands of Mortgagees, as Securities for Money borrowed of them.'

They worked hard upon the widows and children, who crop up again and again in their protests; they complained bitterly that 'Coals which ought from their Locality to be brought to the Birmingham Market, may be conveyed into Worcestershire, Gloucestershire, etc., without any equivalent Advantage or Prospect to any of the Inhabitants of Birmingham';[3] they accused the Worcester & Birmingham of seeking to get its water from the Dudley and not from the Severn—in other words, of seeking to ease the handicaps it had itself imposed—and finally sneered: 'If another Branch of Canal to the Netherton Coal-Mines should be thought necessary, the Proprietors of the Birmingham Canal are willing to make it.'

Indeed, in 1793 they gave notice to make a canal from Oldbury to Netherton, but knew themselves so unpopular that they did not proceed to a bill, because 'the opposition thereto was sufficiently powerful to have quashed any proceedings thereon'.[4] Instead, the Dudley bill went through, and by 1798 the junction had been made with the Worcester & Birmingham. In 1802 Dudley coal could reach the Grand Junction via Kingswood, and at the end of 1815 the Severn.

The canal mania brought forward other proposals that were to affect the Birmingham company. The first, for the Wyrley & Essington Canal (see p. 94), with a line from Horseley Fields junction near Wolverhampton to Sneyd, where one branch would run past Essington to Wyrley Bank, and one to Birchills near Walsall, did not trouble the Birmingham company. They exacted small compensation payments, protected their water, and raised no objection to the Act of April 1792; nor to the extension authorized in 1794 to join the Birmingham & Fazeley at Huddlesford junction.

Secondly, there was the Warwick & Birmingham, which was kept under Birmingham influence and allowed to join the Digbeth branch on payment of small compensation tolls of 3d per ton for traffic inwards to Birmingham and 6d outwards, which included the use of water and the right to navigate as far as Farmer's Bridge toll-free. Digbeth thereafter became the main wharf for lower Birmingham.

Finally, there were the several moves to provide a connection between the Birmingham Canal and Walsall. In mid-1793 the Birmingham company had proposed an extension of their existing line at Broadwaters as far as Darlaston, and a line from Broadwaters to Wolverhampton. At the same time a separate committee, led by the Hon Edward Foley, were proposing a Walsall Canal from Broadwaters. The Birmingham negotiated with Foley's group, and agreed to build the canal and pay the promoters' costs. However, opposition developed, and the final line ran from the Bradley branch at Moorcroft junction by Darlaston to Walsall, and was completed in June 1799 'on which occasion a boatload of coal was given by the Hon. Mrs. Foley and Mrs. Whitby, and distributed to the poor of the place'.[5]

Thought was also being given to a straightening of the Birmingham's main line by a cut from Bloomfield to Deepfields to save four miles over the curving length of canal to the north-east of Coseley, which would 'open valuable Coal Mines'.[6] This was authorized in 1794, but was not then built, probably because money was so difficult to raise.

No connection had been made between the Birmingham and the Worcester & Birmingham canals at the former's insistence. Instead, a physical bar 7 ft 3 in. wide and 84 yd long separated the Birmingham from the basin of the Worcester & Birmingham, and goods to be transferred were lifted by crane from one side of the Bar to the other. Only the northern part of the W & B had been completed when in 1805 that company asked the Birmingham to remove the bar. They agreed on conditions, but the bill was then thrown out by a combination of the Dudley, Staffs & Worcs and Warwick & Birmingham companies, all of whom had their reasons for wanting it to stay. In 1810 the W & B raised the matter again, but were quoted such stiff terms that they promoted their own bill, which failed. In 1814 they tried again, and in 1815 the Birmingham agreed to a junction in return for heavy tolls on coal on to their water, and lower ones on goods in either direction 'as a Compensation for the Diversion of Trade and for the Expences attendant upon the said Communication',[7] after fierce opposition by the Staffs & Worcs. The Act[8] was passed in 1815, and the communication lock opened on 21 July,[9] though the Worcester & Birmingham itself was not completed throughout till 4 December. The bar tolls remained a grievance throughout the canal age. They were reduced in 1835 and 1839 under threat of rail competition, and more in 1846[10] when the Birmingham company was anxious that its arrangement with the London & Birmingham Railway should not be opposed.

In 1824 the company owned more than 70 miles of canal and branches built round the original Autherley–Birmingham–Fazeley lines. The connections that had been made with the Coventry, Warwick & Birmingham, Worcester & Birmingham, Dudley, Wyrley & Essington and Staffs & Worcs canals all brought additional traffic, and congestion showed itself particularly on the old curving main line between Wolverhampton and Birmingham. Earlier there had been talk of improvements and, as we have seen, a Bloomfield–Deepfields cut-off had been authorized, but the prosperity of the times, and probably also the promotion of a railway from Birmingham to Liverpool by way of Wolverhampton, as well as preliminary planning for the Birmingham & Liverpool Junction Canal, brought about action.

The Committee called in Telford to make a survey and give his opinion; this is what he wrote in his autobiography:

'I found adjacent to this great and flourishing town a canal little better than a crooked ditch, with scarcely the appearance of a haling-path, the horses frequently sliding and staggering in the water, the haling-lines sweeping the gravel into the canal, and the entanglement at the meeting of boats incessant; while at the locks at each end of the short summit crowds of boatmen were always quarrelling, or offering premiums for a preference of passage, and the mineowners, injured by the delay, were loud in their just complaints.'[11]

A hostile railway pamphlet of 1825[12] alleged that the main line to Wolverhampton had been stopped for frost, maintenance, etc., for the following days each year:

Year	Days stopped
1820	54
1821	33
1822	8
1823	22
1824	27

and said that flyboats from Birmingham to Liverpool took 44 hours for the 93 miles via Fazeley to Preston Brook (where it was necessary to tranship Liverpool goods to the Duke's flats) and 47 hours for the 96 miles via Wolverhampton. Ordinary boats took three to four days.

Telford recommended a large new reservoir at Rotton Park, shortening and improving the line between Birmingham and Smethwick, abolishing the summit at Smethwick by cutting through the hill, and making a new canal from Smethwick to Tipton on the Birmingham 453 ft level which passed under the old one, and then on an embankment to Tipton, where it rose by three locks to the Wolverhampton level, and a deep cutting between Bloomfield and Deepfields to cut off a wide circle of old canal. The canal company accepted the recommendations, to be carried out in stages, but a letter to *Aris's Birmingham Gazette* was less than ecstatic:

'I could almost imagine that the Canal Proprietors consider the elegant sinuosities of their line to be, like the Birmingham corkscrew, "ne plus ultra" of science and art, except for the recent publication of their intended improvements. Surely no more decisive confession can be made of the disadvantages under which the mercantile and agricultural interests have long laboured, than the great alterations now about to be effected?'[13]

The writer clearly thought railway projects were responsible for the sudden activity.

The reservoir and the improvements to the Birmingham–Smethwick line were first carried out, the latter being completed in September 1827,[14] when many carriers and others who attended the opening thought that 'the facility and dispatch afforded by the double Towing path, the walling of the sides of the Canal, the capaciousness of the Bridges, and strength and solidity of the Masonry, and the rapid and masterly manner in which the whole had been executed, had obtained general approbation, and that it had been stated of these Works . . . that they were second to no other Canal Works whatever in the Kingdom'.[15]

Next the new Smethwick–Tipton canal past Dudley Port was begun, and between March 1827 and the end of 1829 the great cutting was made through the hill at Smethwick.

'The greatest depth of cutting is seventy-one feet; the waterway of the canal is made forty feet wide, and five feet six inches deep; it is walled with stone on each side; and (has) a towing-path, twelve feet wide on each bank. . . . At the place of greatest excavation is erected the largest canal bridge in the world; it is made of iron: the arch is one hundred and fifty feet span, and over it passes a public roadway twenty-six feet wide.'[16]

The Smethwick cutting was opened on Friday 18 December 1829. The local newspaper recorded that when built the canal distance from Birmingham to the Wednesbury collieries had been 9¼ miles, and the journey time past the twelve locks at Smethwick at least 5¼ hours. The distance was now 7¼ miles, there were no locks, and the journey took two hours. Yet toils had not been increased.

Lastly, the construction of the Bloomfield–Deepfields line seems to have been begun,[17] but to have been left unfinished, work on the Island Line being also stopped. Then in 1834, probably because the completion of the Birmingham & Liverpool Junction was at last in sight and much additional traffic was expected, a new plan was made to replace part of the cutting between Bloomfield and Deepfields by a 360-yd tunnel with a double towpath at Coseley. This was authorized in 1835, and work re-started on this and on the Island Line, speeded by the unsuccessful revival of the Birmingham Dudley & Wolverhampton Railway project in 1835 and 1836. The Bloomfield–Deepfields line and tunnel was opened on 6 November 1837, and the Island Line completed from Smethwick junction to Tipton Factory junction on 2 April 1838. Brindley's original line, 22⅝ miles long, had been reduced by successive improvements to 15⅝ miles.

In 1838 the canal manager reported that a great part of the coal trade from the Wolverhampton level was using the new line,

'and the intersection of the Tipton Green and Toll End communications by the Island Line, affords a direct additional communication between the same Level, and the Walsall Level. By the operation of these Lines and Improvements, the Locks at Smethwick, formerly so much overpowered, have been completely relieved, and are enabled in consequence, to afford full accommodation to the Coal Trade from Rowley and Oldbury, and from the new and extensive district in the Titford Valley',[18]

the Titford branch having also been recently opened on 4 November 1837.

The remaining section at the western end, from Deepfields past Wolverhampton to Aldersley junction, was improved and deepened, but not reconstructed, during 1838 and 1839, and the company was then free to turn to the far more difficult problem of the congestion at Farmer's Bridge locks, and to a lesser extent at Ashted and Aston. The thirteen locks at Farmer's Bridge, at the eastern end of the main line, carried all traffic from the Birmingham system and the Worcester & Birmingham Canal that was destined for the Warwick & Birmingham, in which case it turned right at the bottom of the locks at Aston junction and continued down the Ashted flight, or for the Fazeley line, when from the junction it moved down the Aston locks to Salford. This through traffic was heavily supplemented by that to and from local works and wharves. To by-pass this congested section had been part of the plans of the original Birmingham & Fazeley promoters, and later, in 1793, a Bradley to Fazeley canal had been proposed. In 1810 and 1811, the Birmingham company had deposited plans for a canal from Danks Branch, off the Wednesbury line, to Salford to join the Fazeley line. The projects were opposed by the Worcester & Birmingham, probably to bring pressure for the removal of the bar, and by the Warwick & Birmingham, which feared diversion of trade on to the Fazeley and Coventry lines, but failed 'principally from the District not being ripe for the Measure, the extent of the Mineral Basin along the Tame Valley, and the Value of the Mines, not being then ascertained'.[19] In the autumn of 1838 this plan, which would enable traffic from the main line west of Tipton and from Wednesbury to by-pass the Tipton–Farmer's Bridge–Salford section, was revived as the Tame Valley line, with the prospect also of serving 'the great and principal Works of Birmingham (which) are become seated in the lower part of the Town', and of being a step towards a waterway to bring coal from 'the inexhaustible Mines of Cannock Chase'[20] to lower Birmingham.

The case in favour was set out publicly in 1839.[21] Although the Farmer's Bridge locks, it stated, 'are kept open day and night, and also upon Sundays, & several Branches of Trade, to avoid delay at them, have been diverted through other Channels, the pressure upon them during the Autumnal and Winter months is excessive, from Twenty to Thirty Boats being frequently found at the top, and as many at the bottom of the Locks, waiting for a passage'. The statement went on to say that 'nearly 70 Steam Engines, and about 124 Wharfs and Works are already seated on the Banks of the Canals, between Farmer's Bridge and Aston', and that there was no room to build parallel locks. An Act[22] for a canal from Danks Branch via Perry Barr to Salford was passed in 1839, and another[23] in 1840 to vary the line. The 8¼ mile long line, which had cost £400,000, was opened on 14 February 1844, and on the same day also the Birmingham & Warwick Junction which enabled traffic for the Warwick line to avoid the Aston and Ashted flights by continuing to Bordesley. In 1847 the building of the Rushall Canal joined the Tame Valley to the former Wyrley & Essington's

Hay Head branch and so to the Cannock Chase mines. The great improvements were almost done. These extensions and improvements had included further efforts after adequate water. The supply of water pumped into the canal was increased, and a number of new engines provided for pumping back, notably at Ashted, Rotton Park, Ocker Hill, Titford and Perry Barr. On the other hand, the original reservoirs at Smethwick were given up about the middle 1840s.

We must now return to follow the company's financial history from the point at which we left it. By 1800–1 a dividend of £34 per £140 share (24¼ per cent) was being paid, though the company's policy of borrowing to pay for all improvements, rather than issuing more shares, had piled up a considerable debt. In this year they began to reduce their commitments, and by 1818 could refer to 'the financial Arrangements of this Company whereby in the Course of a few years they have been enabled to discharge a heavy Load of Debt with which the Undertaking was encumbered'.[24]

By the year 1810–11 the dividend had become £42 per £140 share (30 per cent), with the likelihood of further increases, and the company therefore took powers[25] to subdivide the original 500 shares into 1,000 nominally of £70, which in 1813 were changing hands at £585 each.[26] A further subdivision to 2,000 shares took place in 1820, and to 4,000 in 1824, such an eighth share of £17 10s 0d nominal value being worth £360 in 1825,[27] giving the original £140 share a value of £2,840. In 1836 another subdivision to 8,000 shares took place. The table on page 91 records the changes made.

These dividends were paid in spite of the costliness of the improvements of 1825 to 1838, which in 1839 the company stated[28] had cost £700,000 without additional tolls having been asked. Part had been paid for out of revenue, but by 1835 the company's indebtedness reached £568,000, which was dealt with in accordance with an Act[29] of that year, which also recast and lowered tolls. The total debt was divided between the 8,000 shares, each being charged with £71. The holder was then expected to pay up £71 on it to redeem his portion of the debt. Those who did not do so had the interest payable on the amount of debt due from them deducted from their dividends. By November 1837 £247,435 had been received from the shareholders.[30]

For the years 1835–6 onwards, therefore the dividends paid to those who had contributed their £71 were higher than they would otherwise have been because they included money formerly paid as interest. For instance, in 1836–7 £9 16s 0d was paid to such, but from this sum £3 11s 0d was deducted in cases where shareholders had not paid the levy, to give a true dividend of £6 5s 0d, equivalent to £100 per £140 share of the original capital.

Y.e. 31 March	No. of shares	Dividend			Equivalent on original £140 shares		
		£	s	d	£	s	d
1810	500	42	0	0	42	0	0
1811	500	42	0	0	42	0	0
1812	1,000	26	5	0	52	10	0
1813	1,000	26	5	0	52	10	0
1814	1,000	28	2	6	56	5	0
1815	1,000	30	0	0	60	0	0
1816	1,000	36	0	0	72	0	0
1817	1,000	36	0	0	72	0	0
1818	1,000	36	0	0	72	0	0
1819	1,000	40	0	0	80	0	0
1820	1/2,000	30	10	0			
1821	2,000	22	10	0	90	0	0
1822	2,000	22	10	0	90	0	0
1823	2,000	24	0	0	96	0	0
1824	4,000	12	10	0	100	0	0
1825	4,000	12	10	0	100	0	0
1826–35		unchanged					
1836	4/8,000	10	3	6			
1837	8,000	6	5	0	100	0	0

Receipts and tonnages carried from 1833 to 1844, averaged over three-year periods, were as follows:

Years	Receipts £	Tonnage Carried tons
1833–5	104,672	2,641,012
1836–8	113,702	3,174,994
1839–41	122,960*	3,696,112*
1842–4	112,884	3,310,448

* An amalgamation with the Wyrley & Essington Canal took place during 1840.

A number of subordinate figures can also be compared for the years 1832 and 1845, and show some interesting changes (the amalgamation with the Wyrley & Essington in 1840 must not be forgotten).

	1832 £	1845 £
Revenue from merchandise	17,525	20,529
The distant coal trade	42,666	28,954
Coal trade to Birmingham town and works	23,296	31,178
Trade within the mining districts	20,766	46,337
Wharfages etc.	1,509	1,463
Totals	105,762	128,460
	tons	tons
General merchandise	552,435	1,093,553
Birmingham coal	324,564	489,599
To Worcester, coal	179,122	178,504
To Warwick, coal	218,765	131,665
To Coventry Canal at Fazeley	51,416	4,414
From Whittington*	12,156	6,380
To Staffs & Worcs, coal	66,304	56,658
Coal within mining district	718,552	1,166,341
Ironstone within mining district	194,781	450,911
Sand within mining district	27,613	64,461
Lime and limestone	151,952	283,860
Road materials and manure	60,683	99,453
Totals	2,558,342	4,025,796

* Junction with the isolated section of the Coventry Canal.

These figures, which derive from the minutes of evidence upon the bill for the arrangement reached in 1846 between the Birmingham company and the London & Birmingham Railway Company, show especially the great increase in the iron industry that took place between 1832 and 1845; this caused expansion in the local consumption of coal, ironstone, sand and limestone. We can note also the falling away of coal traffic to the Warwick line, in competition with Moira, Warwickshire, Derbyshire and Leicestershire coal, and the virtual ending of the Staffordshire coal exports along the Coventry Canal which had been the main reason for its extension to Fazeley. Finally, road improvements on the one hand, and the growth of nightsoil shipments from Birmingham on the other, account for a 60 per cent growth in thirteen years.

Let us now consider some other matters that occupied the company in the later part of our period. In 1824 the committee had written to other companies about a proposed railway from Birmingham to Liverpool, and had been assured by the Coventry that it would co-operate 'in all measures calculated to protect the

Interests of the several Canal Companys likely to be affected by the proposed Measure'.³¹ In November they summoned a conference of these concerns at Birmingham. In December a newspaper comment referred to 'the general alarm which has been excited among Proprietors of Canals connected with Birmingham by the projected Rail-road from that town to Liverpool; the Old Birmingham Canal Shares, we are assured, have fallen £400 and other Canals have been more or less affected ... the Birmingham and Liverpool shares are at a premium of £7'.³² In March 1825 the Coventry company wrote to their local Members asking them, if a bill were introduced, to satisfy themselves 'of the practicability, utility and necessity for such measure at the present time for the Commerce of the Country'.³³ They added that at the time canals had been promoted, their supporters had had to prove to the Parliamentary Committee that they were of national benefit. In fact, a railway was not authorized till 1833, when the Grand Junction obtained its Act, nor opened for goods traffic from Birmingham via Perry Barr, Willenhall, and Wolverhampton to Stafford and Warrington till January 1838, to be followed on 12 November by the London & Birmingham Railway, and on 12 August 1840 by the Birmingham & Derby line from Derby to Hampton on the L & B R.

Meanwhile a notice had been issued in 1825 for a new canal, the Birmingham, Walsall & Liverpool Junction, from Birmingham via Perry Barr and Walsall to the Wyrley & Essington at Wyrley Bank and then to Otherton near Penkridge on the Staffs & Worcs, with branches to Wolverhampton and Cannock Chase, 'to make a more direct navigable communication ... to join the Grand Trunk Canal to Runcorn and then to the Port of Liverpool'. It seems to have had no strong backing and to have disappeared after a year.

No one could call the Birmingham a company popular with their colleagues. The causes lay partly in their power, and willingness to use it, and partly in the comparisons they were fond of making between their own efficiency and the backwardness of others, which did not always take into account the advantages they had of an enormous local trade. In 1838, for instance, they remarked that 'if a reduction on the continuous lines be required to meet railway competition ... the other Companies can (never) have any claim on the Birmingham Canal Company, until full amends shall have been made by them for the loss & inconvenience arising from their supineness, & want of spirit'; and in 1841: 'the circumstance ... of the Birmingham Canal being kept in a navigable state during the Winter, whilst the neighbouring Canals were closed, affords strong proof of what can be done by energy and determination, and is well calculated to add to the impression, now rapidly gaining ground, that the low price of Canal stock and diversion of Trafic, is less to be ascribed to opposing railways, than to the inactivity, want of foresight, and absurd jealousies of the Canal Companies themselves'.[34] The unkindest cut of all, however, was the remark that 'a considerable fall of rain having taken place, and the neighbouring Canals being now navigable . . .'.[35]

In 1840, the Birmingham company and the Wyrley & Essington agreed to amalgamate. There had been negotiations in 1820 and again later, but it seems to have been rivalry in 1838 over opening up the Willenhall district that brought the two companies together, 'each Canal intersecting a considerable portion of the Mineral District of Staffordshire; each looking to the same Markets; and each being alike interested in the opening of the unwrought district lying between them'.[36] Maybe it was the urgent need for the Tame Valley Canal, which could as well have been a project of the Wyrley & Essington as of the Birmingham that helped to bring the greater company to the altar. The terms were that the 800 shares of the W & E were to rank *pari passu* with the 8,000 of the Birmingham. Each W & E share was, however, to pay £49 towards debt reduction, as in 1835 each B.C.N. shareholder had been asked to pay £71. The bill was opposed by the Trent & Mersey, Coventry and Warwick & Birmingham companies, who feared that the prospective Walsall link might reduce their trade, and that the toll reductions authorized in the Act[37] might form an awkward precedent. It passed, and a formidable combination was created. (*To continue the history of the Birmingham Canal Navigations, turn to* p. 252.)

Wyrley & Essington Canal

The original intention of the promoters was to build a canal from the main line of the Birmingham in order that the products of the collieries at Wyrley and Essington could be brought to the towns of Wolverhampton and Walsall,[38] and 'to render the conveyance of coal, corn, ironstone, limestone and other produce less expensive'.[39] The Act[40] of 1792 provided for a level line from Horseley Fields junction near Wolverhampton to Sneyd junction near Bloxwich, where one branch was to run up 5 locks at Sneyd to Wyrley Bank (with a branch again up 4 locks to a colliery at

Essington) and another to Birchills near Walsall. Shorter branches were also authorized.

The capital was to be £25,000 in 200 shares of £125, with power to raise a further £20,000 if necessary, much of which was subscribed in Wolverhampton, the bankers Hordern and Molineux taking a prominent part, but with support also from the colliery-owning Vernons of Hilton Park. The Molineux's had been connected with the Staffs & Worcs Canal from its beginnings, and that company supported the formation of the Wyrley & Essington. There seems at first to have been a wish to be independent of the Birmingham company, for at the first meeting it was decided that 'no Person being upon the Committee of any other Navigation communicating with this is eligible to be elected on ye Committee'.[41] However, six months later the decision was rescinded, perhaps to decrease tension as a result of the announcement by the Birmingham company of their plans for canals from Broadwaters to Wolverhampton and from Broadwaters to Walsall. The first was dropped, but the second proceeded with, in direct opposition to the W & E's intended Birchills branch. An independent scheme for a Bradley–Fazeley canal, supported at a meeting at Sutton Coldfield in January 1793, soon dropped.

In 1794 the Wyrley & Essington company obtained a supplementary Act[42] for an extension of their line from Birchills junction, near the end of the Birchills branch, to run between Bloxwich and Pelsall to the colliery area of Brownhills, and then by 30 falling locks past Lichfield to join the Birmingham & Fazeley at Huddlesford junction, with branches to Hay Head limeworks (the Daw End branch) and quarries (the Lord Hay's branch). The Act authorized a further £75,000, and £40,000 if necessary. This project also was mainly financed from Wolverhampton, but obtained some support in Walsall, for whose coal it provided an alternative outlet towards Lichfield and the Fazeley line. The Act had provided that 400 £125 shares should be made available to the public; it was therefore decided that 600 new shares should be created, 200 of which would be allotted free to the old proprietors, the balance to be subscribed for by new proprietors, who would be expected to sustain calls to the same amount as those on the old shares. The two capitals were for the time being kept separate, each building its own section of canal, but 'the Erection of all Buildings, the Purchase of Land for Wharfs and the making the same, and also all Collateral Cuts Basons Reservoirs Engines and all other Works and Conveniences' were to be paid for 'by the Old and New

Proprietors jointly agreeable to the number of shares they respectively hold'.⁴³

William Pitt was the engineer. A portion of the original line seems to have been open by August 1794, and by November of that year the Committee were empowered to buy boats and trade in coal 'in order to introduce and establish a Trade'.⁴⁴ In May 1794 work on the extension was ordered to start as soon as possible. The regularity of the trade envisaged—some had probably begun—is shown in by-laws issued in May 1795, which provide that all boats going away from Wolverhampton shall give way to those (which would be loaded) going towards it, that no boat shall go more slowly than 2 mph or faster than 3 mph, that each boat should have only one horse, and that boats going the same way 'shall follow in regular order without any attempt to pass or injure one another'.⁴⁵ By June 1796 the proprietors of the new shares had subscribed £100 each, the same as had the old. The whole 800 shares were then amalgamated, and further calls made on the combined capital till £125 had been called on each share.

The main line was opened throughout to the junction with the Fazeley line at Huddlesford on 8 May 1797.⁴⁶ However, water seems to have been very short, for a canal meeting of 5 April 1799 ordered further advertisements to be inserted in newspapers to say that the canal was complete and that plenty of water would be put in; seemingly the Norton bog near Chase Water was drained to form a supply.⁴⁷ Water again handicapped the company when in the summer of 1799 the Sneyd reservoir burst and caused much damage; 'the water swept everything before it in the line it took through Shenstone, Hopwas, Drayton, etc., till it fell into, and overflowed, the Tame at Tamworth'.⁴⁸ There were complaints of water shortage on the main line until the Cannock Chase reservoir was built about 1800.

The extremity of the branch to Birchills was open about 1798, but after the opening of the Birmingham Canal's Walsall branch in June 1799 was little used. John Farey says that when he visited the district in the spring of 1809 'the Walsall branch had been dammed off from the line, and been dry some years; the water therefrom, having broke down into Birch-hill Colliery Works, under it'.⁴⁹ In 1818 Mr Willoughby was applying for its reinstatement.

The original line planned to Wyrley Bank had probably only been built for a short distance, with the four locks up to the colliery at Essington which were open by July 1798. In this year

V. The Smethwick cutting on the Birmingham Canal Navigations: (*above*) Galton bridge, with the Western Region railway bridge beyond, in 1955; (*below*) the 453 ft level on the left, the 473 ft higher and to the right, and the original 491 ft level on the extreme right, from Brass House Bridge in 1963

VI. Birmingham Canal Navigations: (*above*) Great Bridge railway interchange basins on the Walsall level at the bottom of Rider's Green locks, in 1964; (*below*) Winson Green toll office in 1955

Henry Vernon, himself a large shareholder, threatened to seek an alternative outlet for his coal from his Essington mines, and in September issued a notice for a bill for a railway or roads from Essington to the Staffs & Worcs Canal near Penkridge.⁵⁰ The bill was introduced, but was defeated, the Wyrley & Essington saying that Vernon had been bankrupt in 1789 and had handed over his lands to Hordern, the company's chairman and banker, and that the canal had been built on the assurance that Vernon's coal would be carried upon it. The price of withdrawal was an agreement between Vernon and the canal company by which the latter agreed to pay some of his expenses, and to build a 1½ mile long canal in the direction of the original Wyrley Bank line, and a tramroad to his collieries, the latter of which was in place by December 1799. It seems that this branch was closed by 1829, but later it seems to have been rebuilt and extended farther towards Great Wyrley.

The Wyrley & Essington Canal had been built through a comparatively underdeveloped part of the country, and had to wait till quite late in the nineteenth century, when the Cannock Chase coalfield was developed, to reach full use. Meanwhile it served many purposes. It brought cheap coal to Lichfield, created a regular traffic thence with Derby and Burton, and enabled a boat from Wolverhampton to call there three times a week on its way to London.⁵¹ Round Bloxwich the collieries and limestone quarries were developed, and the local industries of bit-making, locksmithing and tack-making were benefited. The Goscote ironworks were established, and fuel from Goscote and other collieries to the Sneyd brick-kilns meant that bricks could be made in large quantities for the new housing required in Walsall.⁵²

About 1800 the Hay Head (Daw End) and Lord Hay's branches were completed. The canal now had 23½ miles of main line with 30 locks, all of which were on the stretch rising from the Coventry Canal to Cannock Heath, the rest of the main line to Horseley Fields being on the 473 ft level, together with the Lord Hay's, Daw End and Birchills branches. The Hay Head branch was 5⅜ miles long, Lord Hay's 1¼ miles,* the Wyrley Bank branch as finally built 3½ miles from Sneyd, the Birchills branch ¼ mile, and the Essington branch ¾ mile. The Hay Head branch had been planned mainly to serve limestone quarries, which were described in 1795 as being 'on a very extensive plan, inexhaustible as quantity, and of a very superior quality'.⁵³ When Farey saw the canal in 1809, he

---

* Farey says the branch was 2½ miles to Lord Hay's colliery, east of Great Wyrley, but it seems only to have been built to the A34 road.

says that the old Hay Head limeworks were disused, and that the new railway to the new quarries was unfinished owing to the death of John Wilkinson. There was therefore no navigation south of Daw End wharf. That they opened later is shown by an advertisement of 1822: 'Brindley's British Cement prepared from the Hay-Head Waterproof Lime—the Old Birmingham Canal, and most other Companies, have exclusively used Hay-Head Lime.'[54]

The construction cost of the whole canal seems to have been between £80,000 and £90,000. From about 1800 revenue began to increase, and improvements to be paid for out of tolls, though trade still had to be encouraged, and the company was never prosperous. In December 1801 and October 1803 dividends of £3 per share had been declared, and in November 1804 an advertisement for the sale of shares said that the canal was 'in receipt of a revenue paying 5 per cent on the expenditure, and would soon be in a state to make liberal and regular dividends'.[55] In 1825 6 per cent was paid, and the shares stood at £135.

In 1820 the Birmingham company had made unsuccessful soundings upon amalgamation. In 1822 the Wyrley & Essington's committee proposed to seek 'causes of the present decline in Tonnage—to inquire what new Avenues and Channels of Trade may be opened—What are the best Means of using our surplus Water—What Communication it would be prudent and practicable to make with other contiguous and collateral Canals',[56] and in 1825 it was suggested that the line ought to be surveyed with an eye to improvements or extensions. The problem of surplus water was solved. From 1835 onwards the company were regular suppliers to the Birmingham & Liverpool Junction, and also sometimes sold water to the Staffs & Worcs and Dudley companies.

At the 1825 meeting, mineowners had suggested a junction with the Birmingham Canal near Walsall, and in 1826 and 1827 surveys were made of possible lines to the Staffs & Worcs, with whom the company shared several committeemen and was in close and friendly contact, and the Birmingham. These were not followed up, but in 1829 there was an application from the 'Landowners, Mineholders, Coalmasters, Ironmasters, Carriers and others in the Town and neighbourhood of Walsall' to extend from Birchills Old Wharf to the Birmingham Canal near there,[57] which led to a suggestion that the committee 'take an early opportunity of enquiring of the Birmingham Canal Company whether they feel disposed to open a Treaty for the Union of the Wyrley and Essington Canal with the Birmingham and to unite their Interests in one general Concern'.⁵⁸ They probably got little encouragement then, and in 1835 the B.C.N. were unwilling to include a junction canal in their own proposals. However, in 1837, after a deputation from the Walsall Town Council had attended a committee meeting, they agreed to support such a plan if the W & E would supply the necessary lockage water. In May 1838 some Wyrley & Essington proprietors then took part in a meeting with 'Gentlemen friendly to the Junction' at Walsall, at which it was suggested that the Birmingham should make it, the W & E supplying the water, but that if both refused to make it, then an independent company should do so.⁵⁹ The W & E then approached the Birmingham rather on the general issue of amalgamation than specifically on the Walsall junction, and were told the latter were not prepared at present to submit any plan. They then gave notice of a bill to make the junction themselves, and this seems to have gained the Birmingham's quick agreement to amalgamation, perhaps because they did not think their attitude would stand up well to Parliamentary scrutiny. The agreement was signed on 9 February 1840, and the necessary Act passed in April. Within a short time the amalgamated company was able to authorize no less than three junctions between the systems: the Walsall link, the Bentley Canal from the B.C.N.'s Anson branch near Walsall to the W & E line at Wednesbury, and the Rushall Canal joining the W & E's Daw End branch to the Tame Valley line. Co-operation between canal interests had come at last, but the time was late. (*To continue the history of the Wyrley & Essington canals within the Birmingham Canal Navigations, turn to* p. 252.)

CHAPTER VI

The Black Country Canals

Stourbridge Canal

WE left this well-situated concern at the point when it had obtained a dividend guarantee from the newly authorized Worcester & Birmingham. The company had paid a maiden dividend of £3 9s od per £142 6/7 share in 1785, and had paid £9 for 1789 and £8 10s od for 1790, the two years before the Worcester & Birmingham's Act of 1791. That canal was finally opened in December 1815, and caused the Stourbridge's dividend to fall from £16 in 1815 to £9 10s od in 1816 and 1817. After that the tendency was again upwards, and only in 1832 and 1833, at £8, did it fall below the guaranteed minimum. There is no evidence that a claim was made for these two years. Finally, as a result of that northwards growth of industry that had among its effects the opening of the Stourbridge Extension Canal in 1840, the dividend rose suddenly from 1836 onwards to reach £20 per £142 6/7 share in 1840. The figures are on the following page.

The company sought also to increase trade by establishing, probably soon after the resolution of 1783, a company at Stourport managed by a sub-committee, for many years under the chairmanship of Isaac Pratt, to promote the sale of coal off their canal. The management was inefficient, for in February 1792 the sub-committee was asked for a 'proper account of their Debts, Credits and Stock',[1] and the following month were wound up, the boats and other assets being sold to Pratt. Other traffic on the canal included rod and bar iron and nails, ironstone and limestone for the ironworks, glass, clay for bricks and earthenware, and bricks.

The planning of the Dudley tunnel extension, the opening of which would make the two canals part of a through route, brought the companies closer together. From 1785 they shared the same engineer, and in 1788 discussed amalgamation, though the talks came to nothing. When the Dudley embarked upon their second extension to the Worcester & Birmingham at Selly Oak, however, the Stourbridge company, who thought some of their trade might be diverted, extracted a guarantee of £3 upon their dividends above the £9 already guaranteed by the Worcester & Birmingham, once the extension was navigable and the Dudley shareholders had received £5 on their own shares. As they failed to do so till 1839, though the extension was opened in 1798, the guarantee was of no use. Fortunately, it was not needed, for the inactive Stourbridge company was far more profitable than the enterprising Dudley.

Years	Average dividend per £142 6/7 share		
	£	s	d
1785–7	5	7	4
1788–90	8	3	4
1791–3	10	1	8
1794–6	9	3	4
1797–9	10	12	0
1800–2	11	19	0
1803–5	8	3	4
1806–8	11	16	8
1809–11	12	13	4
1812–14	12	16	8
1815–17	11	13	4
1818–20	12	0	0
1821–3	10	10	0
1824–6	14	13	4
1827–9	11	13	4
1830–2	9	0	0
1833–5	10	0	0
1836–8	17	10	0
1839–41	19	13	4

In 1796 the canal was carrying 100,000 tons a year, and thereafter its prosperity slowly increased, partly because of the expansion of iron and other works and collieries near their own canal, partly by the extra through traffic that followed the opening of the two Dudley extensions. In 1802, for instance, they contributed to enlarging the Dudley's Gad's Green reservoir, and about the same time began to make contributions towards the cost of mine pumping if the water were run into their canal. In 1807, again, they decided to enlarge Stourbridge basin as 'the Trade . . . has of late considerably increased'.[2]

The opening of the Worcester & Birmingham at the end of

1815 caused a new trade to start—iron from the Coalbrookdale area travelling to Worcester and also, more important, to London via Stourport, the Stourbridge Canal and Selly Oak, and in July 1816 the Staffs & Worcs, Stourbridge and Dudley companies agreed to grant a joint bounty of 1s 9d a ton, shortly afterwards raised to 2s on iron carried through to Selly Oak, and also to reduce tolls on iron off the Severn. At the same time they started to give bounties on coal from their canals and going down the Severn, presumably to compete with the Worcester Canal.

From 1797 onwards, and especially from about 1820, there was a steady development of the works and collieries in the Shut End area north-east of Kingswinford, which led to the building of several wharves at the Wide Waters at Brockmoor on the Fens branch, to which point the coal was brought by road and later by tramroad. Two such were built from Shut End to Brockmoor by Gibbons & Co and Homer & Co, and a third ran from Daniel Horton's mines near Bromley. All these were built by 1829, when the canal company issued a Parliamentary notice of a bill to extend their powers to construct lines (limited to 1,000 yd from the canal), but they did not proceed with it, probably because of the plans being made for what later became the Stourbridge Extension Canal. This was opened in 1840, and made the lines unnecessary.

The company's financial control was not of the best. In 1810 Francis Homfray, who had succeeded his father Francis as treasurer, died owing the company £2,088, and when they attempted to recover it from his first surety, Thomas Homfray of The Hyde, Kinver, the latter went bankrupt in 1819 with the debt unpaid. However, as the company's account was transferred after 1810 to the Stourbridge Bank, one of whose partners was Homfray's other surety, Thomas Hill, all may have come right. In 1831, though, Henry Price, who in 1829 had been appointed Clerk Collector and Agent at £120 p.a. and who handled all the tolls collected, was found to be £1,250 short in his money. He was dismissed, and application was made to his sureties, who presumably paid up. Edward Brewer was appointed in his place, who bettered the example by absconding to New York in September 1833 with over £1,200. This time the company were fairly roused. Having learned that William Craig, the Stourbridge police officer, had failed in his pursuit both of Brewer and the cash, their solicitor sent William Eberhardt to New York in pursuit. Ten weeks later he returned triumphant with the culprit, the former to collect £50 reward, the latter to face criminal proceedings. As the sureties were only good for £600, the company lost heavily on Brewer. Yet another case occurred in 1863, when the company's accountant clerk absconded with nearly £2,000, of which only half was recovered from the surety.

Trade was good. A symptom was the rise in pay given to the lock-keeper at Stourton in October 1830 in consideration of him 'keeping open these Locks all night and on Sundays';[3] he of the sixteen locks got a similar rise for the same reason in April 1834, and a much larger one in July 1836. In that year the canal carried 144,606 tons of coal alone, 64,220 tons of which was for the Staffs & Worcs and the Severn, and 80,386 tons for consumption on the Stourbridge line. Much else was passing; one example is the clay and brick trade, to the Oxford Canal for the south, upon which the Warwick canals gave a bounty in 1832. Prospects looked good, and were to be improved by the opening of the Stourbridge Extension Canal. (*To continue the history of the Stourbridge Canal, turn to p. 264.*)

Stourbridge Extension Canal

In the first days of 1820 the Stourbridge Canal company learned that Gibbons & Co had opened a colliery at Shut End and wanted wharf accommodation on their canal, to which they were presumably going to carry by road. The shareholders, with the coal and ironstone deposits at Shut End in mind, thereupon ordered a survey to be made by Samuel Hodgkinson for either an extension canal to their summit level or a railway. This was done, but the report was shelved in July, and about 1825 the firm built their own tramroad to Brockmoor where, as we have seen, wharves were built to be served also by other lines.

The canal company's failure to take efficient action led to Lord Dudley in 1826 proposing to build a railroad from Kingswinford to the Staffs & Worcs Canal at Hinksford, with the enthusiastic support of that company. In 1829 it was opened as the Shutt End* Railway. In the meantime the Stourbridge committee had called in W. A. Provis who, together with William Fowler and J. U. Rastrick, put forward proposals for a canal extension towards Shut End. Rastrick's line was adopted, but then the company learned of Lord Dudley's hostility, not unnatural in view of his own line, and the project lapsed.

Nothing further happened till early in April 1836, when it was

* This was the contemporary spelling of what is now Shut End.

resolved 'That a new Survey be immediately made by Mr. James Green of Exeter from the Summit of this Canal to ... Gornal with a report as to the expediency of connecting it with the mining district'.[4] The survey was made, though apparently by William Fowler and not by Green, and resulted in a proposal to link the Stourbridge to the Birmingham Canal. A separate company with a capital of £125,000 was formed by some of the Stourbridge shareholders and other local businessmen to build a Stourbridge, Wolverhampton & Birmingham Junction Canal, 5¾ miles long from the Stourbridge near Brockmoor past Corbyn's Hall and Shut End works to Straits Green and Cotwallend south of Sedgley, and then through a mile long tunnel to Bloomfield near the junction of the old Birmingham Canal with the new improved line.

The argument for the project was to open up mines of good quality coal round Shut End, especially as those on the Stourbridge Canal were becoming worked out, and to carry this coal not only south to the Severn, but north to 'those numerous Iron Works, which are clustered on that part of the Birmingham Canal which it is proposed to enter, while those Works are in the greatest need of a constant supply of Coal, which can no longer be obtained in their own Neighbourhood'.[5] The proposal was given urgency by a contemporary scheme for a railway with coalfield branches, proposed from Stourbridge to Birmingham and then as the Grand Connection Railway from the Birmingham & Gloucester Railway near Worcester to the Grand Junction Railway near Wolverhampton. Certainly it would have represented an improvement on the canal line by way of the Dudley tunnel, for which reason it was opposed by the Dudley company. The Staffs & Worcs also disliked it because it would increase competition with its own route via Aldersley and threaten the coal trade along the Shut End railway. It therefore itself gave notice of a branch from Hinksford to Gornal Wood near Oak Farm, rising 104 ft by 13 locks,[6] which was supported by Lord Dudley, and also of another branch into the proposed canal.

However, in all this turmoil the promoters were unable to fill their subscription list, unsupported as they were by Lord Dudley or the Birmingham Canal company, and the project was cut down to one from Brockmoor to near Oak Farm, just beyond Shut End. In January 1837 the Stourbridge company offered to build this line themselves, but the promoters decided to go ahead as a separate company, though with Stourbridge support. Rastrick made an estimate of £32,404, including a Sandhills branch, and a future revenue of £4,960 was considered likely—in fact, an accurate forecast. The ironmasters and colliery owners were unanimous that a canal would be cheaper than the railroads; the Shut End line was quoted as costing 11d a ton from Shut End, and Gibbons's tramroad 5d from Corbyn's Hall. In June 1837 an Act[7] was obtained, one of the considerations being a promise to purchase the Corbyn Hall–Brockmoor tramroad for £3,000 as soon as the canal was finished. This was done in 1841, when the top end was taken up, and the almost useless lower end let at a nominal rent.

Six of the twelve members of the first committee were also on that of the Stourbridge company, so a close link existed. The biggest shareholders were Sir Stephen Glynne of Hawarden Castle, ironmaster at Oak Farm and M.P. (£5,200), James Foster of Stourton Castle, ironmaster (£3,000), Francis Rufford of Prescot, clay merchant (£3,000), who became chairman, and Thomas Wight of Kingswinford (£2,000), who became clerk. Rastrick was asked to be engineer, but evidently declined, for William Fowler was appointed until in September 1838 he was replaced by Benjamin Townshend and then by William Richardson of Dudley. James Frost of Wednesbury was the contractor.

The main line, 2 miles long to a point at Oak Farm slightly beyond the originally intended terminus, seems to have been opened on 27 June 1840, and the Sandhills branch later in the same year. This was 5 furlongs long and ended at the Kingswinford–Sandhills road, where wharves and limekilns were built. The 2½-furlong long Bromley branch, not authorized in the Act, was added probably in 1841. The only lock on the canal was on the main line near the Bromley branch, originally a stop-lock with four pairs of gates, two facing in each direction, later a combined stop and weigh lock with two guillotine gates.[8] The cost had been £49,000.

In November 1839, while the Extension canal was being built, the Staffs & Worcs met Lord Dudley's representatives to discuss a possible canal from Hinksford to Lord Dudley's mines at Barrow Hill, which lay to the east of the Extension company's lines. Notices were issued, but the project dropped after a meeting between the Extension committee and the S & W. The Stourbridge company seemed to suspect the S & W of wanting to join up with the Pensnett Canal, which Lord Dudley's trustees were then building near the Stourbridge's reservoirs on Pensnett Chase, to join the Dudley Canal near Dudley tunnel. Finally, in 1841 there was a proposal to revive the old idea of extending the Oak Farm line to the Birmingham Canal, but the time was past. What had been built, however, was of great benefit to the Stourbridge company, which entered a period of greater prosperity than ever before. (*To continue the history of the Stourbridge Extension Canal, turn to p. 266.*)

Dudley Canal

Within a few months of completing Dudley tunnel the shareholders of the Dudley Canal had decided upon a further major expansion.

On 31 August 1792 a meeting, probably influenced by the canal mania, had been held in Birmingham under the chairmanship of Isaac Spooner to promote a canal from near Birmingham to the Netherton collieries, and had resolved to negotiate with Lord Dudley and the Dudley Canal company. The canal's committee met the following day and promptly decided 'that an extension of the present Dudley Canal to the Town of Birmingham and the Worcester Canal will be highly advantageous to the Interests of this Company and is proper to be carried into execution',[9] the shareholders adding two days later that the 'intended Canal was in contemplation of this Company as an extension of the Dudley Canal prior' to the current proposal. There is a map in the Birmingham Reference Library by James Sheriff, dated 1792, which probably refers to this proposal. It shows not only the Selly Oak line and Lappal tunnel (given as 3,330 yd long) but also a Netherton tunnel (2,078 yd) and a communication to the Birmingham Canal at Oldbury.

Contact was first made with W. A. Roberts of Bewdley, the solicitor to the Worcester & Birmingham and, this having presumably been satisfactory, a meeting with the promoters of the scheme of 31 August was arranged, at which it was agreed that the Dudley company would make the extension, that the existing Dudley shareholders would be paid interest on their shares while it was being built, and would subscribe £28,500 to it, and that the Birmingham promoters would raise the balance of the £90,000 estimated to be required among themselves or from elsewhere. The line was surveyed by John Snape, and an Act[10] obtained in 1793. It seems a little odd that after it had passed, the company voted 500 guineas to W. A. Roberts and £150 to Charles Henry Hunt, the treasurer of the Stratford and probably related to their own solicitor, Thomas Hunt, for their trouble and attendance on the Act. Neither represented the Dudley company, but each companies whose complaisance was important. We shall come across another instance of odd behaviour by W. A. Roberts later.

The authorized line was level from the Dudley Canal at Netherton by way of Halesowen and Lappal to the Worcester & Birmingham at Selly Oak, with two branches, one from Windmill End to Baptist End near Dudley, the other from Cabbage Hall in Dudley to the first branch. The main line was $10\frac{7}{8}$ miles long and included the 3,795 yd long Lappal tunnel, the fourth longest in England, as well as one of 557 yd at Gosty Hill. Bradshaw's map of 1830 also shows a 29-yd tunnel near Halesowen through a spur of hill, but from examination of the site it seems likely that a shallow cutting and bridge were built instead.

The Act permitted new subscribers and such old ones as wished to join them to raise £90,000, and £40,000 more if necessary, in shares of £100, which after completion of the extension were to rank *pari passu* with those existing. A guarantee of 12 per cent dividend was given to the Stourbridge company after the Dudley shareholders had received 5 per cent, and goods travelling south on the Worcester & Birmingham from Selly Oak were to pay the same toll as if they had come from Birmingham. The Act contained two curious provisions: the first, for lump sum and not mileage tolls for nearly all goods through the tunnel, mostly 1s 9d or 2s per ton; the second, that the company should repurchase the shares of such shareholders as 'may not chuse to be concerned in the said Undertaking' at the sum subscribed plus interest at 5 per cent plus 'such further Sum of Money (not less than One hundred Pounds upon each Share) as the . . . Commissioners . . . think reasonable or proper'.

The bill was strongly opposed by the Birmingham company, who explained how much they had spent on their own canal, the value of whose shares might be affected, and who themselves proposed to put forward a bill for a canal from Oldbury via Rowley to Netherton. The Staffs & Worcs opposed it, and so did the iron and other manufacturers of Wolverhampton, who did not wish the cheap coal they enjoyed to find a more extended market. These virtuously considered 'that the increase of Canals must also increase the price of Coals' and that 'the Speculation upon Canals is now carried to an enormous Extent, that, instead of promoting the Public Good with laudable Enterprize, it is become a new system of Gambling'.[11] A newspaper report says that '13,000 of the principal inhabitants and manufacturers of Birmingham petitioned the House in favour of the Bill' and 'in its final stages the petition presented against it was signed by no more than 250 people'. However accurate the figures, they probably represent dissatisfaction with the monopoly position of the Birmingham company. The bill indeed had a rough passage through the House of Lords, Lord Porchester leading the attack on the grounds that it cut through and attacked private property without public benefit'.[12] However, it passed, and soon afterwards that for the Stratford-upon-Avon Canal opened wider hopes of a line to London as well as to the Severn.

Josiah Clowes was now appointed engineer at 3 guineas a day and 4 guineas a journey expenses—so quickly had the pay of competent engineers risen—with William Underhill as resident at £150 p.a. and a house, helped by Thomas Green as superintendent and agent. The surveyors setting out the line were told to avoid all deep cutting and substantial embankments, presumably for fear of subsidence, and early in 1794 work began.

At the beginning of 1796 Clowes died, and Underhill carried on for a year. Robert Whitworth was then asked to make an inspection of the works. After his visit Underhill was given charge of the tunnel and of the aqueduct at the Leasowes near the junction with the old line, and Benjamin Timmins of the rest. Lappal was, of course, a major tunnelling job, with thirty shafts and three steam engines for pumping. Thomas Brettell, the company's clerk, on 16 June of this year, writes of:

> 'the difficulties we have had to encounter in the execution of the Lapal Tunnel, by reason of the great quantity of Water which has been found in almost every Shaft that has been sunk, as also by the running sand, which has extended itself more or less for three fourths of the whole line of the Tunnel . . . our Engineer has been very unequal to the undertaking in point of Judgment and conduct, but now that he has had the advantages of experience, and is perfectly acquainted with the whole of the Works, it is thought more prudent to continue him under the direction of the Committee of Works, who have had an Augean Stable to cleanse and nothing but their almost turning Miners themselves could have accomplished it'.[13]

The Halesowen–Netherton section had been built a foot or so too high, a mistake that had now to be rectified. That done, a public wharf was opened at Halesowen early in 1797, where coal and lime were to be sold, and coal delivered in the town, presumably by the canal company.[14]

By May 1796 the whole of the authorized £90,000 had been raised, and the company began to make additional calls upon its shareholders for the supplementary £40,000 under the 1793 Act, though many older calls were in arrear. By September it was clear that still more would be required, for which a new Act was needed. This in December 1796 recorded the existing capital as £175,325 plus £2,000 in mortgages, and authorized another £40,000 in more of those complicated financial clauses for which the Dudley Acts are remarkable. Meanwhile Abiathar Hawkes the treasurer resigned for health reasons, and Dixon & Amphlett, bankers of Dudley (Amphlett was on the committee) were appointed instead. The finances of the Dudley must have taxed the spare time of a businessman such as Hawkes, and also his cash resources; in their thanks for his services, the company especially mentioned his liberal assistance in lending money to enable the works to be carried on.

By 28 May 1798 the extension was reported 'completely open'.[15] The payment of interest had ceased on 1 September 1797, and in September a final call was made on the new shares, which gave them a value of £162 10s 0d, against £118 15s 0d on the old ones, or a total capital of £207,361, though further small borrowings took place, culminating in one of £10,000 in 1802. A share exchange later took place to give all shares the nominal value of £100. The canal having been opened, Lord Dudley resigned from the committee. He and his predecessor had sat there since the company began, and he presumably felt his personal influence was no longer needed to keep it on a path which would suit his interests. Instead, they became accustomed to make use of his mine agents for many engineering matters; first Charles Roberts, and later Francis Downing, who sat on the canal committee from 1822 to 1843.

The company had spent most of twenty-two years in canal construction, during which their capital had increased from £7,000 to over £200,000, and had not yet paid a normal dividend. Their first task was therefore to build up a trade in coal through Lappal tunnel, but little could be done till the Stratford Canal's junction with the Warwick & Birmingham was completed in 1802, and opened a route towards London. Better markets were found when the Worcester & Birmingham was completed to the Severn at the end of 1815, the Stratford Canal was opened to the upper Avon in mid-1816, and the Stratford & Moreton Tramway was finished in 1826. A first dividend of 1 per cent was paid for the year ending 31 July 1804. Payments did not rise above 2 per cent till 1819, then rose steadily to 4¼ per cent for 1826, and afterwards fluctuated between 2½ and 5 per cent until the end of the canal's separate history in 1846. Here are the figures; each 1 per cent of dividend required £2,060 15s od.

Years Y.e. 31 July*	Average dividend per cent
1803–5	⅔
1806–8	⅔
1809–11	1
1812–14	2
1815–17	1⅓
1818–20	2⅔
1821–3	3
1824–6	4
1827–9	3⅙
1830–2	2½
1833–5	3½
1836–8	4⅙
1839–41	5
1842–4	4⅓

*1822–3 seems to have been an eight months year, after which the financial year probably ended on 31 March.

We must now return to the earlier extension line. The Dudley tunnel was a favourite thrill with sightseers. The Rev Luke Booker, in his *Dudley Castle*, 1825[16] referred to 'The steersman of the boat, even to his very garb, is the exact counterpart of Charon'. W. Harris, in *Rambles about Dudley Castle*, 1845[17] says of the canal: 'Deeply sunken amid rocks and caves, the sunbeam seldoms warms its sullen waters; and the pallid beings who are occasionally seen propelling boats into the apertures of invisible passages, clad in their barracan mine dresses, cameleon like, appear to derive their hue from the rocks which surround them.'

The limestone quarrying did not help the transit of boats wanting a quick passage. In 1797 it was said that boats were impeded 'by the Loading of Limestone into Boats at Charles Starkey's Quarry in the Tunnel, By empty Limestone Boats being left afloat in the Tunnel and By Boats Loaded with Limestone being left in the Canal near to the Stop Lock at Tipton'.[18] About this time the clerk to the Burton Boat Co complained about impediments to a trade between the Dudley Canal and Burton via the Wyrley &

Essington Canal, and was told by the Dudley's clerk: 'I understand the Tunnel itself is more commodious than the Hare Castle. The objection is the effect of prejudice arising from interested Motives in the Boatmen.'[19] Complaints of obstruction from limestone boats end after 1799, so presumably additional space and better regulation had ended the trouble.

They could not, however, affect the two main disadvantages of the tunnel. The first was subsidence due to the coal mining that went on near it, which caused more stoppages for repairs than were convenient, though not as many as at Lappal. Indeed, subsidence and mining problems were such that the canal company had their own Inspector of Mines. The other was the length of time a loaded boat took to get through it. The tunnel rules allowed four hours for a flow of traffic one way, after which the direction was reversed for the next four hours. In 1830 the rules were altered to allow only three hours, and a penalty was threatened if boats were not worked 'with all due diligence'.[20] The threat of the Stourbridge, Wolverhampton & Birmingham Junction Canal (see p. 104) in May 1836 caused the committee to study 'whether further improvements can be made so as to render the passage thro' Dudley Tunnel more convenient and expeditious'.[21] At this committee meeting Thomas Brewin, the superintendent, complained that 'a practice has obtained in passing Boats ... of linking several Boats together and employing only two men or Boys for all such Boats whereby the passage of Boats is impeded in consequence of such Boats not being passed within the time prescribed'. It was decided to enforce the by-law that each boat must have two men, and in 1837 a number of boatmen were summoned for disobeying it. In 1840 Brewin suggested some mechanical means of haulage, perhaps by cable, to reduce the passage of time to three hours at a cost of £6,000, but the company ruled it out as too expensive.

For some years after its opening Lappal tunnel was a source of trouble, mainly from subsidence. It was closed for two months in the spring of 1801, again at the end of the year, and in 1805 for over four months. When this happened, trade stopped, and the pressure to reopen was heavy. 'The men are much tired, some of them ill &c, a long and almost sleepless application to the Job has injured the health of several of them, particularly Mr. Green, who I apprehend will sink under the pressure of the Business. He wants rest very much.'[22] Indeed in 1815 the company actually authorized a tramroad from Netherton to Selly Oak, presumably thinking it would enable traffic to keep going while the tunnel was being repaired. They did not, however, build it.

As with the Dudley tunnel, the four hours needed to pass a loaded boat through Lappal was a handicap. The first step towards improvement was taken in 1820 when each steerer of a boat going east with at least 15 tons was paid 1s 6d to hire legging help. In 1829, shortly after the tunnel rules had been altered to allow only three hours for the passage, this was increased to 3s if the boat was carrying 18 tons. Then in 1841 a steam pumping engine was placed near the mouth of the tunnel which, combined with the use of stop locks at each end, was able to create a current to help boats through. This ingenious contrivance worked well. In September 1842 Brewin was presented with £50 worth of plate for his care and assiduity, and 'for the advantage which the Canal has derived from the late contrivance for passing Boats through the Tunnel'.[23] Pumping continued until 1914.

The opening of the Stratford Canal's junction with the Warwick line at Kingswood brought trade to the Dudley and that company became accustomed to making joint arrangements with the Worcester & Birmingham and Stratford for reduced tolls on certain articles under certain conditions which, they hoped, would keep as much traffic originating on the Dudley or coming from the south of that line to London as possible, rather than on the Dudley tunnel, Tipton, Farmer's Bridge and Bordesley route. In addition, the opening of the Worcester & Birmingham in late 1815 caused the Dudley to give drawbacks on coal to the Severn to compete with that carried by the Staffs & Worcs. A considerable preoccupation was also to persuade the trade, much of it in iron, from the upper Severn and Stourbridge to pass to Birmingham by way of Lappal, and the return trade to take the same route, because more Dudley tolls were to be earned. In 1810, for instance, the company leased their wharf at Birmingham to Danks & Co, the carriers, who guaranteed to carry 80 tons a week via Lappal. After early trouble, when Danks held tolls back because of the state of the tunnel, the agreement was maintained for many years, and in 1821 the company built the firm a new Birmingham warehouse. All the same, one gets the impression that the Tipton route was the more used. For instance, in 1827 John Greaves & Son of Stratford were carrying grain to Dudley via the Birmingham Canal and Tipton, and then loading coal to return the same way, because the tolls were less. The tendency of Lappal tolls was therefore to fall. In 1831 all coal eastwards to the Worcester &

VII. Dudley Canal: (*above*) Delph locks, with the line of old locks to the right; (*below*) Brewin's tunnel, now opened out, and High Bridge on the extension line to Selly Oak

VIII. Early and late: (*above*) from Castle Mill basin looking through the Earl of Dudley's original tunnel towards Tipton; (*below*) the south portal of Netherton tunnel

Birmingham was down to 1s a ton, half the Parliamentary rate.

The removal of Worcester Bar in 1815 helped the tendency for trade to prefer the Tipton route. The Dudley company had therefore allied themselves with their old enemies the Birmingham company against their friends the Worcester & Birmingham to oppose its ending. Indeed, in 1813 the Birmingham had actually proposed amalgamation with the Dudley to avoid increased price-cutting should it be removed, and the construction of a new tunnel between Oldbury and Netherton. After a stop-lock had been substituted, the Dudley company reduced tolls on most merchandise traffic passing it by 4d a ton. For some years after the Lappal line was opened the company itself traded in coal (and to a smaller extent in lime and limestone), having a contract with Lord Dudley for a regular supply from his collieries at Park Head and Bumblehole, and two sub-committees, one to oversee the trade in the Birmingham market, and one in Halesowen, Selly Oak and elsewhere. It was not always easy to get enough coal. Before the tunnel was finished the company asked Lord Dudley and others to 'consider the propriety of opening their Mines on the Line of the Canal as being of the utmost importance to this concern'.[24] About 1802 in reply to their protest about insufficient supplies, Alexander Raby wrote on behalf of the Earl:

'It may probably be supposed that exertions have not hitherto been used to effect this purpose, but, let me assure you, that has not been the case. The real fact (exclusive of the difficulties already stated) is the want of Colliers owing to the great increase not only of Furnaces lately erected, but to the various openings that have been made in every direction throughout the Country by the new Canals. Colliers and Miners cannot be raised like many other Trades but by time; Increase of Wages, we all know (tho' that has been tried) does not always increase work done.'[25]

From Lady Day 1799 to 1 August 1803 the company sold 76,656 tons of coal, as well as 894¾ of lime and 8,057 of limestone, and made a profit on this trading of £909.[26] They had also bought five shares in the Hockley Coal and Boat Co, which were sold in 1805. They gave up trading and the consequential carrying from August 1803, presumably because they felt traders had got used to using the Lappal line.

Thomas Brewin, who had been concerned in coal mining, was a member of the Stourbridge and Stratford Canal committees when he was appointed superintendent in 1812. He then resigned from the Stourbridge, but kept his membership of the Stratford committee, and later was to join the board of the Stratford & Moreton Tramway also. After he had been employed for a year he arranged himself a salary of £250 p.a. and 5 per cent of the tolls over £10,000 up to £15,000 p.a., and soon afterwards was navigating stone and sand on the Lappal line at his own risk. In 1819 his commission was abolished; he was given £300 p.a. instead, and allowed personally to trade in coal wholesale to the Worcester & Birmingham and the Stratford canals. Through Brewin the company therefore kept an indirect interest in the coal trade. So much did the company appreciate his services that in 1833 they agreed to build him a bathroom and closet, if he paid for the fittings himself. In 1839 they acknowledged his services further by raising his salary to £400 p.a. and saying of his management that the company's 'present welfare and prosperity is in a great degree attributable' to it.[27] Brewin was himself a considerable shareholder in the Dudley. In 1841 his holdings reached their maximum of 53¾ shares, plus another 47 held by Mary Brewin, probably his wife.

The company never built its two authorized branches from the Lappal line towards Dudley itself, except for a very short length of the first branch from Windmill End in 1803. They would have required heavy lockage. Apart from short colliery or works cuts, some of which were fed by private tramroads, other improvements carried out were two cut-offs near Dudley Wood in 1836, which shortened the canal by 200 yd, a new cut-off about 400 yd long, with a 75-yd tunnel called Brewin's, at Lodge Farm that cost about £8,500 and was opened in 1838, and the ¼-mile long Withymoor branch in 1842. The Lodge Farm diversion enabled a storage reservoir and pumping engine to be built there. In 1839 the company claimed to have spent £17,000 on new works since 1835. (*To continue the history of the Dudley Canal, turn to p. 253.*)

Pensnett Canal

The Pensnett, or Lord Ward's Branch, Canal runs from Park Head basin on the Dudley near the south end of Dudley tunnel, level for 1¼ miles to a point just beyond the Wallows engine shed on the Pensnett Railway at Brierley Hill, where there was a wharf and railway siding. It was built by Lord Dudley's trustees in 1839–40, and probably opened in the latter year, to serve the Round Oak and other ironworks belonging to Lord Dudley. (*To continue the history of the Pensnett Canal, turn to p. 263.*)

CHAPTER VII

The River Severn

✦✦

IN this chapter and the next we shall look briefly at the Severn itself between 1790 and 1842, when the Severn Commission was established, and at the effect upon the river, as upon themselves, of various canals and river navigations that connected with it: the Staffs & Worcs Canal, the Droitwich, the Worcester & Birmingham, the Upper and Lower Avon Navigations, and the Coombe Hill Canal. For completeness however, we must remember two other groups of waterways, below and above those described. The story of those below will be found in my *The Canals of Southern England*. The Stroudwater Canal had been opened in 1779 from Framilode on the Severn below Gloucester to Stroud, in 1789 to be extended by the Thames & Severn Canal to the Thames. By this route, which had been financially supported by the Staffs & Worcs and Stourbridge companies, a few of the exports of Coalbrookdale, Stourbridge and south Staffordshire found their way to the Thames and London, for no other route was then available.

The first barge to travel all the way from Coalbrookdale arrived in London in July 1800, having taken 14 days.[1] Soon afterwards the Thames & Severn company put on barges from Bristol and Stourport to London,[2] and in March 1802 a firm announced weekly boats from London taking 20–25 days to Stourport.[3] However, at the end of 1800 an all-canal route (except for the tramroad at Blisworth) was available from Stourport to London, via Aldersley and Digbeth, and from May 1802 another via the Stourbridge Canal, Lappal tunnel and Lapworth. The carriers on the longer route by way of the Thames & Severn, using the unimproved Severn and the Thames that was not much better, found it almost impossible to compete. In August 1804, for instance, this advertisement appeared:

'Canal Carriage between Bristol, Glocester, Worcester, Stour-

port, etc. and the Hambro' Wharf, London. The several Owners of Boats upon the Thames and Severn Canal, respectfully inform the Public, that they have made some important Arrangements for the more Speedy Conveyance of Goods between the above Places, whereby the Delays that have been lately complained of are effectually removed; and they can assure their Customers of every possible exertion being used to establish the Trade upon the most regular footing. They also hope, that when the expence of Carriage by this Conveyance is compared with any other, they may reasonably expect a preference of the public Favor.'[4]
They were not to get it and soon after the opening of the Blisworth tunnel in March 1805 we find advertisements for fly-boats from Stourport via Wolverhampton and the Grand Junction to Upper Thames Street or Paddington.

The opening of the Thames & Severn Canal helped to stimulate the development of the Forest of Dean collieries, so that we find the Bullo Pill tramroad opened in 1810,[5] and the Lydney Canal, shipping place for the Severn & Wye tramroads, in 1813.[6] From opposite Gloucester the Herefordshire & Gloucestershire Canal was completed to Ledbury in 1798, and eventually reached Hereford in 1845.[7] Others in the neighbourhood were projected, but never built: a canal from Tewkesbury to Winchcombe in 1793[8] and another from Tewkesbury to Cheltenham in 1801. We shall see later the effect on the Severn of the effort to by-pass a part of the river notorious for the difficulty of its navigation by means of the Gloucester & Berkeley ship canal, authorized in 1793, but not opened till 1827.[9]

Above Stourport, the Coalbrookdale works of the Darbys, and others in the area, had increasingly depended upon the river for transport since their foundation early in the eighteenth century.[10] In 1791 the tub-boats of the Shropshire Canal began to bring down to Coalport for transhipment to Severn craft the products of the collieries and iron works on its line, such as Ketley and Donnington, and to carry back goods brought upstream for Wellington, Newport and neighbouring places. Hulbert says that in May 1836 he counted 72 vessels 'loading and unloading their various cargoes, chiefly Coal. . . . A commodious Warehouse, five stories in height, has been erected by the Lord of the Manor . . .'.[11] Much the same was true of Ironbridge, which he describes as having the appearance of an inland port: 'the most extraordinary district in the world; the banks on each side are studded with Iron Works, Brick Works, Boat Building Establishments, Retail Stores,

Inns, and Houses, perhaps 150 vessels on the river, actively employed or waiting for cargoes'.[12]

We can get an idea of the traffic on the lower part of the river near the beginning of our period from the registration of boats over 13 tons owned in Gloucestershire under the Registration Act of 1795. Thirty-seven were listed as working partly or wholly on the river, 15 being based at Brimscombe Port, the main transhipment centre for the Thames & Severn Canal, 7 at Framilode, 6 at Tirley, 2 at Stroud, and one each at Maisemore, Ashleworth, Berkeley, Arlingham, Frampton, Oldbury and Tewkesbury. The normal run was between Stourport and Tewkesbury, Gloucester, Brimscombe Port or Framilode (the entrance to the Stroudwater Canal), or between places from Tewkesbury down to Bristol, and occasionally on to Newport or Cardiff, with calls also at Chepstow. Of the 37 craft, 5 were of 20 tons or less, 6 of 21–30 tons, 2 of 31–40 tons, 5 of 41–50 tons, 17 of 51–60 tons,* and 2 of 61–70 tons. The normal crew of a 51–60 ton craft was three men if working upwards from Framilode or Brimscombe Port to Stourport, but five men if going to Bristol or beyond.

In spite of the great additional trade that the canals brought upon the river, it remained unimproved, except for the building of horse towing paths, in face of mounting criticism, with many cargoes having to be transhipped at Tewkesbury, Gloucester and elsewhere. One target for this was the section of river between Gloucester and Sharpness, which big craft could only navigate at spring tides, and then with difficulty. Only too often a news paragraph such as this would appear:

'The Heart of Oak trow ... on her passage from Bristol ... lost on Nass Sands ... cargo of groceries, hides, oats, etc, the property of persons at Tewkesbury and Winchcomb, nearly ... entirely lost; but the crew ... saving themselves in the boat. The vessel took the ground in the early part of the flood, when the tide, rushing up with great impetuosity, washed away part of the sand under her, and she soon after broke her back and parted.'[13]

One result of this criticism was the discussion in Bristol during the canal mania of a canal, the Bristol & Severn, to Gloucester with a possible extension to Worcester,[14] and the authorization of the Gloucester & Berkeley ship canal in 1793 as a by-pass for the worst section; another symptom was the discussion at the begin-

* Ten of these were barges, and two trows, owned by the Thames & Severn Canal Co., the barges having probably been built as part of a nearly uniform fleet.

ning of 1825, when it was nearly completed (it was opened in 1827) of a possible extension upwards to the canal at Worcester, this Worcester & Gloucester Union project being strongly supported by the Worcester & Birmingham company, who hoped that with its help boats would be able to reach Gloucester on the second day from Birmingham. 'From the state of the navigation ... between this (city) and Worcester, which is alike impracticable in dry seasons and in times of flood, the establishment of such a Canal has long been deemed a desideratum,' said the *Glocester Journal*.[15] Telford surveyed it, and estimated it at £200,000,[16] but the boom of 1825 came to an end, and nothing was done. In connection with this scheme it was thought that 34,060 tons of coal and 22,445 tons of merchandise then passed annually between the two cities.[17]

The opening of the Gloucester & Berkeley made a great difference to the river traffic above Gloucester by freeing it from dependence upon the spring tides and improving punctuality, while dock and wharf improvements at Bristol increased traffic there. For instance, in September 1827 Pickford's advertised: 'The Gloucester & Berkeley Canal being of sufficient width to admit Vessels of large burthen, Pickford & Co's trows will sail to and from Worcester and Bristol without transhipment of Goods.'[18] By 1828, so much had traffic grown, it was said that 230 craft averaging 50 tons burthen belonged to Gloucester.[19]

A steamboat, described as the first, was carrying passengers and luggage between Gloucester and Worcester in 1814, making the downward trip in 4½ hours.[20] Steam towing was introduced in 1830, when the *Sabrina*, owned by Brown & Son of Tewkesbury, built with shallow draught and able to negotiate bridges in flood time, when on trial in February saved 48 hours on the run between Gloucester and Worcester towing a vessel with a load of 60 to 70 tons at 8 mph.[21] Two years later the tug was certainly operational, for she sank the trow *Neptune*, 90 tons, after a collision.[22]

In 1831 the Worcester & Birmingham Canal company, whose improving business was threatened by the Forest and Welsh coal whenever river navigation was interrupted, had themselves dredged some shallows, and in 1834 and 1835 carried out experiments based upon a model of part of the river. At the beginning of 1836 they thought the Gloucester–Worcester section in which they were interested could be improved by dredging at moderate cost, and 'with no charges or tolls of any magnitude'.[23]

This was in reply to a prospectus that had just been put out by a proposed Severn Navigation Company. This concern, with Rhodes as its engineer, proposed to put weirs across the two branches of the Severn at Gloucester, with a lock in the east channel, another lock near Upton, and three more between Worcester and Stourport. Assuming a depth of 12 ft were provided to Worcester, and 6 ft thereafter to Stourport, enough for 100-ton barges, the cost was estimated at £200,000; for 10 ft to Worcester at £168,248; and for sufficient depth to take existing craft efficiently £111,544. A toll of 6d a ton was proposed for the full scheme.

Immediately sides were taken. The Worcester & Birmingham company was only concerned with the river below Worcester, only wanted 5 ft depth (the craft in which they were interested drawing about 3 ft 6 in.), and wanted trustees and not a private company. The merchants of Worcester were in favour, for they saw themselves replacing Gloucester as the head port for seagoing craft. The Staffs & Worcs company at first supported it warmly and agreed to take 100 shares, for they badly needed extra depth in the river below Stourport for the 300,000 tons of traffic that entered that port each year. Later they became cooler as the opposition hardened of the Stourport traders, who feared that the proposed toll would endanger the narrow margin in favour of Staffordshire coal over that from the Forest, and thought big craft should pay a higher toll than small—'If the Worcester traders want a Ship Canal, they ought to pay a higher rate of Tonnage on Ships, and not tax Stourport whose Traders cannot have any advantage from a Ship Canal'.[24]

The Midlands ironmasters were in favour, because their cargoes would get more easily to the sea and their imports more efficiently return, but the Shropshire merchants and ironmasters were solid in opposition, on the grounds that they did not need the facilities and that a toll would be unjust. Also in opposition was the Gloucester & Berkeley company, who feared the transfer of trade to Worcester and a possible lessening of traffic due to the toll. To be on the safe side, however, they opposed the improvements because they were to be made by a private company, which would be 'an interference with the free rights of the River Severn by individuals for their exclusive profit'.[25] They were supported in opposition by the Gloucester merchants, who wanted only a 5 ft improvement up river so as to preserve their own transhipment trade, the Monmouthshire Canal, who thought tolls on the river

340

GLOUCESTER AND WORCESTER
HORSE TOWING-PATH COMPANY

HAW BRIDGE.

Sept 20 1902

Vessel called the *Blanch*
Owner *Ball*
Master
No of Horses   belonging to
Driver
From *Hun*
To *Diglis*
                           S. D.
Miles Toll   5   6

R   Received for said Co. *EB*

---

would injure the Newport coal trade, and the Herefordshire & Gloucestershire Canal company, who would have been cut off from Gloucester by way of the lower parting by the proposed weir, and whose boats would have had to get there by the more difficult upper route.

Meanwhile the Worcester & Birmingham company, still objecting to a greater depth than 5 ft, had in January 1837 promoted the Severn Improvement company to obtain this depth between Worcester and Gloucester without locks, partly by dredging the shoals and partly by providing side cuts to be used in times of low water, for £50,000, which sum they were prepared to borrow themselves. With their allies, the Gloucester & Berkeley and those who opposed a private company, they successfully defeated the Navigation's bill of April 1837.

The promoters now took the advice of the Staffs & Worcs to consider a barge rather than a ship canal, and in October 1837 agreed to a revised proposal for a depth of 6 ft 6 in. to Worcester and 6 ft to Stourport, with five locks, but with no works other than dredging lower than 17 miles above Gloucester. These proposals were estimated to cost £150,000. They also made an interesting estimate of traffic and income, after the improvements,

	tons
Timber, slates, salt, etc.	134,583
Groceries, corn, etc.	207,000
Coal *ex* Worcs & Birmingham Canal	68,000
Coal *ex* Staffs & Worcs Canal to Worcester	35,000
Coal *ex* Staffs & Worcs Canal below Worcester	35,000
	479,583

yielding an annual revenue of £15,370. In December 1840 William Cubitt gave the actual traffic on the river as 380,000 tons.

The Navigation company then came to an agreement with the Worcester & Birmingham. A new Improvement company was formed, which in April 1838 introduced a bill to improve the navigation from Worcester to Gloucester at an estimated expense of £75,000; there was to be a movable weir at Saxon's Lode, 17 miles above Gloucester, but no locks, and an average depth not exceeding 5½ ft. Craft trading above Worcester to pay no tolls. The company structure was retained, but Commissioners were to be appointed to inspect the completed works, see they were kept in repair, and have access to accounts, these to be representatives of the Worcester & Birmingham and Gloucester & Berkeley companies, and of the towns of Worcester, Gloucester and Tewkesbury.

The support of the Worcester & Birmingham had been gained, but the Staffs & Worcs, much interested in the Stourport-Worcester section, now decided to oppose. In despair, the committee of the newly formed company obtained the Gloucester & Berkeley's support only by agreeing that the company should give way to Commissioners—none of whom were to be representatives of canal companies—who should borrow for improvements at up to 5 per cent. Unfortunately for these plans, the shareholders of the company refused to commit suicide by ratifying the agreement, and proposed to go ahead with the bill as it stood; thereupon their own committee refused to act, and all efforts came to a stop.

In the autumn of the same year of 1838 meetings in support of a Commission were held, to which E. Leader Williams, now engineer to the scheme, reported upon a revised plan of improvement from Gloucester to Stourport. But no one took action, and therefore in 1839 the Worcester & Birmingham company once again started to dredge the river themselves at Upton, so badly was action needed. Towards the end of 1840, when this shoal had been dealt with, the corporation of Worcester, describing themselves as conservators of the river, threatened legal action unless the canal company stopped work, on the grounds that dredging the shoals below Diglis might injure the river above. Indeed, there seems to have been real doubt on the advisability of what the canal company were doing, and they stopped.

At last, in the autumn of 1840, steps were taken to wind up the old company, and then to call a public meeting at Worcester on 12 October, at which the Severn Improvement Association was formed to press for a bill to establish a Commission, with Lord Hatherton, chairman of the Staffs & Worcs Canal, as chairman of its committee. By November the Staffs & Worcs and Stourbridge companies agreed to support the new initiative, and most of the carriers were reported to have become subscribers.[26] Soon afterwards the Droitwich and Monmouthshire Canal companies, the Droitwich Patent Salt Co, the British Alkali Co, the Newport Dock Co and the Gloucester and Worcester Chambers of Commerce were named as supporters.[27] In December the Gloucester & Berkeley company met the Association, to which William Cubitt had been appointed engineer and Leader Williams sub-engineer, and were told its plans for obtaining a depth of 7 ft to 7 ft 6 in. to Worcester and 7 ft to Stourport. Broadly, these followed those of 1837. There was to be a lower lock and weir at Upton, 18¼ miles above Gloucester, and four others between Worcester and Stourport, each about 94 ft by 20 ft. The cost would be about £150,000. Again they decided to oppose, on the grounds that the scale of the proposals was too great and that the river might silt up, but this time they were on the losing side.

A bill was prepared by the Association, and was supported by most interests, though not by the Worcester & Birmingham, who wanted two separate Commissions, one for the stretch below Worcester and one for that above, no lock below the canal en-

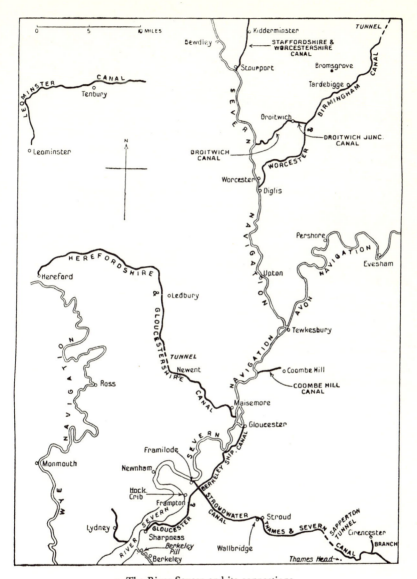

9. The River Severn and its connections

trance at Diglis but only dredging, and lower tolls. They complained sadly that their deputation to London was swamped by Worcester citizens, Stourport traders, and Staffs & Worcs supporters.[28] The bill, after being put into abeyance by the dissolution of Parliament, was finally passed in May 1842. It had been agreed that no lock should be put lower than Diglis, just below the Worcester & Birmingham's entrance, but that below the river should be dredged. The Shropshire interests were given exemption from toll as long as no cargo was loaded or unloaded within the improved portion of the river.

So, at the very end of the canal age, a Commission representative of towns and navigation interests was set up. Though the river had remained so long unimproved, we must not forget towing-path construction.

The rule, to Shrewsbury and beyond, was bow-hauling by men. The first step to provide a towing-path for horses seems to have been taken privately by Richard Reynolds of Ketley, who sometime before 1797 built a path for two miles from Coalport to Ironbridge along rugged banks and over bad fords, and so demonstrated the practicability of such building.[29] He considered that bow-hauling was not only degrading, but 'a means of harbouring and collecting persons of bad character, and facilitating a system of plunder injurious to the trade and destructive of the morals of the people engaged in it'.[30] Opposition came mainly from those who disliked the idea of a toll. Nash, the historian of Worcestershire, summed it up when he wrote: 'Various have been the attempts to introduce horses, but the banks are often so steep, the line must very often change sides . . . the laying a tax upon a free river, and many other objections, have rendered, and I trust will always render, this scheme abortive.'[31]

In 1799, the year that Nash's book appeared, under the influence of the growing canal traffic and the scarcity of 'towing men',[32] the powers of the measure of 1772 were renewed by a four-clause Act[33] which made no changes except to alter the meeting-place of the trustees from Bridgnorth to Madeley. This time they were used, the path being reported complete for the 24 miles from Bewdley Bridge to Meadow Wharf, Coalbrookdale, in August 1800.[34] The capital of the Severn Towing Path Company was £5,000 in £50 shares, but as only £30 seems to have been paid up, and as 35 were forfeited for failure to pay calls,[35] it is likely that the actual cost of the path was only about £2,000. The company were accustomed to let their tolls in up to three lots, the toll being at first 6d per horse per mile, reduced in 1833 to 4d[36] and also to let their contracts for repairing the path and its gates, bridges and walls, fences and watercourses.[37]

At the end of August 1801 a meeting was called by owners of vessels trading on the Severn to consider extending the Bewdley–Coalbrookdale path downwards,[38] and soon afterwards an extension as far as Gloucester was being considered.[39] The scheme was then modified, and in July 1802 a subscription was opened for a path to Worcester.[40] The Act was passed in 1803,[41] it having been stated in evidence that about 150 men were employed in bow-hauling, the cost being 3s a man pulling 3 tons, and that one horse would pull as much as six men at one-third less cost. The authorized capital was £5,000, and £6,000 more if required.

This Severn Horse Towing Path Extension was built not by trustees, but by a company which was connected with the Staffs & Worcs, and also included a number of the canal and river carriers. The path was probably open to Diglis in 1804;[42] a newspaper correspondent reported that that charge for towing upstream was 1s per horse per mile, plus 6d per mile payable to the landowners, downstream towing being free. If more than one horse were used, it had a separate attendant and line to the boat's mast. Horses usually worked 10 or 15 miles a day, and were stabled at night at convenient public houses. The concern seems to have been a profitable one, for an advertisement of 1810 offered several shares 'in this very successful Undertaking, the Dividends of which have been regularly made half-yearly, and the next . . . is expected to be very considerable'.[43] In 1840 the charge was 6d per horse per mile, which was that authorized in the Act. In 1809 another Act[44] was passed to authorize a path from Meadow Wharf, Coalbrookdale, to Mardol and Frankwell Quays, Shrewsbury. The trustees appointed to build and manage it included the Mayor, Recorder, Town Clerk and Stewards of Shrewsbury for the time being; they were empowered to build a path 6 ft wide and provide horse ferries, raising the money they needed by mortgage; to take tolls up to 2s per mile per horse; and to pay dividends up to 10 per cent. William Hazeldine the ironmaster of Bridgnorth invested £500; he was appointed surveyor, and got the path and its attendant gates, bridges and culverts open on 1 December at a cost of £5,000. The charge was settled at 1s a horse per mile.

The figures below summarize the fortunes of the path in terms of dividends and of the number of horses paying toll. Business was steady until the opening of the Newport branch of the Birmingham & Liverpool Junction Canal in 1835, which connected the Shrewsbury Canal to the main network; so doing, it greatly lessened the upper Severn trade. In the following years the trustees opposed river tolls, and helped to get the exemption for Shropshire trade that was written into the 1842 Severn Act. In that year, curiously for a towing-path concern, the trustees paid for the river to be dredged at Preston near Atcham, where a scour had made it impassable. The cost was £160.

Years*	Average dividend per £100			Average number of horses paying toll
	£	s	d	
1809–11†	4	10	0	
1812–14‡	3	16	8	331
1815–17	3	0	0	276
1818–20	3	16	8	286
1821–3	2	17	0	349
1824–6	2	16	8	394
1827–9	3	0	0	354
1830–2	2	13	4	327
1833–5	2	1	8	299
1836–8	1	6	8	188
1839–41	1	10	0	179
1842–4		8	4	130

* Dividends, calendar year; figures for horses, year ending Michaelmas.
† 1810 and 1811 only.
‡ 1814 only.

Before the Shrewsbury Act, however, in 1807, a news item had appeared in the Worcester paper about a contemplated path thence downwards to Framilode, the entrance to the Stroudwater Canal; 'the great facility and dispatch, regularity and certainty, with which mercantile people now transmit their merchandise between the towns on the present line of Towing Path . . . induces us to express our earnest wish and desire, to see farther extension of this beneficial principle'.[45] A bill for a path to Arlingham was introduced in 1811, but the opposition in Parliament by the Gloucester & Berkeley company and the City of Gloucester forced an amendment to end the path at the Lower Parting at Gloucester. The Act[46] authorized a capital of £10,000 in £25 shares for the Gloucester & Worcester Horse Towing Path company.

Its course was typical of such paths. It ran from Worcester bridge on the east side of the river to Upton, crossed on the bridge and ran on the west side to Lower Lode and on to Ashleworth. Here a ferry took it to the east side, where it continued to Gloucester bridge. It crossed again on the bridge, and continued to its end at the parting. The company made a bad start, for in 1826 it was reported that a few years earlier its shares could have been had as a gift. By 1824, however, £17 paid up, they received their first dividend of 10 per cent,[47] and in 1826 one of 14 per cent.[48]

So much for the Severn; now let us turn to the waterways which had throughout the canal age connected with its unimproved channel. (*To continue the history of the Severn Navigation, turn to p. 282.*)

CHAPTER VIII

The Tributaries of the Severn

++++++++++++++++++++++++++++++◆++++++++++++++++++++++++

Staffordshire & Worcestershire Canal

UNTIL 1792 the Staffs & Worcs was the only communication by water between the Severn and Birmingham. The company had strongly opposed the building of the Dudley tunnel, but in fact, trade was so buoyant that they were little affected when it opened. For Midlands trade, the route from Stourport via Aldersley was supplemented in 1798 by that via Lappal, but again there was little effect upon the canal's very satisfactory dividend figures, and in the early 1800s the Stourport basins were extended and barge locks built. The completion of the Worcester & Birmingham at the end of 1815, however, permanently diverted much of the coal and other trades between Birmingham and the Severn; it caused a sharp drop in S & W dividends from an average of £43 16s od for the previous five years to £33 in 1816 and 1817, and though they climbed to an average of £40 for the next ten years, they rose no higher.

From 1815 onwards we see the canal company slowly moving into the increasing competition that resulted from the more widely developed transport system that followed the end of the wars. First, there was slow pressure by the carriers, competing in speed and rates, to extend the hours during which the canal was open. It began when 'boats laden with Spring Goods for Bristol Fair'[1] were allowed to travel day and night and on Sunday evenings; soon afterwards boats to catch the spring tides on the Severn were allowed to travel day and night for 48 hours before and after the full moon. Apart from these special trades, the normal canal hours were 5 a.m. to 9 p.m. on moonlit nights, and 6 a.m. to 8 p.m. otherwise. From April 1816, however, boats licensed at £5 annually could pass at any time, and the first of what was to become a fleet of fly-boats appeared. In May 1820 it was decided that all craft could pass between 4 a.m. and 10 p.m. during the summer, and in June that any boat could pass at any time on payment of 2s extra per trip. In September 1828 the committee learned that the Birmingham company worked boats all night and 'keep an extra set of Men to conduct the night Trade',[2] and promptly ordered a baulk of timber to be put across their canal after hours to keep out the Birmingham boats. In March 1830 they changed their minds and ordered all locks to be open throughout the night, and soon afterwards were employing nightmen, and paying the lock-keepers extra for night work. One sympathizes with William Bagnall after the order 'That the Bed in the Nighthouse at Heywood be taken away and that our Clerk do warn William Bagnall to be more vigilant in his Duty and not permit any Boat to pass without his knowledge'.[3]

Competition showed itself also in the growth of a complicated system of drawbacks on tolls for specified cargoes carried to specified places or along specified routes, in order that they might be helped to compete at the places where competition from other canals was keenest. One finds one drawback on coal from the Birmingham Canal, and another on that from the Stourbridge, if it passed on to the Severn, and a further reduction if it went as far as Droitwich or Worcester. Such coal was competing with that carried down the Worcester & Birmingham, that from the Shropshire collieries or Coalport, and, farther down, with Forest coal. There is a drawback on iron entering the canal at Stourport—presumably from Coalbrookdale or Coalport—and passing by way of the Stourbridge and Dudley canals into the Worcester & Birmingham at Selly Oak, probably on its way to London. The drawback encouraged it not to travel by Worcester, and helped it to compete with that from Birmingham.[4] On the other hand, another drawback was given on Stourbridge iron carried into the Severn and bound for Bristol, or carried to Aldersley for Birmingham, or later to Great Haywood for Liverpool, and on iron from Birmingham also bound for the Bridgewater Canal, and intended to compete with Welsh iron brought by sea to Liverpool. One drawback led to another, till one is lost in the maze. It all led to protests from the short-distance carriers, who often had to pay more tolls per mile than those carrying goods farther, and made it almost impossible for anyone to know in advance what a rate was, and for how long it would remain unaltered, because each company was busy adjusting its own tolls in the light of others' actions, which in turn were caused by their own in an endless regress.

I

This kaleidoscope was moved not only by canal competition, but, as we have seen earlier, by that from coastal craft. Road competition became increasingly severe after 1815 as surfaces improved and waggons became faster: for instance, at the end of 1825 Pickfords were advertising that 'they have established Waggons for the Conveyance of Goods to and from Kidderminster and Birmingham, from whence their Fly Boats Sail to various parts of the Kingdom'[5] in direct competition with the Staffs & Worcs.

Meanwhile a short off-shoot had been built. In 1798 a rather elaborate branch to Stafford had been considered, with aqueducts over the Sow and Penk, and a notice issued,[6] but a horse tramroad was built instead from Radford wharf to Stafford and opened on 1 November 1805.[7] It cannot have been satisfactory, for in September 1810 Owen Hall got permission from the canal company to make the rivers Penk and Sow navigable to Stafford, and a lock at Radford. The navigation must have been made soon afterwards, for the Stafford Railway was sold in July 1814, its effects including two canal and two river boats. The connecting lock does not seem to have been opened until 19 February 1816;[8] it was built farther north than Radford, and opened directly into the River Sow, and not into the Penk.

The lock was not the property of the canal company, but with the navigation seems to have been owned by Lord Stafford, and leased by Fereday of Gornal colliery and later by the Moat Colliery company. It seems that navigation was intended to be restricted to firms' boats, for in July 1825 a special charge for other firms' boats passing the Sow lock was levied when Fereday could not supply the coal, and much was also landed at Radford wharf to be carried to Stafford by land. Later, the Moat Colliery company did not much value the navigation, for in 1838 they agreed to assign their lease from Lord Stafford of the land on which the lock stood, the Sow Navigation and its buildings to the Staffs & Worcs for £50. The canal company then improved the branch and reduced tolls.

At the beginning of 1825 the first was heard of a new project that was to have a great effect upon the Staffs & Worcs, when 'Mr. Thomas Eyre Lee attended and stated a project was in Contemplation for making and maintaining a Canal from the Staffordshire & Worcestershire Canal at or near Autherley to Nantwich'. The S & W stood to lose traffic from the Autherley–Great Haywood section of their canal to the new Birmingham & Liverpool

Junction, and also water. The latter sounding better, the committee decided in May that the 'projected Scheme . . . will be of serious detriment to this Company . . . unless an adequate Compensation be given to the Company for loss of Water'.[9] Early in 1826 the new company agreed to 2s per ton on most commodities, and this compensation toll was included in the Act of that year authorizing the new canal. In 1830, before the B & L J was opened, the Staffs & Worcs agreed to reduce this charge to 1s a ton on everything except manure (6d) and lime (4d). They regarded the toll as including permission to take a lockful of water for each boat passed into or out of the B & L J, but not as payment for it, since when the S & W later themselves became short of water till new reservoirs were built, permission was withdrawn, and the B & L J had to buy supplementary supplies from the Wyrley & Essington.

The B & L J was opened from Autherley to Gnosall on 12 January, and throughout on 2 March 1835. It was new and efficient; the Birmingham was rebuilding its own main line to take the expected additional traffic; the abortive London & Birmingham Canal was being promoted to continue the modernized line to London; and railway competition was in the air. But lying across this up-to-date line was the short section of the Staffs & Worcs between Autherley and Aldersley, with its compensation tolls, all the more irritating because at Christmas 1834 that company had reduced their own tolls but not those at Autherley. Therefore a group, made up of notabilities of the B & L J and the Birmingham companies and of promoters of the London & Birmingham, stiffened by some Staffordshire iron and coalmasters, got together to propose the Tettenhall & Autherley Canal and Aqueduct, one mile long, to cross the Staffs & Worcs by an aqueduct from the B & L J to the Birmingham, and to take a toll of 3d only. It was advertised only four months after the former's opening, and seems to have taken the Staffs & Worcs by surprise. They hurriedly issued a statement showing how little toll they had taken and how much water they had provided, and drew attention to their agreement to halve the authorized compensation. In December they were disturbed enough to send a delegation to meet representatives of the Birmingham company, the result being 'by no means satisfactory'.[10] In February 1836 a bill was introduced, and early in March was about to be read a second time. The Staffs & Worcs' nerve gave way, and a delegation was despatched to London to come to terms with the promoters; it agreed that the compensation should be reduced to 4d a ton, upon which the bill was withdrawn. The same threat of an aqueduct was to be used twice more, by the B & L J in 1842 to get more water, and by the Shropshire Union in 1867 to get a toll reduction to 2d and another water agreement.

Another concern of the company's was a proposal by Lord Dudley and Ward to make a tramroad from the pits near Kingswinford to the S & W at Hinksford. When they heard of it, they offered to make it themselves as a railway or a canal, but Lord Dudley took no notice, and opened it on 2 June 1829 'when an improved Loco-motive Engine called the "Agenoria", made under the superintendence of Mr. J. U. Raistrick, was started, which drew to the head of an inclined plane 131 tons in carriages, wagons, etc. at the rate of nearly 3½ miles an hour'.[11] The line then ran from Shut End colliery down an inclined plane, through Wall Heath, and down another incline to the canal at Ashwood (then sometimes called Flotheridge) basin. Some traffic was lost when the Stourbridge Extension Canal was built, and some when the upper end of the line was connected with Lord Dudley's Pensnett Railway. However, the line was still carrying a great deal of Lord Dudley's traffic in 1856, and was in use till at least 1926.

Finally, thanks to good relations with the Wyrley & Essington company from the 1820s onwards, the Churchbridge or Hatherton branch was built. The germ of this lay in a proposal for a tramroad from Mr Vernon's collieries near Wyrley to the S & W made in 1798,[12] for when the canal company first considered the branch they borrowed Vernon's original plan. Surveys were made in 1826 and 1830, and then in 1837 the Staffs & Worcs ordered a survey for a branch to Churchbridge. It was satisfactory, and they decided to go ahead without an Act, perhaps because of the attitude of Lord Shaftesbury, chairman of Committees of the House of Lords, to the bills of companies levying compensation tolls. This meant seeking consents to all land purchases, which took time, but on 4 April 1839 Robert Frost's estimate of £12,345 and his plan for a level branch to Churchbridge was accepted, and in honour of the company's chairman, Lord Hatherton, the new branch was given his name. In April 1841 it was reported 'in a fit and proper State for Boats of heavy Burthen to navigate the same',[13] and after some water supply difficulties worked satisfactorily. Towards the end of 1842 the company had built a tramroad from Cheslyn Hay near Churchbridge to Great Wyrley, mainly for coal traffic. The locks were not to be built for another twenty years.

The branch and tramroad had been financed from income, for the canal was flourishing. In 1838 it had carried 680,479 tons of goods, received £37,625, and paid out £23,800 in dividends. Few early figures of dividends exist, but in 1801 these seem to have been running at £40 per £140 share.[14] Here are the averaged figures from 1806 onwards:

Years	Average dividend per £140 share £	Years	Average dividend per £140 share £
1806–8	38¾	1824–6	40
1809–11	41⅓	1827–9	38⅓
1812–14	44	1830–2	
1815–17	36¾	1833–5	36¾
1818–20	40	1836–8	38
1821–3	40	1839–41	36

(*To continue the history of the Staffordshire & Worcestershire Canal, turn to p. 276.*)

Droitwich Canal

We left the Droitwich company beginning negotiations with the promoters of the Worcester & Birmingham, who had included a Droitwich branch in their 1789 proposals, and might here notice a very peculiar character, Wilson Aylesbury Roberts, solicitor of Bewdley. He had acted for the original Worcester & Stourbridge promoters, and later did the same for the Worcester & Birmingham, in which company he was a substantial shareholder. Yet he claimed and received fees from the Droitwich company for keeping them informed of the intentions of the Worcester & Birmingham, the interests of which were by no means the same. In 1791, for instance, he was given 50 guineas' worth of plate by the Droitwich for watching their interests in the Worcester & Birmingham's Act, which contained clauses protecting them, in 1804 asked for and obtained another 50 guineas for doing the same in relation to recent W & B bills, and in 1808 the same, though at the time the Droitwich was engaged in an action against the Worcester & Birmingham. It seems odd.

In March 1790 agreement was reached, whereby the Worcester & Birmingham agreed to guarantee 5 per cent (£8 per share) on Droitwich shares valued at £160 from the passing of the Act, and to buy shares offered at this price. As in November 1789 they had sold at £130, and as in February 1790 the company had themselves valued them at £140, the rise to £160, made at Roberts's suggestion, seems to have deliberately worsened his own company's position. It was to prove expensive. Since the Droitwich were not earning £8 per share, the guarantee came into force as soon as the 1791 Act was passed, £300 being claimed for the twelve months from mid-June 1792, and £291 for the next twelve, long before any competition could have resulted. Thereafter a claim was made yearly.

The fall in the Droitwich's revenue was probably caused by road competition and the absence of a practicable horse towing path, towing seemingly being done by men. In 1805 they agreed to a W & B suggestion that their toll on coal should be reduced from 1s 6d to 6d a ton, and in 1806 to make a path usable by horses. In spite of these moves, the Worcester & Birmingham held up guarantee payments on the grounds that the Droitwich were not trying hard enough to encourage trade, till in 1808 the latter brought and won an action to recover them.

Given that the Worcester & Birmingham had to make up the dividend, it evidently seemed simpler to let them manage the canal, and in November 1810, though the W & B was not yet open to the top of Tardebigge locks, let alone to Worcester, it was agreed that they should have 'the controul and management of the said Droitwich Canal Navigation under the inspection of the Committee of the Droitwich Canal'.[15] An additional motive may have been that they were at this time considering finishing their canal with a tramroad from Tardebigge which was planned to join the Droitwich Canal.[16]

The arrangement lasted uneasily till 1821. When the W & B opened it did indeed affect the Droitwich's trade, so that the annual payments rose to between £600 and £800 p.a., and in the year ended mid-1820 reached £1,118. In July 1820 the W & B proposed amalgamation, and the two companies agreed to seek the consent of Lord Somers, the landowner principally concerned, who strongly opposed it. The Worcester & Birmingham's committee then dropped the idea as not of sufficient importance to warrant unnecessary expense, and went on to say that they were not satisfied with the management of the Droitwich, and could not recommend the payment as compensation of sums 'they themselves neglect to collect'.[17] Then they called on the Droitwich to raise their tolls to the full Parliamentary level. This the latter's shareholders thought would be disastrous, apart from needing the consent of the Commissioners under the original Act, most of whom were dead. They finished by minuting that the W & B 'have upon several occasions inter-meddled with and attempted to direct and controul the management and concerns of this Company'.[18]

Things now took a turn for the better. The salt trade had begun to grow even before the partial repeal of the salt duties in 1822 and their ending in 1825, which was followed by toll reductions in 1829. Abolition caused the company to earn its dividend for the last years of the 1820s, and thereafter to make only occasional and small claims on the Worcester & Birmingham. After 1830, however, salt began to come from the new workings at Stoke Works on the W & B; this they carried upwards, the Droitwich company being left with the Severn trade, but in 1836 this traffic also was attacked by the W & B when, by agreement with the Droitwich Patent Salt Co, they reduced the toll on salt going down the Severn to Gloucester and Bristol so drastically that, with $1\frac{1}{4}$ miles of land carriage from Droitwich added, it was no greater than the charge made by the Droitwich Canal company.

The sudden growth of the salt business caused the import trade in coal to Droitwich to become more competitive, for sales of salt enabled bargains to be struck for the back-carriage of coal. In 1825, for instance, the Severn & Wye company gave a drawback on coal going above Tewkesbury with this end in view, which was extended in 1830 and 1833 for bulk sales of Forest coal to Droitwich works, but was ended in 1836; in 1839 the Droitwich Patent Salt Co was asking the Staffs & Worcs for a similar drawback. The old canal was still seeing life. (*To continue the history of the Droitwich Canal, turn to p. 270.*)

Worcester & Birmingham Canal

In 1789 the idea of a canal to Worcester was revived, but no longer by way of Stourbridge. The line now ran by Tardebigge, and in theory offered great advantages: it was 30 miles shorter than the old route by Aldersley and Stourport, 15 miles shorter than the not yet opened Dudley tunnel line, and avoided the navigation of the Severn between Stourport and Worcester. A pamphlet of 1790 claimed that the distances and tolls would be:

Via the Staffs & Worcs	$60\frac{7}{8}$ miles	12s 6d ton
the Dudley	$46\frac{5}{8}$ miles	11s 8d
the Worcester & Birmingham	$31\frac{1}{4}$ miles	5s

It went on to describe 60-ton barges as being used, so that 'The Merchandize to Bristol, without unloading, may be conveyed in the same Vessels, which will deliver Goods in Bristol, or Birmingham, for Eight Shillings and 6d per Ton, and nearly as soon as by Land Carriages, which costs Four Pounds per Ton: and Coals, through the Line of the Canal, nearly One Third cheaper than at present. . . . The roads in the country through which this canal is intended to pass are intolerably bad, and coals dear, and at a great distance.'[19]

On the other hand, the proposal threatened the maximum disturbance of vested interests, so that its mere threat had caused the Dudley company to apply for a reduction of the compensation tolls on its new tunnel line. The Birmingham joined with the Staffs & Worcs and others to defeat the first bill of 1790. In spite of similar opposition in 1791 from as far away as Oxford, the company got its Act,[20] aided by a petition from Birmingham that was 14 yd long and had 6,058 signatures. It was said to have cost its promoters £10,000 and its opponents £20,000, being one of the most expensive till then presented to Parliament. The news of its passing was brought to Worcester by post-coach, the arrival of which 'with the display of a flag, announced the gladsome tidings . . . a general joy seemed to have diffused itself through all ranks, which was testified by the ringing of bells, bonfires, etc.'.[21]

A local poet burst into song:

> Come now begin delving, the Bill is obtain'd,
> The contest was hard, but a conquest is gain'd;
> Let no time be lost, and to get business done,
> Set thousands to work, that work down the sun,
>
> With speed the desirable work to compleat,
> The hope how alluring—the spirit how great?
> By Severn we soon, I've no doubt on my mind,
> With old father Thames shall an intercourse find.*
>
> With pearmains and pippins 'twill gladden the throng,
> Full loaded the boats to see floating along;
> And fruit that is fine, and good hops for our ale,
> Like Wednesbury pit-coal, will always find sale.

* The Thames & Severn Canal had been opened at the end of 1789.

So much does the rage for Canals seem to grow,
That vessels accustom'd to Bristol to go,
Will soon be deserting Sabrina's fair tide,
For shallows and shoals sailors wish to avoid.*

As freedom I prize, and my Country respect,
I trust not a soul to my toast will object;
'Success to the Plough, not forgetting the Spade,
Health, plenty and peace, Navigation and Trade'.[22]

Disturbance of vested interests is always troublesome, and the new company found it so. They began life under severe handicaps.

The worst of these was the prohibition in their Act of a physical junction with the Birmingham Canal: 'Nothing in this Act contained shall . . . cause the said intended Canal . . . to be carried or made nearer than to within the Distance of Seven Feet from the Birmingham and Birmingham and Fazeley Canal without (their) Consent.' This was the famous Worcester Bar, over which all interchange goods had to be physically transhipped, ostensibly to prevent the Birmingham losing water, in fact to force trade to pay toll for a longer distance on the Birmingham line.

Another set of interests thought to be in jeopardy were those of the Stourbridge and Dudley Canal proprietors, whose Dudley tunnel line was threatened, and who feared competition with their coal trade. They were placated by an agreement that, once the W & B had been opened, the dividend of the Stourbridge would be made up to £9 a share, and that should the average receipts of the Dudley between 25 September 1792 and the opening of the W & B be diminished subsequently, the amount would be made up. In fact, the W & B was saved from these commitments: that to the Stourbridge did not become operative in the lifetime of the Worcester & Birmingham (though when the Sharpness New Docks company took it over in 1874 the guarantee went with it), and that to the Dudley was repealed in 1793. The occasion of this repeal showed the other side of the coin. Once the Worcester & Birmingham's Act had been passed, the Dudley company saw the advantages of uniting with it, and in their bill for the Selly Oak extension the clause was repealed.

Because it appeared to George Perrott, the owner of the Lower

* Presumably an allusion to the contemporary schemes for canals between Worcester and Bristol.

Avon Navigation, that his profits would be diminished by the building of the W & B, he got inserted into the 1793 Act for the Stratford-upon-Avon Canal a clause that until that canal was completed he should be guaranteed by the W & B that his current rent of £1,227 p.a. for the Lower Avon should be made up if necessary, and that after opening he should be paid a perpetual £400 a year. The guarantee never became operative, but the £400 p.a. was paid by the Worcester & Birmingham and its successors, and now finds its way from the British Waterways Board's accounts to those of the Lower Avon Navigation Trust.

We have just seen the nature of the dividend guarantee that the W & B had to give to the Droitwich Canal. Finally, Worcester Corporation climbed on to the bandwagon and obtained £40 p.a. as water bailiff's toll.

The Act authorized a capital of £180,000, and £70,000 more if necessary. The two biggest shareholders were Thomas Hooper and Isaac Pratt. Pratt had been for some years on the committees of the Stourbridge and Dudley canals, and had recently joined that of the Oxford, but on appointment to the committee of the Worcester & Birmingham he resigned from the first two. Hooper, who had been one of the promoters of the 1785 Stourbridge and Worcester project, held 48 shares and Pratt 50. Most other shareholdings were in 20 shares or less, four being by committeemen of the Birmingham Canal. The whole capital had been subscribed by July 1791. The shares became speculatively popular during the canal mania, a newspaper report of July 1792 saying: 'Navigation shares are so universally sought after that a holder of that kind of property may consider himself truly fortunate. Ten shares in the Birmingham and Worcester Canal were, on Wednesday last, sold by auction, by Mr. Boot, for a premium of two hundred and ninety-four pounds.'[23]

The surveys for the canal line had been done by John Snape and Josiah Clowes. The company originally intended to build a broad canal so that craft suitable for the Severn could reach Birmingham, but by mid-1794, probably influenced partly by cost and partly by the intended junctions with the narrow Dudley and Stratford canals, they had decided to construct broad tunnels and bridges, but narrow locks. The engineering was mainly done by Thomas Cartwright till he was succeeded in July 1809 by John Woodhouse who, with William Crosley who followed him in mid-1811, finished the summit level and built the rest of the canal to Worcester.

Work began from the Birmingham end, and the canal to Selly Oak was opened on 30 October 1795, when the chairman at the opening ceremony greeted Hooper as 'the father and protector of the Canal . . . saying that but for his Endeavors no Meeting for the present Occasion wd have taken place'.[24] It was not altogether a joyful occasion, for by the end of the year £154,067 had already been spent, and though the company agreed to raise the additional £70,000 by calls, they were, along with many other canal companies, becoming concerned 'that the number of Defaulters increase so much'.[25]

The line reached the Stratford junction at King's Norton in May 1796,[26] and West Hill tunnel (2,726 yd) was opened on 27 March 1797, 'the execution of which, with the stupendous embankments and dry cutting necessary between Birmingham and the commencement of the Tunnel, had been a matter of ridicule as an almost impracticable scheme'.[27] The tunnel opened, barges of 60 and 70 tons passed through to Hopwood wharf.

An Act of 1798 authorized higher tolls, the raising of more money, and the cessation of interest payments on calls. Little cash actually came in, however, and some had unintentionally gone out, for 1797 was enlivened by the discovery that Dr Thomas Hooper, the Treasurer, owed the company a great deal. Though a motion to remove him failed by 568 shares to 653, one of his sureties paid £5,000 to reduce his indebtedness, and at the end of the year Hooper resigned. In mid-1799 he still owed £8,800, and his executors were not entirely clear in 1815.

Work went on very slowly. So difficult did the rest appear that in mid-1799 Benjamin Outram attended in response to a suggestion that the line should be completed by a tramroad, and 'stated to the Company his opinion on railways in general and the proposed Railway to Worcester in particular'.[28] A year later a single line was approved, but in May 1802 the canal was still only completed to Hopwood wharf, 8¾ miles from Birmingham, and nothing had been done about the tramroad. Another Act of 1804 to raise money by further calls was passed, and at the beginning of 1805 a contract was signed with Thomas Cartwright to finish the canal from Hopwood wharf to the entrance of the cutting leading to Tardebigge tunnel. But, though agreement had been reached with the Birmingham company for the removal of the bar, the bill was heavily opposed and failed, and the company's own bill of 1811 for the same purpose was also defeated.

On 30 March 1807[29] the canal was opened to Tardebigge old

wharf, between Shortwood and Tardebigge tunnels, where 'a commodious Bason, Wharf, Weighing Machine, etc. are prepared ... for the accommodation of the Trade'.[30] From here a trade by land carriage, much of it in coal and corn, was built up with Bromsgrove, Droitwich, Worcester, Redditch, Alcester and Evesham. In June a Worcester firm advertised that they carried goods in 1½ to 2 days from Birmingham to Worcester by the Worcester & Birmingham and Droitwich Canals 'upon terms equally as low as by way of Stourport',[31] in May 1808 Thomas Sherratt the Birmingham carrier was advertising that he was carrying by water on the canal and then by land to Worcester, and in future would do so every weekday in 36 hours,[32] and in June it was stated that in the fifteen months since Tardebigge old wharf had been opened, 'the tonnage has increased progressively, and that the last month's tonnage was upwards of £274, which is after a rate of £3,500 per annum, being full treble the tonnage it produced before it was opened to Tardebigg'.[33] A passenger boat also ran between Alvechurch and Birmingham.

Prospects looked better, and another Act in 1808 offered attractive terms for new money, to be subscribed for in £40 shares to rank *pari passu* with those already issued, existing shareholders to be entitled to subscribe for two new ones for each share held. The authorized £168,000 at these terms had all been subscribed by 4 January 1809, and for a short time shares were at a premium of 5 guineas.

Several things happened. Cartwright was paid for what he had done under his contract, several new members were elected to the committee, reservoir construction was authorized, and the company agreed to try an experimental canal lift invented by John Woodhouse, an engineer on the Grand Junction, and to pay for excavation and masonry, if Woodhouse erected it at his own cost. They hoped, if the experiment were successful, to reduce the number of locks needed between Tardebigge and Worcester from 76 to 12, and to solve some of their water supply problems. Woodhouse now replaced Cartwright, whose health had caused him to resign, as engineer, and began to build his lift, which stood where the summit lock of the Tardebigge flight now is.[34] It was ready on 24 June 1808. It had a 12 ft lift, and a wooden tank large enough to take a narrow boat—this weighed 64 tons when filled with water—counterbalanced by a platform weighted with bricks, the two being connected by eight chains passing over the same number of cast-iron wheels. Wooden paddles at each end of the tank, and sealing off the canal, were raised to allow boats to enter and leave. The lift was then moved by two men who wound the tank up or down.

Serious testing began in 1810, though this could not be under operational conditions until the Tardebigge tunnel was finished at the end of the year. On 26 February it was said to have passed a boat in $2\frac{1}{4}$ minutes, and thereafter was repeatedly tested. By July 1810 however, it was clear that the company had decided in their own minds that they would build locks, and on 1 January 1811 this was formally decided, Woodhouse having been brought to acquiesce. A sizeable group of proprietors disagreed. They did not think the committee had given the lift a proper trial, and doubted if there was enough water on the summit level to supply locks and avoid pumping up from the Severn. They called Jessop in, who said 'that it will be for the interest of the Canal Company to adopt the Lifting Machine in preference to any other Mode that can be devised',[35] and tried to form a shareholders' association with local branches.

A good deal of discussion then took place, mainly turning upon Jessop's doubt about the sufficiency of summit water and his very high costs for pumping it. After what seems to have been some mild sabotage of the lift, it was then agreed that a public trial should be arranged from 25 February to 16 March, the lift working from five to twelve hours on each day. In numbers of boats passed the best performance was on 15 March, when it passed 110 boats in twelve hours, using two men. Finally, Rennie was called in, and his report[36] was probably fair: 'The lift does not, in fact, perform better than I expected it would, when worked for the short time and in the manner it has been done, and I doubt not, if carefully attended, it will work for a considerable time to come. My objections are that it is too complex, too delicate in its parts and requires much more attention and careful management than can possibly be expected to be given when in general use on a Canal; that its parts are subject to frequent derangement, and the repairs consequent thereon will be very heavy, and the trade of the canal frequently stopped.'

A joint meeting at the end of March agreed that should the committee be satisfied that there was enough water at or near the summit—without pumping from the Severn—then locks should be built. Meanwhile the lift should continue to give demonstrations. In fact, it was found possible to provide the necessary water, and from the beginning of 1812 construction went ahead along most of the line, new energy being provided by the Dudley family, already well represented on the Dudley, Stourbridge and Stratford canals, who bought 80 shares, Isaac Spooner junior, a Birmingham banker, who became chairman in 1813, and John Mabson, a Birmingham factor. They borrowed some money, and opened the canal to the top of Tardebigge locks in 1813, soon afterwards being involved in unsuccessful opposition to the Stratford's proposed junction with the Avon, which they feared might open a fourth route from Birmingham to the Severn.

By the beginning of 1815 they owed the bank £27,000, and the latter refused to advance any more. They therefore obtained another Act to enable them to raise money, but it contained a unique clause that unless they repaid the bank loan before 29 September they must sell the land they had bought for the reservoirs. In this difficulty they acted as the Stratford company had done a little earlier, and raised £36,000 by annuities at 10 per cent per £100, redeemable after three years. It was expensive, but they could carry on. Crosley had finished the main work on the two reservoirs at Cofton and King's Norton by the end of 1813. In 1814 an agreement had been reached with the Birmingham company for the removal of the bar which, though onerous, was better than nothing, and in July 1815 a lock through the famous obstruction was finished. The old plan of a principal basin at Lowesmore was changed to one at Diglis, served by two barge locks from the river, Woodhouse's lift was replaced by a lock in 1815, and on 4 December of that year the whole line was opened. Almost immediately afterwards, the Worcester & Birmingham's shareholders were told that 'Goods have already passed . . . direct from Bristol to Liverpool, and from Manchester to Bristol'[37] by their canal, and in February 1816 Pickfords were advertising flyboats. The new competition at once caused the Staffs & Worcs, Stourbridge and Dudley companies to grant bounties on coal passing down their lines to Stourport and the Severn.[38]

Up to 27 May 1815, £597,394 had been spent, so that the total cost at opening was probably some £610,000. The company was now in a very shaky position. In spite of having paid off all but £4,700 of its debt to the bank, it owed £27,000, and had to meet interest payments on the annuities and on £40,000 worth of loans. As further loans at 5 per cent could not be raised because of the company's bad credit, and as annuities at 10 per cent were ruinous, a further call of 5 per cent on the shareholders was made and the tolls on coal reduced to encourage traffic quickly and counter the drawbacks of the other companies. These tolls were low: 2s 6d from Birmingham to Tardebigge, and 3s for that going beyond to the Severn—only 6d for all the lockage downwards from the summit.

As completed, the canal was 30 miles long, the summit level being 14½ miles. Leaving Birmingham, one first passed Edgbaston tunnel (105 yd), the only one with a towpath, then the junction with the Dudley Canal extension coming in on the right at Selly Oak, then, 2¼ miles farther on, that with the Stratford Canal at King's Norton on the left, then West Hill tunnel and, at 9 miles from Birmingham, the ¼ mile long Bittall arm, at 12¼ miles Shortwood tunnel (613 yd) and finally Tardebigge tunnel (580 yd). Beyond it began the great flight of thirty locks that took the canal down from the Birmingham plateau, followed by twelve others to Hanbury wharf, at first the transhipment point for land carriage to Droitwich, later the connection point for the Droitwich Junction Canal (see p. 271). Thence the canal passed Dunhampstead tunnel (230 yd), by fourteen more locks to Diglis basin, Worcester, and by two barge locks to the Severn, a fall of 428 ft in all. Here at Diglis a steam engine was installed in 1818 to pump water back from the Severn to the basin; by 1820 this had had to be enlarged, and, thanks to the close connection with the Droitwich company, 'Warehouses and other accommodations for the Salt Trade as well for the Salt intended for Manure as that for Household purposes'[39] were built there.

Though the canal was an expensive one to maintain, with its five tunnels and heavy lockage, finances slowly improved. In 1818 the annuities were replaced by loans, which saved about £1,800 p.a. In 1820 the tolls were £14,625,* and at the beginning of 1821 the company declared its first dividend of £1 per share. The amount of money paid on each share varied with the issue, from £166 on the 1800 original shares down to about £42 on the most recent of the remaining 4,200. Later, Samuel Salt gave the average subscription on the shares as £78 8s 0d[40] in 1842.

Toll receipts slowly rose as traffics, especially in salt, improved, but by 1825 a long-term threat showed itself: 'whether the Canal will be able to retain its trade amidst the many projects for conveying Goods on Railroads, time can only determine . . . one obvious mode of rendering such Schemes unnecessary is, for Canal Companies to adopt and use every means in their power to improve the line of their Canals and to afford all the facilities they

* Year ending 30 November.

can for the passing goods with the greatest possible dispatch'.[41] Some of the shareholders thought all railways should be opposed, others that it was impossible to obstruct all improvement, and that opposition should be limited to cases where projected lines immediately threatened the canal.[42] In January 1825 the company welcomed the promotion of the Worcester & Gloucester Union Canal (see p. 118) to by-pass the Severn and link their waterway directly with the Gloucester & Berkeley, now at last well on the way to completion. At the same meeting they decided to take over a lease of the Coombe Hill Canal from John Mabson and others connected with their own company at £250 p.a. for seven years from 29 September 1822. It was stated that Mabson and his partners had lost £100 on the lease, but that 4,093 tons of additional traffic had passed over the W & B.[43] Later in this same little railway mania year of 1825, they do not seem to have been impressed by a resolution of the Bristol Rail Road Co 'to carry their line no further than Worcester, intending to open a communication with Birmingham by the Worcester Canal'.[44]

In 1825 also, after some earlier discussions, plans were put before the committee by H. Jacobs, a Birmingham surveyor, for a branch canal from near Dunhampstead tunnel for about 4 miles to end on the Worcester–Alcester road, to serve the limestone quarries at Broughton Hackett near Upton Snodsbury. Previously, between 1819 and 1821, there had been discussions with quarry owners about the possibility of a tramroad, which had come to nothing because of the shortness of the quarry leases. The shareholders adopted the proposal for a branch and in January 1826 agreed to seek a bill, and to raise £12,000 on mortgage to make it. However, in Parliament the proposal, like so many others of the time for canal improvements, ran foul of Lord Shaftesbury, the chairman of the House of Lords Committee on such bills, who was determined to get the favourable rating position of the main canal altered as the price of the branch. The company therefore dropped it.[45] In 1832, however, a tramroad was built from the canal to limestone quarries in Himbleton parish; by 1850 it was disused, and lifted in that year. One might mention here also a line about 500 yd long built at some time before 1861 by the company from a wharf on the north side of the canal just below the top lock at Tardebigge to a nearby quarry, which was probably in place till the 1880s.

In 1827 the Gloucester & Berkeley Canal was opened, and the new port of Gloucester benefited the Worcester & Birmingham in

IX. The experimental canal lift built at Tardebigge on the Worcester & Birmingham Canal

X. Shrewsbury Canal: (*above*) guillotine gate at Trench lock in 1954. The weight counterbalancing the gate falls into a pit to the right; (*below*) the iron aqueduct at Longdon-on-Tern in 1954

drawing trade to itself. About this time, also, the improving trade in salt which had followed the partial repeal of the salt duties in 1822 had its effect in making the Droitwich Canal independent of the payments which the W & B had had to make from its earliest days. More important was rock salt from Stoke Prior. In 1828 Jonathan Fardon had bought land there, but in 1830 was encountering difficulties in sinking shafts. But in August 1830 'the pits recently sunk by Mr. M'Allister, on the opposite side of the Worcester canal, to the mine of rock-salt, lately found at Stoke Prior, are now complete . . . every preparation is being made for commencing operations within the present month'.[46] These deposits made it possible to compete in the Bristol and Gloucester markets with salt exported from Lancashire and Cheshire ports, and gave the canal good prospects of trade. Shares, which had stood at £45 in January 1825, were selling at £90 in July 1831 and again in December 1833.

Receipts increased rapidly, as did dividends. The former grew from £20,254 in 1826 to £44,478 in 1836, the latter from 30s to £4 per share. Here are the figures, averaged over three-year periods:

Years (y.e. 30 Nov.)	Average receipts £	Average dividend per share £ s d		
1824–6	20,254*	1	10	0
1827–9	27,684	2	10	0
1830–2	33,774	3	13	4
1833–5	36,891	3	16	8
1836–8	43,488	4	0	0
1839–41	45,459	3	16	8

* 1826 only.

In 1830 the company decided to lease the Lower Avon from Tewkesbury to Evesham for 21 years at £880 p.a. net. The motives for doing so were not stated, but may have been two: first, the coal trade down the W & B to the Severn was increasing, and control of the Lower Avon would mean that places on it could be supplied via the canal and Tewkesbury rather than via the Stratford-upon-Avon Canal and its own leased waterway, the Upper Avon. Second, the plans discussed from 1828 onwards for a new canal from the Stratford to the Oxford or the Grand Junction probably suggested that the route from Bristol by way of the Avon to the West Midlands might become more important. Developing trade also caused the company to open a new reservoir, their seventh, at upper Bittall in 1832,[47] and a branch canal near it in 1836.

In October 1830 a prospectus appeared for a Gloucester & Birmingham Railway,[48] and a notice of a provisional committee for another line, the Birmingham, Worcester, Gloucester & Bristol;[49] they were accompanied by a news item that canal shares, which had stood at £105 in July, were now offered for £80.[50] A week later they were being advertised at £75. This threatened competition must certainly have been one reason why the company began taking a greater interest in the navigability of the Severn, both because of its own trade down it, and because any interruption benefited the competing Welsh and Forest coal, and in 1831 made the first of a long series of moves that were to be completed by the formation of the Severn Commission in 1842.

Before that, however, they were in railway trouble. In 1835, in anticipation of the Act of 1836 for the Birmingham & Gloucester Railway, the Birmingham company had reduced the coal toll at the bar from 4d to 2d, and in 1839 took off many of the bar tolls. By the end of 1840 the railway was open to Camp Hill, Birmingham, and throughout for goods traffic in October 1841, so that the canal company could note that: 'in consequence of the formation of the Gloucester Railway, a considerable portion of those Goods and Merchandise which would otherwise have waited the breaking up of the frost and the re-opening of the Canal were during the continuation of the frost forwarded by the Railroad'.[51] The remaining 2d on coal through the bar was removed in 1844, leaving 3d on other goods. (*To continue the history of the Worcester & Birmingham Canal, turn to p. 270.*)

The Upper Avon

The Warwickshire Avon[52] never succeeded in establishing itself as a through navigation; it was too winding, too awkward a line. Therefore the Lower Avon was considered a branch of the Severn, so falling under the influence of the Worcester & Birmingham company, while the Upper river, from Stratford down to Evesham, was associated during most of our period with the Stratford-upon-Avon Canal company.

There was a short time, however, when to establish the river as a through navigation between the East, the Midlands and the Severn seemed a possibility to William James,[53] and in 1813 he bought the shares.[54] Being influential in the Stratford company, and at that time in charge of getting the canal built to Stratford, it was probably he who persuaded the shareholders to seek a junction with the Avon there, instead of ending their canal in the town, as they intended. This took place on 24 June 1816. Though he could ill afford it, James spent £6,000 in 1822 on improving the upper river, mainly by repairing the locks. He went bankrupt, and in 1824 the upper river was bought by a syndicate of seven closely connected with the Stratford company. It was probably this group who added a second lock below Lucy's at Stratford, so making it a staircase pair. Certainly in 1827, they built three new locks, and did much dredging to make the navigation suitable for 30-ton barges. Trade then improved, but it was local, mainly in coal from Stratford for wharves down to Evesham.

From 1830 onwards the syndicate found themselves competing against the Lower Avon to carry coal to Evesham, till in 1842 the Stratford company itself took a lease of the upper river for five years. (*To continue the history of the Upper Avon, turn to p.* 269.)

The Lower Avon

At the beginning of our period the Lower Avon was owned by George Perrott of Fladbury, and leased at a rent of £1,227 p.a. At first he planned to sell it, but when the Stratford Canal was promoted thoughtfully had a clause added to compel the Worcester & Birmingham company to make his rent up to that figure till the Stratford should be completed, and afterwards to pay him £400 p.a. to compensate for his expected loss of tolls. He died in 1806, and was succeeded by George Wigley Perrott, who in turn was followed in 1831 by Edmund Thomas Perrott. From about 1808 the navigation was leased to Thomas Milton.

Coal from the Worcester & Birmingham coming up river from Tewkesbury began to compete briskly with that coming down from Stratford. The tolls of the Upper Avon suffered, and so did Perrott's, till in 1830 he leased his waterway to the Worcester & Birmingham company for 21 years at £880 p.a. net. (*To continue the history of the Lower Avon, turn to p.* 269.)

Coombe Hill Canal

The growing spa of Cheltenham needed coal, which had to be carried from the Severn by land till in June 1792 this broad canal was authorized from the river some six miles above Gloucester to the foot of Coombe Hill, so shortening the road distance to about five miles. The proprietors were three, William Miller and Sarah Mumford of Cheltenham, and Thomas Burgess of London, the capital £5,000, with £2,000 more if necessary.[55] It seems likely that the canal was open by February 1796. It was certainly so by March 1798, when the company offered a site at Coombe Hill wharf at a peppercorn rent to anyone willing to build a warehouse and dwelling-house. It was then stated that 'any quantity of the best Staffordshire and Shropshire Coal may be had at reasonable rates'.[56] Although the first meeting to appoint a clerk and establish the high toll of 2s 6d a ton was not held till 20 July 1802,[57] an advertisement of earlier the same month had offered the canal on lease, and stated its trade as 7,000 tons of coal in three years.[58] The proprietors' confidence in charging a high toll may have been due to the lack of success of those who, the previous year, had called a meeting at Cheltenham to promote a canal thence to Tewkesbury.[59] The canal was 2¾ miles long, had two locks at the entrance into the Severn, and took barges of 50–70 tons. It cost about £5,000,[60] and does not seem to have got off to a good start, for in 1808 the proprietors said that 'it has till within the last 2 years been very unprofitable so as almost to be ruinous to them'.[61]

By 1806 it was clear that the canal, while some use, was no solution to the problem of supplying the rapidly growing town with coal, because of the cost of land carriage, which may have been especially high because of the difficulty of the steep 'driftway and bridle road' that connected the basin to the main road at Coombe Hill, as well as to the rest of the journey. Two schemes were therefore brought forward to improve the position.

On the one hand Mr Trye, a director of the unfinished Gloucester & Berkeley Canal, a landowner, and the owner of a limestone quarry at Leckhampton, proposed a horse tramroad from the canal basin at Gloucester to Cheltenham, with a branch to Leckhampton, and a plan was made. This was opposed locally, altered, and the second plan introduced as a bill in the session of 1808–9. Though both claimed to be first, this plan probably antedated plans by the Coombe Hill proprietors, first to extend their canal to Cheltenham and then, when the principal landowner disapproved and the cost seemed too formidable, a tramroad, apparently linked to the canal either by a tunnel or an inclined plane.

It is likely that behind the Coombe Hill extension project were Staffordshire coal interests, who had hitherto been supplying Cheltenham by water. Behind the tramroad from Gloucester was

Forest coal, to be carried by the projected Severn & Wye tramroad[62] to Lydney or by that already begun to Bullo Pill,[63] and thence by barge to Gloucester. The promoters of the extension argued that it was 'extremely hard that the Town and Neighbourhood of Cheltenham should be deprived of the great Benefit it would derive from having a Rail-road in another Direction where Water-carriage is within Five Miles, whereas by the Gloucester Rail-way, Water-carriage would not be within Ten miles',[64] but opinion was against them. The corporations of Gloucester and Cheltenham, the Gloucester & Berkeley company, and various influential landowners petitioned against it, and in favour of the other line, by which it was estimated 22,000 tons p.a. would be carried, yielding a revenue of £1,925 p.a.[65] Both bills reached Parliament, but only that for the Gloucester & Cheltenham tramroad[66] was passed, in the same year that the Severn & Wye and the public portion of the Bullo Pill lines were also authorized.

In spite of the Act, it seems that the idea of extending the canal to Cheltenham was again considered, for a plan of 1810 exists. In this same year the waterway was leased at £400 p.a. to a group of three probably concerned with the Staffordshire coal trade.

Tramroad competition was the probable cause of reductions of canal tolls that by April 1822 had reached 6d. In that year the canal was leased to a Birmingham group, all of whom were committeemen of the Worcester & Birmingham; these raised the toll again to 10d, and seem to have competed successfully from the point of view of that company, which gained additional traffic. In 1825 the W & B was assigned the remainder of the lease, it being then said that the Gloucester & Cheltenham tramroad company had tried to get control of the Coombe Hill Canal.[67]

In 1826 the Worcester & Birmingham encouraged the coal trade by allowing a drawback of 1s a ton on their own line, and in 1829 renewed their lease, now at £500 a year, for another 21 years. (*To continue the history of the Coombe Hill Canal, turn to p. 281.*)

CHAPTER IX

The Canals of East Shropshire

THE Donnington Wood or Duke of Sutherland's Tub-boat Canal, the building of which was described in Chapter II, was the first of an interconnected group of small-boat canals linking Shrewsbury, Donnington Wood, Pave Lane, Ketley, Coalport and Coalbrookdale, all of which were completed by 1796, with a combined length of 38¼ miles. In 1797 and early 1798 a proposal was made to connect them to the main canal system by an 18-mile long canal from Pave Lane, or 'from the Lime works at Lilleshall, to join the Trent-Mersey canal at or near Stone, with a branch to or near Market Drayton',[1] some of it following closely the line of Sir Richard Whitworth's earlier Ternbridge scheme. It came to nothing, and a connection had to wait till the Newport branch was built to the Birmingham & Liverpool Junction in 1835.

Donnington Wood Canal

The Marquess of Stafford was a principal participant in the Lilleshall Partnership, formed in 1802, later to become the Lilleshall Company. The partnership took over the furnaces at Donnington Wood which had been built by Richard Reynolds, as well as the colliery with its underground levels, and the canal was leased to it. Later the Lodge furnaces were built at Donnington Wood, and a short branch was made to them.

The canal's water supply on the main line came from the collieries, and on the branch from Limekiln and Wilmer pools. (*To continue the history of the Donnington Wood Canal, turn to p. 238.*)

Wombridge Canal

About 1787[2] William Reynolds of Ketley ironworks, part of the Coalbrookdale group,[3] found coal and ironstone near the surface at Wombridge. By that time the Coalbrookdale company had built up a considerable system of horse tramroads between the Severn and its works at Coalbrookdale, Horsehay and Ketley,[4] and Reynolds presumably decided upon a tub-boat canal instead of a tramroad to carry these products past Wrockwardine Wood to the furnaces at Donnington Wood because of the prior existence of the Donnington Wood Canal. The Wombridge Canal was about 1¾ miles long and level, beginning just south of Wombridge church and communicating with the Donnington Wood. It was probably completed in 1788, and cost £1,640.

A few years later the Shrewsbury Canal company was formed, of which William Reynolds was a director and shareholder. It paid the Ketley company £840 for 1 mile 88 yd of the Wombridge Canal from its junction with it just above what was later the Trench inclined plane to Donnington Wood, which then became part of the Shrewsbury's line. That company's Act provided that Reynolds's internal traffic on the Wombridge Canal could pass free of toll.

Furnaces were built at Wombridge in 1819, and it is probable that the unincorporated section of canal went out of use soon afterwards.

Ketley Canal

At the same time that William Reynolds was building the Wombridge Canal, he and Richard Reynolds were engaged on another to carry coal and ironstone from Oakengates to their works at Ketley. This was a tub-boat canal 1½ miles long, completed in 1788, which, after passing through a 20-yd tunnel,[5] reached the top of Ketley inclined plane. From its foot the canal continued past a 60-yd tunnel to the Warehouse Pool at the works.[6]

The Ketley plane had a fall of 73 ft. The boats were carried in cradles on two sets of tracks, the motive power being the weight of the loaded boats, as almost all traffic was downwards.[7] The incline had no reverse slope; instead, a boat at the top entered one of two locks, and settled upon a cradle as the water emptied. This incline was the first to be built to carry boats on a canal in Great Britain, though earlier examples had been constructed on the

Continent and, unsuccessfully, on the Tyrone Navigation[8] in Ireland. Reynolds may have known of these,[9] of the inclined slide on the St Columb Canal,[10] or of Edmund Leach's proposals to use planes on the Bude Canal authorized in 1774;[11] or he may have adapted the idea from tramroad planes. The boats used were 20 ft by 6 ft 4 in., to carry 8 tons. Rees[12] tells us that 'several of these small boats linked together are towed along the level by one horse, and to guide them round the projecting turns of the bank, sliderails are placed thereon'.

When the Reynoldses built the Ketley Canal, they had it in mind that it would become a branch of the Shropshire Canal. William wrote to his brother-in-law, William Rathbone junior, on 16 January 1788: 'Indeed I have my hands full—we are making a canal from Oakengates to Ketley & have between 2 and 300 men at work upon it & as I am head and subschemer, Engineer and Director & have besides one in contemplation from the same place to the river wch I have been obliged to Levell & relevell, survey & resurvey I have had scarce time to do anything but think of them.'[13] And in an agreement of 22 May 1788 with the Lilleshall partners Richard said he 'and his Copartners have begun and nearly completed a Navigable . . . Canal . . . to communicate . . . with a Navigable Canal proposed to be made' to the Severn.[14]

This indeed happened. The Shropshire Canal was authorized in June 1788 from Wrockwardine Wood to Coalport on the Severn; it was at once decided to build it downwards from Wrockwardine Wood, and at the same time 'that the Hands be first employed in extending a Branch from the Ketley Canal made by Mr. Reynolds and Company, on the Line of the new intended Navigation'.[15] The hands had probably only just finished the Ketley Canal. The extension was a short one, but a lock had to be put in, as the level of the Shropshire Canal was 1 ft higher.

William Reynolds died in 1803, and in 1816 Joseph Reynolds dismantled the Ketley works. It is likely that the canal then became disused, for Dutens the French engineer found it so in 1818.[16]

Shropshire Canal

Before the main project, an effort seems to have been made early in 1787 to cut a level from the Severn bank under The Hay hill, reputedly for several miles, to serve local collieries, partly as a drain, and partly as a navigable canal. A news item headed 'Coalbrookdale Navigation' of 25 June tells us that after 300 yd had been tunnelled, tar and pitch was struck, and a reservoir was built to hold the yield of 70 to 80 gallons a day. Farther in, however, headings were filled with brine, and work was abandoned,[17] though the oil continued to be tapped.

It is probable that the idea for the Shropshire Canal came from William Reynolds, and arose from his need for better communication with the Severn. All he had was a horse tramroad that connected his works with those of Coalbrookdale and led to the river wharf there, his competitors at Lilleshall, who were associated with the owners of the Snedshill collieries, also having a tramroad to the river. The greater carrying capacity of a canal would therefore attract him, and he had a working example of what he needed at Donnington Wood. The great difficulty was the hilly nature of the country and the lack of enough water for heavy lockage. Once he had made sure that his inclined plane at Ketley would work, he knew the solution.

In the event the canal was promoted mainly by Coalbrookdale group interests, but partly also by the owners of the Donnington Wood Canal. Whereas the three previous waterways had been built privately, this much bigger one was not. Of the £50,000 capital reported to have been raised at the first general assembly on the day after the Act had been passed, £39,100 was subscribed within Shropshire, £16,000 by Reynoldses, Rathbones and Darbys, £3,000 by the Marquess of Stafford and Thomas Gilbert, and much of the rest by people associated in one way or another with the two concerns, such as John Wilkinson. The management reflected the Coalbrookdale preponderance—except for a curious episode in 1825—throughout the period. At the first meeting a seal was chosen to show 'The Iron Bridge with the Motto of "The Shropshire Canal Navigation",' Samuel Darby was appointed first Treasurer, and preliminary work at the top end was authorized.

This tub-boat canal had been surveyed by William Reynolds, but Jessop supported it with evidence in London, and so must have helped with it. It rose 120 ft from its junction with the Donnington Wood Canal* by the Wrockwardine Wood inclined plane, 316 yd long, to its summit level. Thence it ran past the coal and ironstone mines at Wrockwardine and Snedshill, the junction with the Ketley Canal, and other ironworks to Southall Bank, where the Coalbrookdale branch left the main line. Just below the junction was the Windmill plane with a fall of 126 ft in a length of 600 yd, which took the canal past Madeley to the top of The Hay

* Not the Wombridge till 1794, when the Shrewsbury Canal bought part of it.

plane. Here the line dropped 207 ft in 350 yd to Coalport, where it turned sharply at right angles to the river, but above it, and ran for ¾ mile past warehouses and wharves which had short railway inclines for transferring cargoes to river craft. There was a short tunnel under the London–Holyhead road at Oakengates, and two longer ones, at Snedshill (279 yd) and Stirchley (281 yd), each 10 ft wide at surface. As can be seen, the line ran past a number of works and collieries, and others, like the Langley and Madeley Court furnaces, were later connected to it by tramroads. The branch ran in a northerly curve past Horsehay works to Brierly Hill above Coalbrookdale. The Shropshire Canal's line ran 'over high and rugged ground, along banks of slipping loam, over old coal-mines, and over where coal-mines and iron-stone are now actually worked under it'; Telford regarded it as proof that canals could be built over almost any ground.[18]

In spite of Reynolds's Ketley plane, the committee decided 'That a Reward of Fifty Guineas be offered by an Advertisement to that Person who shall discover and communicate to the Committee . . . the best Means of raising and lowering heavy Weights from one Navigation to another'.[19] A month later they asked Boulton & Watt the same question. A number of models were sent in, and James Watt and John Wilkinson helped a sub-committee to judge them. In the end Henry Williams of Ketley and John Lowdon of Snedshill each got £50, while some entries were given consolation prizes. Lowdon had already been appointed surveyor, and from the circumstances of the award one feels that Williams must have been associated with Reynolds in building the Ketley plane.

The planes built on the Shropshire Canal differed from that at Ketley in having a short reverse slope at the top instead of a lock, so preventing any loss of water, and in being steam-powered. The Hay and Windmill planes worked mainly by counterbalancing, the engine being used to haul the cradles up the reverse slope and in both directions over the summit sill, though it could if necessary work the main plane if the loads could not be counterbalanced. That at Wrockwardine Wood, however, carried the heavy traffic upwards from Donnington Wood, and was normally worked by an engine with little help from counterbalancing. The problems of working this plane may have led to the adoption on the Shropshire Canal of boats of the same length and breadth as those on the Ketley, but shallower, to take 5 or 6 tons according to bulk instead of eight.

At the foot of the main incline were two docks into which ran parallel rail tracks, each pair laid with plate-rails 72 in. long, 8 in. wide, 2 in. thick and with 3 in. flanges, spiked to wooden sleepers. These rails ran up the slope, over the sill at the top, and down to another pair of docks. On each track ran a wheeled cradle, to the platform of which a boat was lashed with chains. It was made of heavy timbers strengthened with iron, and had side struts supporting an overhead beam; from the struts ran bridle chains to the main haulage chain.* The front wheels of the cradle were 27 in. diameter and the back wheels 16 in., so that the platform with its boat was held nearly level as it was pulled up the slope. On the same axle as the smaller pair were two other wheels of 24 in. These were only used on the reverse incline, when they engaged a special set of rails fastened to the upper dock walls at such an angle that the cradle was still kept nearly level.

Above the sill was the main winding drum, around which the chain was coiled, one end being fastened directly to a cradle, the other being taken over a pulley above the upper dock before being attached to the second cradle. Connected to the drum was a brake-wheel that could be held by a timber brake-shoe working on half its circumference and actuated by a lever: this brake controlled the speed of the descending cradle. A secondary winding drum, also braked, and detachable chain pulled the cradles up the reverse slope and over the sill. The engine drive could be applied to either drum through sliding gear wheels. The total weight was normally $8\frac{1}{4}$ tons, made up of cradle (2 tons), boat ($1\frac{1}{4}$ tons) and cargo (5 tons).

Each incline required four men: one at each dock to fasten and unfasten the boats, an engineman, and a brakesman who also fixed or unfixed the chains connected to the smaller drum. It was possible for them to pass six boats an hour in each direction.[20]

The section of canal from the top of Wrockwardine Wood plane to the junction with the Ketley Canal was completed early in 1789, while the owners of the Donnington Wood Canal cut at their own expense from their canal to the bottom of the plane. Early in 1790 the work had been completed to Southall Bank, but the pace had been too hot for Lowdon, and he resigned. After two others had tried to cope with the distinguished and efficient committee, Henry Williams took over in February 1794, and stayed till he retired in 1839. Tolls began to be received on 3 September 1790, and about this time the Wrockwardine Wood plane and

* Rope at first.

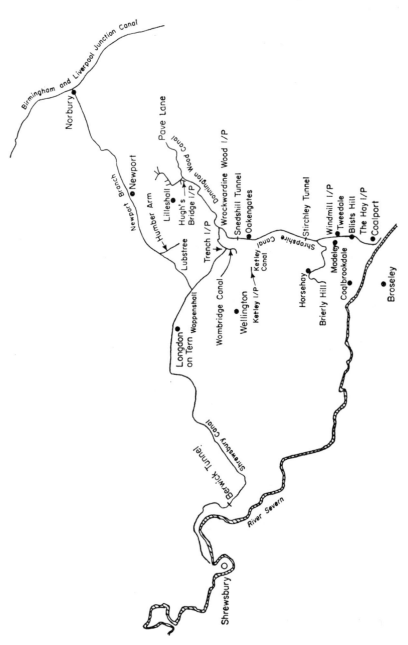

10. The canals of east Shropshire

steam engine seem to have begun work. The rest of the main line to Coalport appears to have become available during 1791, the Hay and Windmill planes being worked by horses till steam engines were substituted in 1793, when special tolls were levied for the use of the planes and apparatus. Piling for the Severn wharves was being done in May 1792, and the whole canal was probably open and in working order from the end of that year.

The branch to Coalbrookdale was possibly opened in 1791, more probably in 1792, and provided a means of interchange between Coalbrookdale, Ketley, Horsehay, Old Park, and Donnington for iron, iron ore and limestone. It ended above the Dale at Brierly Hill, where during 1792[21] the Coalbrookdale Company built two vertical shafts 120 ft deep and 10 ft wide down which coal and iron were lowered by cranes in iron crates each carrying up to two tons from the canal boats to waggons standing on a tramroad in the tunnel below, and limestone raised for the use of the furnaces on the line. Each boat carried four crates. No power was used, the descending load counterbalancing the crate that came up. This apparatus, which had cost £2,742, was probably working by 4 October 1792, when the Shropshire company minuted that they were unwilling to take over the shafts and tunnel from the Dale company, but agreed to them charging tolls for their use not exceeding 3d a ton for letting articles down and carrying them to the tunnel mouth, and 2d a mile for transport between the end of the company's canal* and the Severn. The existing account book[22] starts from 24 January 1793, and shows that the shafts and tunnel were quite heavily used. For instance, in the six weeks from 2 September to 10 October 1793, 1,801 tons of coal alone were lowered.

The mode of getting the crates into and out of the boats was unsatisfactory (Telford, writing in Plymley's *Shropshire*, describes it), for a letter of 25 May 1793 from John Curr of Sheffield suggests new methods. Instead, the Dale company decided to replace the shafts and tunnel with a counterbalanced inclined plane to carry waggons, not boats. Some work had been done by the end of 1793, and entries for the shafts and tunnel in the account book are not made after 26 September 1794, when the inclined plane probably began work. This became something of a local sight, and was visited by the Prince and Princess of Orange when they saw the Coalbrookdale works in August 1796.

* The phrasing of the minute implies that there was a length of Dale Company's canal to the top of the shafts.

The length of the completed main line was 7¾ miles, and of the branch 2¾ miles. The £50,000 raised at the beginning seems to have sufficed, for various authorities give its cost as either £47,000 or £47,500. It is almost unique in having been built with the money first raised, and in having a board composed almost entirely of businessmen, without the usual admixture of landed gentlemen, peers, members of Parliament and clergymen. The first recorded dividend, of 2½ per cent, was declared in April 1793; after that payments were made regularly at a satisfactory rate, especially if one remembers that the company, being controlled by industrialists, were keeping their tolls low in their commercial interests:

Years (y.e. 31 March)	Average dividend per cent		
	£	s	d
1791–3	2	10	0
1794–6	4	3	4
1797–9	4	0	0
1800–2	4	0	0
1803–5	4	16	8
1806–8	5	3	4
1809–11	6	6	8
1812–14	4	16	8
1815–17	6	10	0
1818–20	7	10	0
1821–3	7	3	4
1824–6	7	3	4
1827–9	7	6	8
1830–2	8	0	0
1833–5	7	13	4
1836–8	7	16	8
1839–41	8	0	0

The Coalport area was industrial even before an Act of 1777 authorized a bridge, and by 1786 there were extensive coal wharves near this on both banks of the river. After the canal opened Coalport soon acquired two potteries, a chain-making business, and others for making ropes and bags, which employed 400 people.

The inclined planes of Shropshire, except for the one inside Worsley mine, were the only ones in Britain carrying boats between the time they were built and at any rate 1819. They were a source of interest to visitors and, sometimes, of excitement to those who worked on them, as when at The Hay

'on the chain snapping we have known a canal boat with five

tons of iron pigs on board gain such velocity that on coming in contact with the water in the lower canal it has broken away from the iron chains which held it to the carriage, bounded into the air, clearing two other boats moored on the side, together with the embankment, and alighted in the Severn, close to the ferry-boat, into which it pitched some of the iron pigs it contained'.[23]

In between the planes the boats travelled in gangs. Stephen Ballard visited the canal in 1829, and said: 'one horse generally draws 12 loaded Boats or 60 tons, and not unfrequently 18 or 20 loaded Boats of 5 tons each, the Boats are chained to each other and are guided by a man who walks on the towing path with a Hook shaft'.[24]

To obtain the annual traffic of about 50,000 tons of coal and a considerable carriage of iron,[25] one competitor had been eliminated in 1815 for a payment of £500 and the guarantee of favourable rates, the tramroad from Donnington Wood to the Severn at Sutton wharf owned by the Lilleshall company. The success of the main line was not, however, matched by the section of branch beyond Horsehay wharf. Once the inclined plane had been substituted for the shafts and tunnel at Coalbrookdale it became obvious that it would be more sensible to run tramroad waggons all the way from Horsehay to Coalbrookdale and the Severn without transhipment from boats. The old tramroad by Jiggers Bank was therefore probably replaced about 1800 by one along the towpath from Horsehay, tolls being paid to the canal company for goods carried on it. The canal beyond Horsehay then became disused.

Thereafter all went easily till the railway mania year of 1845. (*To continue the history of the Shropshire Canal, turn to p. 232.*)

Shrewsbury Canal

While the Shropshire Canal was building, another was suggested to bring coal to Shrewsbury, which town 'and the country immediately around it', Plymley tells us, 'are supplied with coal principally from the neighbourhood of the Oaken Gates, and which has hitherto been conveyed by land-carriage, about fourteen miles along the London road; and this part of the road, from the constant succession of heavy coal carriages, had become almost impassable, notwithstanding that large sums of money were annually laid out upon the repairs of it. The price of coals at Shrewsbury continued to rise year after year'.²⁶ The local newspaper agreed, for in 1794 they referred to the townspeople, 'who have been for some time so grievously imposed upon by the Jaggers, and proprietors of coal teams, both in the price and quality of the coals, brought from Ketley and its vicinity'.²⁷

George Young of Worcester surveyed the canal in 1792, and in 1793 an Act²⁸ was obtained. The promoters were nearly all local people, mainly those who had already built Shropshire canals. William and Joseph Reynolds were active, and John Wilkinson took shares and sat on the committee for a year. The three Lilleshall partners, the Marquess of Stafford, John and Thomas Gilbert, between them subscribed £5,000. Later, however, the manufacturing and mining interests seem partly to have given way to those of consumers in Shrewsbury itself, till in 1830 this coal-carrying waterway had on its board two clergymen (one an archdeacon) and two doctors.

The canal ran from Shrewsbury, where it had no connection with the river, for 17 miles by way of Wappenshall and Trench to join the Wombridge Canal, 1 mile of which, leading to Donnington Wood, was bought by the Shrewsbury company. It was intended for tub-boats, carrying 8 tons, of about the same size as those on the Shropshire Canal, though smaller craft were, of course, also used. Shares were standing at £40 premium when work began in 1793, Josiah Clowes being the engineer under William Reynolds till he died in February 1795 and was replaced by Thomas Telford. By November 1795 tolls were being taken, in October 1796 a maiden dividend of 3 per cent was declared, and in November 1796 it was reported that 'the cutting and works . . . are now completed, and it will be opened for the passage of canal-boats as soon as it has filled with water, within a few weeks'.²⁹ It was opened in February 1797; the cost had been between £65,000 and £70,000, £125 having been called on each £100 share.

The canal had four features of great interest, the locks, the aqueduct at Longdon-on-Tern, the inclined plane at Trench, and the Berwick tunnel. The eleven locks present a mystery not yet solved. Telford, who was then the engineer, wrote in 1797 in Plymley's *Shropshire* that 'the locks are so formed as to admit of either one, three or four boats passing at a time, without the loss of any more water than what is just necessary. . . . This is accomplished by having gates that are drawn up and let down perpendicularly . . . and each lock has three gates, one of which divides the body of the lock'. This could mean that each lock had

XI. Trench inclined plane on the Shrewsbury Canal in 1921: (*above*) the engine house, showing an empty tub-boat arriving at the top of the plane; (*below*) cradles ascending and descending

XII. Ellesmere Port: (*above*) in 1890; the iron ore wharf is to the left; (*below*) the three wings of the warehouse built in 1843

three lifting gates, or that it had ordinary gates at each end and a lifting gate between them. The length of the locks, 81 ft upwards, and their width of 6 ft 7 in. upwards, is consonant with Telford's description, for such a lock would hold four tub-boats. But there is no record of the lifting gates having been moved to the lower ends, where we later find them (with ordinary gates at the upper ends), nor clear present traces of intervening gates ever having existed. In default of new evidence, one can only conclude that when Telford wrote he described what was intended, and not what was actually built. The original pattern of lifting gate was counterbalanced by chains leading over wheels above the gate to a centre weight falling outside the gate. Starting in 1840, however, the counterbalancing was altered so that an iron weight sank in a well at the side of the lock as the gate was raised, and all gates other than that at Hadley Park were finally converted to this design.

In the early 1830s, when the building of the Newport branch from Wappenshall to the Birmingham & Liverpool Junction, then under construction, was imminent, the Shrewsbury company planned to widen their locks and bridges to take standard narrow boats. This proved too expensive, however, and only the two Eyton locks were converted to a width of 7 ft 4 in., together with the bridge openings on the Wappenshall–Shrewsbury section. The locks and bridges between Wappenshall and Trench were not altered, and special narrow boats only 6 ft 4 in. wide were used on this section.

Clowes originally began to build a masonry aqueduct at Longdon-on-Tern, but the works were destroyed by the abnormal floods of early 1795.* Clowes had just died, and been replaced on 28 February by Telford, then 'General Agent' of the Ellesmere Canal. A meeting on 14 March 1795 'Ordered that an Iron Aqueduct be erected at Longdon (agreeable to a plan to be approved by Mr. Telford) by Messrs. William Reynolds & Company' at a cost not exceeding £2,000. The minute implies that the idea was not Telford's, and this.is supported by Telford himself writing in Plymley's *Shropshire*, his account being later reproduced in Rees's *Cyclopaedia*. 'The idea of having this aqueduct made of cast iron was first suggested and recommended by Thomas Eyton esq. then chairman of the committee: after due consideration, it was approved by the committee, and the principles of construction, and the manner in which it should be executed were referred to Mr.

* A second aqueduct, probably Clowes's, lies a little to the east.

L

William Reynolds, and the writer of this article, who, after several consultations, and forming and considering various plans, at last determined' upon what was built. Yet Telford, in a letter dated the day before the meeting, wrote: 'I have just recommended an aqueduct of iron, and it will be executed under my direction.'[30] Either he was not bothering to explain the full circumstances, or in his public account he was not taking credit due to him. If one reflects, however, that Telford was a mason by training, with great knowledge of stone, that the minute first calling him in was dated less than three weeks earlier, on 23 February, and that on the Shrewsbury Canal he found himself among ironmasters, his public account seems most likely to be correct. To add to the confusion, Telford in the same account says: 'I believe this to be the first aqueduct for the purposes of a navigable canal which has ever been composed with this metal.' But it was not, for the iron aqueduct at the Holmes on the Derby Canal, which is Outram's, was completed in February 1796, one month before Telford's, though one does not know the date of its conception. And Benjamin Outram had been for five years the partner at the Butterley ironworks of William Jessop, the greatest canal engineer of the age and the man for whom Telford was then working on the Ellesmere.

Wherever the original idea came from, the iron for the plates was cast at Ketley, and the aqueduct was built, 62 yd long and 16 ft high, its masonry ends possibly being those of Clowes's original work.

The Trench inclined plane was 223 yd long, and had a fall of 75 ft downwards towards Shrewsbury. Soon after the authorizing Act it was decided 'That an Engine similar to the one at Donnington Wood be erected at the Head of the intended inclined plane at Wombridge, and that Mr. William Reynolds be requested to order the Engine from the Coalbrookdale Company'.[31] Shortly afterwards, his company was asked for cast-iron rails at the same price as those provided for Windmill Hill.

The plane was similar to those on the Shropshire Canal, the boats being carried one at a time in cradles. The traffic being almost wholly downwards towards Shrewsbury, the cradles worked by counterbalance, the steam engine being used only to pull the cradles over the top of the plane, as at Windmill and The Hay. In 1840 it was converted to use edge rails set in chairs fastened to stone sleepers, and another engine, this time a 'high pressure Steam Engine on the Cornish plan capable of Working

THE CANALS OF EAST SHROPSHIRE

from 15 to 25 Horse power'[32] was bought from the Coalbrookdale company in 1842. This plane remained in use until 1921, the last in Britain.

The Berwick tunnel (970 yd) was remarkable for being the first of any length to have a towpath built through it. This was 3 ft wide, of wood carried on bearers set in the wall. The waterway of the tunnel was rather over 10 ft wide, and the projecting towpath allowed the full width to be filled with water, so reducing the resistance of passing boats. The tunnel was designed by Josiah Clowes, but the towpath was added at William Reynolds's suggestion. It was removed in 1819.

The traffic was almost entirely coal to Shrewsbury, paying 1½d a ton a mile to begin with, and 1d to pass the plane. This was too high for a new venture, however; boats had to be built to let to those who were willing to trade, and in 1797 tolls were reduced to 1d. Other encouragements followed, William Reynolds being allowed for a time to carry iron and other things free, and limestone being also passed toll-free (except over the plane), temporarily if for burning into lime beside the canal. By 1799, however, the company was well enough established to raise its tonnage rate to 2d. That winter the local newspaper complained that the carriers had a monopoly, and that more boats ought to be built: 'the hopes of being benefited by water conveyance have been so far from being realised that the town pays 2 to 3 shillings per ton more than it did before'.[33]

One immediate effect of the canal's construction was to make it unlikely that the Ellesmere Canal would be extended from Weston to Shrewsbury. In 1800 Jessop wrote of it: 'though the lime will command a market, the coal will be met by that from the Shrewsbury Canal'.[34]

The canal's history was uneventful, and its prosperity solid. Dividends rose slowly to reach £8 per £125 share about 1805, at which level they remained till about 1815, when they moved slowly upwards again to reach £10 about 1823 and £11 in 1829. The opening of the Newport branch brought a sudden jump to £16 for 1836, which by 1841 had fallen back to £13 and 1843 to £10.

In 1827, the Clerk of the Birmingham & Liverpool Junction Canal, authorized in 1826 from the Chester Canal at Nantwich to the Staffs & Worcs at Autherley, with the support of the Duke of Sutherland, attended a Shrewsbury Canal meeting to deposit a plan for joining that canal to his main line, so promising a physical link between the little east Shropshire Canal system and other waterways. For many years, however, the B & L J was too busy with its own troubles on the main line to think more about the branch, and it was not till 1831 that Henry Williams, who had become engineer and superintendent in 1797 while remaining also employed by the Shropshire, reported on the cost of altering the locks and bridges on the Shrewsbury to take narrow boats. As we have seen, two locks only were widened. The branch was opened on 12 January 1835 from Newport to Wappenshall, and on 2 March the B & L J itself was complete, and new prospects had opened.

Trade through the Newport branch, to Shrewsbury or to the foot of Trench plane, was now done in the special narrow boats referred to, though tub-boats had still to be employed for traffic past the plane, the cargoes being transhipped at Trench wharf to narrow boats if they were bound in the Newport direction. A contemporary description of tub-boat operation says: 'by dividing the load among a number of small boats, one horse is enabled to draw 120 and 140 tons, and at the same time all the boats are managed by one steersman. The single steersman is placed in the foremost boat of the train; at curves and turns the second boat follows the direction of the first, making exactly the same turns; the third boat follows . . . and so with the whole train'.[35]

I doubt whether trains were often of this length, but the exertions of a boatman's life can be imagined from a minute of 1838:

'when two trains of Boats shall have entered the Tunnel at the same time the party which shall have first passed the Centre of the Tunnel shall proceed and the other party shall return so as to allow the other to pass where both are laden but when one train is unladen such train shall turn back'.[36]

After a boatman had turned back a loaded train two or three times, his language must have been worth hearing.

How far the control of the canal had passed from the hands of the producers can be seen from a letter signed by the prominent coal owners in 1843 saying that there has been a 'very great reduction in the sale of Coal at the Shrewsbury and other Wharfs' and attributing this to high tolls, which, they said, were double those on the B & L J 'along which some of the competing coal passes' and one fourth higher than those on the Ellesmere & Chester, 'which is now one of the principal sources of competition with the Shropshire Coal Trade'. Clearly the making of the Newport branch had not been all gain. They ended that the high tolls 'enables the land Carriers to undersell their Coal in the Market'.[37] The company replied briskly that if they charged no tolls at all the sale of coal at their wharves would not be materially increased, because the coal-owners were charging too much for it. There must have been something in it, for the following year they reduced their price by 2s 6d a ton delivered in Shrewsbury, and the canal company reduced their toll by ¼d a mile to 1½d, still a high toll on coal for that time.

But major changes were on their way. (*To continue the history of the Shrewsbury Canal, turn to p. 232.*)

CHAPTER X

The Ellesmere
and its Connections

✦✦✦✦✦✦✦✦✦✦✦✦✦✦✦✦✦✦✦✦✦✦✦✦✦✦◆✦✦✦✦✦✦✦✦✦✦✦✦✦✦✦✦✦✦✦✦✦✦✦✦✦✦

IN 1791 a small group interested in iron, coal and allied works near Ruabon, encouraged by the current interest in canals, projected a line from their industrial area in one direction by Chester to the Mersey at what is now Ellesmere Port, and in the other to the Severn at Shrewsbury, with branches to ironworks at Bersham and Brymbo, limestone quarries at Llanymynech, and past Whitchurch to Prees. A diversion was caused by a rival group who proposed to get the same result by a branch from the Chester Canal near Tattenhall to run by Whitchurch to Ruabon, with lines also to Llanymynech and Shrewsbury. The projects of the first group were supported, and they began work.

Some twelve years later, the ideas of the losing group had mainly prevailed. Canals had been built from Ellesmere Port to Chester, from the Chester Canal at Hurleston by Frankton to Plas Kynaston and Trevor near Ruabon, with a navigable feeder to Llangollen, and branches to Whitchurch, Quina Brook near Prees, Ellesmere and Llanymynech. The Shrewsbury line had only been cut to Weston, and that between Ruabon and Chester not at all, except for a section of the Brymbo branch.

Westwards the line to Llanymynech had been continued by the Montgomeryshire company as far as Garthmyl between Welshpool and Newtown. In 1815 a new Western Branch company was established to build an extension to Newtown, the original concern becoming the Eastern Branch.

In 1813 the Ellesmere and the Chester companies united to form the Ellesmere & Chester. Their prospects were much improved when in 1826 a company encouraged by the Birmingham Canal proprietors obtained an Act for a canal from the Staffs &

166

Worcs at Autherley to join the Ellesmere & Chester at Nantwich. Taken with the improvements carried out and projected on the Birmingham's own line, the new canal offered a good water route from the Midlands to the Mersey and Liverpool. The Ellesmere & Chester company were therefore encouraged to link their canal at Barbridge to the Trent & Mersey at Middlewich, so that trade from the new waterway could have access to Manchester also. But meanwhile the Birmingham & Liverpool Junction was running into serious engineering difficulties, and by the time it was completed, in 1835, railway competition was close.

The two companies worked closely together to develop Ellesmere Port and build up an efficient carrying trade, using steam tugs on the canal and the Mersey, till they united in 1845. By this time, however, a still larger scheme of amalgamation and expansion was already in preparation, that for the Shropshire Union.

Ellesmere Canal

As early as 1789 proposals for what became the Ellesmere Canal were put forward by a small group: Col John Kynaston (later John Kynaston Powell), William Mostyn Owen and the Rev J. R. Lloyd of Aston, all three interested in industry near Ruabon, together with a local engineer, John Duncombe of Oswestry, and Charles Potts, solicitor of Chester. They brought a gleam of hope to the struggling committee of the Chester Canal, for a junction of their waterway with the new scheme would 'enable us either to make something by it for Mr Egerton,* or he may dispose of it *then* for some Advantage'[1]

The scheme was launched at a public meeting at the Royal Oak in Ellesmere on 31 August 1791, which appointed a committee headed by the Earl of Powis, and including the mayors of Liverpool, Chester and Shrewsbury. The line the promoters had in mind was one from Netherpool† on the Mersey to the Dee, which gave access to the Chester Canal, and then by Overton (five miles north of Ellesmere) to Shrewsbury, with a branch from Overton to Ruabon and Llangollen, and from it to Bersham; another to Llanymynech, and possibly ones also to Whitchurch and Wem. Duncombe and Joseph Turner[2] produced an estimate of £171,098,

* The mortgagee.
† The name Ellesmere Port occurs as early as 1796. The popular local name, however, was Whitby Wharf or Whitby Locks, the railway station being given the latter name when it was opened in 1863. As late as 1921 traffic shipped to Ellesmere Port from Old Quay Dock, Liverpool, was known as 'Locks goods'.

of which £67,456 was for the main line. At the August meeting William Turner of Whitchurch, also an engineer, suggested an alternative line which would make use of the Chester Canal and then cut westwards past Whitchurch, and Duncombe was ordered to survey it.

The promoters now decided that they needed 'an Engineer of approved Character and Experience'[3] to advise them, and William Jessop was called in, with Duncombe and William Turner to help him. In August 1792 he recommended the western or original route as 'best adapted to the Accommodation of the Country with Coal and Lime and to the General Commercial Interests of the Public'.[4] His line differed from Duncombe's. The Wirral line remained; the canal was then to run from the Dee opposite the Chester Canal basin east of Pulford and Trevalyn to Wrexham, Bersham, Ruabon (with a 4,607-yd tunnel), over the Dee at Pontcysyllte, under Vron limeworks with a tunnel 1,236 yds long at Chirk, then by Frankton and Weston (476-yd tunnel) to two points at Shrewsbury. There was a rise of 303 ft to the summit at Ruabon, and a fall of 150 ft to Shrewsbury. In his report, Jessop drew attention to the difficulties of the long tunnel and the proposed aqueduct at Pontcysyllte; if the latter were to be built on the level, he said, it would be 970 yds long and 126 ft high, but by building three locks at each end it could be reduced 24 ft in height, so saving one-third of the estimated cost. The Wirral line, and possibly that from Chester to Wrexham, should be built broad to take Mersey craft; the rest narrow to save expense on tunnelling. His estimate was £179,898 for the main line, or £196,898 including branches to Llanymynech and Holt.

It was the time of the mania. The subscription was opened in September, and in 1805 Rowland Hunt, the chairman, wrote of it: 'The paroxysm of commercial ardour of the memorable tenth of September, can never be forgotten by the writer, who had the honour to be left to defend the hill near the town* . . . from the excessive intrusion of too ardent speculation:—the books were opened about noon, and ere sun set a million of money was confided to the care of the Committee.'[5] Indeed, £967,700 had been offered by 1,234 subscribers, and £246,500 accepted, applications being scaled down according to their size. How widespread was the area from which subscriptions had been drawn can be seen from the company's instructions to its solicitors to return excess deposits at Derby, Leicester, Northampton, Stony Stratford,

* Ellesmere.

Coventry and Birmingham. Leicestershire provided an especially large group of investors: at the beginning of 1793 they were said to hold £60,000 worth of shares, and that year had four representatives on the committee.

The supporters of the eastern line did not accept defeat, but sought subscriptions with the support of the Chester company. To counter them, the Ellesmere promoters put in hand a survey for a connection from their Whitchurch branch to the Chester Canal, while Jessop decided that his great tunnel could be avoided by carrying the line on a higher level. In February 1793 the two groups decided to amalgamate; a bill was introduced in a great rush of deviations, surveys and alterations, and the Act[6] passed on 30 April, authorizing a capital of £400,000 and £100,000 more if necessary. The committee had decided to build the canal with broad locks, but finally had to substitute narrow while the bill was going through. The engineer was William Jessop helped by John Duncombe, his assistant Thomas Denson, and William Turner, but on 30 October an addition to the staff was made, when Thomas Telford, aged 36, was appointed 'General Agent, Surveyor, Engineer, Architect and Overlooker of the Works'. His duties were mainly to set out the line and to superintend building, he 'to submit . . . Drawings to the Consideration and Correction of Mr William Jessop'.[7] His salary was £300 p.a. and he worked part-time, still retaining his post as Surveyor of Public Works for the County of Shropshire, to which he had been appointed in 1788.

The Wirral line was begun in November, and on 1 July 1795 packet-boats began to use it.[8] The three locks to the Mersey were finished early in 1796, and in February the first flats arrived at Tower wharf, Chester, with coal.[9] The junction with the Chester Canal there was made in January 1797,[10] access to the Dee being obtained through the Chester Canal's basin with the consent of the river Dee company. The branch was supplied with water partly from the Chester Canal, and partly by a small steam engine at Ellesmere Port. It was 8¾ m. long, and soon gained a good passenger and goods trade.

The passenger-boats on the Wirral line were popular and long-lasting. They were run by lessees, who in 1810 paid £1,300 p.a. for the franchise, and each carried up to 200 people, the fare being 1s 6d for the best end of the boat, and 1s at the other, at times to suit the Mersey tides, printed timetables being issued in 1796.[11] Passengers were served with tea, coffee and refreshments, and tipping was forbidden. At Ellesmere Port passengers changed to Patrick (later Mrs) Coffield's boat to Liverpool, which cost them 1s in the best and 6d in the fore cabin. From the middle of 1797 a smaller boat began to carry parties to the Mersey and back at the same fares. Packet-boats ran till at least 1834, and perhaps till the opening of the Birkenhead Railway in 1840. For a time, also, connecting boats ran from Chester to Nantwich, but these seem to have been taken off soon after 1797. Commercial traffic slowly built up on the Wirral line, helped by toll-reductions. In 1801 new basins at Chester were finished, and in 1802 a tide-lock to the Dee gave access to the previously tidal basin from the canal at all times, and reduced silting in it.

Cutting from Hordley, near Frankton, westwards towards Llanymynech began early in 1794, to get access as soon as possible to the limestone quarries there, and because the bill for an extension into Montgomeryshire was already in Parliament. This length, 11 miles from the bottom of Frankton locks past Llanymynech to the junction with the Montgomeryshire Canal at Carreghofa, with three locks at Aston, cut a year earlier, was opened in the autumn of 1796, and enabled a limestone trade to be brought on to the rest of the Ellesmere system, and other goods from Liverpool, Chester and elsewhere to be passed to the Montgomeryshire company.

The section from Pontcysyllte to Chirk and on towards Hordley was also begun. In August 1793, before Telford's appointment, William Turner had been asked to 'prepare plans and Estimates of the aqueducts at Pontcysyllte and pont faen*', and he, Duncombe and Arthur Davies the surveyor produced plans of this line and 'the Sections of the Aqueduct over the Ceiriog and the Dee' in September. In January 1794 the committee agreed to the great three-arched masonry aqueduct at Pontcysyllte that Turner had designed 'with such Alterations therein as Mr. Jessop shall communicate to Mr. Thomas Telford',[12] the latter being asked to do the specification and working drawings. At the end of March he produced his plans and sections 'which have been settled and approved by Mr. Jessop,'[13] and was told to prepare final specifications and find a contractor. James Varley, mason, was engaged to quarry stone and work it.

Locks had been proposed at each end of this aqueduct to reduce its height, but on 14 July 1795 William Jessop produced an exciting report:

* The original point for crossing the Ceiriog; later altered to Chirk.

'It had been proposed to save expense in the Aqueduct at Pont-cysyllte to reduce the height 50 feet and descend and ascend by Locks, but . . . I must now recommend to the Committee to make this saving by adopting an Iron Aqueduct at the full height originally intended . . . 125 feet above . . . the River Dee . . . the arches . . . of the Aqueduct may be seven of 50 feet each the remainder may be raised by an embankment.'

Jessop must have got informal approval in principle, for almost immediately afterwards the foundation stone with its well-known inscription [14] was laid on 25 July. On 10 August the formal committee meeting was held, at which Jessop repeated his recommendation, and 'It is ordered that the recommendation of Mr. Jessop in that respect shall be adopted'. The surveyor, Telford, was asked to do plans and sections of 'the improvements proposed by Mr. William Jessop in passing the said Valley by means of an Iron Aqueduct.'[15] In his report of 14 July, incidentally, Jessop had also recommended an iron aqueduct at Chirk, considering that such would be preferable to an embankment; indeed, 'instead of an obstruction it would be a romantic feature in the view', and therefore the landowner might permit the canal to cross the Ceiriog at Chirk instead of Pont-faen. This in fact happened.

What had probably occurred to cause these choices of iron was this. On 28 February 1795, as we have seen, Telford had been appointed to succeed Josiah Clowes as engineer of the Shrewsbury Canal; there an iron aqueduct at Longdon to replace that of masonry just destroyed by floods had, it seems likely, been suggested to him by Thomas Eyton and had been approved on 14 March. As Eyton was also one of the treasurers of the Ellesmere Canal, it is not impossible that, after the decision had been taken about Longdon, Telford mentioned to Eyton the problem of the great masonry aqueduct at Pontcysyllte, with its approach locks at either end. For the first time in his life Telford had been among ironmasters, and he came back to Jessop on the Ellesmere full of the advantages of iron.* Jessop, too, was an ironmaster, who had been since 1790 a partner in the Butterley ironworks, and probably he took up the idea enthusiastically and worked it out with

---

* Telford's new enthusiasm for iron was not confined to Pontcysyllte. On 28 February, the day of his appointment to the Shrewsbury, he was ordered at a Sessions meeting to prepare plans for a new road bridge at Buildwas to replace one swept away in the floods. On 25 April he proposed an iron bridge; it is interesting that the justices submitted his plan to John Wilkinson and William Reynolds (both, we may note, members of the committee of the Shrewsbury Canal at the time), who approved it.

Telford, especially as about the same time Benjamin Outram, his partner at Butterley, was building a small iron aqueduct on the Derby Canal, about which Jessop must have known. On 26 July, for instance, he writes that he is 'looking forward to the time when we shall be laying the Iron Trough on the piers'.[16]

This kind of action would account both for the words of the oration of 1805 on the aqueduct: 'Mr. Telford who, with the advice and judgment of our eminent and much respected Engineer Mr. Jessop, invented, and with unabated diligence carried the whole into execution,' and the fact that Jessop, the most unassuming of men and the least likely to take credit where it was not due, did not mention Telford's name in his report or before the committee. He was the ironmaster and the principal engineer, and he was taking full responsibility for the major proposal he was putting forward. If we remember that Telford had previously had no experience with iron, had never been a canal engineer until his appointment to the Ellesmere, and was sufficiently a man-of-all-work to be sent round the Midlands in October 1795 to collect outstanding calls on shares, one may think that William Jessop, at that time at the peak of his reputation as the greatest canal engineer of the age, has not been given due credit for his part in Pontcysyllte. His 'advice and judgment' were probably vital. When he was elderly and looking back, Telford forty years later in his *Life* had almost forgotten what had really happened. He described the committee as 'pleased to propose my undertaking the conduct of this extensive and complicated work'* and went on: 'my previous occupations had so far given me confidence; and in regard to earthwork, I had the advantage of consulting Mr. William Jessop, an experienced engineer.' He goes on: 'I had about that time carried the Shrewsbury canal by a cast-iron trough . . . and finding this practicable, it occurred to me, as there was hard sandstone adjacent to Pont-y-Cysyllte, that no very serious difficulty could occur in building a number of square pillars, of sufficient dimensions to support a cast-iron trough.' He had forgotten how quickly the decision to use iron at Pontcysyllte came after that for Longdon; forgotten that the stone for the original masonry aqueduct—which he does not mention—was already cut; and indeed forgotten that he was not principal engineer.[17]

Varley's contract to build the stone aqueduct had fallen in; there was an attempt to associate him with the new work, but it seems

* The Ellesmere Canal.

to have failed, and he left the project. A decision was taken to increase the number of piers to nineteen, in order to reduce the span of the arches from 50 ft to 45 ft and also the length of the approach embankments, a start was made on the piers, and then work stopped in favour of the aqueduct at Chirk.

Given that Pontcysyllte would take a long time to build, the company were anxious to open a line from Chirk, near the Vron limeworks, with access to coal, and to which the products of the Ruabon area could be brought by road, to Frankton. The contract for the aqueduct was let in January 1796 to William Hazeldine—who supplied the iron plates—John Simpson and William Davies; it was completed in 1801, and opened a waterway 8 miles long from Chirk basin at the northern end of the aqueduct to the bottom of Frankton locks. There were four of these, including a staircase pair, and two at New Marton. By June 1802 the line had been extended through Chirk tunnel (459 yds) and Whitehouses tunnel (191 yds) to the southern end of Pontcysyllte.

Chirk aqueduct was 600 ft long and 70 ft high with ten arches of 40 ft span, and cost £20,898. The Report of 1801 said of it:

'there is no earth or puddle made use of; the water-way is formed with a cast iron bottom, and square masonry on the sides; the spandrels of the arches are hollow. By this mode of construction, a very considerable proportion of the masonry is saved in the breadth of the Aqueduct; the risque of expansion or contraction from puddling is avoided. In case of any leakage, the water may find its way through the spandrels, without injuring the Work; and every part of the Masonry and the bottom of the water-way, may be readily examined at all times.'

I do not know why, after an iron trough had been decided upon for Pontcysyllte and suggested for Chirk, this mixed form of construction was adopted. Perhaps neither engineer yet felt confident enough to design such a long iron trough.

In July 1795 contractors were sought for the section of the Shrewsbury line from Hordley to Weston; this was opened in 1797, and 'a wharf, four lime kilns, a public house, stables, a clerk's house, and weighing machine'[18] were built. It was hoped that, by burning limestone from Llanymynech here with coal from the Chirk line, 'the adjacent country would, by degrees, be accustomed to look to the Canal for Coals and Lime, while the more tedious works were completing'.[19] In fact, the canal got no nearer to Shrewsbury, because lime from Weston had to compete with that brought along the Shrewsbury Canal from Donnington, and the coal did not materialize till Pontcysyllte had been finished. From time to time thereafter an extension from Weston to Shrewsbury was reconsidered along various routes, but sufficient revenue could not be foreseen, and no action was taken.

Telford had re-examined the Ruabon–Chester line to a running fire of argument from the landowners, had had his proposals approved by Jessop in August 1795 and authorized in an Act[20] of 1796. From Pontcysyllte the line was now to rise 76 ft by locks to Plas Kynaston, and then run level past Ruabon and Bersham to Pool Mouth above New Broughton, whence a long flight of locks fell past Stansty, Gwersyllt, and roughly on the line of the Wrexham–Chester railway to the Dee opposite the canal basin. Branches were intended from Pool Mouth on the level past Ffrwd to a flight of locks, reservoir, collieries and limestone quarries below Llanfynydd, and another from near Pulford to Holt and Farndon. In June of the same year part of the first branch, on the same level as the summit of the main line, was started, about 2¼ miles being built from the Moss–Gwersyllt road to a basin half a mile from Ffrwd at a cost of £9,135. It was filled with water and equipped, but probably never used. After 1809 it was progressively dismantled.

Early in 1794 Edward Rowland and Exuperius Pickering, both of Ruabon, the former a shareholder and the latter a substantial land and colliery owner, patented an idea for a canal lift.[21] They then offered to build it experimentally, and the company ordered Telford to point out a place on the line between Pontcysyllte and Chester where it could be constructed. If it worked, the committee would pay; if not, the inventors.[22] An advertisement of May 1796[23] announced that the lift was in a state of forwardness, that a successful trial had been made, and that the proprietors would, for the inspection of engineers, have it working every Monday morning and Thursday evening. It was not till April 1800 that the inventors asked for payment. Jessop and Rennie had meanwhile examined it and reported. They probably said that, like other lift prototypes, it worked well under favourable conditions, but was not robust enough for daily use, for the company paid £200 of the £800 it had cost. Perhaps somewhere along the ghostly line its inexplicable remains still stand, waiting to be found.

The principle was that of a float contained in a well of water supporting a number of iron pillars upon which rested a tank full of water containing the canal boat. The two were balanced, so that the action of a rack and pinion or a capstan would be suffi-

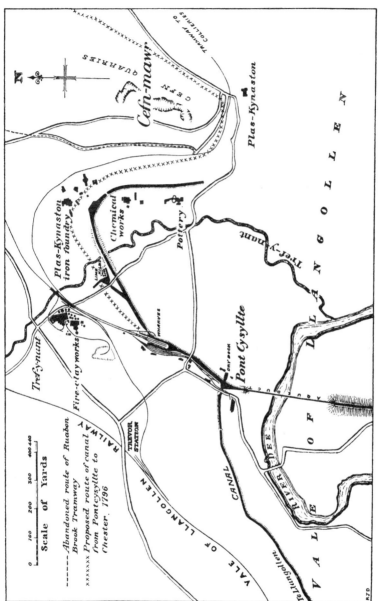

11. The Plas Kynaston Canal

cient to raise or lower the tank. The same principle is used today for the two great Henrichenburg lifts at Dortmund and the Rothensee lift at Magdeburg.

Apart from the Ffrwd branch and the lift, there was much activity but no action on the Ruabon–Chester section. Inclined planes were considered, as were tramroads, till in his report for 1800 Jessop wrote that: 'change of circumstances . . . since . . . the Act, have shown it to be wholly inadvisable to execute a Canal between Pont Cysyllte and Chester, and especially since the extensive opening of the Collieries between Hawarden and Flint, which will communicate by Railways with the Dee, so as to deliver coal at a much less price at Chester than formerly.'

In 1800, with Chirk aqueduct nearly finished, tenders were accepted for completing the pillars and abutments of Pontcysyllte. In the following year the committee decided to build a tramroad from the works north of it to the canal, but could not decide whether to carry it over the aqueduct as well. In November they decided upon a canal to Trevor to meet the tramroad there, and only then let the contract for the ironwork to William Hazeldine. The great aqueduct was opened at a ceremony on 26 November 1805, not the least of the attractions being the salute by cannon, formerly belonging to Tippoo Sahib, that were fired by the Artillery Company of the Shropshire Volunteers. It was 1,007 ft long, 126 ft 8 in. high, and had cost £47,018. The main canal line ended 300 yds beyond it at basins, whence the tramroad ran past the Plas Kynaston stone quarries to Acrefair. Opened on the same day as the aqueduct with coal from Hazeldine's collieries at Plas Kynaston, this was a double-track plateway. It was extended to Plas Madoc colliery in 1808, and later to near the Afon-eitha brook. In August 1820 Exuperius Pickering junior was given permission to make a private canal from Trevor basin towards Plas Kynaston. This seems to have been partly built soon afterwards, but not to have been completed till about 1830.

While canal building was taking place on the Llanymynech, Pontcysyllte and Shrewsbury lines, the Chester Canal company was suffering from hope deferred. Its prospects had looked brighter after a clause permitting the construction of a branch from the Ellesmere to the Chester if the landowners agreed* had been included in the former's Act of 1793, and after the Wirral

---

* If they did not, the Ellesmere company bound themselves to seek an Act, and, if it were passed, to build the connection within two years of the completion of their canal from Frankton to Fens Hall near Whitchurch.

branch had been built. In December 1794 the company compounded with their principal creditor, Mr William Egerton,[24] to take £8,000 for the £20,000 capital and £14,108 interest they owed him, and in February 1795 with the River Dee company for £1,000 in settlement of their debts there. Calls to raise these sums were made upon the shareholders, but even the brief added prospects given by the Commercial Canal project (see p. 198) only produced £3,300, others preferring to forfeit their shares. Despairingly the committee wrote: 'Let the Blessings of Peace return, with them will return to this Land the Spirit of Industry, Enterprize and Commerce . . . Can the Waters of Cheshire alone be useless, and its Agriculture unfurnished with the means of Improvement?'[25]

The company were trying to raise the £9,000 in £50 preference shares when they read the parliamentary notices for the Ellesmere's 1796 bill, which failed to mention the connection. They thereupon decided themselves to seek an Act to enforce the junction, and meanwhile to cancel their agreement to supply water to the Wirral line: 'our Water has been at their service continually . . . neglect & contempt are the returns we receive'.[26] The Ellesmere company reacted at once, agreeing to insert clauses requiring them to seek an Act within two years, and to a joint engineering survey. Water was restored, and in 1797 a line was set out and estimated at £36,478. Jessop pointed out, however, that until the Whitchurch branch had been made and water could be got from the main line beyond Pontcysyllte, there would not be supplies for the junction cut. The Ellesmere company then inserted into the Act powers to abandon the old Whitchurch line, and to make a new one to Sherryman's Bridge near the town, with a branch to Prees Higher Heath and another to the town of Ellesmere.

The Chester company now managed to raise the money to pay its debts and start putting its canal in good order. The Ellesmere got its reluctant agreement to further delay, but did actually start to build from Frankton towards Whitchurch in February 1797, and had got to Tilstock Park, 4 miles short, in 1804. The work was difficult, with embankments and cuttings, the crossing of Whixall Moss, and an 87-yd tunnel at Ellesmere. There was a ¼ mile branch into Ellesmere itself, and at the junction the canal company built their offices. From this line at Whixall Moss the Prees branch ran south-east; it was intended to reach Prees Higher Heath on the road to Market Drayton and Wellington, but by about 1806 had only been made for 3¾ miles to Quina

Brook on the Whitchurch–Wem road, where limekilns were erected.

After final agreement with the Chester in November 1802, work began on the junction line from Tilstock Park to Hurleston, and was completed on 25 March 1805. The necessary water was obtained under an Act of 1804[27] which authorized a navigable feeder from the north end of the Pontcysyllte aqueduct past Llangollen to an intake from the Dee at Llantisilio,* itself governed by a regulating weir at Bala. It was completed in 1808. The junction seems to have been opened at the end of 1805, for a newspaper of New Year's Day 1806 reported that 'Six vessels, heavy laden, with oak timber, from the Ellesmere Canal, along the old Chester Canal, arrived at the Tower Wharf in Chester on Monday last, the first that have gone by the conveyance since the communication between these canals'.[29] Five came from the Weston branch, and one from the Montgomeryshire Canal. Once the connection had been made, trade grew rapidly, though it must be remembered that the whole Ellesmere and Montgomeryshire system was self-contained except by way of the Mersey or the Dee. The new line was 12⅛ miles long from Frankton on the level to Tilstock Park, and 16⅞ miles thence to Hurleston with nineteen locks, six of them at Grindley Brook and four at Hurleston. One further extension was made, from Grindley Brook, 2 miles from Whitchurch, to Sherryman's bridge on 6 July 1808, and into the town at Castle Well in 1811.

In anticipation of increased prosperity, the Ellesmere in 1804 offered to buy the Chester for 1,000 shares, making 5,000 in all, and the assumption of debts up to £4,000, but the Chester asked 1,300 and the negotiations fell through. By now the purposes of the Ellesmere company had changed from their original concern to provide an outlet for the limestone of Llanymynech and Trevor, the iron of Ruabon and Bersham, and the coal of Chirk, Ruabon and Wrexham, to Chester and Liverpool in one direction and Shrewsbury in the other. Their current function was to distribute coal, limestone, lime and building materials within the limits of their self-contained system of 68¼ miles of canals, together with the Montgomeryshire, though with a subordinate and increasingly important trade from this area to and from Liverpool by way of the additional 8½ miles of the Wirral canal.

* In 1810 there was a hopeful proposal (the Merionethshire Canal) to extend it to Barmouth, to open a conveyance 'for the treasures of the mines of Merionethshire to Liverpool and the Metropolis'.[28]

Jessop had left about 1801, and Telford remained as part-time general agent, with Thomas Denson as resident engineer. The financial position at the end of 1805 was that £410,875 had been raised by calling 133 per cent on 3,330 shares, less arrears, and £48,586 received in toll and other income, all of which had been spent on works, expenses or interest. No dividends had been paid. In 1807 receipts were £12,568 and the estimated debts £31,102; in 1809 receipts had risen to £15,707 and debts fallen to £29,500, including nearly £18,000 in optional notes. By 1813 these had been repaid. The Chester company in 1807 also started paying off old debts, and by 1811 had much improved their position. Holding a key position between the two sections of the Ellesmere's line to Liverpool, it is surprising that they agreed so easily to amalgamation on terms much worse than they had rejected in 1804. However, they welcomed it, and in 1813 an authorizing Act[30] was passed, on the basis of 500 Ellesmere shares, 2½ to each holder of Chester £50 preference shares, ¼ to each £100 ordinary share. On 1 July the United Company of Proprietors of the Ellesmere and Chester Canals came into existence.

Ellesmere & Chester Canal

The large general committee elected in July 1813 tried to represent the unusually wide spread of shareholding interests, including the persevering group from Leicestershire. Having done right by the gods in adopting a seal with the likeness of the late Duke of Bridgewater, the company adopted a forceful commercial policy, encouraging long-distance traffic by allowing free passage after a certain distance, or very low long-distance rates. A steam packet, *The Countess of Bridgewater*, owned by the company, was put on in 1816 between Ellesmere Port and Liverpool: her movement was majestic, her structure was elegant, her principal cabin spacious, and her ladies' apartment handsome;[31] but she failed, and was sold in 1819. Also on the debit side was the collapse of an embankment in 1816 which flooded Chirk colliery, fortunately when no one was at work. On the credit was the use of iron for lock-gates, starting about 1819 with some at Frankton, and the construction in 1827 of two new locks, the lower being entirely of iron, and a short new section of canal at Beeston to get rid of the endless trouble that had occurred there with unstable and leaking foundations.

In 1824 the Earl of Bridgewater died, having been chairman

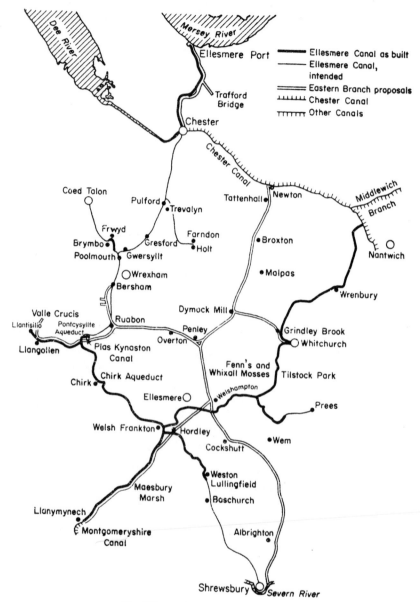

12. The Ellesmere Canal as planned and built

ever since Pontcysyllte had been opened; he was succeeded by Lord Clive, already chairman of the Montgomeryshire Canal (Eastern Branch), and the following January new stirrings began. Some were at the prospect of the Birmingham & Liverpool Junction, a line from the end of the old Chester Canal at Nantwich direct to Autherley to join the Staffs & Worcs almost opposite the Birmingham, the construction of which would provide a much more direct line from the Midlands to Liverpool. Talks began upon this project, and it seemed sensible also to sound the Trent & Mersey and the Bridgewater trustees upon at last making a connection between the old Chester line and Middlewich, so that the new canal would have direct access to Manchester.

The Bridgewater trustees had no objection, but the Trent & Mersey refused to consider a line that they saw as prejudicial to their own trade until the B. & L. J. had obtained their Act. That passed in 1826, the Ellesmere & Chester then promoted their own for a canal from Barbridge to Wardle near Middlewich to join a short branch from their main line which the Trent & Mersey had agreed to build after having imposed stiff compensation tolls. It was authorized in 1827[32] by an Act which also repealed all old Ellesmere and Chester legislation, and substituted a new consolidation. Wharves and transhipment warehouses were built at Barbridge, and the new branch was opened on 1 September 1833, at a cost of about £129,000, but carried little trade till the completion of the B. & L. J.

On 2 March 1835 the Birmingham & Liverpool Junction opened, and in August 1836 the Ellesmere & Chester's committee reviewed the company's patterns of current trade. Limestone was carried from Llanymynech to be burnt for agricultural use with Chirk small coal at the many limekilns on the line. Household and industrial coal from the fifteen or so pits at Chirk was also carried, but competed with that from Flintshire coming up the Dee through Chester. Iron from Ruabon could be carried to Chester by less than 20 miles of land carriage; the canal route was 58 miles plus up to four on the tramroad, and therefore tolls were low, and only brought in £1,000 p.a. Staffordshire ironmasters carrying their iron to Chester or Liverpool by the Trent & Mersey's line had the privilege of buying very cheap fluxing limestone from the Caldon quarries; the Ruabon ironmasters used Trevor stone, but this was accepted by Staffordshire and Shropshire ironmasters only as back carriage in boats that had taken their iron to Chester or Ellesmere Port in a triangular trade. The stone paid very low tolls to the Ellesmere & Chester and was carried toll-free on the B. & L. J. On the Middlewich branch comparatively high tolls had to be charged to avoid undercutting the Wirral and Chester line from Ellesmere Port, the importance of which was steadily growing at the expense of Chester. The iron trade was the most important; in 1838, 60,406 tons of iron were carried by the Ellesmere & Chester to Liverpool, 38,758 tons from Staffordshire, 11,687 from North Wales, and 9,961 from Shropshire, three-quarters being manufactured. The Middlewich branch carried another 10,370 tons to Manchester, mainly from North Wales.

OPENING OF THE NEW DOCK, ELLESMERE PORT.

13

In 1830 the company had obtained special carrying powers on the Mersey, and in 1832 agreed with two firms (later one) to carry all goods offered to and from Ellesmere Port and Liverpool at agreed rates for five years after the opening of the B. & L. J., they to provide boats and warehouses and to pay £2,000 p.a. to the company for its existing accommodation at Ellesmere Port. Although the company supported the carriers, there were many complaints of delay and unfair dealing, and in November 1836 the company agreed to buy the business for £25,000, the price to include 25 flats and 1 lighter. At the same time, on the recommendation of Telford, they decided to make large improvements at Ellesmere Port to match the accommodation for the general and timber trades they had already provided at Liverpool.

At the Port two locks led down from the canal to a dock which gave access to the warehouses, and a third from this dock to a tidal basin open to the river past two pier heads. It was now agreed to build a sea-lock leading out of the tidal basin into a separate and much larger still-water dock, 435 ft × 139 ft, behind the warehouses; to build a second flight of canal locks; and to make various lesser improvements.

Work began with W. A. Provis as contractor and William Cubitt as Telford's successor, and the improvements were opened in September 1843:

'A few years since, there were upon this site but a public-house, three small cottages, an excuse for a warehouse, and one set of locks. Now it has upwards of seventy houses . . . a church, schools, two or three inns, two sets of locks; a splendid and most ample range of warehouses, erected on arches over various branches of the canal . . . besides the vast new dock. The port is now open to any coasting trade that comes to Liverpool . . . for towing the vessels up, two powerful steamers leave Liverpool two hours and a quarter before every tide, and remain there an hour, returning at the top of the ebb.'[33]

By 1844 revenue was only being kept up with difficulty, and it was clear that the fortunes of the company were so bound up with those of the Birmingham & Liverpool Junction that an amalgamation was desirable, especially because of 'the material alteration which the construction of Railways has made and the interference which they are likely to create with Canal property'.[34]

Birmingham & Liverpool Junction Canal

In the summer of 1824 the trade of the Birmingham Canal was 'unprecedented',[35] and its committee asked Telford to recommend improvements. He did so in September, and probably also suggested that if the traffic from the more efficient line he was proposing was to find adequate outlet westwards, a new canal to carry it straight to the Mersey ought to be built, for a few months later he was described as its 'originator and proposer'.[36]

It was also the summer of the little railway mania, and among the projects much discussed in Birmingham was a line thence to Liverpool. Some stimulation from railway promotion, as well as from their own proposed improvements, probably acted upon the Birmingham company. They promptly took up the idea, and by the end of the year their agent, Thomas Eyre Lee, was seeking support for the new canal, to run from Autherley on the Staffs &

Worcs not far from its junction with the Birmingham Canal to Nantwich, where it would join the Ellesmere & Chester for a clear run to the Mersey at Ellesmere Port by way of Chester. Naturally the Ellesmere & Chester were all in favour, and as Telford was their consulting engineer, coordination would not be difficult. The companies to suffer would be the Staffs & Worcs and the Trent & Mersey. The first concentrated upon negotiating compensation tolls and protecting their water; the second, whose new tunnel at Harecastle had been authorized in 1823, hurriedly had it resurveyed and then began construction in February 1825, ironically enough with Telford as their engineer.

The Birmingham & Liverpool Junction project was thoroughly canvassed during 1825. On 22 September a subscription meeting was held at Newport, and in May 1826 the Act[37] was passed, authorizing £400,000 capital and £100,000 more if necessary. The shareholders were widespread. The Marquess of Stafford had taken the trouble to assess the relative merits of railways and canals, and had eventually decided for the waterways: he held 200 shares and his principal agent, James Loch, sat on the board. On the other hand, the Marquess understood the public pressure and feeling behind railways, and had so far yielded to it as to support the Liverpool & Manchester, though it competed with the Bridgewater Canal, the revenue of which went to him.[38] Lord Clive of the Ellesmere & Chester and the Montgomeryshire, who succeeded his father as Earl of Powis in 1839, was in the chair. On the list were such committeemen of other companies as P. P. Bouverie and William Rickford of the Grand Junction, John Tomes of the Warwick canals, John Woodcock, Thomas Little and John Twist of the Coventry, Samuel Mills of the Grand Union, S. T. Galton, James Watt and seven others of the Birmingham, C. H. Molineux of the Wyrley & Essington, J. W. Whateley of the Stratford-upon-Avon, Samuel Dawes of the Worcester & Birmingham, E. J. Littleton and Sir John Wrottesley of the Staffs & Worcs, Timothy Smith of the Dudley, Stourbridge and upper Avon, Thomas Lister of the rival Trent & Mersey, John Bather of the Shrewsbury, and a number, of course, from the Ellesmere & Chester. There were also John Freeth, the clerk of the Birmingham company, and Thomas Brewin, superintendent of the Dudley. The clerk was Thomas Eyre Lee, solicitor to the Birmingham.

The canal was to some extent a test case, built by existing canal proprietors and interests against the prevailing public mood. The project received very little support from the railway-minded

THE ELLESMERE AND ITS CONNECTIONS

correspondents of Midland newspapers, with whom high canal dividends and tolls were most unpopular. Sir John Rennie, in his *Autobiography*, recalls that his brother, with Josias Jessop and William Chapman, had planned the Birmingham to Liverpool railway along a similar route to that later taken by the canal. 'The public', he says, 'were not quite prepared for such an undertaking . . . it was in advance of the time, and for a while fell to the ground. Canals had not fallen into disrepute . . . Telford, having been bred in the old school, and having seen the triumph of canals, could not, or would not, believe in the efficacy of railways . . . indeed, he laughed heartily when he had succeeded in supplanting my brother's line of railway from Birmingham to Liverpool by a canal.'[39] Work started from the Nantwich end towards High Offley, with John Wilson as contractor and Alexander Easton as resident engineer.

A link with the Donnington area and Shrewsbury was now considered. A possible extension of the Donnington Wood Canal for $7\frac{3}{4}$ miles to Gnosall was first surveyed, but was found impractical and unwelcome to the Lilleshall company, and so a branch from Norbury to join the Shrewsbury Canal at Wappenshall was chosen instead, and authorized by an Act[40] of 1827. This was $10\frac{1}{4}$ miles long, with 23 falling locks from the main line, 17 of them in the Norbury flight. Two branches were authorized from it, one to Edgmond that was never built, and one, to be a cut with 7 locks or a tramroad, to Lilleshall. This, on a different line and without locks, became the Humber Arm, $\frac{3}{4}$ mile long, leading to the Marquess of Stafford's Lubstree wharf, which opened for business in 1844. It seems to have been connected with Lilleshall by road till the later locomotive line was built.

During 1827 and early 1828 the promoters' prospects were brightened by the authorization of the Ellesmere & Chester's Middlewich branch, which offered the B. & L. J. access to Manchester for such goods as they could get past the Trent & Mersey's compensation tolls, and by the first plans for the projected London & Birmingham Junction Canal as a complement to their own. In 1829 a contract for the High Offley–Church Eaton section was let to W. A. Provis, and early in 1830 for the Newport branch and Humber Arm also. Later that for the Church Eaton–Autherley section went to John Wilson and, after his death, to W. Wilson.

In 1831 the Staffs & Worcs agreed to reduce their compensation charge at Autherley from 2s to 1s, which improved prospects. But towards the end of the year, with expenditure at £442,000, the committee had to apply to the Exchequer Bill Loan Commissioners, and in November a loan of £160,000 at 5 per cent was agreed, repayment to begin after three years. A further £24,600 came from them in 1832. At the beginning of 1832 the situation looked manageable, and it seemed as if the canal would be open by the end of the year. 'As much expedition has been used as is consistent with prudence and the permanent stability of the undertaking,' the shareholders were told.[41] By the end of the year Knighton reservoir had been finished, Belvide begun, and all works except the Shelmore embankment were well ahead. The struggles of the ailing Telford and of William Cubitt, called in to help, with Shelmore have been told in L. T. C. Rolt's *Thomas Telford*. More and more money was needed, not only that from the Commissioners, but raised from the shareholders. At last the canal was opened from Autherley to Gnosall on 12 January and throughout, including the Newport branch, on 2 March 1835. The cost had been about £800,000 excluding arrears of interest.

The B. & L. J. was 39½ miles long from Autherley to Nantwich, with a stop-lock at Autherley and 28 others, mainly grouped in the flight of 15 at Audlem. Other features were the great cutting at Tyrley and an 81-yd tunnel at Cowley. It shortened the route from Birmingham to the Mersey by 19⅞ miles and 30 locks, and to Manchester by 5¼ miles and 30 locks, compared to that by the Trent & Mersey. After the Macclesfield Canal had been opened, however, the B. & L. J. route to Manchester became 4¾ miles longer, but had no less than 50 fewer locks. Shrewsbury, now connected to the canal network, was 102⅞ miles and 60 locks distant from Manchester, and 80⅜ miles and 87 locks from the Potteries. On the main line, goods from Birmingham to Liverpool could be delivered in about 45 hours by using the new route.

In 1833 the Grand Junction Railway from Warrington to Birmingham was authorized, and in 1834 enabled to join the London & Birmingham line there. Competition was coming even before the canal was open, and the initial tolls had to be lower than had been envisaged: ½d on lime and limestone, and 1d on everything else. By May 1836 most commodities except coal and iron were at ½d. Cubitt was ordered to enlarge Belvide, and support was given to the Aqueduct company (see p. 131) as a means of putting pressure on the Staffs & Worcs to reduce their compensation toll further—which they did. Early in 1838 the Birmingham Canal completed its main line improvements. But the financial position was bad: in October 1839 the company owed the Exchequer Bill Loan Commissioners £184,600 in capital and £67,521 for interest, and also £100,555 to others.

In July 1837 the Grand Junction Railway was opened to Birmingham, began to convey goods in January 1838, and in May offered to carry between Birmingham and Liverpool at canal freight rates. We can get a picture of the canal's trade, still building up, just before the railway affected it, from figures for the first half of 1836.[42] In this period 5,144 boats passed, and the following tonnages were carried:

	tons
General merchandise	22,732
Iron	25,685
Coal and coke	9,631
Building materials	4,532
Lime and limestone	8,546
Road materials, manure, etc.	279
Total	71,405

Belvide now became written on the hearts of the committee-men, because without it there was not enough water for the traffic. Indeed, in 1835, 2,000 locksful had to be bought from the Wyrley & Essington for £800. 'Upon this reservoir depends the prosperity of the Company.'[43] The Commissioners agreed that £20,000 could be spent on it before payments were made to them, and its 208 acres were opened in 1842. Meanwhile other useful prospects appeared. There was talk of a Middlewich–Altrincham Canal to save 18 miles to Manchester, badly needed as a rival to the newly-opened Macclesfield, and the Birmingham company had announced plans for a Tame Valley line and a junction between their own navigations and the Wyrley & Essington. Tolls had, however, to be kept well below those contemplated when the canal had been promoted.

The opening of the Newport branch meant that iron from the Coalbrookdale area, previously limited to land carriage within about 30 miles or to shipment down the Severn for export, could now be sent by canal anywhere in England. The Horsehay company, for instance, established a number of depots throughout the country. At first they put their products into tub-boats on the Coalbrookdale branch of the Shropshire Canal at Dawley for transhipment at Wappenshall. Then they found it more sensible to improve the direct road (about 5 miles) and send goods direct to Wappenshall for loading, usually in their own boats.[44]

In 1842 the canal company obtained powers to carry passengers and goods and to provide haulage facilities for the boats of other carriers, in advance of the adoptive Act of 1845, as a result of experiments carried out by Alexander Easton and their superintendent Samuel Skey. These, with a steam tug to haul narrow boats, seemed early in 1843 to show that 'the expense of moving Trains of Boats by Steam power is . . . likely to be less than Horse power'.[45] In late 1843 they started to work boats in trains through from Autherley to Ellesmere Port, hauled by one of eight steam tugs, and by August 1844 could report that 'the Steam Tugs of the Company have been actively at work throughout the main line of Canal and the System of hauling Boats in trains has been carried out to a considerable extent'.[46] In the following year, however, the Ellesmere & Chester, excited about railway conversion, said that 'the system of working boats in Trains though used with great advantage . . . is not cheaper than locomotive power now is upon Railways with a good gradient'.[47] The method only seems to have lasted for a few years before being replaced by a contract for horse haulage given to a single contractor, William Bishton. The company's carrying department seems to have indulged in freight price-cutting, for a carrier told the Staffs & Worcs in December 1843 that the B. & L. J., 'as General Carriers, had offered to convey Goods of all Descriptions at so low a Rate of Tonnage, that the Canal carrying Trade will not be worth following by the Old Carriers'.[48]

In January 1844 agreement was reached between the company and the Bridgewater trustees whereby the latter were leased the company's tugs and flats, their Ellesmere Port warehouses and some of their Liverpool accommodation, for £4,122 p.a. plus a share of certain profits.[49] This was presumably done to free it to concentrate on organizing carrying on the canal itself.

The company paid no dividends. The revenue figures for its short life are set out on the opposite page.

Early in 1844 discussions began between the committees of the Birmingham & Liverpool Junction and the Ellesmere & Chester upon amalgamation, and agreement was reached in August, on the basis that revenue would be appropriated in order to the following three classes of stock:

(*a*) a dividend of 4 per cent (the rate that had ruled for some years) upon the 3,575¾ shares of the Ellesmere & Chester, requiring £14,303 p.a.;

(*b*) interest totalling £4,713 p.a. upon the share bonds of the

THE ELLESMERE AND ITS CONNECTIONS 189

B. & L. J., being those sums of £25 each above the nominal £100 of the shares that had been subscribed by its shareholders to finish the canal;

(c) the surplus to be divisible between the shareholders of each company in proportion to the debts of each.

The new company would borrow at 4 per cent to pay off the debt owed by the B. & L. J. to the Exchequer Bill Loan Commissioners.

Y.e. 31 March	Revenue £
1836	11,706
1837	16,001
1838	18,662
1839	28,923
1840	30,859
1841	28,576
1842	27,796
1843	22,170
1844	23,404*

* Includes some carrying revenue.

On 8 May 1845 the amalgamation Act was passed, and the united company was formed, taking the name of the Ellesmere & Chester. Even before the Act had been passed, however, a further change was envisaged, when at the end of April a sub-committee was set up to consider the future of the company and the possibility of railway conversion. The Shropshire Union idea had been born. (*To continue the history of the Ellesmere & Chester Canal, turn to Ch. XIII.*)

Montgomeryshire Canal

While the controversy over the Ellesmere's eastern or western lines was at its height, a meeting was held at Welshpool on 23 October 1792 to support an extension of the Llanymynech branch to that town, which moved the Ellesmere committee to recommend their shareholders to support it 'either by a consolidated Stock or by a separate independent Company'.[50] After another meeting on 18 October 1793 that decided upon a line to Newtown, a company was formed and an Act[51] obtained in March 1794. This authorised a canal from near the Porthywaen limestone quarries to Newtown, with a branch from near the quarries to Llanymynech, and another from Burgedin to Guilsfield. John Dadford was the engineer, with his brother Thomas

Dadford junior to advise him, the two being jointly paid. A proposal of 1793 for a connecting canal 40¼ miles long from the Montgomeryshire near Garthmyl to the Leominster Canal at Woofferton came to nothing.[52]

Agricultural development was the main motive behind the canal's promotion. Lime was needed for the rough lands that were being enclosed. Land carriage of limestone and coal was expensive, and the horses used for it consumed so much grain that not enough was left to increase cattle numbers. Some turnpike roads had been built, but durable materials for their repair were scarce, and the wear upon them heavy. A pamphlet of 1797 said: 'This Canal was not undertaken with the view of large profit accruing from the Tolls; for there is not even a Probability that any such can arise; and therefore the Subscribers were the Noblemen and Gentlemen either possessed of estates in this County, or resident therein, who had for their Object the Extension of Agriculture, the Reduction of Horses . . . the Increase of Horned Cattle, and the Preservation of the Roads; with the consequent Advantage to the Public.'[53] So the Act limited dividends to 10 per cent.

Out of the 720 shares of £100, 711 were subscribed, and work began on two aqueducts, that over the Vyrnwy having five arches of 39 ft span, and over the Rhiw at Berriew two of 30 ft, with two land arches. The contractors for the former were John Simpson and William Hazeldine, soon to be concerned with work for the Ellesmere company. There was talk of the latter seeking powers to make a branch from their line by Oswestry to Porthywaen, but until they did so, it seemed wiser for the Montgomeryshire company to plan for a junction north of the Vyrnwy with the Ellesmere's Llanymynech branch, and to leave the section to Porthywaen, which was likely to be costly, on one side. It was never built; instead, the Porthywaen tramroad was made for 2¼ miles from the quarries to the Ellesmere Canal at Crickheath.

Work went on well. In early February 1796 the first boat was ceremoniously launched near Welshpool, and named *The Royal Montgomery* amid libations, sheep-roasting, ale-drinking, bell-ringing and gunfire. By the beginning of July 1797 the junction at Carreghofa had been made, and the Llanymynech branch of the Ellesmere was navigable though leaky; by August the canal was open to Garthmyl beyond Berriew and near Montgomery, and probably also the Guilsfield branch, in spite of John Dadford having resigned some months before and gone to America. He was replaced on Thomas's initiative by their father, old Thomas

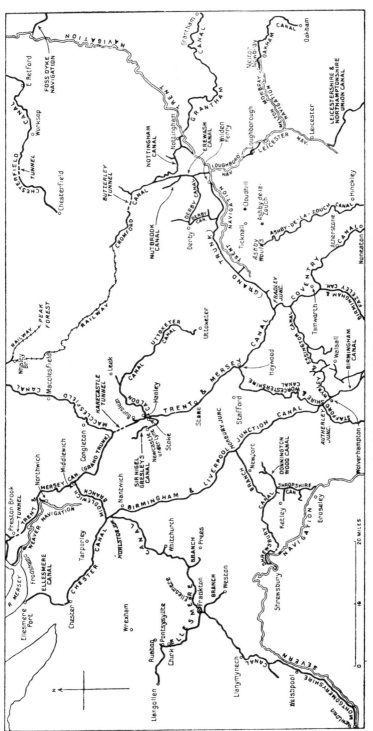

14. The canals of the north-west Midlands and their connections

Dadford, 'under whom they were bred, and who has had great experience in Canal works'.[54] There had been trouble with the Vyrnwy aqueduct (there was to be more), one arch of which had collapsed, with that at Berriew over the Rhiw, and with some minor works, and the committee were critical of their engineers, but Jessop, called in, soothed them by saying such teething troubles were normal.

To get to Garthmyl and build the branch £71,100 had been spent, and there the canal remained for many years. It was $16\frac{1}{4}$ miles long from the junction with the Llanymynech branch at Carreghofa to Garthmyl, with four falling locks from Carreghofa to Burgedin, and nine rising thence to Garthmyl. The level Guilsfield branch was $2\frac{1}{4}$ miles long.

Being an agricultural canal, the main trade was in limestone brought down from the Llanymynech and neighbouring quarries by tramroads to the canal, and then boated upwards to be burnt at waterside kilns. These were built at Belan and elsewhere, the lime trade being encouraged from 1800 onwards by the high wartime prices for grain, which in turn encouraged extensive enclosures of the Welsh hill-lands, which again led to heavy demands for lime. Road carriage was cheaper for some coal, however, till the Chirk and, even more, the Pontcysyllte aqueduct was opened. There was also a slow growth in profitable merchandise traffic from the Ellesmere Canal. Other traffics were in building stone, slates, timber and bark. A traveller between Newtown and Welshpool in 1801 remarked that the roads were 'so torn up and destroyed by the wagons loaded with stones and coal to which may be added immense trees for ship timber that are in constant motion to and from the . . . Canal, that they are almost impassable'.[55]

The principal shareholders and supporters of the canal were the Earl of Powis and his son Lord Clive. On the one hand they were concerned as landowners with agricultural development; on the other they were owners of quarries at Llanymynech and Porthywaen, and of mills at Pool Quay. Their interest in the Montgomeryshire led the Powis family to the successive chairmanships of the Ellesmere & Chester, the Birmingham & Liverpool Junction, and the Shropshire Union companies, in a series that lasted nearly a hundred years.

The first dividend, of $2\frac{1}{2}$ per cent, was paid for 1805;* thereafter, with two or three missed years, dividends ranged up to a

* Year ending 30 June in all cases.

XIII. The Shropshire Union: (*above*) 'rocket' bridge over Tyrley cutting on the Birmingham & Liverpool Junction Canal; (*below*) an experiment with locomotive towing carried out in 1888 on the Middlewich branch of the Ellesmere & Chester Canal

XIV. Montgomeryshire Canal: *(above)* Vyrnwy aqueduct; *(below)* Berriew aqueduct

maximum of 5½ per cent for the rest of the company's independent life. Once Pontcysyllte was open, and as long as the war continued, the demand for lime was high and the canal did well. In 1806, 24,082 tons of limestone and 6,757 tons of slack with which to burn it were carried; by 1814 these figures had risen to 44,592 and 11,560 tons. Peace brought a collapse of demand; in 1817 limestone traffic was down to 23,463 tons and slack to 7,046. Here are average figures:

Years	Tolls £	Dividend per cent	Limestone tons	Total tonnage tons
1806–8	3,160	2½	27,315	46,941
1809–11	3,923	4	38,218	65,738
1812–14	4,804	5⅓	43,786	75,217
1815–17	3,973	3½	31,478	56,810
1818–20	4,792	1¾	38,036	73,848

By now a new source of income was about to show itself. In 1812 and 1813 an extension onwards to Newtown, then beginning a period of rapid population and business growth, by canal all the way, or by canal to Bryn-derwen and a tramroad beyond had been considered. A strong group favoured it, and in October 1813 the shareholders voted the extension by the narrow majority of 92 votes to 86. Josias Jessop was called in, and made an estimate of £28,268; he was later to be accused of having omitted to include the cost of puddling and lining the canal throughout.[56] In July his report was accepted, and the company agreed to seek powers.

Now a strong opposition appeared, which requisitioned a special meeting in September to choose a new committee, and to consider introducing into the proposed bill clauses 'to prevent any reduction in the Dividends or Profits of the present Proprietors, by the projected extension, and to provide that the money, necessary for completing such extension, be raised by the creation of new shares, or by Mortgage to be secured solely thereon' and 'to prevent any Union of Interests between the Proprietors of the present Canal and the Subscribers to the proposed Extension, until the latter shall have produced a Dividend equal to the former'.[57]

Neither this nor another requisition of January 1815 succeeded, but both sides, almost equally balanced, got their way, for on 3 February 1815 it was agreed that a virtually separate company having its own committee and accounts should build the Newtown extension. The old company, now to be called the Eastern

Branch, would transfer to the new their Severn feeder that ran to Garthmyl, and any profits they made above those needed to pay a 5 per cent dividend should go to build the extension. On completion, management but not accounts would be united, the surplus over a 5 per cent dividend on the Eastern Branch would be added to the profits of the Western, and when these also permitted a 5 per cent dividend, the two concerns would be finally consolidated. On this basis an Act[58] was passed to authorize the raising of £40,000 in addition to the unused capital powers of the original company, though lack of enthusiasm and failure to pay deposits were evident while the bill was still in Parliament.

The result was peculiar, for, in spite of provision in the Act for exchange of information, the new Western Branch proprietors so conducted themselves that in July 1818 the Eastern could minute: 'Of the Western Branch of this Canal, the Committee cannot say anything Official, having never received any Report of its proceedings, until this morning. . . . Of the Trade on that Canal, your Committee have received no authentic information.'[59]

The Western line was built by John Williams as resident engineer from Josias Jessop's plans. It was finished to Newtown in March 1819, 7⅜ miles long with 6 rising locks, though it was not reported fully completed until 7 December 1821. A 24-ft waterwheel and reserve steam engine near Newtown provided the basin and upper section with water from the Severn; the rest came from a feeder and weir at Penarth.

It seems that the cost was £53,390. Only £22,300 had been raised in shares; of the rest, £6,000 had been borrowed from the Exchequer Bill Loan Commissioners, and most of the rest had been lent by William Pugh, who in 1823 was described as 'everything in that concern',[60] a few other creditors, and the treasurers. Revenue proved small, and the concern could not in its early years pay interest on its debts. By December 1832 it was split into two parties, one led by Pugh, who thought that since opening John Williams and some of the committee had muddled the accounts and were wasting money; the other anti-Pugh, complaining that he had borrowed beyond Parliamentary powers without authority, and wanted to make use of the Loan Commissioners, that they might 'thro' the strong arm of Government, come at all the Books and Papers and have time to go through a real and efficient audit of the whole receipt and expenditure of W.P. and his assistants' during the construction period.[61] Both agreed that they wanted George Buck of the Eastern Branch as clerk and engineer.

He was appointed in December 1832, with instructions to investigate the accounts.

He reported in November 1833 to a meeting at which Pugh was not present, and which took no action. Pugh thereupon paid off at £3,268 the principal and interest due to David Pugh for land at the basin and elsewhere not paid for, and himself took over their possession and the handling of the company's receipts, counsel's opinion supporting his action. He was owed £30,351 in principal and interest, which included £4,800 of repayments to the Loan Commissioners, who were still owed £1,200 and £1,400 interest; to this had to be added the money he had paid David Pugh, and also £4,397 he paid the treasurers to extinguish their claim on the company. This total of £38,016 he then agreed to take as to £25,000 by mortgage, and as to £13,000 in shares, and himself obtained an Act[62] to validate his position and that of other creditors for £2,549, and to enable the company to raise their tolls.

In June 1835 the trade of the Western Branch was said to be producing more than sufficient to pay interest on all the mortgages,[63] but the figures we have for gross tolls for 1836–1842* give an average of £2,389, which can have left little margin after expenses and interest. As far as I know the shareholders never got a dividend. One difficulty was that the trade was unbalanced; estimated figures for the calendar year 1844 show a total tonnage of 37,010, of which all but 961 tons was upwards to Newtown. The principal items were 18,137 tons of limestone, 5,840 tons of slack and 7,667 tons of household coal. The main downwards traffic was 565 tons of timber. The provisions for amalgamating the two companies were later repealed, and each continued separate to the end.

Like the Ellesmere, the Eastern Branch from 1819 began to use iron lock gates.† In 1823 extensive repairs were done to the Vyrnwy aqueduct, which had, the committee reported, been badly built of bad materials. Every arch was fractured, and it had to be strengthened with iron bands that can still be seen. This work was carried out by George W. Buck, who had been appointed engineer of the Eastern Branch in 1819. He was from the start interested in railways, visited the Stockton & Darlington and the Liverpool & Manchester, and reported fully and perspicaciously upon the latter to his proprietors, so much so that in

* Year ending 30 June.
† A pair can be seen at the British Waterways Museum at Stoke Bruerne.

December 1833 he resigned to become one of Robert Stephenson's assistants.

Though the improvement of local roads caused many farmers to send teams direct to the limestone quarries, trade was good, helped by lowered tolls on the Ellesmere, and in 1832 the Eastern Branch carried a record number of craft. In 1836 fly-boats were running from Newtown to London. All went well till 1840, when the Eastern Branch's tonnage reached 119,562. Trade depression followed till 1844; then a revival began, thanks to the absence so far of railway competition. Here are averaged figures for the later years of the Eastern Branch:

Years Y.e. 30 June	Tolls £	Dividend per cent	Limestone tons	Total tonnage tons
1821–3	4,581	2½	32,894	74,186
1824–6	6,218	2½	48,657	100,549
1827–9	5,923	4	50,494	99,429
1830–2	5,397	4	50,275	100,083
1833–5	5,209*	4¼	53,745*	102,821*
1836–8	NK	4½	NK	NK
1839–41	5,773†	5	56,501†	113,580†
1842–4	4,748	5	47,486	97,441

* 1833 and 1834 only.   † 1840 and 1841 only.

In January 1845 a sub-committee was set up to protect the company's interests against a proposed Shrewsbury to Newtown railway, who had written to propose a deal. The committee were then told by Lord Powis that he had heard the London & Birmingham Railway were prepared to cooperate in the Ellesmere & Chester's plans to convert their canals to railways, and decided themselves to ask William Cubitt to consider whether their own canal was suitable for such conversion. Within a few weeks they had been offered £110 per share by the Ellesmere & Chester, had accepted it, agreed to participate in the Shropshire Union, and suspended their survey.

Pleasantly, they then gave 100 guineas to their clerk and engineer, 5 guineas worth of plate to the wharfinger at Carreghofa locks, and an annuity of 5s a week to their pensioner, Jane Roberts. Dividing among themselves the balance of cash in hand, they completed the transfer of the Eastern Branch to the Shropshire Union on 1 January 1847. For the time being the Western Branch remained independent and controlled by the mortgagee. It followed on 5 February 1850. (*To continue the history of the Montgomeryshire Canal, turn to Ch. XIII.*)

CHAPTER XI

The Grand Trunk and the Macclesfield

++++++++++++++++++++++++++++++++++++◆++++++++++++++++++++++++++++++++++++

FOR some fifteen years from 1790, the Trent & Mersey company was the centre of much intrigue, as it tried to extend its own influence while preventing others from cutting into its increasingly lucrative trade. We must look at the events of these years against the background of rapid canal expansion: in 1789 the link to Birmingham by way of Fradley and Fazeley was opened, and in the following year that to Oxford and the Thames. From 1789, when the Cromford Canal was authorized, to 1794, when agreement was reached upon the improvements to the River Trent, a whole waterway system was laid out in Derbyshire and Nottinghamshire. In 1793 the Grand Junction Act thrust a broad canal as far as Braunston, and in the next year that for the Ashby gave hopes that it might be continued to the Trent, and sparked off the only serious effort made to by-pass the Trent & Mersey till the promotion of the Birmingham & Liverpool Junction, which in its turn was answered by the Macclesfield.

The company's plans to extend their line eastwards from Derwent Mouth to Nottingham by means of the projected Trent Canal while simultaneously blocking the efforts of the Burton Navigation to extend upwards to the Coventry, and those of the Grand Junction company in the 1790s to persuade the Oxford, Coventry and Trent & Mersey to widen portions of their lines, and so make a broad canal to Manchester and Liverpool, have been described in *The Canals of the East Midlands*. Because it seemed obvious that the Trent & Mersey were not going to be so persuaded, and because their line, obstructed as it was by Brindley's Harecastle tunnel with its laboriously-legged boats moving first in one direction and then in the other, already seemed old-fashioned to modern-minded men, the Commercial Canal was promoted in the autumn of 1795.

Surveyed by Robert Whitworth, and later re-surveyed by Jessop, its promoters seem mainly to have been Sir Nigel Gresley, as canal and colliery owner, the Burton Navigation, some supporters of the Ashby and the Chester Canals, and certain pottery manufacturers anxious for transport competition. A barge canal was planned from the Chester Canal at Nantwich (whence there was broad canal connection to the Dee at Chester and the Mersey via the Wirral line) through a tunnel a few miles south-west of Harecastle to join Sir Nigel Gresley's canal or its extension the Newcastle-under-Lyme Junction, then to cross the Trent & Mersey at Burslem and later the Caldon branch, and pass by the Dilhorne and Cheadle coalfield to Uttoxeter and so down the Dove valley to join the wide portion of the Trent & Mersey below Horninglow. Thence it would cross the Trent below Burton and join the Ashby Canal. It thus offered the Potteries an alternative line both east and west, though if it were to serve its full purpose as a broad canal by giving Trent craft access to the Grand Junction a small part of the Coventry, and the Oxford to Braunston, would also have had to be widened.

Controversy became heated. A meeting of the Commercial promoters in October 1796 decided to seek a bill 'regardless of any party shafts that may be directed against them'; these seem to have come from the Trent & Mersey, the report of whose meeting on 17 September was said to appear 'to contain some very illiberal insinuations against the Promoters of this Undertaking'.[1] As a second string to invective, the T. & M. also made proposals to extend its Caldon branch to Uttoxeter in country the Commercial was proposing to develop. This was of course the Grand Junction's chance, but their line was still building, and it had come too soon. All they could get from the Trent & Mersey was a promise that if the Grand Junction were completed, and if the Oxford and Coventry companies would then widen the necessary sections of their lines, the Trent & Mersey would widen from Fradley to Harecastle within two years. However, it was enough to cause the Commercial's bill to fail, and so the scheme ended. The Ashby company tried to save something by a plan of its own to extend to the Trent at Burton and on to the Trent & Mersey at Shobnall, and the Chester by wondering whether it could extend as far as the Potteries, both with the support of a group of Staffordshire manufacturers, but neither had the necessary resources.

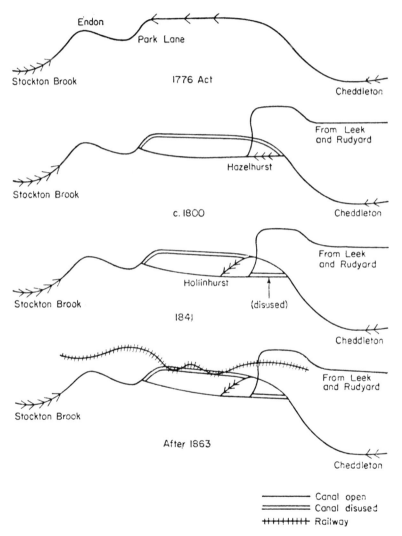

15. Plan showing successive changes in the layout of the summit level of the Caldon branch

In 1796 the Trent & Mersey, disturbed by criticisms from Commercial Canal supporters that they were unable to carry all the traffic offering, promoted a bill for a branch from the Caldon line to Leek, and a feeder thence to a reservoir at Rudyard. A large water reserve was now necessary to them, for in dry seasons they had had to draw water from the Caldon branch to supply the main line, and mitigate the disturbance to traffic by offering toll allowances for limestone carried during the winter. Certainly existing supplies would not support any increase in main line traffic. The main purpose of the bill was the reservoir, not the branch: indeed, 'The Cut is not a matter of Choice in the Company, but rather a Burthen laid upon them, by the Town and some of the Landowners, as a condition for their Consent to the Reservoir'.[2]

The bill failed, and was then briefly rivalled by a bigger scheme, with Outram as its engineer, for a line from the Peak Forest Canal near Marple to run above Macclesfield and by Rudyard to the Caldon branch about 4 miles from Leek, which also included a reservoir at Rudyard. The Trent & Mersey's bill was reintroduced in 1797 and passed in March.[3]

At that time the Caldon branch had a short 1½-mile summit between the top of Stockton locks and Park Lane, whence it fell by three well-spaced locks to Cheddleton. Since the Rudyard water had now to be taken into the top level of the Caldon, the company built a new canal south of the old line from above the first falling lock at Park Lane to Hazelhurst above Cheddleton. Here the Leek branch was continued across the old canal on an embankment, while a 3-lock staircase linked the new construction to the former line to Caldon. The old canal between Park Lane and Hazelhurst was then disused.

About 1841,* presumably because the staircase was delaying traffic, a part of the old line was reopened by cutting through the embankment of the Leek branch, the Denford aqueduct being substituted. Three separate locks were built at Hollinhurst (they kept the old name), above which the canal rejoined the previous line, the staircase being closed. Later, the Stoke–Leek railway covered portions of the original 1776 canal.

In June 1797 an Act[5] authorized an extension of the Caldon branch from Froghall to Uttoxeter, 13¼ miles long. It seems that the company first thought of building a canal, then about 1800 decided upon a railway, and then, after another Act of 1802 to vary the line, eventually started upon a canal in 1807. It was

* The date on the Denford aqueduct.

completed to Oakamoor in August 1808, Alton in May 1809 and Uttoxeter on 3 September 1811. On that day a procession of boats travelled from the town to the Churnet crossing, where their passengers picnicked and listened to speeches and songs. 'About five o'clock the company embarked on their return to Uttoxeter. . . In the evening bonfires were lit in the market place, two sheep were roasted and distributed to the poor with a suitable quantity of bread and ale.'[6] There were 17 locks on the branch from Froghall to Uttoxeter, and a 40-yd tunnel at Alton. The River Churnet was crossed on the level, with controlling locks on each side, and the Tean on an iron aqueduct. A tramroad ran from the collieries at Woodhead Hall, Cheadle, to a wharf near Jackson's Wood. Of Uttoxeter itself, a directory of 1818 said: 'The wharf belonging to the Grand Trunk Canal Company, with several large warehouses enclosed by a brick wall . . . has contributed much to the prosperity of this small but flourishing town.'[7] In 1813 there was talk of a branch from Rocester to Ashbourne, and in 1824 of a canal from the Uttoxeter branch through Ashbourne to Little Eaton on the Derby Canal, and in 1839 of another from Uttoxeter to the Trent & Mersey at Burton. Nothing came of them.

Between Froghall and the Caldon quarries a third rail line was authorized by an Act of 1802.[8] This was a double line of plateway[9] 4 miles long, on which inclined planes were used by John Rennie, the engineer, to overcome part of the 649 ft rise, and a steady upward inclination of the track the remainder. The line ran from the basin to the bottom of Froghall plane, which like the others, was worked by the weight of the descending waggons. Above it was a second bigger plane, Great Froghall. Thence the line ran to two more planes at Whiston and a fifth at Coton, after which it joined the 1780 line to enter the quarries. Finally, on the Caldon branch itself, an Act of 1831[10] allowed a straightening and widening between Oakmeadow and Flint Mill locks. At some time also before 1809 a private canal 5 furlongs long, with 1 lock, was built from the Caldon line at Foxley to Ford Green ironworks. From the terminal various tramroads ran to the ironworks and to Norton Green colliery.

There had also been developments in the Potteries. We shall come later to the independent Newcastle Canals (see p. 206). Under the Act of 1802 the Trent & Mersey company obtained powers to make railways from Stoke to Lane End, Longton; Etruria to Hanley; and Dale Hall to Burslem, and to take tolls on them.[11] That from Stoke to Longton (Lane End), the longest (2⅝ miles) left the canal a little south of City Road bridge, and rose over 150 ft to a point near Longton station where it divided, one short branch going along Market Street and another (2¾ f) down to Edensor Road. That from Etruria to Hanley (6¾ f) left Etruria wharf (on the Caldon branch below the first locks), and rose 115 ft in 7 f to Trinity Street, Hanley, with a branch to the point where Sun Street meets Broad Street. The third line left the Burslem branch canal (which had been authorized in 1797 and completed in 1805) just short of its termination, and ran up Navigation Road for 5¾ f to a point near St. John's Square.

Many other wharves were strung out along the canal in the Pottery towns. For instance, towards the middle of the century there were at or near Longport four public wharves, as well as those of four carriers, Henshall & Co (the canal company itself), the Anderton Co at Port Vale, Geo Appleby & Co at Smallbridge and Samuel Bache at Middleport. Near Etruria, and at the lower end of Shelton, there were 'spacious warehouses, sheds and accommodations . . . held by various carrying companies.[12]

Let us now pick out some events from the general history of the concern, which can only be fragmentary in the absence of the company's own records.

In April 1798 the company voted a donation of £1,000 to public funds in the crisis of the war, thereby combining patriotism with keeping up with the Oxford Canal, whose proprietors had voted a similar sum the month before. In November 1800 the committee, 'desirous of contributing their endeavours to relieve the distress of the Poor, and labouring parts of the Community, by giving encouragement to a considerable Importation of Corn, have . . . Agreed, that all Wheat imported and brought upon this Navigation after the 25th instant, shall be permitted to pass FREE of TONNAGE, and all other dues, for the space of Two Months'. This good piece of public relations combined with public feeling brought a newspaper editorial to say that 'the Utility of Canals has never been more conspicuous than at the present period. For some months past the neighbouring counties have been principally fed by wheat brought by water from Liverpool, Hull, etc.'[13]

In 1810 the company opposed the bill for the Grand Union Canal, which was supported by the Grand Junction, because the latter company was favouring the proposed High Peak Canal to connect the Cromford and Peak Forest Canals and so provide an alternative route from London to Manchester. Each agreed not to annoy the other.

In March 1816 Lord Stanhope presented to the Regent's Canal company a plan for saving water by using locks with six compartments, these being equivalent to a series of interconnected side ponds. The minute book of that company says that these 'resemble what are called the combination Locks on the Grand Trunk Canal, which we are told have been found inconvenient in practice, from the delay they have occasioned in the passage of the Trade, and are in consequence—as we are informed—about to be altered for the Common Locks'.[14] Early in the nineteenth century the staircase of three locks at Lawton was replaced by four single ones, and some curves straightened out. Most of the duplicate locks west of Harecastle were put in during the early 1830s.

We get a picture of the company's affairs from the report for the year ending 20 June 1812.[15] Income from tolls was £107,457; carrying profits £2,721; those from selling limestone £1,119, and warehousing dues £2,954. Total revenue was £114,928, the amount allocated to dividends £58,500, and the debt £116,820. Three years later,[16] tolls had risen to £123,707, total revenue to £132,362, and the dividends to £71,500. In 1820 the debt was extinguished, no less than £61,520 having been paid off in that and the previous year.

In 1823 an Act[17] authorized the building of a second tunnel at Harecastle within ten years, and a special toll of 1½d per ton per mile on goods using it. The company were also empowered to raise £60,000 on mortgage, and to build a new reservoir at Knipersley. Plans to duplicate or by-pass Harecastle had been made in 1807,[18] and the need for a second tunnel had been amply shown by a survey made by John Rennie in 1820. He recommended that the old tunnel should be closed for twelve months for repair, and in order that this could be done, suggested a tramroad over the top, or a by-pass along the Bath Pool valley, or a second tunnel. The company's report of October 1820 had, however, said that the 'proposed Tunnel is not a case of immediate urgency'. Then Rennie had died, so causing a bill to be postponed; finally it was again surveyed by Telford, on whose estimates the Act was obtained. The new tunnel, larger in section than the old, and with a towpath, was 2,926 yds[19] long. Telford was responsible for its construction, with James Potter as engineer in charge; work began in February 1825 and was completed when the tunnel was opened on 16 March 1827, having cost £112,681.[20]

It was just in time, for in May 1825 the Cromford & High Peak Railway was authorized to run from the Cromford Canal to the Peak Forest, as part of a through line from London via Leicester to Manchester, with good connections also to Nottingham and the Trent; which at the time looked like threatening seriously the Trent & Mersey's Manchester trade. A year later, the Act for the Birmingham & Liverpool Junction Canal was passed, a line which would offer a shorter and more efficient route from Birmingham to Liverpool than the Trent & Mersey. Faced with these threats, the company offered much less opposition than might have been expected to the Macclesfield Canal Act, which had been passed in April 1826. Although it, like the Cromford & High Peak, offered a shorter route to Manchester than the old Grand Trunk line via Preston Brook, it did at any rate join the Trent & Mersey, which would therefore carry for some distance on its own line goods from the Staffs & Worcs or the Coventry. However, in order that the Macclesfield should know its place, that company's Act forbade boats to pass from it through the regulating lock to the Trent & Mersey if the water level in the latter was lower, without T & M agreement. In addition, the T & M's own Act of 1827[21] empowered them to make the first 1½ miles of the Macclesfield's authorized line to Hardingswood lock, and to take 1¼d per ton thereon upon coal.

It will be remembered that the original Chester Canal Act of 1777 had empowered that company to build a line to a point at Middlewich not nearer than 100 yds to the Trent & Mersey. The latter's Act of 1827 also empowered them to build the short Wardle Green branch, with one lock, to span this distance, and join the Ellesmere & Chester's proposed Barbridge–Middlewich line to their own canal. They were, however, empowered to charge 9d per ton on coal, limestone and salt, 9½d on stone, timber and slate, and 10½d on other goods. These were stiff terms.

The canal was a highly profitable one. Under the Act of 1802, the 650 £200 shares were split into 1,300 £100 shares, and under that of 1827 into 2,600 of £50. In 1806 the £100 shares were standing at £840, the dividend being 40 per cent, and by 1811 these had risen to £1,170 and 45 per cent. In 1822 the dividend had reached 75 per cent. In 1845, when the railway threat was acute, it was still 30 per cent on shares that had been halved. The tolls were reported as £139,000 in January 1812, about the same in 1826, and were £136,450 in 1846.

Until the opening of the Macclesfield in November 1831 the company had the only line from the Midlands to Manchester and Liverpool, and not until the opening of the Birmingham & Liverpool Junction in 1835 was there a complete alternative. This monopoly position brought the usual penalties. In the course of a discussion on the projected Birmingham & Liverpool railway of 1824, a Potteries manufacturer wrote of his grievances: 'It should be observed that out of £74,580, £47,680 are lost to the Potteries, not from the regular charge of Canal freight, but because our manufacture happens to be of a bulky description, and not adapted to the Canal Company's rule of 15 tons to each boat, a boat only being capable of receiving 7½ tons of earthenware; and because the Duke's agents monopolize the carriage from Liverpool to Runcorn; and also from the necessity of carting all raw materials from the canal wharf to the various manufactories, averaging a mile of uphill draughts.'[22]

The first railway threat, apart from the projected Liverpool and Birmingham line of 1824, was that of the Grand Junction Railway from a junction with the Liverpool & Manchester at Newton Bridge (now Earlestown) to Birmingham. Though not authorized till 1833, toll reductions on general merchandise, coal and malt on the canal were made in 1832, presumably in the hope that the railway's profitability would appear less attractive. Ironstone tolls followed in 1834. The railway was opened for goods in January 1838; it and the Birmingham & Liverpool Junction Canal together brought about a steady trickle of announcements of toll reductions from 1838 onwards.

These reductions were welcomed by the carriers. One of them, Edward Bate, writing in October 1838, after saying that he had about 25 boats a week over the Trent & Mersey and Bridgewater Canals, praised the Bridgewater authorities, but said 'the Trent and Mersey Company . . . have rather sought to cripple carriers than afford them any facilities in the dispatch of their business. Things are however altered now, and what would have come better from them as a boon will now be forced from them; because competing lines will make them more accessible to reason, and an absolute necessity to protect their own interests will be the master-key to their long-needed improvement.'[23]

Let us end this section by looking at the canal's long-distance trade in and out of the Potteries as it was in the year ending 30 June 1836. Tonnage inwards totalled 143,610, made up of 129,800 tons from the Mersey, including 70,000 tons of clay and stone from Devon, Dorset and Cornwall, and 30,000 tons of flintstones from Gravesend and Newhaven, 8,260 tons from south Staffordshire, 7,000 of which was iron, 3,050 tons from London, and 2,500 tons from Manchester. Tonnage outwards totalled 184,500, of which 61,000 went to the Mersey, 51,000 being earthenware and china, 59,500 to Manchester, including 30,000 tons of bricks and tiles and 25,000 tons of coal, 15,000 tons of ironstone to south Staffordshire, 6,000 tons to Birmingham and the west of England, 1,000 tons of earthenware and china to Chester and north Wales, and 42,000 tons to London, including 30,000 tons of coal and 12,000 tons of earthenware and china. Local trade must have added well over half a million tons. Yet the busiest days of the canal were yet to come. (*To continue the history of the Trent & Mersey Canal, turn to p. 221.*)

The Newcastle Canals
(Sir Nigel Gresley's, the Newcastle-under-Lyme, and the Newcastle-under-Lyme Junction Canals)

Though a branch to Newcastle had been suggested at the time of the bill for the Trent & Mersey, its prospects were diminished by the authorization of Gresley's Canal in 1775, for the controlled prices for coal sold in the town that its Act established for 42 years gave its proprietor a virtual monopoly of the trade. When, therefore, in 1795 a separate company obtained an Act[24] for the Newcastle-under-Lyme Canal to run from Stoke on the level in a long curve to a basin at Brook Street, Newcastle, a clause provided that no coal should be carried along the new canal to the areas named in Gresley's Act as long as he was bound by minimum prices, except that for earthenware manufacture sold at under 8s a ton. Other traffics had to be sought, such as limestone from Caldon for the neighbouring ironworks and to be burnt for agricultural use in the kilns that were built at the basin. The authorized capital was £7,000 in £50 shares, with £3,000 more if necessary.

It is said[25] that the canal was completed early in the nineteenth century. Before that, the Commercial Canal project of 1796 had come and gone. As far back as 1780, the Gresleys had agreed to supply coal to the Chester Canal, presumably having it carried by land from Newcastle to Beeston,[26] and Sir Nigel Gresley probably supported the Commercial project in order that his mines could be linked directly to Nantwich. That having failed, the Newcastle-under-Lyme Junction Canal was authorized in 1798, to provide

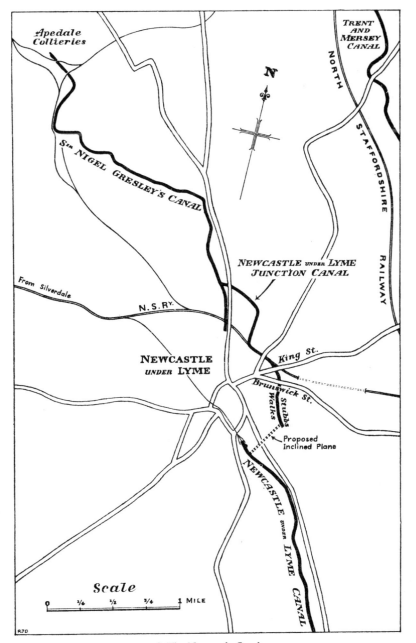

16. The Newcastle Canals

transport lines to the Trent & Mersey for Gresley's and other collieries and also local ironworks. The line was surveyed by Charles Roberts in 1797, and his map[27] shows four proposals: a railway ½ mile long from the end of Gresley's Canal at Apedale to the Partridge Nest ironworks; a canal to leave Gresley's a little short of its terminal basin alongside Liverpool road, Newcastle, and to run through the town to Stubbs Walks, 1⅛ miles long and on a level with Gresley's; a railway ¼ mile long from this point downhill to the Newcastle-under-Lyme Canal near its basin; and, quite separately, a railway from Leycett colliery to Silverdale ironworks, ¾ mile long, and another, 1⅛ miles long, from there to the Newcastle Canal basin on the opposite side to the line from Stubbs Walks.

By the time the Act[28] was obtained in 1798, the last proposal had been dropped, and the map annexed now shows the Apedale line of railway passing a little beyond Partridge Nest to Bignall End, to serve 'the Coal and other Works of Sir John Edensor Heathcote, Knight, and Thomas Kinnersly, Esquire, at Partridge Nest, and John Wedgwood,* Gentleman, at Bignall End'.[29] These three, with Sir N. B. Gresley, were the principal promoters. The authorized capital was £8,000 in £50 shares, and £4,000 more if necessary. As in the Newcastle Canal Act, the carriage of coal for local consumption (except cheaply for the earthenware manufacture) was prohibited so long as the limitation on Gresley's price remained, unless his mines proved insufficient.

It seems that the canal part of the work was soon done, though no railways were built, and in July 1799 the shareholders met to consider how best to form a communication with the Newcastle Canal,[30] and to audit their accounts. They came to no conclusion. By 12 March 1802, 97 shares had been subscribed, which would have raised £4,850 if fully paid up, and £290 had been borrowed. From that date it is unlikely that another meeting was held till April 1825, when one that had been requisitioned sought to find out the company's assets and liabilities, and appointed a part-time clerk and agent, each at £5 a year. Because their connecting railway between Stubbs Walks and the Newcastle Canal had never been built, the only traffic was probably some coal to Marsh wharf opposite Water Street, rather more centrally situated at Newcastle than the terminal basin of Gresley's Canal. The Stubbs Walks-Marsh wharf section was probably not used at all.

* This John Wedgwood was the son of John who died in 1780, and who was an uncle of Josiah Wedgwood.

XV. An account of what Hugh Henshall & Co. carried for Wedgwood's during two months of 1806

XVI. Trent & Mersey Canal: (*above*) the Kidsgrove end of the Harecastle tunnels in 1958. The new (Telford) tunnel is on the left, the old (Brindley) entrance on the right; (*below*) the abandoned Uttoxeter branch near Lord's bridge, Alton, in 1958

The first twenty years of the Newcastle-under-Lyme Canal itself were little better. Because of the failure of the Junction Canal, there was no through trade, and its finances were hopeless. The share capital of £7,000 had been raised, together with £3,518 in loans. Probably about 1815, having accumulated also a bill of £1,582 for unpaid interest, the company reduced their debt to about £2,000 by issuing 64 new £50 shares, each in exchange for £40 of debt, and paying off some in cash. At that time the gross income of the company was about £300 p.a. from rents and tolls, and £63 p.a. from the limekilns, and the reconstruction enabled them to meet interest payments on the reduced debt, to pay the not extravagant combined salaries of £15 15s od p.a. to their clerk and treasurer, and to have a small surplus. Not till November 1840 did the company manage its first modest dividend of £1 per share; for its shareholders hope had indeed been deferred.

Sir Roger Gresley, son of Sir Nigel Bowyer Gresley, died in 1837, but some ten years before that his canal had passed to Robert Edensor Heathcote, also a shareholder in the Junction Canal, and who now with Thomas Kinnersly became a partner in the Apedale mines. The restrictive clauses of the original Gresley Act having expired some years before, in 1831 the shareholders of the Junction Canal resolved once more to consider making a railway from Stubbs Walks to the Newcastle Canal's basin. A group of those interested then looked over the ground, and suggested instead that it might be more sensible to convert both Gresley's Canal and the Junction into railways, because otherwise 'the opening of a Railway between this Canal and the Lower Canal will be productive of little advantage to the Company'.[31]

Heathcote, the Junction and the Newcastle companies each paid one-third of the cost of seeking George Stephenson's opinion on the practicability of conversion. On 6 January 1832 Heathcote presented Stephenson's report, which recommended against conversion because the canal curves were too steep for a railway, but suggested a steam-operated single-track inclined plane to carry boats from one canal to the other at a cost of £2,206 plus land, cutting and embanking. At this point the shareholders tried to get Heathcote to lease the canal and the proposed inclined plane, but he refused on the grounds that they had no power to lease for more than seven years, a period too short to interest him.

So the Junction Canal continued semi-moribund, its only recorded achievement within our period being the repayment of the £290 debt of 1802 with five years arrears of interest, and the New-

o

castle struggled towards the birth of its first dividends. About Gresley's there is no information, but I assume a steady but small trade to the town of Newcastle. (*To continue the history of the Newcastle Canals, turn to p. 217.*)

Macclesfield Canal

Many projects preceded the actual construction of the Macclesfield Canal from the Peak Forest Canal at Marple to the Trent & Mersey at Hall Green west of Harecastle tunnel. Germs of the idea are perhaps in a proposal of 1765, for a canal from Macclesfield to Congleton and Northwich,[32] and later, in a letter from 'Constant Reader' in the *Derby Mercury* for 5 December 1793, who proposed a Caldon branch–Leek–Macclesfield line. This was followed in 1795 by a proposal for a canal from the Poynton collieries to Stockport that became one 'thro' Poynton and by Macclesfield to the Trent & Mersey Navigation near the Red Bull in Lawton and to the Caldon Low Canal near Leek'.[33]

At the request of 'Gentlemen of Leek, Congleton, Macclesfield, Manchester, Stockport and the West Riding',[34] Benjamin Outram, the engineer of the Peak Forest, surveyed a line and reported to a meeting on 11 March 1796 at Macclesfield. There it was agreed that a canal from the Peak Forest by way of Rudyard to the Caldon line at Endon would be advantageous, together with a branch canal or railway from Poynton and Norbury to Stockport. Outram's estimate of cost had been £90,000 and of revenue £10,175 p.a., and a subsequent meeting in April resolved to proceed. However, there was a cry of caution from those who doubted the success of the Peak Forest itself, and opposition from the Trent & Mersey, itself promoting its own branch from the Caldon line to Leek. The canal mania was over, finance was becoming difficult to raise, the mild support the project had received died away, and the Trent & Mersey were left to build their Leek branch and Rudyard reservoir.

Again, in 1799, the Peak Forest company sought powers for a branch from Marple to Poynton and Norbury collieries, but the clauses were struck out of the bill, and in 1805 and 1806 they looked round for support from the Trent & Mersey or elsewhere if they themselves were to build a line by Macclesfield to the Trent & Mersey near Lawton, and tried to find the papers and maps of the original project. There was another scheme in 1810,[35] and once more, between 1814 and 1818, the project was languidly revived.

The movement that was to build the canal began with a meeting at Macclesfield on 6 October 1824.[36] Although Mr. Wakefield 'entreated that due consideration might be given to the important question of whether a Rail Way would not be a better answer', the meeting 'seemed decidedly in favour of a canal'. Sixty thousand pounds was immediately subscribed, the committee promising to consider both ideas. They must have settled quickly on a canal, for in November a deputation of promoters visited the Peak Forest committee and were told that they foresee 'prospects highly beneficial to this concern and feel cordial interest in the success of the . . . measure'.[37] The timing probably had relevance to the simultaneous promotion of the Cromford & High Peak Railway, which was authorized in May 1825, and which was thought liable to attract much of Manchester's trade with the Nottingham–Leicester–Burton area and towards Chesterfield and Sheffield. The Peak Forest stood to gain either way, but the Trent & Mersey stood to lose less from traffic via the Macclesfield than from that taking the C. & H. P. R.

All went well. In April 1825 Telford 'most unequivocally' declared in favour of a canal[38] after having produced two reports and an estimate, and in April 1826 the Act[39] was passed, the preamble sticking to local arguments for better transport: 'Whereas the Towns of Macclesfield and Congleton . . . and their respective Neighbourhoods, are very populous, and contain therein many large Mills for the manufacture of Silk and Cotton, and other Commercial Establishments. . . .'

Among the canal's shareholders were some of the Peak Forest's supporters, notably Samuel Oldknow, behind whom stood Arkwright. Thomas Telford had done the original survey, decided between the widely-differing tenders for construction, and subscribed £1,000. He seems, however, to have taken no active part thereafter, and William Crosley must be given most of the credit for a magnificently-engineered canal. He had given up his previous job as resident engineer, north end, of the Lancaster Canal to which he was appointed in May 1817, and for which he was being paid the high salary of £500 p.a. and £50 travelling expenses, to take the post. The canal was opened on 9 November 1831[40] by two processions of boats, 25 from the north and 52 from the south, complete with bands, banners and artillery. The cost seems to have been about £320,000, not much above the estimate of £295,000.

The canal is 26⅛ miles long from Marple where it joins the

Peak Forest Canal just above the top lock of the Marple flight, to the junction with the Hall Green branch on the summit level of the Trent & Mersey. The only locks are the twelve at Bosley which carry the canal up to the 518-ft summit level, and the all-important stop lock at Hall Green that prevented loss of water from the Trent & Mersey. By the new route, a water line to Manchester was provided, 10 miles shorter than that by way of Preston Brook, but with twenty more locks.

It was born into competition, with the Trent & Mersey in Manchester goods and iron from Staffordshire, and with the Cromford & High Peak Railway, also opened in 1831, in malt and flour carried to Manchester from the Nottingham area. In 1837 the pressure of the Grand Junction Railway was also to be added.

The company's authorized rates were reduced immediately the canal opened, the Peak Forest having been persuaded also to make reductions 'without which . . . the Carriage of Goods and Merchandise betwen Macclesfield and Manchester will not be brought upon these Canals'.[41] The Trent & Mersey then cut their rates, and the Macclesfield company was back with the Peak Forest asking for a further reduction. Again in July 1833 reductions had to be made, after which limestone was being carried for ¼d per ton per mile, lime for ⅓d, coal for ¾d, and merchandise for 1d. Later, when the Trent & Mersey cut tolls, it often excluded the Hall Green branch. However, for the year 1833–4 the company paid its first dividend of 1 per cent upon its 3,000 £100 shares; the rate rose to 2½ per cent for the three years 1836–7 to 1838–9. After that competition from the Grand Junction Railway, opened in 1837 between Manchester and Birmingham, was added, bringing the rate down to 1½ per cent for 1840–1, after which no further dividend was paid till the canal was sold, but the net income (stated to have been £5,135 in 1844–5) used to reduce debt.

Following the opening of the Grand Junction Railway, a meeting of canal companies and carriers on the Manchester–London route was held to consider steam power 'applied for the purposes of Canal Navigation'[42] and in September 1838 a proposal, supported by the Birmingham & Liverpool Junction and the Ellesmere & Chester, was put forward for a canal 16 miles long with a capital of £500,000 from the Bridgewater at Altrincham to Middlewich to join the Ellesmere & Chester there. This canal,[43] the Manchester & Birmingham Junction, was surveyed by W. A. Provis, and would have provided a shorter route from Manchester to the Potteries than the Macclesfield, with less lockage and tunnels than the Trent & Mersey, as well as a shorter route from Manchester to Birmingham by eliminating the canal loop based on Preston Brook and avoiding the Trent & Mersey's compensation toll at Wardle. The Macclesfield, Peak Forest, Trent & Mersey and other companies therefore met at Stone and decided to oppose it, and the project came to nothing before reaching Parliament.

At the end of 1838 the Peak Forest company, energetic and concerned, sent its agent and another on a visit to all the canal companies on the London route. They reported back on 30 January 1839 to say that they had found the Staffs & Worcs sympathetic, but clear that 'if the Canal Companies did not reduce their Tonnage Rates the Trade would certainly leave them as the Railway Company were using every possible exertion to obtain it'; the Grand Junction was helping the Warwick line against the Coventry–Oxford and so indirectly the Trent & Mersey–Bridgewater line against the Macclesfield–Peak Forest–Ashton line, because the Coventry company, and even more the Oxford, would not reduce tolls; the Coventry vacillated, on the one hand fearing lest the Oxford might get the benefit of reductions, on the other so hating the Grand Junction that they had asked: 'Why the Devil we had not joined them in Blackguarding Bouverie,' the manager of the Grand Junction; while the Oxford, when its committee members had been run to earth in the colleges that they dignified, thought it was all a scheme by the carriers to play the railways off against the canals, and get lower tolls, and would do nothing. An accompanying table showed that the prevailing toll was 1d per ton per mile on the Trent & Mersey and Macclesfield, 1½d on the Peak Forest, 1½d on the Grand Junction, Coventry and Birmingham, and 2d on the Ashton and the Oxford,[44] a total of 28s 5d (28s 5½d via Preston Brook) on the London–Manchester line via the Macclesfield Canal. The meeting therefore decided on behalf of the Macclesfield, Peak Forest and Ashton companies to write to the Grand Junction, Coventry and Oxford companies to ask for toll reductions, and later in the year the total tolls on the route were reduced to 21s. 6¾d, or 21s 8¼d via Preston Brook. Another meeting on 27 March 1839 heard that for the nine weeks ending 2 March Pickford's had carried on the three associated canals only half the tonnage of the previous nine weeks, and later hoped that the toll reductions just made would bring 'a large quantity of heavy goods on the Canals which usually go by sea, and thereby replace the light goods which the Railway Companies are now taking'.[45] However, in 1840, the Peak Forest shareholders were told that lower receipts were due not only to depressed trade, but to the loss of 'a portion of the Birmingham and London Trade which has been taken by the Railways, and of the Staffordshire iron trade, which had been taken by the coasters bringing iron from Scotland'.[46]

So, in this cloud of competition from the railways and other waterway companies, and in the midst of the inter-canal disputes which contributed to loss of trade, the Macclesfield entered the last few years of its independent life. (*To continue the history of the Macclesfield Canal, turn to p. 219.*)

PART THREE—1845-1947

CHAPTER XII

The Grand Trunk Continues

Sir Nigel Gresley's Canal from the Apedale mines had never been joined to the Trent & Mersey by way of the Newcastle-under-Lyme Junction and Newcastle-under-Lyme Canals. R. E. Heathcote, its owner, sought better transport, and on 13 January 1835 a meeting under his chairmanship had proposed a Potteries Railway, with a branch from Etruria to Newcastle to connect with his canal to Apedale.

Then the North Staffordshire Railway, incorporated in 1846, was in the same year empowered to build a branch from Stoke to Silverdale. This probably brought the Junction company to life. It had held no meetings for many years and found its accumulated funds enough to pay a dividend of 5 per cent. In 1849 it closed and drained the Stubbs Walks section of canal, and in the same year began negotiations with the North Staffordshire Railway to sell part of the rest for conversion. In May 1851 the railway company agreed to buy the section between Brampton Lane and Hassell Street Bridge* for £1,000, the portion from King Street to Hassell Street being a siding which made use of the canal's Marsh wharf, still used by Heathcote as his depot for Apedale coals carried on Gresley's Canal. Meanwhile Ralph Sneyd of the Silverdale ironworks, seeing no probability of the branch being built, had himself constructed a line through his own lands to carry coal and iron from Silverdale to Pool Dam in Newcastle, half a mile from the basin of the Newcastle-under-Lyme Canal.

The N.S.R. branch to Newcastle was opened in 1852, and extended in the same year over the canal property to join the Silverdale & Newcastle Railway at Knutton junction, on the strength

* The railway siding seems to have extended a little on the Stubbs Walks side of Hassell Street bridge, where a small section of canal was retained as an 'Engine Pond', and is shown on Malabar's map of 1861.[1] Later the branch was contracted to the section ending beside Water Street at Brunswick Street, and the two bridges filled in.

of a guarantee by Ralph Sneyd. From this line a branch to the Apedale collieries was opened in 1856, after which Gresley's Canal probably ceased to be used. Meanwhile, at Newcastle, Heathcote's wharf was transferred to the siding, and the Junction company then proceeded to sell the rest of the canal bed piecemeal for about £545, to repay a total of £19 5s 9d on each share. It probably ceased to exist about April 1864.

The Newcastle-under-Lyme Canal itself, having managed to pay its maiden dividend of 1 per cent in 1840, seems only to have paid four others: 25s in 1843 and 1848, £1 in 1849 and £3 in 1852. For the years 1851–2 and 1852–3 the tolls were let for £480 p.a., the company maintaining the canal, and a similar arrangement may have been made for other years. For the last few years of its independence we have the following averaged figures of total revenue:

Years	Average revenue £	Years	Average revenue £
1852–4	563	1858–60	566
1855–7	479	1861–3	737

The canal company in May 1853 authorized the building of a short line, the Canal Extension Railway, to be worked by horses, from their basin to join Sneyd's railway at Pool Dam, Charles Trubshaw being the engineer. It cost £1,725, which was found from income and borrowing. The line was clearly intended to offer Sneyd a cheaper alternative to the N.S.R. branch but, as we can see, at first it had no effect upon canal receipts.

In 1859, however, Sneyd obtained the Silverdale & Newcastle Railway Act, which enabled him to run the line as a public one, and *inter alia* empowered him to agree with the canal company over the Extension Railway. He did, to the tune of 2d per ton, and for the year ending 30 September 1863 he contributed £430 to the company's tolls. However, a North Staffordshire Act of 1860 had empowered them to lease and work the Silverdale & Newcastle Railway. They later did so, and in 1863 the canal company, faced with North Staffordshire ownership of the Trent & Mersey at one end, and lease of the railway at the other, agreed to lease their own property also from 1 July.

The lease provided that the N.S.R. company should 'for ever hereafter uphold and maintain the Canal Undertaking in good and efficient Repair and working Condition'; they were to take over responsibility for canal rents and £2,000 of debt, and to pay an annual rent of £536 10s, or over 5 per cent on the share capital of

£10,200, this payment to rank before ordinary dividends or those on future preference shares. The shareholders could think themselves lucky.

The canal was then worked with the Trent & Mersey. In 1913 the N.S.R., who were thinking of building a light railway from Trentham through Newcastle to Pool Dam and the branch to Silverdale, asked the canal shareholders if they would object to partial closure. This was agreed, but the line was never built, and not till 1921 did a N.S.R. Act authorize the closure of the portion from Trent Vale bridge to Newcastle basin. The rest was abandoned under a Stoke-on-Trent Corporation Act of 1935, as unnecessary because for some years it had not been used for navigation. The land was given by the N.S.R. to the Corporation, and some was used for road widening.

Farther to the east the Macclesfield company was less active than the Peak Forest in trying to organize canal resistance to railway competition. Except for the steam boats they seem to have encouraged, and a fast passenger craft that was put on in 1842 and ran at least till 1846, they did little but make staff cuts and wage reductions, and reduce tolls until much merchandise was passing at ¾d or ½d. No dividends were paid after 30s for 1840.

When, however, the North Staffordshire Railway was promoted, the canal company in July 1845 followed the familiar gambit of threatening themselves to build a railway 'between the Macclesfield Branch of the Manchester & Birmingham railway and the lines of the proposed railways near Harecastle'.[2] It had the desired effect, for in the same month the North Staffordshire company offered them 1,000 shares to abandon their scheme and help the railway to get its Act.[3] The North Staffordshire having already agreed to buy the Trent & Mersey, the Macclesfield therefore replied that as they could 'work the Traffic on the two Canals jointly with more advantage to themselves and the Public than can be done by Companies having separate Interests',[4] the committee would recommend shareholders to lease the Macclesfield to the N.S.R. for £2 per share p.a. if the latter were willing to make such an offer.

In October the North Staffordshire proposed instead that the Macclesfield should subscribe £40,000 to their company and appoint a director, and should give the railway an option to buy within five years at 50s. a share plus payment of the debt, the canal company in any case having as favourable rates on the Trent & Mersey as any other. The shareholders rejected these terms, and authorized the committee to make a better arrangement with any railway company, or to seek powers to make a line of their own. In December the committee did indeed produce a better offer, from the Sheffield, Ashton-under-Lyne and Manchester Railway* to buy at a perpetual yearly rent of £6,605, being 50s a share on 2,642 shares, together with the payment of £60,000, the figure to which the indebtedness had been reduced.

An authorizing Act was to be sought, but in the meantime the Trent & Mersey put on pressure, 'it appearing' to the committee in March 1846 'that the Trent & Mersey Canal Co. are now charging Tonnages in a manner which is very prejudicial to the Interests of this Company as it abstracts Traffic which ought naturally to pass along the Macclesfield Canal'.[5] However, the bill went through,[6] and the canal, together with its neighbour the Peak Forest, became the property of the Sheffield, Ashton-under-Lyne & Manchester Railway, though the canal company remained in being to take the rents until 1883. Almost immediately the railway company in another Act[7] obtained powers to sell water from either canal, a practice they had already begun. The last meeting of the canal company was held on 15 July 1847. It seems that soon afterwards Farnall, the manager of the Navigation Department of the North Staffordshire, made approaches to the M.S.&L.R. for possible purchase from them, for in December officers of the latter met Ricardo of the N.S.R., who denied Farnall's authority to make any such proposition, and the interview ended without result.[8]

In 1848 the canal had a revenue of £9,049. Soon afterwards the railway company started carrying in a small way on its three linked waterways, the Ashton-under-Lyne, Peak Forest and Macclesfield, in connection with its goods trains at Guide Bridge near Manchester. In 1854, 6,894 tons were so carried on the Macclesfield out of a toal tonnage of 214,445. These carrying services were continued until 1894, and then ended on the grounds that the company was unable to get sufficient backloading of finished goods to balance the raw material, mainly cotton, being carried.

In 1905 the canal was carrying coal, though some local collieries were closing; unmanufactured cotton; grain from Manchester and other docks to local textile and flour mills; and stone. But traffic was small, and by 1954 when the Stoke-Marple coal trade ended, it had disappeared, to be succeeded by a growing number of pleasure craft.

* Later the Manchester, Sheffield & Lincolnshire, later still the Great Central.

The Trent & Mersey's trade between the Potteries, the Mersey and Manchester had not been seriously threatened by the Ellesmere & Chester's Middlewich branch, thanks to the compensation tolls at Wardle. It had been affected, however, by the opening of the Cromford & High Peak Railway in 1830, the Macclesfield Canal in 1831, and much more by the Grand Junction Railway for goods traffic in January 1838. In 1837 also there was another canal threat, the proposed Manchester & Birmingham Junction. This brain-child of the Birmingham & Liverpool Junction was proposed from the Middlewich branch of the Ellesmere & Chester near that place across the Trent & Mersey and then by Knutsford to the Bridgewater Canal at Altrincham. It would have provided a shorter route from Manchester to the Potteries than the Macclesfield, one with less lockage than the Trent & Mersey, and a shorter route also from Birmingham to Manchester by eliminating the Preston Brook loop. For this reason the Trent & Mersey, Macclesfield and Peak Forest companies opposed it, and it never came to Parliament.[9]

Tolls were steadily reduced, though often not on the Wardle or Hall Green branches in order to hamper competition from the Ellesmere & Chester and the Macclesfield. In September 1844 Pickfords asked the Staffs & Worcs and the Trent & Mersey to reduce all tolls to ¼d per ton per mile. The latter refused, and soon afterwards Pickfords ceased to carry by canal. Ironically enough the reduction was made by the company in 1847, after it had passed into railway hands.

When, in April 1845, the promoters of what was to become the North Staffordshire Railway had decided to bring together three railway schemes still on paper, the Churnet Valley, the Staffordshire Potteries and part of the Trent Valley that had been dropped by that company's sponsors, they announced bills for the 1846 session for lines from Macclesfield to Colwich, Stone to Norton Bridge, Harecastle to Crewe and North Rode to Uttoxeter, these to connect with other railways. Such complete coverage of the district naturally threatened the Trent & Mersey, and the company therefore suggested that the railway should acquire their canal; the alternative would have been Parliamentary opposition that might have curtailed, but would not have defeated, the measure. The North Staffordshire promoters were willing, for 'this amalgamation brought the North Staffordshire project into such direct and complete competition with the Trent & Mersey Canal Company—the Shareholders in which are, to a great extent, composed of influential Landowners, Bankers and Manufacturers on the Line, who had successfully resisted several attempts to form a competing Line of Railway, that it became incumbent upon your Directors to endeavour to effect some amicable arrangement with the powerful interests therein comprised'.[10] They also estimated that ownership of the canal would save them £300,000 in construction costs.

An agreement was signed on 12 July 1845. The canal shareholders secured what amounted to a guaranteed 30 per cent dividend (their current rate) until the whole North Staffordshire line were opened. Their shares were then to be exchanged for railway 5 per cent preference stock to give them 22½ per cent thereafter, with proportionate participation in further profits (until they reached 30 per cent again) after railway shareholders had received 5 per cent. It was also provided that three of the nine railway directors were to hold their qualification in canal shares. The transfer of the Trent & Mersey to the railway was to date from 15 January following the railway's Act. This[11] was passed in June 1846, the North Staffordshire taking over on 15 January 1847. The railway line was opened on 13 July 1849, and two days later the share exchange took place, the canal shareholders receiving 58,500 £20 railway shares, which gave the canal a nominal value of £1,170,000.

When the directors of the N.S.R. had come to their arrangement with the canal company, they had reported to their shareholders: 'They have no reason to believe that their tonnage will diminish after the construction of the railway, and it was considered possible, though experience can only demonstrate the fact, that by making arrangements, so that the Railway and the Canal might become mutual feeders, the one to the other, the profits on the Canal might be augmented.' An example was the interchange basin built before November 1850 at Willington junction.[12] While themselves anxious to promote rail-water interchange, the N.S.R. were equally anxious to discourage it in cases where the rails were not theirs. A business had grown up in canal company days of transferring pottery traffic from the canal to the Grand Junction Railway at Madeley station to be carried to Liverpool. The widening of the canal was considered as a means of cheapening rates and regaining the traffic; a committee reported that the cost of widening from the Potteries to Preston Brook to take 60-ton craft capable of navigating the Bridgewater Canal and also the Mersey would be £80,000.

The financial crisis of 1847 took the N.S.R.'s mind off widening, but the company encouraged canal trade in several ways. Tolls were reduced to ½d a ton, and a decision was taken to re-start carrying. Hugh Henshall & Co, the company-owned carrying concern of the Trent & Mersey's proprietors, was still in existence in 1845, though seemingly it had for many years been worked only on a small scale. It probably closed down at the time of the railway transfer, and in that case its disappearance led to a quick increase in freight charges, for, in deciding to start carrying again in July 1847, the railway reported: 'The Tonnage dues of the Navigation cannot be maintained in competition with Railways, while the freightage of Goods on the Canal is exclusively in the hands of common Carriers: the profits obtained on freights being the principal element at present in the cost of canal conveyance.'[13] The North Staffordshire Railway & Canal Carrying Co was then organized, and by the beginning of 1848 it had offices, a warehouse, and a collection and delivery service in Birmingham, for it then agreed to act as carrying agents there for the Worcester & Birmingham Canal.[14] In 1849, however, the Birmingham boats and carts were transferred to the Bridgewater Trustees, who used them to provide services for the Great Western and Shrewsbury railways.[15]

Other decisions were to cut carriers' credit, raise the charges for limestone* to the South Staffs iron trade to its economic price, introduce strict indexing and gauging, pass traffic through the canal at all hours, repair the canal property at Gainsborough and put an agent there, try to regain the Lincoln and Newark flour, malt and grain trade, and some part of the salt and timber trade between Hull and Liverpool, and later to use joint staff to operate both railway and canal. The waterway was hard worked, and its profits, over and above payments to the canal shareholders, formed for many years a substantial part of the railway's income. There was one exception; the Uttoxeter branch from Froghall was abandoned by the N.S.R. Act[16] of July 1847. The Churnet Valley line, which was seen as an effort to reach Burton and so as part of the shortest rail route from Manchester to London, was built partly in its bed.

The North Staffordshire had been planned to link together the lines of three independent railway companies, the Grand Junction, London & Birmingham and Trent Valley, but almost immediately

* Evidence on the 1847 Act gave 150,000 tons of limestone as carried annually from Froghall.

after its Act had been passed, all these, with the Manchester & Birmingham, became one concern, the London & North Western Railway. It was therefore necessary either to amalgamate or to break out. First, negotiations for amalgamation were begun, and were taken to a bill, which was defeated in 1854 by canal opposition, led by the Grand Junction Canal company. In order to try again, the two railways then asked the opposing concerns to buy or lease the Trent & Mersey. However, though they had opposed the amalgamation, and though tolls on the Trent & Mersey were higher than those of the complaining canal companies, the latter decided that purchase or lease was impracticable, and that they would settle for an agreement on the maximum tolls to be charged; the Grand Junction then threatened to appeal to the Railway Commissioners. However, the amalgamation proposals themselves were dropped, and the N.S.R. sought a means of breaking out of the ring.

The directors therefore 'entered into negotiations with the trustees of the Duke of Bridgewater for obtaining possession on a perpetual lease of the whole of their canals,* stations, wharves, dock accommodation, and warehouses,'[17] in order to get facilities at Liverpool and elsewhere for the collection and delivery of goods. The Bridgewater Canal was then feeling the full force of railway competition, and the N.S.R. reckoned that, just as they had increased the tonnage on their own canal since purchase, so by working the two canals together, they could raise that carried on the Bridgewater also. In this year of 1856 the Trent & Mersey carried 1,284,222 tons, and earned £82,658 from tolls. The proposed rent was the average profits of the Bridgewater for the previous three years, less 10 per cent.

A bill was deposited in early 1857, but later in the year the directors had to report that 'the Trustees of the Duke of Bridgewater considered themselves precluded from furnishing the complete vouchers for a large part of their estimate of the net earnings of the navigation, and the absence of these accounts, and the unfortunate calamity which occurred in the death of Lord Ellesmere, and the refusal of the trustees to agree to the nomination of an arbitrator in his stead, made it impossible to fix the rental payable for the perpetual lease of the Bridgewater navigation, and so to prosecute the bill'.[18] So the scheme fell; J. L. Ricardo, the N.S.R's chairman, and G. P. Bidder its engineer, with others subsequently

* The Bridgewater, the Mersey & Irwell, the former Manchester & Salford Junction, and the Runcorn & Weston.

considered a considerable widening programme and the running of barges on fixed services, but Ricardo died, the pressure on the N.S.R. eased, and nothing was done.

The company's carrying business probably succeeded in its aim of keeping down freight rates, even though it only carried a very small proportion of the tonnage—in 1856, for instance, 56,811 tons out of 1,481,071. For many years it made about 10 per cent on the turnover, and then declined both in profitability and in the tonnage handled. Another small source of canal revenue was from sales of limestone from the Caldon quarries: these rose from £10,709 in 1855 to £14,146 in 1865.

Though the canal was fully worked, a slow transfer of traffic to rail took place as old works and collieries were replaced by new. After 1858, when agreements ended the N.S.R's ruinous competition with its neighbours, the company had less incentive to work the canal fully, but they continued to do so, and were willing to enter into toll agreements with others, such as that made in 1864 to cut certain rates in conjunction with the Erewash, Loughborough and Bridgewater. In 1861, however, canal profits were only just enough to pay the guaranteed dividend to the canal's ex-shareholders, and the company reported that 'while encouraging to the utmost the trade for which water-carriage is adapted, the Board have at the same time felt it incumbent upon them in no way to sacrifice for this purpose the resources of the Railway.'[19] In 1864 the Newcastle-under-Lyme Canal was added to the system.

The fall in tonnage carried was less than in the revenue obtained. Here are some averaged figures:

Years	Average tonnage carried tons	Average tolls received £	Average per ton carried £
1862–6	1,611,264	86,204	12·81
1867–71	1,519,635	73,841	11·68
1872–6	1,449,941	61,189	10·09

At the beginning of 1874 the directors reported that: 'the canal has been unfavourably affected by the declining trade in potters' raw materials and in earthenware, and also, because traffic is more and more being transferred from the water to the Railway. The Railway Revenue is thereby benefited to a certain extent, but not equal to the tolls lost by diminishing trade on the Canal,'[20] and a year later that the canal tolls were no longer covering the guaranteed dividends, a situation which was 'engaging the anxious consideration of the Directors.'[21]

In the following chapter we shall see that though the opening of the Anderton lift in 1875 diverted trade from the Trent & Mersey, the N.S.R. did their best to minimize loss of revenue, as far as possible at the expense of the Shropshire Union and its backer, the L.N.W.R. In 1886 the maintenance of the canal, which since the early days of ownership had been in railway hands, was separated, a canal engineer was appointed, and the deepening of the canal to 4 ft 6 in. to cost £3,000, was approved. In the following year the company supported the bill for the improvement of the Trent, and agreed to widen the canal from Shardlow to Burton.

The building of the Manchester Ship Canal created interest in other big canal projects, among them the Birmingham & Liverpool Ship Canal, 64¼ miles long from the Weaver at Winsford to Stafford, Wolverhampton and Birmingham by way of the Potteries. It seemed wise to the North Staffordshire to make sure that, should the interest be maintained, their own canal would form part of the route. They therefore introduced a bill in 1891 to widen and straighten the Trent & Mersey between Stoke and Preston Brook, replace the existing 35 locks by 21 new ones, each 135 ft by 15 ft by 6 ft, which could take a steam barge carrying 40 tons and towing a dumb craft carrying 50/80 tons, remove the towpath through Harecastle tunnel to enable larger craft to pass, and provide compulsory tunnel towage. A petition against the bill was presented by the Chamber of Commerce for the North Staffordshire District and supported by others; they considered 'that the proposals in the Bill are not *bona fide* . . . but are made with the view of preventing the passage of the Bill for the construction of the ship canal'. Douglas Phillipps, the general manager of the N.S.R., then gave an assurance that the bill was indeed *bona fide*, though he would not accept a time limit; this was accepted, and the Act[22] was passed.

In fact, it seems that the N.S.R. only intended to move if support for the continuation to Birmingham proved reliable, for then they could foresee an increase in canal traffic that would not be merely a transfer from their own rails. This support failed and so all that was done was to widen bridges and dredge upwards from Anderton so that 50–60-ton craft could work thence to Middlewich, or a narrow boat carry 28 instead of 21 tons, and to duplicate the top lock at Kidsgrove. The company considered the new toll

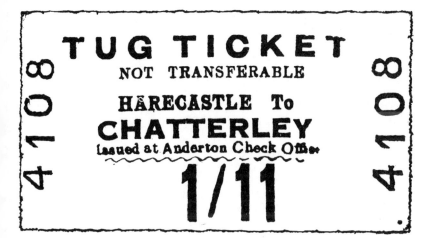

17. Tunnel tickets, Trent & Mersey Canal

schedules issued and enforced under the Railway & Canal Traffic Act of 1888 'will occasion a serious diminution of the receipts of the Canal . . . so as to reduce an income already insufficient to meet the preference interest secured to the Canal proprietors'. In these circumstances, 'it will be necessary to stop, for the time being, the progress of the improvements that were contemplated in the character and capacity of the Canal. The expenses must be limited to the maintenance of a sufficient waterway and to the most simple and essential repairs'.[23] However, a similar plan to the original full scheme was put by Phillipps to the Royal Commission in 1905.

In fact, the receipts did not fall, as can be seen from the figures opposite, due to increased average revenue per ton carried, but the company nevertheless decided to close the carrying business, which had almost always shown a profit, from 1 January 1895. In 1904, however, the company had sufficiently recovered to seek powers to provide haulage through Harecastle by an electric or other tug not driven by steam, and to charge for its use. Though the Chamber of Commerce opposed it on the grounds that traders at present used their horses without payment, and would virtually be compelled to use the tug, powers were granted, and an electric tug eventually started work on 30 November 1914. It consisted of a steel barge carrying two 15 h.p. motors driving winches which picked up a steel cable laid at the bottom of the tunnel invert, and so hauled the tug along. Power was provided by a second barge loaded with batteries weighing 18 tons. There were two such battery craft, one being in use while the other was recharging at the generating station at the south end, where two 77 b.h.p. gas engines each drove a dynamo. The time through the tunnel was halved. Later, about 1920, overhead wires laid on the tunnel roof enabled current to be picked up by the tug, and eliminated the need for the battery boats. A charge of 6d per boat, laden or empty, was made, and in theory 30 could be hauled. The tug remained until 1954, when the remaining boats using the tunnel being self-propelled, ventilating equipment was installed at the southern end of Harecastle, and the tug was removed. Until horse-drawn traffic ceased to justify them, tugs worked through Preston Brook, Barnton and Saltersford tunnels.

Here are figures of tonnage and tolls, averaged in five-year periods:

Years	Average tonnage carried tons	Average tolls received £	Average per ton carried d
1877–81	1,143,541	54,549	11·4
1882–6	1,187,692	55,722	11·3
1887–91	1,099,948	51,810	11·3
1892–6	1,096,982	49,056	10·7
1897–1901	1,190,338	48,201	9·7
1902–6	1,157,774	49,311	10·15
1907–11	1,063,038	49,834	11·3

Interchange figures for 1905, given to the Royal Commission, are of special interest as showing how through traffic, other than between the Potteries and the Mersey, had fallen away:

At	With	On to the T. & M. tons	Off the T. & M. tons
Derwent Mouth	Trent	8,866	10,417
Swarkestone	Derby Canal	3,585	3,258
Fradley	Coventry Canal	2,499	10,179
Great Haywood	Staffs & Worcs	18,945	28,478
Hall Green	Macclesfield	657	15,152
Wardle Lock	Shropshire Union	6,623	8,517
Anderton	Weaver	25,372	764
Preston Brook	Bridgewater	41,917	31,699
		108,464	108,464

(The perfectly balanced trade is just a coincidence.)

In 1849, two years after the North Staffordshire had acquired the canal, they had put in a new cable-operated 3 ft 6 in. gauge railway between Froghall and Caldon quarries to replace the earlier tramroad. It was built nearly straight on a rising gradient with three self-acting planes at Froghall (on the site of the lower plane of the 1802 route), Oldridge and Cotton. A maximum of nine waggons of 6 tons each made up each train, and up to 1,000 tons a day of limestone were carried. There was a little back traffic in coal and merchandise.

By the turn of the century the quarries were moving away from the tramroad towards Waterhouses. The Endon basin, three-quarters of a mile from Stockton locks, was therefore built as a transfer point for limestone brought by rail from the quarries. In July 1905, also, a railway was opened from the new Leek–Waterhouses line at Caldon junction to serve the new workings. Traffic now began to go by rail and caused a substantial drop in canal tonnages. In 1920 the Brunner Mond works at Sandbach, one of the principal users of canal-borne limestone, was closed. A serious slip also occurred on the canal near Froghall, and on 25 March 1920 the cable-line was closed. Transhipment at Endon basin ceased about 1930, and thenceforward the branch was little used commercially beyond Stoke itself.

Under grouping the canal was transferred to the L.M.S.R. Traffic in 1940 was 237,981 tons, most of it for the Potteries. In this year tolls were £14,378 and total receipts £24,617.

The Leek branch was abandoned as unnecessary under an L.M.S.R. Act of 1944. Coal traffic from Foxley to Leek had ended in 1934, and a small tar trade from Leek to Milton in 1939, after which the branch had been disused. On the Caldon itself clay to Stanley and felspar to Milton finished at the end of World War II, and the local coal traffic from Endon to Cheddleton about 1952.

In May 1958 a prefabricated steel tank lock with guillotine gates was opened at Thurlwood—the result of salt-pumping which had more than once cracked the old locks—and a 1,750-ft deviation at Marston. Mines had been dug to the rock salt seams at Thurlwood and Rode Heath. These were later flooded, salt pumping being substituted for mining. After pumping had ended in 1927, the River Wheelock changed its course, and part of it flowed down the shaft, causing subsidence that affected the canal in 1939 and later. By 1950 Thurlwood upper lock was affected, and from 1953 both locks were seriously damaged. To avoid a dangerous area, a new cut was built at Marston, and one of the Thurlwood locks was replaced by the present tank lock, constructed to resist any further subsidence.

CHAPTER XIII

The Shropshire Union

✦✦✦✦✦✦✦✦✦✦✦✦✦✦✦✦✦✦✦✦✦✦✦✦✦✦◆✦✦✦✦✦✦✦✦✦✦✦✦✦✦✦✦✦✦✦✦✦✦✦✦✦✦

IN May 1845 the Act enabling the Ellesmere & Chester to absorb the Birmingham & Liverpool Junction was passed. A month later the combined concern appointed a special committee 'to take the necessary steps either by a modification or extension of the existing Company or otherwise . . . for converting into Railways the whole of the . . . Canals or . . . parts . . . and to promote or undertake the execution of such Branches or extensions as shall be found necessary for the full development of the resources of the proposed lines of Railway and the accommodation of the public'.[1]

It was the year of the railway mania. The company were faced with schemes for railways all over the area within which they operated. They were already working boats on the old B. & L. J. and onwards to Ellesmere Port in trains hauled by a steam tug, and realized that the same system could not be used on the Welsh and east Shropshire lines, and that it was 'not cheaper than locomotive power now is upon Railways with good gradients'.[2] Their engineer, W. A. Provis, had also assured them that their canals could be converted to railways at half the cost of new lines. So, seeing themselves in control of a railway system that would stretch from Birkenhead to Wolverhampton and Newtown to Shrewsbury and Worcester, they decided there was no time to be lost in making an expert examination, getting powers and connecting with the general railway system. 'The steps they propose to take', they minuted, 'are not those of wild speculation . . . but . . . of defence and are intended to preserve a valuable property . . . while in deference to public opinion they avail themselves of the advantages and adopt that system of public conveyance which modern science and experience have shown to be better suited to the present wants and wishes of the country.'

This wholesale abandonment of water transport caused consternation to the Staffs & Worcs, who protested publicly that 'a stoppage of any part of the great chain of inland water communication would cripple the whole system', and decided to oppose it.[3] On the other hand, representatives of the Birmingham Canal, when told that a portion of the B. & L. J. at Autherley would be kept open, and canal traffic transferred to rail there, were personally satisfied, but did not commit their company without consulting the committee or the London & Birmingham Railway.[4] The Shropshire Union proposal probably had some effect upon the London & Birmingham's (subsequently the L.N.W.R.'s) guarantee of the Birmingham Canal Navigations.

On 24 July a meeting was held at Robert Stephenson's. The engineer proposed an amalgamation of interests to avoid Parliamentary competition, George Loch, the Duke of Sutherland's agent and a leading member of the Ellesmere & Chester's board, drew up a scheme, and the Shropshire Union was born. The plan was to bring together a number of railway and canal companies, among the latter being the Montgomeryshire Eastern and Western Branches, the Shrewsbury and the Shropshire. Some would be converted, but between 80 and 90 miles would be kept as waterway, notably the Ellesmere Port–Barbridge–Middlewich line for the salt trade, and the Shropshire and Shrewsbury Canals.

On the construction side, the company's prospectus, issued in October, made proposals for railways (*a*) from Crewe via Nantwich, Whitchurch (with a branch to Wem), Ellesmere, Oswestry and Welshpool to Newtown, to connect with a projected line to Aberystwyth; (*b*) from the North Staffordshire at Norton Bridge or Stone to the Trent Valley and Grand Junction Railways at Stafford, and past Newport, Donnington and Wellington to Shrewsbury; (*c*) from Shrewsbury along the Severn to Worcester to join the Birmingham & Gloucester Railway, with a branch from Ironbridge to Wellington and Donnington; (*d*) from Wolverhampton via Market Drayton and Nantwich to a junction with the Chester & Crewe Railway.

The proposed capital was £5,400,000 in £20 shares. Of the 84 provisional directors named, 13 were on the board of the Ellesmere & Chester, 9 of the Shrewsbury & Trent Valley Railway, and 11 of the Crewe & Worcester. The 14 members of the Committee of Management were headed by the Earl of Powis, chairman of the Ellesmere & Chester, with J. P. Westhead, chairman of the Manchester & Birmingham Railway, as vice-chairman. Of the others, 6 were on the board of the Ellesmere & Chester, 2 of the Crewe and Worcester, 1 of the Trent Valley, and 3 of the Shrewsbury & Trent Valley. The engineers were named as William Cubitt, Robert Stephenson and W. A. Provis.

Three Acts[5] were passed in 1846 for the Chester and Wolverhampton, Shrewsbury and Stafford, and Crewe and Norton lines, the fourth, from Shrewsbury to Worcester, not being proceeded with. They changed the name of the Ellesmere & Chester to the Shropshire Union Railways & Canal company, transferred the Shrewsbury to it, gave powers to buy the Montgomeryshire, and authorized a subscription capital of £3,300,000 (not counting that already in existence) with £1,100,000 more if necessary. As regards the canals, the 3,573¾ shares of the old Ellesmere & Chester, on which £133 had been called, were valued at £69 18s 4d, or £250,004 10s 5d in all; the 4,000 £100 shares of the old B. & L. J. at £37 10s 0d or £150,000; and the 500 shares of the Shrewsbury, on which £125 had been called, at £150, or £75,000. These were exchanged for paid-up S.U. stock. In addition, there were £800,207 of debts and liabilities, making a total canal capital of £1,275,211 10s 5d.

The foundation members were joined by the Montgomeryshire Canal (Eastern Branch) in February 1847, the £100 shares in which had been bought for £110 each, totalling £78,210.* The Western Branch followed on 5 February 1850, seemingly for £42,000 cash,[6] though the L.N.W.R. accountant in 1851 put the net cost at £33,036 9s 11d, most of the discrepancy being due to an alleged credit from the Western Branch for £7,000 I cannot otherwise trace. The S.U. also paid out the difference between the 1847 and subsequent annual revenues of the concern up to the transfer date. The Shropshire Canal was reported to be making £4,000 p.a., and the S.U., who had originally intended to buy it for £72,500, instead of proceeding with the purchase bill, leased it from 1 November 1849 at £3,125 p.a.

The company began with the Shrewsbury and Stafford railway which between Shrewsbury and Wellington was jointly vested in them and the Shrewsbury & Birmingham Railway company and was to be built by them jointly, and between Wellington and Stafford was S.U. alone. This line could be built quickly, and 'while it is much required by the district, its construction will not involve the loss of any revenue from the Canals'.[7]

The Shropshire Union, however, enjoyed only a few months of independence, for it had got itself too involved with ambitious and energetic railway companies. To form it, contacts had been

* £70,290 in cash, £7,920 in S.U. stock.

made, among others, with the Shrewsbury, Wolverhampton, Dudley & Birmingham project first put forward in 1844, who had received an offer to lease from the London & Birmingham. The latter saw the Shropshire Union's proposed line from Wolverhampton to Crewe as an essential part of a main line to Holyhead (with the Chester & Crewe and the Chester & Holyhead), and to Manchester by the Manchester & Birmingham from Crewe. The London & Birmingham, Crewe & Holyhead and Manchester & Birmingham all agreed to co-operate with the Shropshire Union in rivalry with the Grand Junction Railway. When, however, the Manchester & Birmingham forgot its enmity to the Grand Junction, and on 1 January 1846 joined it and the London & Birmingham to form the L.N.W.R., the Shropshire Union scheme became a dangerous rival, which now had to be controlled, to their alternative route to Crewe.

In the autumn of 1846, therefore, the L.N.W.R. offered the Shropshire Union a perpetual lease. They were to receive 4 per cent on their existing canal stock till their railways were built, and then a rent equal to half the ordinary dividends on L.N.W.R. stock on both the canal stock and the shares issued to build the railways. The canal debt was to be serviced by the S.U. out of its surplus revenue from canal operations. There were provisions for sharing surplus profits and for giving S.U. stockholders rights of participation in future L.N.W.R. share issues. Management was to be in the hands of a joint committee with equal representation from the S.U. and the L.N.W.R. At the meeting in December 1846 that approved these terms the directors said they were 'aware that, in the present state of public feeling in regard to new railway undertakings, a guarantee by a powerful Company of a certain profit would be probably more acceptable to the Proprietors generally than the anticipation of a greater profit by carrying out the scheme independently, and as originally intended'.[8]

The Act authorizing the lease was passed in June 1847[9] (though it was not completed till 25 March 1857), and the Shrewsbury to Stafford line was opened on 1 June 1849. By then much had altered. The Earl of Powis had died, and been succeeded as chairman by his son, formerly Lord Clive. The L.N.W.R., hard-pressed by its own growth, did not want the S.U. to expand also, and persuaded it to abandon the Chester and Wolverhampton and the Crewe and Newtown lines, in exchange for amending the terms of the lease to put responsibility for servicing the canal debt on the L.N.W.R. from 1 July 1849, the date when their rental payments began. No further railway works were to be undertaken, and the S.U. shares were eventually consolidated at £6 10s 0d each. The canal offices, which had been installed in newly-acquired premises in Wolverhampton upon the expectation that it would be the nub of the S.U.'s railway and canal system, were now transferred to Chester. One cannot help thinking that the L.N.W.R., in spite of the financial stringency of the time, lost great opportunities by not making use of the Shropshire Union's power to help its own expansions; later it was to lose others by its supine and negative attitude to other railway projects put up by the quite lively S.U. joint board. On the canal side, however, the directors were given a very free hand.

In March 1849 the company extended their own carrying, previously limited to the Autherley-Ellesmere Port run and the Middlewich branch, to the whole of its 200 miles of canal. From a report of 1851[10] we get a good picture of canal trade in the period 3 August 1846 to 30 June 1850. The total toll revenue had been £180,746, and six company-carrying trades were distinguished:

(a) The Staffordshire, carrying mainly iron from around Wolverhampton to Liverpool. Fly-boats were unloaded at Chester and the goods there transhipped to Mersey flats; heavy goods went on to Ellesmere Port to be stored there to await consignees' orders. At this time the trade across the Mersey and much of the accommodation at Ellesmere Port was leased to the Bridgewater trustees; in 1846, however, these also began to carry across the Mersey for the Chester & Birkenhead Railway, and probably for this reason the lease was ended in 1850. After paying tolls, this Staffordshire carrying trade made £9,407 profit in the period.

(b) The very old trade in fluxing limestone for iron making, carried from Trevor rocks above Pontcysyllte or from Crickheath on the Llanymynech branch to Nantwich or Wappenshall. Most of the returning boats loaded iron ore from Golden Hill near Burslem for the ironworks at Ruabon, the stone being carried very cheaply to get this back freight. Profit, £5,043.

(c) General merchandise between Chester and Liverpool in company's boats, but towed across the Mersey by the Bridgewater trustees. Profit, £3,338.

(d) The North trade in general merchandise for Shropshire and North Wales. Profit, £6,574.

(e) General goods from Birmingham to Liverpool. Loss, £429.

(*f*) The Chester coal trade. About October 1848 the S.U. agreed to give up part of their North trade to the Shrewsbury & Chester Railway in exchange for that from the Brymbo collieries up the canal from Chester to Beeston and along the Wirral line. It seems to have failed by 1850, little business being done. Loss, £194.

By 1850 the company was being affected by railway competition, often from lines they themselves had originally intended to build. The Shrewsbury & Chester's line from Ruabon by Wrexham to Chester, with access to a wharf on the Dee at Saltney, was opened on 4 November 1846, extended to Shrewsbury on 14 October 1848, and a branch to Oswestry opened on 23 December. The Chester & Birkenhead opened in 1840; after its extension to Cathcart Street in April 1847 its competition with the Wirral line was only mitigated by its relationship with the L.N.W.R. and, apparently, by a rates agreement reached in 1858. Rivalry was intensified when in December 1850 the Birkenhead, Lancashire & Cheshire Junction was opened from Chester across the Mersey. Farther to the south, traffic from the Horsehay and neighbouring Shropshire works was attracted from the canal at Wappenshall to the S.U.'s own joint line at Wellington station, until the opening of the Wellington & Severn Junction to Horsehay on 1 May 1857 and onwards to a junction with the Madeley line after March 1858, provided still more convenient access. An extension to the Dale was provided in 1864.

In September 1851 Lord Powis had from the chair of a shareholders' meeting attributed the decadence of canals to the number of small companies and to compensation tolls. The Shropshire Union had dealt with the first criticism, and tried to solve a case of the second when in 1852 it promoted a bill to by-pass the Trent & Mersey's Wardle branch by building a new cut 327 yds long to join that canal. The Trent & Mersey had been entitled to charge 9d to 10½d a ton compensation toll at Wardle, and it was maintained that whereas the canal-owners, the North Staffordshire Railway, had reduced many other tolls, they had kept them unaltered on most of the interchange traffic there. This toll, the S.U. argued, made the Middlewich branch 'almost useless, and . . . in effect closes the road between the ports of Liverpool and Chester and the Potteries by means of the Shropshire Union'.[11] However, the bill was withdrawn at the request of the L.N.W.R., as was another of the same year to enlarge the basins at Chester, and make an interchange point with the railways there. A second attempt at getting a bill for a by-pass at Middlewich, this time on a route that would have saved four locks, failed in the House of Lords in 1868.

On 1 September 1854 the Great Western had taken over the Shrewsbury & Birmingham's line through Oakengates, together with its branch, just opened, from Madeley junction to Lightmoor. This weighty threat may have influenced Robert Skey, the canal manager, when in January 1855 he recommended that the Shropshire Canal be converted to a railway: subsidence was affecting it, water was scarce, and the Lilleshall company was complaining. The S.U. board agreed and told the L.N.W.R., who did nothing. In July a collapse occurred in Snedshill tunnel, and in September there was another closure due to the failure of a pit-shaft improperly filled in when the canal line was diverted over it to make the Shrewsbury & Birmingham railway. More subsidences occurred in 1856—seven of them including one at Wrockwardine incline—and in September Skey wrote again that 'If there be an ironmaster who hesitates to incur the cost of connecting his property with the G.W.R., another 3 months stoppage of his Works from the failure of the only means of conveyance open to him will undoubtedly decide him'.[12]

At last the L.N.W.R. took action. It would have cost £30,000 to put the canal into repair; instead they agreed to pay the estimated cost of £80,000 to build a branch of their own to Coalport, and the expenses of the Act that was passed in 1857. This provided for buying the canal for £62,500 or £125 per share, and closing the part from the bottom of Wrockwardine Wood to the bottom of Windmill inclined planes, together with the Coalbrookdale branch, and its use where necessary for the railway. Here is a picture of the traffic on the section to be closed from August to December 1857:[13]

| Month | Boats over | | Est. tonnage at |
	Wrockwardine incline	Windmill incline	5½ tons per boat
August	336	100	2,398
September	883	542	7,837
October	490	928	7,799
November	60	595	3,602
December	776	785	8,585
	2,545	2,950	30,221

Even now the L.N.W.R. were in no hurry, though subsidence was so bad on the Wrockwardine incline that 'The Drum-Barrel &

Winding out Shaft are now so near to the Rails that the Carriage Head touches as passing under; we shall therefore be compelled to raise the whole of the Machinery',[14] and elsewhere leaks were developing, so that only 3 tons a boat could be carried. The authorized sections were in fact closed on 1 June 1858, a temporary road being built to carry traffic to the Shropshire Union Railway at Hadley till the railway branch opened to Coalport in the middle of 1861.

The incline at The Hay and the section above it probably became disused about 1894,[15] and two further sections were abandoned in 1913. The remaining level pound, 1¼ miles long, was used to carry coal from Kemberton and Halesfield collieries to Blist's Hill furnaces until they were blown out in 1912; traffic in 1905 was 29,066 tons and revenue £321. This section was abandoned in 1944. The independent Donnington Wood Canal remained open for a while. The limeworks branch and the inclined plane at Hugh's Bridge were last used in 1873, after which little traffic was carried east of Muxton bridge. After the early 1880's the only active section was the 1¼ miles nearest to the Shrewsbury Canal. This was leased to the Lilleshall company, who made some use of it until the early 1900's.

In 1853 the L.N.W.R. sought an Act for a railway from Shrewsbury by Welshpool and Oswestry to Newtown, but withdrew its bill the following year after making an arrangement with the Great Western. In 1855 the Oswestry & Newtown Railway, with four G.W.R. directors, was incorporated, and got itself open to Pool Quay on 1 May 1860, Welshpool in August, and Newtown on 10 June 1861. It was supported by some of the former shareholders of the Montgomeryshire Canal, who had sold out to the Shropshire Union because they thought that by doing so, the canal would be turned into a railway and they would be provided with better facilities. Canal coal and mineral rates had then been lowered so that tolls and freight together equalled those on the railway, and merchandise charges sufficiently to keep a fair proportion of traffic on the water. This and another competitive line, the Oswestry, Ellesmere & Whitchurch, opened in 1864, became part of the Cambrian Railways. Later, rates understandings were reached by the S.U. with the G.W.R. upon traffic to places such as Llangollen, Ruabon, Chirk and Oswestry, and with the Cambrian; in both cases canal rates were kept slightly below those on the railway.

In September 1861, speaking at the company's autumn meeting,

Skey, looking back, explained that the B. & L.J., the Middlewich branch, and the dock and warehouses at Ellesmere Port, had been built principally for the trade between Staffordshire, Liverpool and—mainly—America, one that had been brought almost to a standstill by the American Civil War, then being fought. He went on to say that by their arrangement with the L.N.W.R. the company was largely confined to this traffic, and could not seek compensation in 'the general mercantile traffic of the country, which had been suffered to be quietly transferred to rails; nor could they make arrangements for the interchange of traffic with companies south of Birmingham without coming into collision with the London & North Western'.[16] He calculated that the company's canals brought about £60,000 worth of trade a year to the L.N.W.R. It was a time when the S.U. were exasperated with their lessor, who was powerfully attacked at the September 1862 shareholders' meeting for failing to use Shropshire Union powers to get railway possession of Shropshire and Montgomeryshire.

Meanwhile, in 1860, the committee had decided to convert the Pontcysyllte tramroad thence to Afon-eitha to a locomotive line. The L.N.W.R. agreed, and it was decided to buy land privately for diversions, and not to seek an Act. Work began at the end of 1861. The line, including an extension to brickworks at Llwynenion, was opened in sections, and completely by 30 January 1867. For a time it was worked by a locomotive provided by the New British Iron Co, but at the end of 1870 the S.U. bought an 0-4-0 shunting engine from Crewe works.

In 1870 the company, anxious to save money on the maintenance of Trench incline, agreed to lease Lubstree wharf on the Humber Arm of the Newport branch from the Duke of Sutherland and pay a wharfage rate of ½d a ton, so that the coal and other traffic from Lilleshall could be shipped there. To carry it, 30 boats were taken from the company's fleet, and others ordered to replace them. New accommodation was provided, and a railway line built from Lubstree to the Lilleshall Company's works.

In the same year also the company, worried about the state of the channel up the Mersey to Ellesmere Port, bought land for a possible canal extension downwards to Pool Hall Deep, just beyond Mount Manisty and half-way to Eastham. They also considered a locomotive line from the Hooton & Helsby line of railway to the docks at the Port, but because they could not decide which side of Whitby Locks station would make the best junction, they laid down a temporary horse railway along the road from the station to the Port. This was completed in the autumn of 1870, and carried mainly coal, for which a coal tip was provided.

Occupying property at Chester basin, Liverpool, the company was engaged in cross-river barging not only to Ellesmere Port but also to Birkenhead. In 1869 they suggested that the L.N.W.R. should transfer to them the railway's cross-river trade with private carriers. This was agreed, and the S.U. thereupon in 1870 bought William Oulton's lighterage business, which operated from Canning Dock. They paid £4,800 for stores and 13 barges varying from 80 to 130 tons. Soon afterwards they concentrated their operations on the Liverpool side by moving most of them to new quarters at Manchester basin. In 1883 the business of the Mersey Carrying Co was also bought for £4,275.

Competition, and the limitation of Shropshire Union carrying to certain trades, had meant that very soon after the L.N.W.R. agreement to lease, the canals had ceased to pay their way, in the sense of being able to provide the full interest on their debt or any dividends. The interest on debt alone was £34,473 p.a., and this figure was not earned in any year after 1850. The balance of interest, and dividends half those of the L.N.W.R.'s ordinary shares, were therefore paid by that company. On the other hand, the canal business did make a substantial surplus over expenses until the end of the sixties. In the following figures it must be remembered that the income is mainly from carrying rather than tolls:

Years	Average receipts £	Average surplus £	Average dividend £ s d		
1848–50	104,638	45,885*	2	12	6†
1851–3	105,120	27,008	2	13	4
1854–6	128,483	25,122	2	11	8
1857–9	115,586	19,730	2	5	10
1860–2	102,800	11,366	2	3	4
1863–5	101,798	11,055	3	0	5
1866–8	123,619	12,266	3	1	3
1869–71	143,976‡	11,727	3	8	9

* 1848 and 1849 only.
† 1850 only.
‡ 1869 and 1871 only.

In 1858, 855,462 tons in total were carried; in 1868, 742,315 tons.

Bishton's contract for horse haulage had continued to the midsixties, when the company took it over, seemingly to give them flexibility in changing to steam should this prove desirable, though in fact very little steam haulage was done except on the Ellesmere

Port to Chester section. Horses were considered to be cheaper, and most of the fleet remained horse-hauled to the end. The carrying business was sizeable. In June 1870 the fleet consisted of 213 narrow boats, 168 of which were moving merchandise and only 45 coal, stone and lime; 65 Mersey flats and 11 floats; 12 tub-boats; and 2 river and 4 canal tugs. Of the 213 narrow boats, 77 worked in the Staffordshire trade, 56 in that to Shropshire and north Wales, 24 to the Potteries, and 45 carried fluxing stone. Few boats were needed for the Chester and Birmingham trades. During the 1870s this fleet was greatly expanded, as the company's turnover grew from £120,066 in 1869 to £193,088 in 1876; it was a brave effort, but the gain was at the expense of profits, which fell between the same years from £12,995 to £1,568. At the end of 1889 the fleet had grown to 395 narrow boats, 197 of which were in the merchandise trade, 66 moving coal, stone and lime, and 88 in the boatage business. There were 101 Mersey flats and 15 floats; 5 tub-boats, and 3 river and 5 canal steam tugs.

Boatage services—that is, carrying to and from railway transshipment basins, mostly on the Birmingham Canal Navigations, the Stourbridge and the Staffs & Worcs Canals—was a business growing in importance. Attached to it were services the S.U. rendered the L.N.W.R. in unloading traffic at the basins, for instance, at Spon Lane, Greatbridge, Tipton and Bloomfield; in managing railway depots; and in providing railway cartage services at Chester and in the Potteries. The contributions of the Mersey cross-river, boatage and cartage operations to total revenue can be seen from these figures for the four months, June to September 1889:

	£	s	d
Tolls	2,159	9	10*
Cartage	3,708	3	5
Cross-river trade	4,764	5	10
Boatage	10,113	4	10
Canal carrying	59,116	12	1
Total	79,861	16	0

* Paid by independent carriers.

In May 1888 an experiment was carried out over about a mile of the Middlewich branch near Worleston, at the suggestion of Francis W. Webb of Crewe works, the L.N.W.R.'s Mechanical Engineer, with the haulage of boats by small Crewe locomotives running on 18-in. gauge track. With two and then four loaded boats the locomotive* moved at 7 m.p.h., and subsequently it pulled up to eight. Two months later G. R. Jebb, who had been appointed canal engineer in 1869, reported on the probable cost of providing rails; after that nothing more was heard of the experiment.[17]

From the 1870s onwards the future of the Welsh lines of canal, that to Weston, and later part of the Shrewsbury Canal, was in doubt. In 1873, for instance, Jebb suggested that the line from Llangollen to Weston be converted to a narrow-gauge railway and extended to Wem. In 1875 and again in 1885 the closing of the Weston branch was considered; in 1887 the Montgomeryshire Canal was examined, and reprieved because it was making the tiny profit of £432; in 1899 the closing of the Eyton–Shrewsbury part of the Shrewsbury was looked into because of the bad state of the Longdon aqueduct. All were in fact kept open, mainly perhaps because of the legal problems involved in closure by a railway company, though by 1905 there was little coal tonnage from Chirk and the old 40,000 tons a year trade in fluxing stone had almost disappeared. The possibility of a different future for the Llangollen line was foreshadowed when in 1886 a second passenger boat was put on the Llantisilio–Newmarton run. In 1905 such boats ran regularly in summer between Llangollen and Berwyn and Llangollen and Chirk; twenty years later horse-drawn boats were running daily between Llangollen and Llantisilio, and twice-weekly from Llangollen to Chirk.

In 1880 the Humber Arm was only carrying fluxing stone, though two years before the iron ore toll from Ellesmere Port had been specially reduced for the Lilleshall Co. Negotiations for its better use followed, and the company agreed to take 300–400 tons a week of limestone and 100–150 tons of ore at agreed rates. The S.U. also hoped for a coal trade outwards, and pig-iron to be carried for transhipment to the L.N.W.R. Business seems to have remained brisk for some time after that, for in 1891, when the wharf lease was renewed, another siding was built. In 1905 it was renewed for another fourteen years.

The company, already operating the Wellington–Stafford line and that at Pontcysyllte, soon found itself working a horse tramway. By an Act of 1870, slate and other interests obtained an Act

* The engine was probably either *Dickie* or *Billy*, which could be driven from either end. These were built by Webb, and were later than five of Ramsbottom's, one of which, *Pet*, is at the British Transport Museum at Clapham.

(not the first) for a horse line, the Glyn Valley, down the Ceiriog valley, but could not raise the necessary £10,000. They approached the Shropshire Union, who agreed in mid-1871 to subscribe £5,000 (in fact, £6,000) on condition that it could control construction and work the line. George Jebb, the canal's engineer, was appointed to the tramway board, and in April 1873 the line was opened to a canal wharf near Gledrid, and exchange sidings with the G.W.R. near Preesgwyn station.

The S.U. bought waggons and in April 1874 put on passenger cars, but though the quarrying of granite setts soon replaced slate as the main traffic, the line lost money, and relations became strained between the tramway shareholders and the S.U. Finally, on 31 August 1881, the S.U. gave up operating the G.V.T., having lost £7,061 by it, and another £2,630 in selling its works and plant, though it realized that by doing so it would lose much of the tramway's trade to the G.W.R. In 1888 the line was converted to steam, with a new canal connection at the Blackpark colliery wharf beyond Chirk tunnel, mainly for shipping roadstone.[18]

In 1879 the extension of the Pontcysyllte Railway beyond Afon-eitha seems to have been disused, for the rails were lifted to renew other sections. Two years earlier the line had carried 17,706 tons and worked at a loss of £248, though, taking canal business into account, there had been an overall profit of £309.

In the eighties, however, works near Pontcysyllte began to close down: in 1882 Kenrick's spelter works went out of business, and in 1887 the New British Iron Co, a main user of the railway, went into liquidation. When, therefore, in 1895 the G.W.R. introduced a bill for a railway from Wrexham to Rhos, and offered to buy the S.U.'s line if the company would withdraw opposition which had probably only been made for the purpose, a sale was agreed on 13 November, and the line and 25 vehicles were handed over on 12 February 1896. The existing train service of two trains a day to the canal wharf was maintained, and differential rates in favour of canal carriage left undisturbed. The line from Rhos to Wrexham was opened on 1 October 1901. The Plas Kynaston Canal, now owned by the Wynn estate, was still open in 1904 but needed repairs; it seems to have been out of use by 1914.

The Weaver trustees had since their Act of 1866 been widening, deepening and improving their river and reconstructing its locks. This potential threat was discussed by the S.U., N.S.R. and Bridgewater trustees, accustomed by now to confer regularly on traffic matters, and in November 1867 the N.S.R. reduced its net rates on earthenware between the Mersey and the Potteries. By 1870 the threat had become real, and in April the N.S.R. and Bridgewater reduced charges for salt in bulk via Preston Brook. In May they again discussed the 'action recently taken by the Weaver Trustees, with a view of diverting Traffic to their Route, and also to the alleged reduction in Rates, which was being offered by that Route'[19] and agreed on cuts in the rates on potters' raw materials, followed in July by those on iron, and in August by the N.S.R.'s decision to charge full Parliamentary tolls on traffic exchanged at Anderton.

In September 1870 the S.U. learned that the Weaver Carrying Co (it was run by a former N.S.R. goods manager) were quoting a 9s. rate from Liverpool to south Staffordshire, but held their own 10s rate firm. Thanks to the N.S.R.'s Parliamentary tolls, the carrying company then retired from business, the S.U. taking over some boats. In March, however, a new carrying business was formed, the Traders (North Staffs) Carrying Co., supported by the chairman of the Potteries Chamber of Commerce, Godfrey Wedgwood, and some ironmasters, to carry via Anderton, seemingly having absorbed the carrying business of Joseph Davies, the originator of the competition on the Weaver route. By January 1872 the Weaver trustees were sufficiently encouraged to seek a bill to build a lift at Anderton, and the opposition of the N.S.R., S.U. and Bridgewater collapsed, some of their rates being raised.

'Large and increasing quantities of goods are there interchanged . . . by means of steam hoists, inclined planes and other machinery', the bill's preamble said, describing Anderton, and elsewhere there are references to salt shoots. Because these arrangements were time-consuming, costly, and led to there being more traffic downwards than upwards, the trustees thought a more efficient means of transfer necessary. The Act[20] passed, and permitted a charge for passing the lift of 1d a ton and 1s a boat. The S.U., still paying 9d to 10½d at Wardle, wrote to the N.S.R. to protest, only to be told that the 1d was not a compensation toll but a charge for the use of the lift, and that the Wardle toll would remain. In fact it survived until the new rates structure resulting from the Railway & Canal Traffic Act of 1888. The lift was opened in August 1875, attracting to itself traffic that had formerly passed by Runcorn and the Bridgewater as well as by Ellesmere Port and the Middlewich branch. In 1886 it was made free to those who had paid Weaver tolls.

In May 1874 discussions upon a pooling agreement for traffic took place between the N.S.R. and the S.U. This grew into the North Staffordshire Conference, to which the Bridgewater also belonged, which was operative by 1890. It covered rates and carrying matters, and had as a principal object the exclusion of private carriers. In 1905 a pooling agreement was also made by the S.U. with the Mersey, Weaver & Ship Canal Carrying Co, to cover Mersey Ports-Potteries traffic. The Anderton Company, also carriers, were included, and in 1912 the agreement was renewed for another seven years, as was another with the Mersey, Weaver and Northwich Carrying Co covering the Liverpool/ Birkenhead and Middlewich traffic.

The Manchester Ship Canal was authorized in 1885. Its line ran between Ellesmere Port and the river, and while it was being built from Eastham a gap was left in the embankment opposite the dock entrance so that ships could get in and out. This gap was closed at the third attempt, and the first Ellesmere Port traffic passed down the ship canal and through Eastham lock on 16 July 1891,[21] passage being free for ships of the size that had usually traded there. The former tidal basin was given double gates at its entrance to the ship canal, along one side of which a new quay wall, 1,800 ft long, at which ships up to 4,000 tons could lie, was built at a cost of £37,850 to the Shropshire Union. The ship canal itself was finally opened on 1 January 1894.

The interest in canal enlargement caused by its construction led the S.U. early in 1890 to estimate the cost of rebuilding their line to Autherley to take larger craft: this Jebb put at £895,475 or about £13,500 a mile. In the autumn, however, they were discussing with the North Staffordshire Railway a contemporary scheme for a large canal from the Mersey through the Potteries to Birmingham, a development of an earlier plan of 1888 for a 300-ton line thence from Liverpool. The N.S.R. were then considering the enlargement of the Trent & Mersey westwards of the Potteries, seemingly to make sure the large canal project did not by-pass them (*see* p. 226), and suggested the S.U. also should improve their route to the Potteries. Though the N.S.R. plan came to little, improved facilities on the Mersey led to a growth in Potteries trade that was reflected in the spending by the S.U. of a good deal of money to provide better wharves and warehousing at most of the Pottery towns.

A plan of Ellesmere Port in 1882 shows a china clay shed and warehouse, grain and iron warehouses, and one for general mer-

18. Ellesmere Port in 1882

chandise; in 1884 a new iron warehouse costing £10,292 was added. In the twenty years from 1892 to 1912, and partly influenced by the Manchester Ship Canal, about £170,000 was invested in Ellesmere Port. Apart from the quay wall, the old horse tramroad that passed from the Hooton & Helsby line along the streets was replaced by a mile-long locomotive branch and the necessary sidings, and a new grain warehouse costing £80,000 was built on the north quay. In the next decade a dock arm was constructed and then extended, and more land was bought.

At the opening of the 6-storey grain warehouse on 10 May 1899, it was said that when the Shropshire Union had been formed, there was a large trade in iron ore and pig-iron brought to the Port by coasting vessels to be carried to south Staffordshire, and a back-carriage of manufactures. Later a new trade had grown up in flints, china-stone and clay for the Potteries, earthenware and iron being brought back. Latterly much foreign grain was being imported at Liverpool and brought to the Port in the company's barges, for which the new warehouse was needed. About 140,000 tons a year of coal was also being shipped, providing back loading for many ships that discharged there. The speaker went on to say that express and fly-boats delivered to Birmingham in 35 hours and the Potteries within 24, and finished by remarking that the traffic from Liverpool to the Port had increased by 85 per cent within the preceding twenty years, 45 per cent of the increase being in grain.[22] Later, in 1906, a new barge dock, to take Mersey lighters drawing 7 ft, was built at the Port.

In 1903, in the course of enforcing the Canal Boats Acts, the company authorized the engagement of 'a Lady Inspector who would be able to visit the Cabins and exert a beneficent influence, especially in seeing that the children attend school.'[23] After consultation with the vicar of Ellesmere Port, a nurse was appointed at £1 p.w. She was a success, and another later succeeded her. The family population of the boats, however, had already fallen considerably, probably as a result of the Acts:[24] In 1884, on 363 boats, there were 189 women and 151 children; in 1902, on 450 boats, only 151 women and 97 children.

In 1905 there were few by-traders, and almost all carrying was done by the company—in that year they handled 469,950 tons. Except for tugs on the Ellesmere Port to Chester section, towing was by horses—328 owned by the company and 94 by steerers— and daily services were run on the main line, with locks open at most hours. From the early seventies to the end of the century the

Shropshire Union canals had only earned small surpluses of receipts over expenses, which took no account of interest payments on debts or of dividends, nearly all of which had to be paid by the railway company. In the 1900s the situation improved, only to collapse with the war. Government subsidies then helped to meet the losses, but as soon as the ending of these was announced, the L.N.W.R., itself soon to be abolished under a measure to regroup the railways, saw no reason to continue financing losses that, owing to the rise in wage rates, were likely to be much larger than before the war. Here are the figures:

	Average receipts £	Average surplus £		Average dividend £	s	d
1872–4	172,660		6,715	3	13	9
1875–7	189,949	loss	6,444	3	6	8
1878–80	172,701	loss	93	3	7	11
1881–3	183,348*		3,674*	3	14	2
1884–6	177,438	loss	1,228	3	5	0
1887–9	190,151		4,327	3	8	9
1890–2	180,352†	loss	7,171†	3	9	2
1893–5	172,067	loss	11,485	3	6	8
1896–8	179,192	loss	1,131	3	11	3
1899–1901	185,425	loss	1,973	3	2	11
1902–4	205,075‡		5,986‡	2	18	11
1905–7	217,983		11,426	3	2	11
1908–10	225,469		13,549	3	0	10
1911–13	251,088		10,246	3	7	11
1914–16	235,110	loss	14,262	3	0	0
1917–19	193,256	loss	139,484	3	8	4
1920–2	227,845§	loss	153,318	3	15	0

* 1881 and 1882 only. † 1891 and 1892 only.
‡ 1902 and 1904 only. § 1920 and 1921 only.

At the end of 1920 the Shropshire Union company had boat families on 202 boats, 127 of them having no other home. The total boat population was 592. On 1 June of the following year the company gave notice that 'as the period of Government Control of this Undertaking ceases on August 14th next, the Company, after serious consideration, much regret to announce that it is found impossible to continue their carrying business under economic conditions'. They therefore proposed to stop all carrying from 31 August, including that on the Mersey 'though until further notice the Waterway will be maintained in the hope that the Public will make use of it by their own or hired Boats on payment of toll'.[25] The principal reasons given were the extensions of the eight-hour day to boat and river men, increased wages, and the higher cost of materials.[26] About 60 men were found employment with the L.N.W.R.; of the rest, the older men were compensated, and those of the younger who had ten years' service. Some of the boats were taken over by local firms. For instance, the Peates of Maesbury Hall mill took eleven, one being *Cressy*, later owned by L. T. C. Rolt. The Chester & Liverpool Lighterage Company began a general carrying business between Liverpool and Chester; former customers for the cross-Mersey services made future arrangements with these or other carriers. Later, the company recorded that by their action they had reduced the loss on their canals from £98,384 in 1921 to £26,473 in 1922. In the same year of 1921 the locks were closed from 10 p.m. Saturdays to 6 a.m. Mondays, being left open but unattended from midnight to 4 a.m. on other days. Next year tolls were reduced by 15 per cent to match similar reductions in railway and road rates.

Other changes also took place. In 1915 passengers ceased to be carried on the Mersey steamers, alterations to which to comply with the Merchant Shipping (Life Saving Appliances) Act 1914 were not considered justified. In 1916 the payment of £36,000 p.a. made to the Shropshire Union by the L.N.W.R. for boatage services in south Staffordshire was increased to £42,500. In 1920, however, for economy reasons, the L.N.W.R. took over cartage at Birmingham and Chester, and in January 1922 the boatage services, 100 craft being transferred to the railway company. The services in the Wolverhampton, Kidderminster and Stourport areas were maintained by the L.M.S.R. and British Railways until 1 November 1950: those in the Birmingham area till 1 April 1954, when the remaining 61 narrow boats were withdrawn.

The Manchester Ship Canal Company now became lessees of the Shropshire Union estate at Ellesmere Port for 50 years, and took over the working of the port, a joint committee with the S.U. (now with the British Waterways Board) being maintained to supervise capital expenditure and the general conduct of business. The Ship Canal company then spent £23,000 on deepening ship canalside berths. Across the river, the carrying department's former accommodation at Liverpool was taken over by the Great Western Railway.

At the end of 1922 the Shropshire Union company was absorbed by the L.N.W.R. A great deal of the S.U. stock had already been exchanged for that of the L.N.W.R., but £352,432 worth remained, of which all but £22,277 10s, held by 29 shareholders, was owned by the L.N.W.R. or its nominees. In accordance with the Railways Act 1921 which grouped the railways, and under the provisions of the L. & N.W.R. (S.U.R. & C.C.) Preliminary Absorption Scheme 1922, the outstanding S.U. stock was exchanged for L.N.W.R. on the basis of £50 L.N.W.R. for each £100 stock. A few days later the L.N.W.R. itself became part of the London Midland & Scottish Railway.

In 1929 the canals still carried 433,230 tons. By 1940 this was down to 151,144 tons; in this year tolls were £17,763, and total receipts £40,985, of which £10,362 came from the Shropshire Union's share of Ellesmere Port. An L.M.S.R. Act of 1944 abandoned the whole of the former Montgomeryshire Canal from Newtown to Carreghofa, together with the Guilsfield branch; the Llanymynech branch to Frankton junction and that to Weston; the line from Hurleston junction, including the Prees, Whitchurch, Ellesmere and Llangollen branches; the old Shrewsbury Canal from Shrewsbury to Donnington, with the Newport branch and the Humber Arm; and the remaining section of the Shropshire Canal.

The Frankton–Newtown line had carried 8,992 tons in 1923. Users in later years were the Chester & Liverpool Lighterage Co., who carried 242 tons in 1930 and withdrew from the line in 1931, and the Peates of Maesbury mill, who imported grain from Ellesmere Port in their own boats. In spite of toll reductions from 4s 5d a ton in 1921 to 2s, they went over to road transport in 1934, greater convenience and the steadily deteriorating condition of the waterway probably both being factors. In 1935 Jones, Evans & Co, flannel manufacturers of Newtown, who used 400 tons of coal a year, closed down, and the sole remaining user was a by-trader, George Beck, who in 1935 carried 974 tons of coal, timber and sand. Then, on 5 February 1936, a burst in the canal bank occurred near Frankton, through which a mile of canal emptied itself. The railway estimated that some £16,000 would be needed to restore the breach and length; instead they paid George Beck £80 compensation, and on 14 July 1937 gave notice of intention to apply for a warrant of abandonment. There were objections (though not on navigation grounds), and the Minister refused his consent in order that the company should seek an Act.

The Weston branch had burst at Dandyfield in May 1917, navigation being thereafter limited to Hordley wharf, ¾ miles from

Frankton. Restoration was estimated to cost £14,000, which the railway company were not inclined to spend. Protests, however, compelled a reference to the Board of Trade, who in 1920 decided that its prospects did not justify restoration. As for the rest of the line, no commercial traffic had passed between Frankton and Llantisilio since 1937, or between Frankton and Hurleston since 1939, and very little since the burst on the Welsh section in 1936.

On the Shrewsbury line, the basin there was abandoned in 1922 to save the cost of a new swing bridge at the entrance. On 31 August of the previous year the Trench inclined plane, the last at work in Britain, had passed its final boat, and the canal above it had become disused; for some years its only traffic had been wheat upwards to Donnington Wood mill. In 1922 the Duke of Sutherland decided to close Lubstree wharf and the rail line to Lilleshall, thus ending traffic on the Humber Arm. A further section of the Shrewsbury was abandoned in 1939, from the old basin entrance to near Comet bridge in the town. No traffic had passed to the town since 1936, though a little coal continued to Longdon till 1939. By 1943 100 tons a year from Newport was the only traffic on the Newport branch. Finally, the remaining section of the old Shropshire Canal, just over a mile near Madeley, had been disused since 1913.

To the abandonment of all the canals listed in the 1944 L.M.S.R. Act, some 175 miles, including others as well as so much of the Shropshire Union system, no one objected on navigation grounds (though early in the war the Montgomeryshire War Agricultural Executive had asked for the restoration of the Newtown line for war transport purposes). The many objectors were all concerned with such matters as water supply and liability for bridge repairs. Out of the clean sweep one line was saved, that from Hurleston to Llantisilio, together with the Ellesmere branch. It was needed as a water channel, and so survived long enough for a water-supply agreement to be sought and negotiated in 1955 by British Waterways with what is now the Mid and South East Cheshire Water Board, so enabling the canal to be kept open for pleasure use also. It has become very popular with holidaymakers.

This, and the main line from Autherley to Ellesmere Port, is all that survives of the old Shropshire Union. The last regular traffic from Ellesmere Port via Chester to the Midlands, the tar boats from Stanlow, ended in 1957–8; much earlier, in 1932–4, the River Dee branch ceased to be used when the Shotton–Ellesmere Port steel traffic ended.

CHAPTER XIV

Birthmingham and Stourbridge

✦✦✦✦✦✦✦✦✦✦✦✦✦✦✦✦✦✦✦✦✦✦✦✦✦✦✦◆✦✦✦✦✦✦✦✦✦✦✦✦✦✦✦✦✦✦✦✦✦✦✦✦✦✦✦

THE Birmingham company's amalgamation with the Wyrley & Essington only succeeded in maintaining the previous level of the Birmingham's receipts. Then came a period of strain, with colliers' strikes, shortage of water on neighbouring canals, and some railway competition. The Tame Valley, Bentley, Rushall and other canals built since the Act of 1835 had cost £636,793 to 1844, when power was taken[1] to raise another £130,307 to complete them. Interest on these sums had to be paid, and the dividends for the April–September half-year of 1843 and the two following years could only be maintained by drafts on reserves; in addition, from the corresponding half-year of 1844, the rate was dropped from 5 to 4 per cent upon the 17,600 shares into which the 8,800 outstanding after amalgamation with the Wyrley & Essington had been divided.

In 1844 the ironmasters near the canal line between Birmingham and Wolverhampton had pressed for a railway to connect with the London & Birmingham and the Grand Junction Railways, so that they could compete with the Scottish and Welsh works. The canal company then suggested that they themselves should build the line, and got the consent of most works proprietors; perhaps they thought of passenger-carrying as an additional motive, following the starting of a 'line of swift packet boats' between the two places in the summer of 1843.[2] The railway idea was taken up by the supporters of a line from Shrewsbury, and became a scheme for a line from that town to Wolverhampton and then beside the canal to Birmingham. This was supported by the London & Birmingham company, who provisionally agreed to lease it as part of their plan to extend to the north-west in competition with the Grand Junction Railway. When, however, the two agreed to amalgamate into the London & North-Western, the London & Birmingham withdrew its offer, and the Shrewsbury & Birmingham, left on its own, reduced its ideas to a line from Shrewsbury as far as Wolverhampton, leaving the difficult section from Wolverhampton to Birmingham to be built by a separate company. On 22 May 1845 the London & Birmingham made a provisional agreement with the Birmingham Canal Navigations jointly to build this line together with a branch to Dudley. The canal company was to sell the necessary land at a reasonable valuation; the railway profits were to go first to maintain a 5 per cent canal dividend, and thereafter to be shared; the line was to be built and worked by the London & Birmingham, but managed by a joint committee. Each agreed to cede one-third of its half interest to the Shrewsbury & Birmingham if that company was itself incorporated in the next session and supported the project.

During the summer the London & Birmingham Railway and and the B.C.N. agreed upon a guarantee of the latter's dividends by the former, and the B.C.N., with L. & B.R. support, then renewed its earlier invitations to the Dudley company to amalgamate. The latter, threatened by the passing of the Act for the Oxford, Worcester & Wolverhampton Railway and by the B.C.N.'s own plans, agreed, seeing no other way of preserving the value of the company's shares, for, 'unless some arrangement of this kind were entered into, the revenues of both Canals would be seriously impaired'.[3] Agreement was reached on 8 October, the amalgamation being ratified by an Act[4] of 1846 after opposition from the Worcester & Birmingham, who wanted a reduction in the bar toll. They got it. The 2,060¾ £100 shares of the Dudley were added to the 17,600 of the B.C.N. to make a new total of 19,660¾, a debt of £24,000 also being transferred. The Dudley company's separate existence ended on 27 July 1846.

On 1 November 1845, a final agreement was made between the London & Birmingham, the Shrewsbury & Birmingham and the B.C.N., by which the three companies agreed to seek powers to make two railway lines, one from Birmingham to Dudley and Wolverhampton and on to the Grand Junction Railway at Bushbury, the other from Smethwick to Stourport, and also to authorize the arrangement already made between the London & Birmingham Railway and the B.C.N., by which the railway company would lease the canal in exchange for a 4 per cent guaranteed dividend on the shares as increased by the Dudley canal amalgamation. Control was to remain with the canal company as long as the guarantee was not called upon, though toll changes or expenditure of more than £500 on new works would require railway agree-

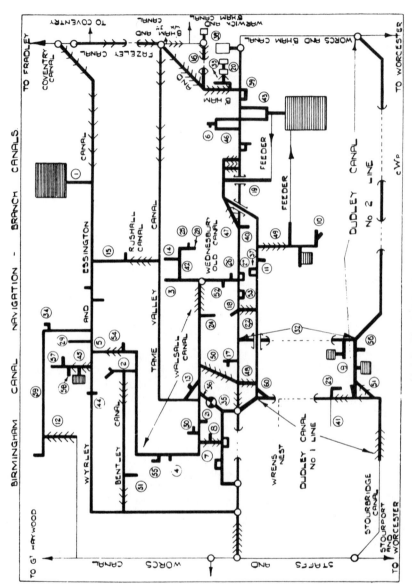

19 (a). The Birmingham Canal Navigations

BRANCH CANALS

1 Anglesey
2 Anson
3 Ball's Hill
4 Bilston
5 Birchills
6 Birmingham Heath
7 Bradley
8 Bradley Locks
9 Bumble Hole
10 Causeway Green
11 Chemical Arm (Houghton)
12 Churchbridge
13 Danks
14 Dartmouth
15 Daw End
16 Digbeth
17 Dixon
18 Dunkirk
19 Engine
20 Gibson's
21 Gospel Oak
22 Gower
23 Grazebrook
24 Haines
25 Halford
26 Izon
27 Izon Old Turn
28 Jesson
29 Lord Hay's
30 Monway
31 Neachells
32 Netherton Tunnel
33 Newhall
34 Norton Springs
35 Ocker Hill
36 Ocker Hill Tunnel
37 Oldbury Loop
38 Old Wharf
39 Oozell's Street
40 Parker
41 Pensnett
42 Ridgacre
43 Rotton Park Loop
44 Short Heath
45 Sneyd Locks
46 Soho
47 Spon Lane Locks
48 Tipton Green Locks
49 Titford
50 Toll End
51 Two Lock Line
52 Union
53 Union (Roway)
54 Walsall Locks
55 Willenhall
56 Withymoor
57 Wyrley Bank
58 Essington Locks
59 Cannock Extension
60 Lord Ward's

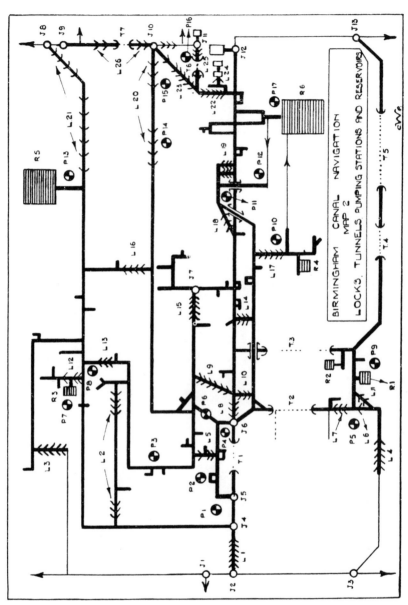

19 (*b*). The Birmingham Canal Navigations

LOCKS

L.1	Wolverhampton	(21)	L.14	Brades		(3)
L.2	Bentley	(10)	L.15	Rider's Green		(8)
L.3	Churchbridge	(13)	L.16	Rushall		(9)
L.4	Delph	(8)	L.17	Oldbury		(6)
L.5	Bradley	(9)	L.18	Spon Lane		(3)
L.6	Blower's Green	(1)	L.19	Smethwick		(2 x 3)
L.7	Park Head	(3)	L.20	Perry Barr		(13)
L.8	Tipton Factory	(3)	L 21	Ogley		(30)
L.9	Toll End	(7)	L.22	Farmer's Bridge		(13)
L.10	Tipton Green	(3)	L.23	Aston		(11)
L.11	Two Lock Line	(2)	L.24	Gibson's		(1)
L.12	Sneyd	(5)	L.25	Ashted		(6)
L.13	Walsall	(8)	L.26	Minworth..		(14)
				Curdworth..		

PUMPING STATIONS

P.1	Stow Heath	(S)	P.11	Smethwick	(R)
P.2	Bradley	(S)	P.12	Smethwick Engine	(R)
P.3	Herbert's Park	(S)	P.13	Cannock	(R)
P.4	Moat	(S)	P.14	Perry Well	(S)
P.5	Park Head	(R)	P.15	Perry Barr	(R)
P.6	Ocker Hill	(R)	P.16	Ashted	(R)
P.7	Sneyd	(R)	P.17	Rotton Park	(R)
P.8	Walsall	(R)			
P.9	Lodge Farm	(R)	*Note:* Supply		(S)
P.10	Titford	(R)		Recirculating	(R)

TUNNELS

T.1	Coseley		T.4	Gosty Hill
T.2	Dudley		T.5	Lappal
T.3	Netherton		T.6	Ashted
			T.7	Curdworth

RESERVOIRS

R.1	Lodge Farm		R.4	Titford
R.2	Gad's Green		R 5	Cannock
R.3	Sneyd		R.6	Rotton Park

JUNCTIONS

			J.7	Rider's Green
J.1	Autherley		J.8	Huddlesford
J.2	Aldersley		J.9	Whittington Brook
J.3	Stourton		J.10	Salford
J.4	Horseleyfields		J.11	Proof House
J.5	Deepfields		J.12	Worcester Bar
J.6	Bloomfield		J.13	Selly Oak

ment. The lease was confirmed in 1846 by an Act[5] which also turned the current level of tolls into maxima, and from the beginning railway influence upon the canal company was predominant.

By this time the L.N.W.R. had replaced the London & Birmingham. In the same year, one of the two projected railway lines, from Birmingham via Wolverhampton to Bushbury with a branch from Dudley Port to Dudley, was authorized as the Birmingham, Wolverhampton & Stour Valley Railway. The B.C.N. had originally agreed to subscribe £277,500 towards its construction, but early in 1847 the L.N.W.R., then arranging to lease that also, agreed that the amount should be reduced to £190,087 10s, upon which the B.C.N. would receive from the L.N.W.R. a dividend equal to two-thirds of that upon L.N.W.R. ordinary stock, which meant in practice that the B.C.N. were allotted £126,725 of L.N.W.R. stock and received the dividends. The Stour Valley's main line was opened for goods traffic in February 1852.

The Birmingham area was notable for the size of the short-haul traffic between mines and works within it. In his evidence upon the O.W.W.R. bill of 1846, Richard Smith, agent for Lord Ward, had estimated that in the Dudley district alone there were about 120 furnaces each making 90 tons of iron a week, each ton requiring about 7 tons of material. These furnaces alone therefore called for about 3,600,000 tons to be carried. It was moved by canal, and by a network of small tramroads varying from 20 in. to 3 ft 6 in. gauge, mostly horse-operated, with a few 4 ft 8½ in. locomotive lines as well. The O.W.W.R. itself were proposing very cheap rates for journeys over 6 miles, but said that they did not want the short-haul traffic, while C. A. Saunders of the Great Western commented that a railway 'is not adapted to receive large quantities of minerals to be carried from works for short distances upon it because it interrupts and obstructs the traffic upon the main line. I do believe a Canal better adapted to short distances of traffic between the Mines and the Works'.[6]

A combination of this theory and the fact that many collieries and works stood beside canals and had no rail access led to the system by which canal boats worked short journeys between them and railway interchange basins, playing rather the same part as a lorry working to a rail depot would now do. For such traffic, therefore, the railway companies were prepared strongly to support canal transport. In February 1855 the traffic manager of the O.W.W.R. urged the completion of railway basins at Tipton and Wolverhampton, 'as it will be impossible to secure the heavy

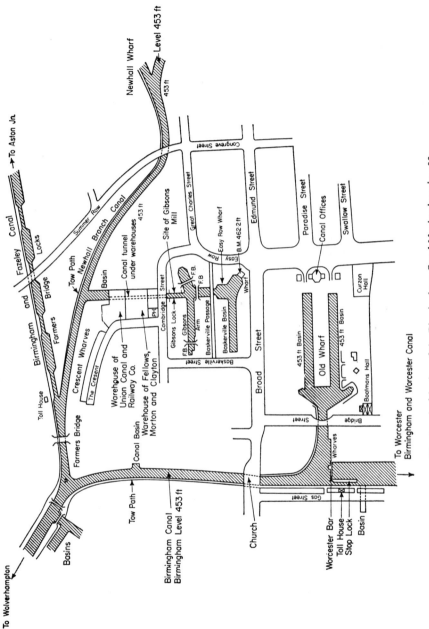

20. The terminal basins of the Birmingham Canal Navigations in 1884

weight of traffic from works on the Canals until we have the means of loading to and from the boats direct into the Railway waggons';[7] six months later he reported them complete, and said, 'we shall shortly be in a position to collect and deliver Traffic at the various Works, almost all of which are on the Canal side'.[8] In February 1856 he reported that his company had itself bought boats to collect iron and other materials, and that traffic was increasing.[9]

The Birmingham company's extensions built since 1840 had proved successful, and in 1854 a further programme was authorized,[10] the L.N.W.R. raising no objection so long as no higher dividend than 4 per cent were paid until the debt on the proposed works had been paid off. It provided for the building of the Cannock Extension Canal from Pelsall to Hednesford, with two tramways joining the canal at Norton Springs and Hednesford from Littleworth, an extension towards Cannock Chase of Lord Hay's branch, an extension of Vernon's branch along the Wyrley & Essington's original line to Wyrley Bank, and the replacement of the Delph locks on the Dudley line. A year later the Netherton tunnel branch between the Birmingham and Dudley extension lines was authorized,[11] together with the Two-Lock line and the Bumblehole straightening.

The Netherton tunnel, 3,027 yds long, was the last canal tunnel to be built in this country. The first sod of the branch was turned on 31 December 1855 by Lord Ward in the presence of 300 or so gentry, ironmasters and others,[12] and the tunnel was opened on 20 August 1858. It was exceptional in having two towing paths (the Coseley tunnel, 360 yds, on the B.C.N. and the second Newbold tunnel, 250 yds, on the straightened line of the Oxford canal also had double towpaths), and unique at the time in being lit by gas, later replaced by electric light. It was also wider than any other canal tunnel built in Britain, 27 ft at water level, including the paths, against the 26 ft 6 in. with towpath of the Strood tunnel of the former Thames & Medway Canal, by this time used for trains.[13] Strood with its one towpath had, however, a water width of 21 ft 6 in. against Netherton's 17 ft, and a height from the bottom of the invert of 35 ft against 22 ft 9 in. The estimated cost had been £238,000, but 'the district through which the tunnel went was peculiar, the land was perforated by mines, and liable to sinking and shaking'. The company 'did not expect to be compelled to carry an invert for more than three-fourths of the length; but they have been obliged to do so for the whole distance, and to build heavy and massive retaining walls at each end'.[14] The final cost was about £302,000, and a tunnel toll was imposed to help pay for the extra expense of maintenance and interest on capital.

The building of the Netherton tunnel was accompanied by improvements to the Dudley Canal. The Two Lock line joining the original and extension lines was built, Brewin's tunnel opened out, and the old flight of nine locks at Delph replaced by eight,* all in 1857 and 1858. Later, in 1893–4, the two locks below the junction with the Lappal line at Park Head were replaced by the present single Blowers Green lock. About the end of 1857 also, the Wyrley Bank branch was completed, and at the beginning of 1863 the Cannock Extension, the company hoping that 'the facilities thus afforded for developing the mineral resources of that very important district, will . . . secure early attention on the part of the public, to the advantages which it holds out'.[15] About this time also the 1¼-mile feeder to Cannock reservoir was opened out into a navigable canal, the Anglesey branch, which entered at the top of Ogley locks. It tapped new coal-mines that were being sunk by the Marquess of Anglesey.

In 1864 the company summarized what it had done since 1825. The improvements of 1825–9 had cost over £500,000, and had reduced haulage charges by 4d a ton; those of 1835–9 had saved 6 miles in haulage charges and had reduced tolls by 9d; including the Titford Canal, they had cost £200,000. In 1839–43 the Tame Valley, Bentley and Rushall Canals had cost over £570,000; in 1855 the Cannock Extension and Wyrley Bank branches over £100,000; and in 1855–8 the Netherton and other improvements over £350,000. The total was about £2m, and except for the tunnel toll there had been no increase in charges, and some reductions, while the dividend had been reduced from £5 to £4.

Receipts, which had averaged £176,161 in 1851–3, had risen to £196,290 for 1864–6, but the gap between them and operating costs and interest payments was narrowing, partly because of the improvements themselves. In respect of the year 1867 the company for the first time could not pay their dividend from income, but by agreement with the railway drew upon a suspense account. In 1868, however, the railway guarantee was called upon. Then the company was once more in surplus till 1874, from which year the L.N.W.R. was to pay an increasing proportion of the canal's dividend, and so to have a greater say in policy.

* The new flight utilized the top and bottom locks of the original flight, and provided six new ones between them.

Tolls as a percentage of total receipts tended to fall, and other income, such as rents, to rise. The amount needed to pay a 4 per cent dividend changed according to the number of shares issued, but it never varied greatly from the sum of £47,314 3s 2d required in 1876. The following figures, taken at five-yearly intervals, show the trends:

Date	Total receipts £	Tolls £	Tolls as percentage of receipts per cent	Working expenses and interest £	Expenses as percentage of tolls per cent
1877	220,162	211,154	96	173,209	82
1882	212,618	NK	—	171,530	—
1887	182,217	172,324	94½	NK	—
1892	192,400	181,335	94	173,140	95½
1897	203,883	191,688	93½	165,278	86
1902	197,546	181,758	92	176,400	97
1907	199,935	179,888	90	173,406	96½
1912	189,270	167,504	88¼	169,448	102
1917	186,695	148,795	84	144,165	97
1922	236,516	188,363	80		
1927	203,648	166,226	82		
1932	148,293	110,150	74		
1937	140,791	104,560	74		

Tonnage carried had meanwhile risen steadily, but with shorter hauls. The 1848 figure of 4,696,192 had increased to 6,982,773 in 1868, 7,713,047 in 1888 and 8,627,074 in 1898, the gross receipts from £114,005 in 1838 to £208,036 in 1898.

Later events can be quickly listed. The Cannock Chase line grew in importance and remained busy till recent times. In 1884 Dudley tunnel was closed and the south end rebuilt; it was re-opened on 23 April 1885, and in its later days carried coal and limestone south, and blast furnace slag north. Between 1886 and 1891 there were meetings and discussions in Birmingham and elsewhere about possible ship canals from Liverpool, the Humber or the Severn. The compulsory review of canal tolls that followed the Railway & Canal Traffic Act of 1888 and resulted in a series of Tolls & Charges Acts in 1894 was thought likely to lead to a considerable reduction in the company's receipts (they did not do so), and this expectation led the L.N.W.R. to refuse to guarantee interest on the capital required to build two inclined planes on the system at Walsall and West Bromwich.

Evidence taken by the Royal Commission gives us information

upon the state of the B.C.N. in 1905. The system then had 159 miles of canal, excluding some 550 private basins and short branches, with 216 locks. Water was supplied from reservoirs at Cannock Chase, Rotton Park, Lodge Farm and Sneyd, but most supplies came from mine pumping by the South Staffordshire Mine Drainage Commissioners or private engines. In addition, the canal company maintained thirteen stations of their own, mainly to pump water back from lower to higher levels of the canal. The cost of all this pumping was about £11,000 p.a.

Traffic in 1905 was 7,546,453 tons, of which 6,170,288 was both loaded and discharged on the canal, the balance coming from or going to one of the connecting canals; the average haul was 8 miles (of coal alone 18 miles), and the average toll 5·52d, a figure we may compare with the 7·61d of 1846. Of the 6 millions odd of internal tonnage, 1,108,172 tons was discharged at, or loaded from railway-canal interchange basins. The G.W.R. had ten of these, handling 469,387 tons; the L.N.W.R. thirteen, handling 481,094 tons, and the Midland Railway three, with 157,691 tons. For this railway basin traffic, in short hauls to and from canal-side works, the average toll was 1·7d (G.W.R. basins), 4½d (L.N.W.R.) and 4·66d (M.R.). The busiest parts of the system were the main line and the Wolverhampton locks, where 24-hour working existed, and on the Netherton tunnel and Dudley extension lines.

In 1894 the Dudley Canal from Blackbrook junction, including part of the top of the Two Lock line to Blowers Green, fell into old mine workings and was closed for a considerable time. The Two Lock line, heavily affected by subsidence, was finally closed in March 1909, and Lappal tunnel since June 1917, when part fell in. Lord Dudley's Pensnett Canal became disused in the 1940s, except for a short section to the Harts Hill Iron Co which lasted until 1950. In 1951 the Dudley tunnel ceased to be used commercially. In 1954 an Act closed the Wyrley & Essington main line between Ogley and Huddlesford, together with the Sneyd, Wyrley Bank, Lord Hays and part of the Hay Head branches. The Cannock Extension, seriously affected by subsidence, ceased to carry commercial traffic in 1961, and was abandoned in 1963 between Watling Street and Hednesford basins.

After the first world war the canal company suffered much from strikes and industrial depression, only managing to keep business by successive toll reductions. Therefore toll receipts slid down, from £272,858 in 1920 to £168,092 in 1925, £132,020 in 1930, and

£115,359 in 1935. Then came a period of more sudden decline, among the causes being the beginnings of coal movement by lorry, the closing down of old canalside industrial premises under rationalization schemes, and the shutting of old power stations. The war accelerated the breaking of old habits, and by 1944 toll revenue was £88,805. Even in 1949, 1,219,607 tons were carried on the B.C.N., 664,385 being coal, much of it to power stations, but by 1964 the figure had fallen to 339,181 tons, of which 153,802 tons were coal.

The South Staffordshire Mines Drainage Commissioners were wound up in 1920, and a new drainage board took over. The B.C.N. were at that time paying by instalments for four plants bought in 1914, of which only Bradley survived in 1965. In that year the water supply of the B.C.N. was maintained from reservoirs at Cannock, Rotton Park, Titford and (if needed) Lodge Farm, Sneyd being no longer used, and also from pumping from the old shaft at Bradley. Plant for pumping back was only maintained at Titford (Oldbury) locks, not so much for the little traffic through the locks, as to lift water from the Wolverhampton level into Rotton Park reservoir via the summit feeder.

Stourbridge Canal

After the Stourbridge Extension Canal had opened in 1840, the dividend of the Stourbridge rose, more water had to be provided, and the hours at which the locks were open increased.

In 1844 the company sent a deputation to the Board of Trade to object to the Oxford, Worcester & Wolverhampton Railway, then proposed, and followed it in February 1845 with a petition to the House of Commons that railway companies should be compelled to charge fairly as between passengers and goods. In the same year the canal committee was allowed to spend up to £1,000 in opposing railways. Nevertheless, the O.W.W.R. was authorized with a main line that partly paralleled the Stourbridge and Dudley Canals, though the opening of that unfortunate company's line from Droitwich to Stourbridge and on to Dudley in 1852, and through to Tipton at the end of 1853, seems to have had little effect for many years. Indeed, consideration in November 1852 of a reduction in tolls 'in consequence of the supposed competition of the O.W.W.R.' resulted in a resolution 'that there is no sufficient evidence . . . to warrant any reduction of tonnages'.[16]

However, the company found in 1854 that at least one private basin was being used to tranship goods from canal to rail, and resolved 'that the most energetic steps be immediately taken to remedy this matter and that legal measures be taken accordingly'.[17] This caused the O.W.W.R. to offer, and the canal to accept, a charge on all goods so transhipped of 1d a ton on raw materials and 1½d on manufactured goods, and in 1858 the railway agreed to put a siding on Stourbridge wharf for transhipment.

In March 1855 the Birmingham Canal company proposed amalgamation with the Stourbridge, perhaps with encouragement from the L.N.W.R. to penetrate the territory of a Great Western satellite. The Stourbridge stipulated five Birmingham railway-guaranteed 4 per cent shares for each Stourbridge share, and frightened the bigger company off. The smaller still had, however, great industrial resources behind it, for in 1856 six ironworks and a tinplate-works were listed on the summit level, apart from those on the Extension Canal, as well as collieries, glassworks and firebrick works.[18]

In 1865 the company obtained an Act to bring their position up to date: it stated their capital to be £90,000 in 900 £100 shares, and gave them power to get additional water and to charge mileage tolls when lockage was not payable, so settling the old summit level dispute. In 1866 it is recorded that 32 boats a day passed the 16 locks. From the sixties a quorum at shareholders' meetings was rare, as the outlook of the concern became narrower. In 1873 the committee were empowered to oppose or make terms with the proposed G.W.R. line from Stourbridge to Kidderminster, and did oppose it in 1875 and 1876. In 1873 the dividend for the first time fell below £12 per share, and the company applied to the Birmingham as successors of the Dudley to make it up, but liability was disclaimed. Learning wisdom, therefore, they opposed the Gloucester & Berkeley's bill to take over the Worcester & Birmingham until a clause was inserted protecting the guarantee the latter had given.

In 1883 the toll revenue was £3,276 and the total revenue £4,121. Takings continued to slide until in 1894 they reached £1,695 for tolls and £2,671 in all. Then the new toll structure created by the Railway & Canal Traffic Act of 1888, which adversely affected so many companies, seems to have benefited the Stourbridge, bringing the toll revenue for 1896 up to £2,718. In 1904 the company began a programme of dredging and improvement which for some years was financed by dividends, but thanks to which, and so to maintained local trade, they did reasonably well till motor lorry days. Their last good year was 1929, with tolls of £3,750, receipts of £5,270 and a 3 per cent dividend (almost 4½ per cent on the original capital). The large difference between toll and total revenue was made up of rents, loading charges, water sales, income from investments, and dredging done on a repayment basis. Thereafter tolls slid away until in 1938 they were down to £1,717. In this year the operational profit was only £222, the dividend being paid from non-toll revenue. In 1946 the toll revenue was lower still at £1,278.

In the succeeding years commercial traffic almost ceased, but the sixteen locks were restored from 1964 onwards by the combined efforts of the Staffordshire & Worcestershire Canal Society and the British Waterways Board, so that the canal might be used by pleasure craft.

Stourbridge Extension Canal

The canal returned a profit of £1,047 for its first full year to 31 March 1842, and paid a dividend of £3 10s 0d a share. Results then fell off due to poor trade, but for the year ending 31 March 1845 the dividend was £4 10s. 0d. The traffic was mainly coal and iron downwards and ironstone upwards, some of the coal being bound for the Birmingham & Liverpool Junction, from which concern the Extension company had some difficulty in getting its money.

Early in 1845 the company was busy watching for dangers from competing railways, and in April petitioned against the O.W.W.R. On 31 May 1845, however, a provisional agreement was reached with that company 'for the conditional sale to the said Railway Company if incorporated of the said Canal',[19] the railway being anxious to get access to such a promising source of coal and iron traffic. The authorizing Act[20] was passed at the end of 1846, the sale doubtless having been facilitated by Francis Rufford of Belbroughton, who was a member of the committee of the Extension canal* as well as chairman of the O.W.W.R.

The Act, which also enabled the railway to buy the Stratford-upon-Avon Canal, provided that both canals were to be efficiently repaired, kept navigable, and supplied with water. Canal charges were not to be higher than those in force at the passing of the Act;† there was to be no undue preference, and power was given

---
* He had joined it in 1844 when Francis Rufford of Prescot died.
† 2d a mile on everything.

to the Treasury or Department concerned with the supervision of railways to intervene, if necessary for the interests of the public, to require the railway to correct or prevent inconveniences or evils which appeared to have arisen as a result of railway ownership, and, if action were not taken within six months, to introduce the necessary legislation at the railway company's expense.

On 24 February 1847 the minute book referred to 'the great traffic now upon the Canal',[21] and on 27 March the O.W.W.R. took possession, the price paid being £49,000, being the share capital repaid at par and the £9,000 of loan debt. It now happened that the Extension canal was, with the Stratford & Moreton Tramway[22] which they had leased, the sole source of revenue of the unfortunate O.W.W.R. It was therefore worked to its utmost, carrying in the ten years 1850–9 an average of 502,013 tons a year, and is an unusual case of a canal under railway ownership greatly increasing its receipts and its profits after being taken over in spite of high maintenance costs due to subsidences. Here are figures:

Years	Average receipts £	Average profits £
1842–4	2,628	768
1845–7	3,926	1,331
1848–50	4,052	2,078
1851–3	5,108	2,956
1854–6	5,905	3,522
1857–9	5,295	3,532

A report of 1856 listed on the canal 6 ironworks together containing 17 blast furnaces, 3 forges and 2 mills, together with several collieries.

On 14 November 1858 a short branch railway was opened to the canal at Bromley basin, and afterwards some of the traffic was transhipped there instead of passing the Stourbridge Canal. This Kingswinford mineral branch was extended from the basin to Oak Farm in 1860, and in 1925 was linked to Oxley junction near Wolverhampton.

In July 1860 the canal passed to the West Midland Railway, formerly the O.W.W.R., and soon afterwards to the G.W.R. In 1888 the tonnage had fallen to 129,656 and the revenue to £1,460, and in 1898 to 163,534 and £1,500, but the canal was still showing a profit. In 1890, out of 117,707¾ tons carried, 67,533 was coal and coke (56,922 tons of it slack), 23,871¼ tons iron, 3,064 ironstone, and 23,239½ tons bricks, sand and other cargoes. Of this same total, 71,030½ tons, including 41,070½ tons of the coal and almost all the iron, was only carried a mile on the canal, and another 22,936¼ tons a mile and a quarter. Only 2,833½ tons went the full distance. In 1905 the revenue was £1,524, and the main traffic was in coal and iron. Not until after World War II did the canal become completely disused.

CHAPTER XV

The Lines to the South

From Birmingham water lines ran to the Severn by Stratford and Tewkesbury, by Worcester, and by Stourport.

The Avon Line

In 1842 the Stratford Canal company[1] leased the Upper Avon for five years, but did not renew it in 1847. Such little traffic as the upper river carried was threatened by the O.W.W.R. as soon as it should be open to Evesham. After its opening traffic died away, and the proprietors failed to sell the navigation to the local landowners for as little as £150. Therefore in 1857 they ceased to take tolls, and the upper river lay virtually abandoned. The local traders then persuaded 'John Broughton the local manager for the O.W.W.R. at Stratford, himself to buy the navigation for £300, though clearly in the interests of his company. Broughton was succeeded by Hudson; the O.W.W.R., after having changed its name to the West Midland, by the Great Western. Less and less was done, till in 1875 the G.W.R. announced that it would no longer take tolls or maintain the works. An application for reopening was made to the Railway Commissioners, but a judgement of 1877 agreed that the railway company had power to surrender the management; after that the navigation slowly decayed. Subsequently, a number of proposals were made to reopen the line, and since the restoration of both the Stratford Canal and the Lower Avon, there has been renewed interest in such a project.

The Lower Avon was first leased to the Worcester & Birmingham Canal company in 1830, and again in 1851 for another 21 years. Trade was maintained to the opening of the railway from Evesham to Ashchurch in 1864, but then fell away until in 1872 the receipts were only £139. The lease was not renewed and under various managements the navigation struggled on, the scarce barges being supplemented by a growing number of pleasure craft.

During World War II the river became unnavigable above Pershore, and it seemed as if the rest would soon follow. In 1950, as the result of initiatives by local interests and by the Inland Waterways Association, the Lower Avon Navigation Trust was formed to restore the navigation. Large amounts of money were raised, and in 1962 the river was once again open to Evesham, and in 1964, after the rebuilding of Evesham lock, to Offenham.

The Worcester & Birmingham & the Droitwich Canals

The opening of the Birmingham & Gloucester Railway in 1841 seriously affected the W. & B.'s trade. The dividend had to come down, there was price-cutting, and even then the railway had 'in some instances . . . taken Minerals and other heavy Goods which seem legitimately to belong to the Canal'.[2] An effort to buy the Coombe Hill Canal in 1844 to safeguard the Cheltenham coal trade was not, however, followed up.

In 1845 the canal company had itself issued a scheme for a railway from Birmingham to Worcester with a branch to Redditch. They received sufficient applications for shares to persuade themselves that, instead of using the plan to invite an offer to purchase, they might actually carry it out. In October they began a survey with R. Boddington as their engineer. Then came the panic of late-1845; applications for shares were withdrawn and the company therefore repaid deposits and settled the expenses.

In 1847 much of the salt from Stoke Works began to be carried by rail, and increasingly the company were to lose a profitable traffic. They realized that they must get the goodwill of traders and 'keep alive the interest now felt in our well doing by the whole commercial community',[3] and therefore began a carrying business in 1848, not, they said, in the interests of profit, but in order to withstand railway competition. In Birmingham they allied themselves with the North Staffordshire Railway & Canal Carrying Co, who were willing in surprisingly modern terms, to 'collect, receive, dispatch and deliver all your Goods for a definite charge per Ton' and to 'have the name of your Company painted on their Waggons'.[4]

The Worcester & Birmingham's lease of the Coombe Hill Canal ended in 1850, and while they were negotiating for its renewal at a reduced rent, the Staffs & Worcs leased it instead. To preserve their coal trade, therefore, they joined the Midland Railway in building a rail siding at Tewkesbury, so that waterborne coal could be sent thence by rail to Cheltenham. It seems not to have succeeded, for it was taken up in 1857.

By 1851 the company were contemplating worse competition when the O.W.W.R. opened, especially in coal to Droitwich and salt thence and from Stoke. They thought their best protection would be a canal from Hanbury wharf to Droitwich to link their line with the Droitwich Canal, and to cut out the land carriage between Droitwich and the wharf by which all coal and salt were transported. In 1852 an Act[5] was obtained by a nominally independent company, the Droitwich Junction, and an agreement then made for a lease of the new canal on completion at a rent equal to 5 per cent on the capital of £24,000. In fact it cost more, and the rent was £1,170 p.a. In 1853 the company also leased the Droitwich Canal itself for 21 years at a rent equal to their statutory liability to pay £8 a share—it amounted to £1,575 p.a.

Meanwhile the Worcester & Birmingham maintained its usual love-hate relationship with the railway-influenced Birmingham company. In 1851 they had asked them for help against the threatened O.W.W.R. competition by cutting tolls on W. & B. traffic, but the B.C.N. had refused. They were left to cut their own tolls, and to complain that they were 'left to their own unassisted efforts in contending against the unscupulous system of opposition adopted by their formidable rivals'.[6] Negotiations for toll reductions began again in 1852, and turned into others for amalgamation by exchanging two W. & B. shares for one L.N.W.R.-guaranteed Birmingham share. At first the L.N.W.R. agreed, but apparently after pressure from the Midland Railway, now owners of the Birmingham & Gloucester Railway, the scheme was dropped. In turn the Midland approached the canal company 'with a view of placing on a more satisfactory footing the traffic of the two Concerns',[7] but meetings had no result. By now the B.C.N. had been alienated, and the W. & B., fearing for its coal supplies, decided to lengthen the locks of the Droitwich Canal to take narrow boats, so that coal could be drawn by way of the Severn without transhipment. This was done by mid-1854, and by the end of the year the Junction canal was navigable. A parallel effort to persuade the Board of Trade to act against the B.C.N.'s coal tolls under the powers of their 1846 Act failed when the Board decided its powers did not extend so far.

The Droitwich Junction was 1¾ miles long, with seven locks

falling 66 ft from the W. & B. Five narrow and deep locks 75 ft × 7 ft 3 in. brought the waterway from Hanbury wharf to Droitwich: the sixth, near the Town Mill, took it into the river Salwarpe, the channel of which was used for about 160 yds, and so to a junction with the Droitwich Canal by a broad lock 75 ft × 15 ft which replaced the previous sluice used to draw water from the river, and which seems to have been built so that the Droitwich Canal barges could lock out into the river to load at a salt works which then lay just below Chapel bridge. This lock was fitted with four pairs of gates, two facing each way, so that it could be used whether the level of the river was above or below that of the canal. The whole lock structure had to be raised about 9 ft in 1875–6 owing to subsidence, and another 5 ft in 1903.

In 1857 a possible canal branch on the level from Tardebigge to Redditch was discussed, but the agent to Baroness Windsor, who owned most of the land needed, would not consider it. In this year also tolls were again cut, but negotiations then began with the O.W.W.R. to end competition that was unremunerative to both sides, and in mid-1858 it was agreed that the railway would lease the W. & B. for 21 years at a rent varying according to income that would yield between 1 and 2 per cent to the canal shareholders. Since railways could no longer lease canals, the O.W.W.R. intended to proceed as the owners of the Stratford Canal under the powers of the Canal Clauses Act, 1845.[8] The Gloucester & Berkeley's committee reported that they 'cannot but view with apprehension' the proposed lease, and 'trust that some step may be taken to induce the Government to interpose and prevent a misuse of legislation which was intended for the protection and benefit of canal and water communications, but which, in this case, is likely to be perverted to their injury'.[9] The Grand Junction Canal company, who had some interest because of the trade via Kingswood, then started a suit in Chancery to restrain the O.W.W.R. from acting on the agreement, but the Court of Appeal eventually confirmed it. Meanwhile the Gloucester & Berkeley's representatives had seen the President of the Board of Trade, and a clause was added to the Cheap Trains Act to prevent railway companies exercising the powers of the Canal Clauses Act.

The agreement therefore dropped, the company taking some comfort from the improved navigation of the Severn now the improvements were completed. For 1862, and from 1864 onwards, they could no longer pay a dividend. In spite of that, they decided in 1864 to promote a railway from New Street station, Birmingham, along the canal banks to a junction with the Midland Railway at King's Norton, with a branch to Harborne and a junction with the West Midland near Halesowen, and paid £300 for a survey. By July they were busy promoting the West Birmingham Railway & Canal Co., and making a contract with it to give the canal company a preferential dividend of 4 per cent. Six months later they sadly reported that the project had failed owing to the 'exceptional state of the money market'.[10]

They now received an offer to buy both their canal and the Droitwich Junction from J. R. McClean, Thomas Brassey and George Elliott, the railway contractors, who wanted them for conversion. The offer was to take over the canal debt (some £100,000) and to pay £3,000 p.a. for two years after the authorizing Act, £4,500 for the next two, and then £6,000 p.a. in perpetuity, with the option to commute for £135,000 if the canal were indeed converted to a railway. It was promptly accepted. The bill was presented in 1866, was opposed by the Gloucester & Berkeley, and failed because the promoters would not agree to maintain the canal in perpetuity or to reduce the Parliamentary tolls.

Another bill was introduced in 1867, was opposed by a number of canal companies, and withdrawn for much the same reasons, after which the promoters withdrew.

The canal company cannot have been grateful for the efforts of their friends. Their financial position was so bad that they could not raise money to repay mortgages falling due, some of the holders applied for a receiver, and one was appointed in 1868.

In 1870 a gleam of light appeared, when a Birmingham group revived the proposal to lay a railway along the canal bank from Birmingham to King's Norton, with a branch also to Harborne, to be called the Birmingham West Suburban Railway and worked by the Midland, and offered a rent-charge of £1,400 p.a. for the land. The Act was passed in 1871 and the Midland, now themselves interested, offered the canal company the guarantee of a 1 per cent dividend in exchange for a lease. This was agreed, and the Midland then sought powers in one of its own bills. Because the matter of canal and railway amalgamations had been referred to a Parliamentary Joint Committee, however, the House of Commons deferred consideration of the transfer clauses till the committee had reported, and, when it did, the M.R. decided to wait and see what Parliament might enact. Though so far frus-

S

trated, the rent for the Birmingham West Suburban* began to be paid from 1 August 1873.

Then, in September, the Sharpness New Docks Company† offered to take over the canal, including its liabilities for the Droitwich and Droitwich Junction Canals,‡ for £6,000 p.a. or £1 per share, later converted to £150,000 of 4 per cent debentures, and the liquidation of the debt of £100,473 or its exchange into mortgages of the amalgamated company. The offer was thankfully accepted, and was authorized by an Act[11] of 1874, the company being thenceforward called the Sharpness New Docks & Gloucester & Birmingham Navigation Company.

By 1875-6 the new owners were engaged in raising its operational standards, including dredging 60,000 tons of mud out of it, and putting on tunnel tugs, one to work through West Hill, and the other from the north end of Shortwood to the south end of Tardebigge. But after only four years the Sharpness company failed to make the receipts, even with the railway rent, balance the expenses together with interest on the purchase price, and later even to balance the expenses alone. Without a subsidy from the ship canal, the Worcester & Birmingham would have closed early in the present century.

In May 1886, at a time when great canal schemes were discussed, an improved waterway from Bristol to Gloucester was proposed§ which had nothing to do with the Sharpness company, and would have involved enlarging the W. & B. to take craft of 200-250 tons. It was supported by the Chambers of Commerce of Worcester, Birmingham, and Wolverhampton, but after investigating it, Birmingham Corporation decided instead to support a better route to London. About the beginning of 1900 the Sharpness company considered enlargement and sought support. Not enough was forthcoming, though the idea became part of the recommendations of the Royal Commission.

About 1926 George Cadbury inaugurated a guarantee fund to provide five annual subsidies not exceeding £2,000 p.a. collected from firms and associations in Birmingham and Bristol towards the trading loss, not counting return on capital, upon the canal, the Docks company agreeing not to close it during the period.

---

* The line originally ran to Lifford on the M.R. In 1875 it was vested in that company, and was then rebuilt on a partly different alignment to Kings Norton, being opened with a single track in 1876.

† Formerly the Gloucester & Berkeley Canal Co.

‡ The lease of the Lower Avon had been given up on 29 September 1872.

§ The Birmingham & Bristol Channel Improved Navigation.

During these five years the average trading loss was £3,605, and the average subsidy given was £1,589.

Here are the averaged figures of receipts from soon after the take-over to 1915, and of tonnages from 1921 to 1945: they include the two Droitwich canals.

Years	Receipts
	£
1876–80	22,187
1881–5	19,962
1886–90	16,332
1891–5*	14,865
1896–1900†	13,754
1901–5	13,168
1906–10	13,007
1911–15	13,072
	Tonnages
1921–5	216,376
1926–30	156,275
1931–5	134,634
1936–40	119,396
1941–5	59,374

* Excluding 1894.   † Excluding 1898.

The Sharpness company had done its best with the Droitwich. In 1881 they had given it a thorough dredging, during which 73,000 tons was removed, 'the accumulation, I should think, of the last half century'.[12] In 1888–9 the sills of the upper gates of all the locks were altered to provide the same 6 ft depth as on the lower sills. Their dimensions then became 77 ft × 15 ft × 6 ft, and they were now capable of taking 115-ton craft against 70 tons before.

However, the canal's fortunes slowly declined. In 1906 revenue did not cover maintenance on either the Droitwich or the Droitwich Junction, let alone make any return on the £2,800 p.a. the Sharpness New Docks company were paying on the lease of the two canals. A writer said in 1914: 'The canal head at Droitwich was, at the time of its prosperity, lined with wharves and bordered by salt works. But the salt trade has deserted this quarter of the town for the vicinity of the railway, the works have been demolished and the wharves are falling into decay.'[13] In March 1938 the Sharpness company, with the agreement of the shareholders of the two Droitwich companies, announced a bill to abandon them. By then the canal had been disused for many years. The Act was passed in 1939.

Commercial traffic—coal from Cannock to Worcester, and chocolate crumb from Worcester to Bourneville—passed until 1960 and 1961 respectively.

Staffordshire & Worcestershire Canal

The company had first heard sounds threatening railway competition in 1830, when they joined the Trent & Mersey and Birmingham companies in opposing the Birmingham & Liverpool Railroad bill. Soon afterwards, in 1832 and 1833, they lowered some tolls. Further reductions had to be made to follow those made by the Birmingham & Liverpool Junction after the Grand Junction Railway began carrying goods on 1 January 1838. In 1844, again, two or three railway companies interested themselves in the Severn, and we shall follow later the story of the Staffs & Worcs company's involvement with the river.

So threatening did railways seem that on 12 December 1844 the S. & W. suggested a meeting with the Birmingham company 'to confer on the propriety of arranging a Coalition of the Canals in this District, in opposition to the projected Lines of Railway, and to take such other Measures . . . as may be thought advisable'.[14] Neither the Oxford nor the Worcester & Birmingham were willing yet to join in opposition, but the S. & W., Birmingham, Dudley, Stourbridge and two Warwick canals agreed upon joint action upon railway bills, at any rate to second reading. A joint fund of 6d in the pound of the net dividends of the S. & W., Birmingham, Dudley and Stourbridge companies was set up, and surveyors and agents to canvass landowners appointed. Joint action did not last long, however, when faced with the financial benefits of co-operation with the railways, for only a fortnight later the Birmingham company wrote to say that 'under all the Circumstances . . . (it is) no longer expedient to carry on any united opposition to the various projected Railways'.[15] So, early in 1845, it was agreed instead that each company should defend its own interests, though in co-operation.

The Staffs & Worcs maintained an anti-railway policy during 1845, and sent out a circular letter to condemn the conversion schemes of the Ellesmere & Chester and the Birmingham & Liverpool Junction, and to stress

'that a stoppage of any part of the great chain of inland water communication, would cripple the whole system . . . at present their ramifications extend into every part of the manufacturing portions of the Kingdom which thus have mutual dependence on each other, and a common interest in maintaining unbroken the existing water communications, and they afford to the public the only salutary check to and control over those charges and regulations which the Railway Companies may at pleasure impose if left uncontrolled by such check'.[16]

They at first decided to oppose the Shropshire Union scheme, but later withdrew it because they feared for their water supplies and compensation tolls. Alas for resolution! In 1847, when many canals had passed into railway hands and, one must suppose, they considered the mischief had been done, the committee agreed that it would be 'highly desirable that this Company should amalgamate with some railway Company on the basis of guaranteeing to this Company their present dividend with the power of taking any further dividend the net profits of the Company may produce'.[17]

Up to 1860 the company's prosperity remained high. Its connection with the Severn, and its links with the Stourbridge, the Birmingham and the Shropshire Union, gave it a strong position, though its connection with the Trent & Mersey was worth much less than had been the case before the opening of the Birmingham & Liverpool Junction. Here are the averaged dividends to 1874.

Years	Average dividend per £140 share £	Years	Average dividend per £140 share £
1842–4	29⅓	1860–2	29⅓
1845–7	28	1863–5	25⅓
1848–50	28	1866–8	20
1851–3	28	1869–71	20⅓
1854–6	28	1872–4	20⅓
1857–9	30		

In 1875 there was a capital reorganization, each share being given a value of £300 and then split into three, after which an average of 4·95 per cent was paid for 1875–90, 3·5 per cent for 1891–1900, and 2·66 per cent for 1900–9.

In 1849 the company had tried to extend its market for Staffordshire coal by leasing the Coombe Hill Canal, and had given instructions to provide 'sufficient Boats to enable the Coal Trade to the Coombe Hill Canal to be carried on with vigour'.[18] By 1867, however, when the lease expired, they had changed their minds, for they refused to renew it or 'to keep the Canal on any terms'.[19]

In 1851 the company decided to enter carrying by buying William Partridge's existing business between Birmingham and Gloucester and operating it under his name. They thought trade could be gained from the Worcester & Birmingham, and that profits would at least equal the £500 p.a. Partridge was to be paid, and the expenses. Another carrier, Devey, was lent £1,500 to restart his business. However, in four years the Partridge business lost £3,000, less the tolls gained to the S. & W. and the Severn, and in 1855 Devey failed.

The company carried on with Partridge and also supported the tug business run on the Severn by Alfred, a son of the Commission's engineer, Edward Leader Williams.* In 1860 they bought two steam coasters of their own, the *Ironside* and the *Cuirassier*, which Edward Leader Williams had designed. Sister ships 94 ft by 19 ft 6 in., plated with iron over wooden frames, each with a drop keel, a single screw and a 40 h.p. engine, *Cuirassier* carried 140 tons of cargo and *Ironside* 120 tons (because of a variation in the layout of bunkers and boilers) between Worcester (later Gloucester) and Irish and French ports for 20 years or so. They seem, however, to have been given up by the S. & W. company in 1864. The latter had in 1861 adopted the Carriers Act, and soon afterwards employed Alfred Williams as their carrying manager, apparently also taking over his tugs. Their business, direct and indirect, was considerable. In 1862 the Severn Commission reported that the maintenance of their tolls in spite of the depression caused by the American civil war was due to the carrying trade of the Staffs & Worcs Canal, which they estimated was providing about one-sixth of their revenue.

In 1890 the Severn & Canal Carrying company, run by Joshua Fellows in partnership with Danks, asked for help, and the S. & W. agreed to buy their craft for £10,000 and hire them back on repayment terms, but after negotiations the carriers went on by themselves. Subsequent negotiations took place, till in 1906 a new company was formed to take over the assets of the S. & C.C.C. to which the S. & W. advanced £5,000, all except £250 in exchange for debentures. They also appointed a director. The Sharpness company now took over towing on the Severn, and in 1909 the carrying company repaid its debentures to the S. & W., and offered control to Sharpness, thereafter operating as a subsidiary of that company.

* He died in 1879. Another son, Sir Edward Leader Williams, was the engineer of the Manchester Ship Canal.

THE LINES TO THE SOUTH

In 1854 the company agreed with the B.C.N. for a junction between the Hatherton branch and the proposed Cannock Extension Canal by a flight of 13 locks at Churchbridge. The land seems to have been bought jointly, but the locks to have been paid for by the S. & W.; they were built in 1858 and 1859, and came into use when the Extension line was opened at the beginning of 1863. About 1860 the South Staffordshire Railway built a railway interchange basin at Churchbridge, the S. & W. having contributed towards the cost. In 1902 the Cannock traffic downwards through the locks was reported as 12,000 tons a month. The Cheslyn Hay tramroad seems to have become disused by the seventies, because it was in 1880 restored to working order at a cost of about £200. It was again disused well before the 1940s, when it was being used as a path.

Apart from skirmishing with the Shropshire Union, water supply questions were not troublesome until in 1864 the B.C.N. gave notice that it proposed to pump back from the foot of Wolverhampton locks, so depriving the S. & W. of the water it gained by their working. The S. & W. sought and obtained an injunction, but lost to the Birmingham company on appeal, a decision that was maintained by the House of Lords. They then agreed to pay £1,500 p.a. for the water, a rate varied later. Because they were so dependent upon the B.C.N.'s water and its trade via Wolverhampton and Churchbridge, the company tended to support the company against other canal concerns in spite of its railway control. For instance, when a meeting was called in 1881 over the matter of the B.C.N. and through tolls, the S. & W. decided 'to give a general support to the Birmingham Canal Company'.[20]

About 1880 a local writer found Stourport

'a sad contrast to its former self. Railways have robbed the Severn and the canal of the traffic, which now passes by instead of into its commodious basin. We found the Company's great commercial hotel, the *Tontine*, a large square block, with rooms sufficient to make up a hundred beds, and equally extensive stabling, diminished to the proportions of one of the smallest inns in the town, its extensive rooms being let off to form dwelling houses. One solitary barge, loaded with sand from the neighbourhood, bound for Newport, was all that the Athlete, capable of tugging a hundred such, could muster on the Monday morning . . . true, it took others in tow, between there and Gloucester'.[21]

In 1881 the company decided to oppose the closing of the Thames & Severn Canal,[22] which 'would destroy a large and increasing Coal Traffic on the Severn'.[23] and after consultation with the Severn Commission, Sharpness company, and Stroudwater, opposed the Midland Railway's attempt to get powers to acquire it. They then protested to the Thames & Severn company about the state of their canal, and in 1895 joined the trust formed with other waterway concerns to put it into order and work it. Thereafter the S. & W. in most years lost a certain amount of money on the Thames & Severn; smaller losses continued after it was taken over by the Gloucestershire County Council.

In 1885 the company bought the Severn Horse Towing Path Extension Company (Bewdley to Coalbrookdale) for a nominal sum.

After the Railway & Canal Traffic Act of 1888, many inter-canal discussions on through rates took place. The Birmingham gave difficulty in spite of the support they had had from the S. & W., and in 1892 the S. & W. approached the Manchester Ship Canal company as owners of the Bridgewater, the Weaver trustees, and the North Staffordshire Railway as owners of the Trent & Mersey, to help in negotiating through rates between Birmingham and south Staffordshire, Liverpool and Manchester. In 1893 and 1894 agreements were in fact reached with the B.C.N. and also with the Shropshire Union. In 1895 a sign of the times was the permission given to Mr. Beach of Compton to keep thirty pleasure boats on the summit level.

In 1897 the Chambers of Commerce of Bristol and Wolverhampton interested themselves in a partial enlargement of the upper Severn locks and the canal as far as Aldersley to take river barges of 170–200 tons. They sought a report from H. J. Marten, engineer of the Severn Commission, who reported that it could be done at a moderate cost.

The Stafford branch ceased to be used in the early 1920s. Boats carrying slack and iron from Ashwood basin and Stourbridge continued to work through the side lock into the Stour on their way to the Wilden ironworks until 1948–9. The Hatherton branch and Churchbridge locks went out of use about 1949, as did Ashwood basin for commercial traffic.

In 1930 Lord Hatherton died, having been a member of the committee for 62 years and chairman for forty-two. In that year the Severn Commission owed the company £65,643 on mortgages, plus £58,892 of interest arrears, and in 1931 were accused by the

S. & W. of having paid money due to them to the new mortgagees under the Commission's 1890 Act. The canal company followed their accusation with a writ, and in 1933 won their case. Thereafter, the Commission's finances improving at the same time, substantial repayments were made each year till in 1943 all arrears had been paid off, and capital repayments began. This inwards flow of money enabled the S. & W. to continue their policy of buying in and cancelling their own securities.

The Commission interest, together with other sources of revenue, enabled the company to pay 2½ per cent up to nationalization, when £210,000 of equity and £51,476 of debentures were outstanding, against which £110,000 were held in mortgages and Government securities. The old concern had ended its long independent life in good order.

In 1905 the canal had carried 722,000 tons, 225,000 tons of which was coal from the Cannock and other coalfields destined for places on the Severn. Thereafter commercial traffic steadily fell away. Just before the war the Severn & Canal Carrying company gave notice to leave the warehouses in Stourport basin because they could not get big river craft up the locks. The S. & W. estimated the cost of enlargement at £12,000–£14,000, and made a provisional agreement with the carrying concern to do the work against a guarantee of tolls and a long lease of the warehouses, only then to change their minds and decide that the expenditure was not worth while, as onforwarding was likely to be by road transport.

About 1949 coal traffic from the Hatherton branch to Stourport power station ended. Today the canal is increasingly used for pleasure purposes.

Coombe Hill Canal

The Worcester & Birmingham Canal company, who had renewed their lease in 1829, were by 1844 much worried by railway competition for the coal trade to Cheltenham, which had reduced their own traffic from 25,000 to 18,000 tons a year. They thought their position would be strengthened were they to buy the canal and extend it to Cheltenham. It was offered them for £12,000; they counter-offered £8,750 on condition that they obtained an extension Act, and indeed deposited a plan. But their solicitor then advised them that their funds ought not to be so used; he was a large shareholder, his views carried weight, no second opinion was sought, and the project dropped. In 1849, while negotiations to renew the lease at a lower figure were going on, the W. & B. suddenly learned that the canal had been leased instead to the Staffs & Worcs, and had to pay £130 renewals upon the ending of its tenancy.

The lease to nominees of the Staffs & Worcs was for 17 years at £400 p.a. They lost money by forcing traffic upon it, and when they gave up their lease in 1867, tonnage at once fell away to some 1,800 tons a year. G. W. Keeling, engineer of the Gloucester & Berkeley, asked to report on it, considered that it could not be made to pay expenses, and had better be turned into an osier bed.[24] However, the little Coombe Hill company first tried to run it themselves, and then sold it in 1871 to Edward Sowerby and Joseph Cockrell for £520. They, having lost money in its operation, resold it in 1873 to Algernon A. de L. Strickland for £1,000. In 1875 Keeling again examined it, and reported that 'the Bridges and Lock Gates were in a far more ruinous condition* and the Canal in a very foul State'. He was right. A summer flood of the Severn carried away the lock gates and caused the water to back up the canal and overflow. The resulting trouble with landowners caused Strickland to seek an abandonment Act. The Sharpness company, some landowners, and the Severn Commission petitioned against its closing—the last-named considering it should instead be continued to Cheltenham—but the bill was passed,[25] and the canal closed on 1 August 1876. The tolls for the first half of 1875, before the flood, had been £8.

Severn River

We get a picture of the river two years before the Act was passed for the Severn Commission, from a report by James Walker for the Gloucester & Berkeley company. He said that in 1840 there was a traffic above Gloucester of 3,328 laden canal boats and 84 empties, 405 partly-laden barges, 296 laden trows and 253 partly-laden. Craft from Shropshire, he said, remained aground at Ironbridge during droughts; when the river rose they came down to Gloucester in fleets of twenty or thirty, getting there in 11 to 16 hours, and unloading as quickly as possible, so that they could get back again before the water level fell.

The Commission's authority extended from the Gladder Brook a little above Stourport to the entrance lock of the Gloucester &

* Than in 1867.

Berkeley Canal on the eastern channel at Gloucester, and to that of the Herefordshire & Gloucestershire Canal on the western channel; 43⅜ miles to Gloucester, and 1⅞ miles of the western channel. The sum of £150,000 had been authorized to build locks at Lincomb, Holt, Bevere just below the Droitwich Canal, and Diglis below Worcester, each 94 ft 7 in. × 20 ft, to take craft carrying up to 150 tons. Below Diglis the river was to be dredged to a minimum depth of 6 ft. The Commissioners appointed William Cubitt chief engineer, but, as they had no power to take tolls until the navigation was complete, and therefore no means of paying interest on capital in the meantime, they got no further until Grissell & Peto, the 'eminent Contractors of Lambeth',[26] offered to do the whole job under Cubitt's superintendence for £139,850, payable in guaranteed mortgage bonds. The Commission estimated that in addition to the contract price they would also need £34,690 for other expenses, and under Acts of 1843 and 1844 an additional £30,000 was authorized, the whole £180,000 being guaranteed by the Staffs & Worcs company. Incidentally, the 1844 Act also gave the Worcester & Birmingham company powers to build a branch from their canal to the river below Diglis locks, for seemingly they feared 'the obstruction which it is supposed may be occasioned by a number of Vessels being collected at the Locks'.[27]

Work began in July 1843; on 21 December Lincomb lock was opened, Holt in June 1844, Bevere and the two locks at Diglis* by the beginning of September 1845. So far so good, but dredging between Diglis and Gloucester was proving difficult through low water and the tenacity of the marl shoals, which had to be blasted with gunpowder. This railway mania year brought several threats to the uncompleted navigation, and in September the Oxford, Worcester & Wolverhampton and the Great Western Railways agreed to guarantee the Commission a revenue of £14,000 a year, 'being the amount proved in Parliament by the Promoters of the Severn Improvement Act as the anticipated revenue of the Commission calculated upon the then existing trade upon the River'.[28] This guarantee was useful, but it only applied as long as the debts of the Commission did not exceed £180,000. Almost at once, however, they decided that something must be done about Upton bridge, which the boatmen considered a danger. In 1846 another Act authorized £30,000 for this purpose and to pay expenses until tolls could be taken. Meanwhile dredging had been going on with

* One 94 ft 7 in. by 20 ft, the other 142 ft 5 in. by 30 ft.

a heavy dredger, and on 17 December 1846 Cubitt certified that the river had a minimum depth of 6 ft at all seasons; tolls were therefore charged from 1 January 1847.

Though the first full financial year of operation to 30 June 1848 showed tolls of £11,336—the highest figure, except for 1851, that the Commission was to take until 1933—and a tonnage of 450,000, traders at once began to complain that the depth was not being maintained. In August 1847 one newspaper said that there was only 4 ft in parts.[29] This Leader Williams, now engineer, admitted, saying that his proposed additional lock at Upton had been struck out of the 1842 Act. Cubitt broadly agreed, but recommended a lock near Tewkesbury instead to benefit the Lower Avon. Disputes inside and outside the Commission followed, and bills to authorize the lock were lost in 1848 and 1849.

The position was now critical, for tolls were falling, and the railway guarantee did not apply. It was now acknowledged to be impossible to maintain the 6 ft depth, because when the rock barriers which held back the water were removed, the water ran out faster. Dredging away channels in the rock barriers was tried but, as Edward Leader Williams said at an 1849 inquiry, these became 'so many mill-races, down which it was difficult to navigate the vessels . . . accidents frequently occur'. During 1850 the depth fell to 3 ft 6 in.: barges had to be lightened, and even then were delayed, Droitwich salt barges being reported as taking three to four days to Gloucester, and a trow two days to cover the 2 miles from Gloucester to the Upper Parting. Trade needed steamers like the 150-ton *City of Worcester* which in 1851 worked to that town, or tugs each taking 500–600 tons of salt downriver in lighters.

In 1852 an Admiralty* report by Captain Beechey and James Walker recommended a lock at the Lower Parting at Gloucester but not at Tewkesbury, and regretted 'that the opportunity has not been employed of treating this great subject in a more practical manner'.[30] This annoyed the Commission and its engineer, who naturally considered that they knew their own river better than the Admiralty, and who, incidentally, had had to see defeated an independent bill to lay down two or more lines of flexible iron bands all the way from Gloucester to Welshpool, which were to be picked up by a tug which would pass them through power-driven rollers and so haul itself along. No one quite understood what would happen at locks. Sticking to their own plan, the

* The Admiralty was concerned because the river was tidal.

Commission got an Act³¹ in 1853 authorizing £53,000 to build a lock at Tewkesbury and to liquidate debts.

Things now looked better. A 30 h.p. steam tug, *The Enterprize*, had started running between Gloucester and Stourport, and the proprietors were so pleased that they had ordered two more. Upton bridge,† to which the Commission had contributed £1,160, had been at last rebuilt by the. Worcestershire authorities, though with an awkward drawbridge 120 ft long and weighing 100 tons, which when raised only produced a navigable opening of 40 ft. In 1854 the Commission reported that 'the traffic on the River having being severely tried by Railway Competition the result has proved that with a well-ordered Navigation the River is at all times best suited for the conveyance of the great products of the District'.³² But it was difficult to raise the money till an Act of 1856 enabled the Staffs & Worcs to lend; they provided £40,000. The bill was supported by the now converted Worcester & Birmingham, who considered that at last they were going to benefit. A new channel to avoid an acute angle of the river was then cut at Upper Lode, Tewkesbury, a weir was built, and a lock 112 ft by 30 ft 3 in., with a pair of gates dividing it from a basin 153 ft by 73 ft 6 in. The lock could be used by itself, but by using lock and basin together a tug and its whole tow could be put through in one operation. It was opened early in August 1858.

Though seven steamers working between Gloucester and Stourport were reported in 1860, the river between Upper Lode lock and Gloucester was still unsatisfactory, partly because the depth over the sill at the canal lock at Gloucester was often not enough, partly owing to the deteriorating state of the Gloucester channel, which was 'an effective bar to the regular employment of an improved class of sea-going vessels, by which alone any great development of the Severn traffic can be looked for'.³³ By 1864 the Commission owed £62,600 of arrears of mortgage interest, and tolls were falling:

Years	Average tolls
	£
1848–52	10,935
1853–7	9,850
1858–62	8,968
1863–4	7,786

† It was rebuilt in 1884 as a swing bridge maintained by the Commission, and in 1942 was demolished, having been replaced by a new bridge.

After manœuvres between the Staffs & Worcs Canal, the Great Western Railway and the Commission, which included a court case, a G.W.R. Act of 1868 embodied an agreement whereby the railway agreed to implement the guarantee of £14,000 p.a., and to apply the arrears of it to paying off the £40,000 raised under the Acts of 1853 and 1856, the arrears of interest upon it, and on some of the principal debt of £180,000. The Staffs & Worcs had already obtained the release of the £30,000 raised under the Act of 1846 (so reducing the principal debt to £180,000) and £23,408 arrears of interest upon it. The future annual income of the Commission, including balances from the guarantee, was to go to reduce the £180,000 to £100,000, to which amount the G.W.R. agreed to limit the mortgages they would receive under section 103 of the O.W.W.R. Act, 1845, for those paid off. Lastly, the G.W.R. were to nominate three Commissioners.

An Act of 1869 embodied proposals based on those made by Leader Williams and Clegram of the Gloucester & Berkeley. It authorized a weir in the Western channel to throw more water into the Eastern or Gloucester channel; the extension of the Commission's jurisdiction to the Lower Parting; a weir and lock at Llanthony a little below the canal lock, and a narrow boat lock at Maisemore on the Western channel for boats to and from the Herefordshire & Gloucestershire Canal. The Staffs & Worcs and Gloucester & Berkeley companies each advanced half of the £20,000 necessary. Encouraged by the prospective improvements the latter began enlargements at Sharpness that were greatly to increase the capacity of the canal.[34] Maisemore weir was finished in 1870, Llanthony lock about early June 1871, and Maisemore lock in the autumn. Ten years after this narrow lock was built, on 30 June 1881, the H. & G. Canal closed, but narrow boats for some time continued to pass through it to a coal wharf at Maisemore.

In 1877 the two towing path companies between Bewdley and Gloucester suggested that the Commission should take them over, the upper one for £750, the Gloucester & Worcester for £800. A battle followed between the Commission and the Great Western as to which should do so—though not at these figures; in the end neither did. The effect of the improvement of the lower river, and the steady growth of steam craft and steam towing that it encouraged after 1854, can be seen in the results of the Gloucester & Worcester path. This company, with seven tollhouses, had in 1859 receipts of £1,670 against a paid-up capital of £6,800, and a surplus of £759 after paying for salaries and wages, the maintenance of the path and gates, and wayleaves to certain landowners. The following figures show what happened to the company, especially after the opening of Upper Lode lock in 1858:

Years	Average receipts £	Surplus £
1858–62	1,413	521
1863–7	922	248
1868–72	686	42
1873–7	497	6
1878–82	388	loss 54
1883–7	NK	
1888–92	NK	
1893–7	134	
1898–1902	145*	
1903–7	112	

* Excluding 1902.

By 1885 the landowners had foregone wayleaves, by 1889 the Commission's lockkeepers were taking tolls, yet from 1875 losses occurred in most years. Few horse-drawn craft worked below Tewkesbury. Out of 1,749 tickets issued in the year ending 31 March 1892, 650 were only for Worcester to Diglis, and most of the rest for points between Worcester & Tewkesbury. By 1902, only 644 tickets were issued for points below Diglis. The last dividend was paid about 1875, but the company struggled on till 1912.

I do not know when the Worcester to Bewdley path closed, though the company still existed in 1906. That between Bewdley and Coalbrookdale ceased to take tolls from 25 March 1884 and sold its shares to the Staffs & Worcs company, relinquishing its rights from 25 March 1885.

From 1845 the fortunes of the Shrewsbury path slowly declined, the final blow being the opening of the Severn Valley Railway on 1 February 1862. The last barge passed to the town in the same year. The trustees relinquished the path on 25 March 1885 and then ceased to meet, but they still owned a little property, and also had liabilities. In 1934 the Shrewsbury Council called a meeting of the remaining ex-officio trustees, who appointed others, and then became for practical purposes a committee of the Council, their small income being spent on the maintenance of the path and river bank near the town. Here are the figures for its last days:

Years*	Average dividend per £100			Average number of horses paying toll
	£	s	d	
1845–7		11	8	127
1848–50	1	1	8	125
1851–3		11	8	88
1854–6		8	4	72
1857–9		6	0	76
1860–2		2	0	NK
1863–5		none		none
1866–8			8	none

* Dividends, calendar years; figures for horses, year ending Michaelmas.

In 1879 the Severn railway bridge was opened. Rail access from the Forest collieries to Sharpness did not immediately affect shipments from Bullo Pill, but by 1902 these had almost ceased, and with them the main reason for building Llanthony lock. In 1882 the Commission opposed the closing of the Thames & Severn Canal, from which they reckoned to get 15,000 tons of traffic and £600 in tolls a year. In 1895 they participated in the trust then formed, and paid contributions after its transfer to the Gloucestershire County Council. By this time there was almost no traffic above Stourport except for a few craft to Bewdley and Arley. Traffic to Welshpool had ended by 1862; in 1856 the Shrewsbury directory advertised only a weekly barge, and there, too, all traffic ended in 1862; the last barge traded to Bridgnorth in 1895.

We saw earlier that one result of the interest of the eighties in canal enlargement was a scheme for the Worcester & Birmingham. The Severn Commission was also encouraged to enlarge its own waterway, especially by the Chamber of Commerce and the Corporation of Cardiff, anxious to encourage 'a through trade to Worcester. The Commission's engineer was favourable, and they decided to present a bill in 1890, on condition that the Sharpness company enlarged their Gloucester lock and that the G.W.R. again stabilized its contribution so that the increased tolls hoped for could be used to pay interest on the new loan that would be necessary. Negotiations changed the position. The G.W.R. quitted the scene, having paid over £100,000 in cash, given up £28,809 in mortgages and its three seats on the Commission, and agreeing not to oppose the bill. The £100,000 was paid to the Staffs & Worcs to reduce the debt owing to them, and the Commission was left with a debt of only £67,164. The Act then passed, enabling them to raise £30,000 more and to lend the Sharpness company the money to lower the sill of Gloucester canal lock by 1 ft 10 in. Work began in July 1891. When it was completed on 30 June 1894, within the estimate, a depth of 7 ft had been obtained from Stourport to Worcester and 10 ft thence to Gloucester, and all the locks from Lincomb to Gloucester canal lock had been deepened, except Upper Lode which did not need it.

For a time there were high hopes, although mortgage interest under the 1842 and 1844 Acts was already falling behind, and none could be paid under that of 1890. The Commission appointed a traffic agent, and negotiated through toll agreements with a number of canal companies. In 1895 the *Atalanta*, owned by the Severn & Canal Carrying Co, and drawing 7 ft 9 in., had discharged 170 tons at Worcester on 28 September. In 1896 the steamer *A1*, able to pass under Westgate bridge at Gloucester and to carry 200 tons, was built by a company of Cardiff and Worcester merchants and put on the run between those cities. But the company soon failed.

In fact, no increase in trade resulted from the improvements, while the schedules of revised tolls under the Railway & Canal Traffic Act 1888, and the recently-negotiated through tolls, tended to reduce receipts. Indeed, Cardiff merchants admitted that they were sending timber by rail to the Midlands at rates that were lower than elsewhere because they were held down by the threat of river competition. All the same, the goods did not go by water, and in 1898 the traffic agent was dispensed with, his work not having made much difference. Revenue fell steadily:

Years	Average tolls £	Years	Average tolls £
1868–72	7,997	1893–7	7,494
1873–7	7,790	1898–1902	6,472
1878–82	7,785	1903–7	6,270
1883–7	8,184	1908–12	6,156
1888–92	8,219		

Traffic fell from 349,393 tons in 1868 to 323,329 in 1888 and 292,326 in 1898: about a tenth was coal, a fifth other minerals, and the rest mostly grain, foreign timber, salt, sand and iron. In this situation the Commission's debt mounted by about £3,000 a year, from £107,549 in 1895, after the improvements were finished, to £232,140 in 1935.

The Royal Commission in 1909 recommended that the Severn be improved to take a 600-ton craft to Stourport and 750 tons to

T

Worcester. There was local interest, but the war came to stop anything that might have been done. An indication of change, however, was the Commission's Act of 1914, one part of which gave powers to control passenger and pleasure craft, including 'intoxication and general disorderly conduct on Vessels on the River'.[35] In 1921 they were empowered to levy tolls on pleasure craft. After the war there was more talk of improvement, and of a Severn Barrage, but no action. The last craft passed through Maisemore lock in the early 1920s, and through Llanthony lock in 1924. By 1927 receipts had fallen to only £4,422, and locks and weirs were in bad shape. Then oil storage wharves began to be built at Diglis, and within a few years the oil and petrol traffic, a little of which had gone on since at least 1882, began to transform the river's finances, helped also by a substantial revenue from the sale of condensing water to power stations, so that by 1939 receipts had risen to £19,123. The carrying company, supported by Cadbury Bros., remained in existence, and benefited from the improved trade. In 1942 their name changed to the Severn Carrying Co. On nationalization, the company was acquired by a concern primarily interested in transporting petroleum; the British Transport Commission therefore purchased that part of the fleet which was used for general merchandise traffic.

Westgate bridge was demolished in 1942 and replaced by a temporary structure that seems to have become permanent. In 1954 the river was carrying motor craft with a maximum capacity of 280 tons to Worcester, and dumb barges with 330 tons. In that year the Commission built the new Diglis wharf, with a quay 320 ft long and a large transit shed. By 1964 the oil traffic had fallen against the competition of pipelines and bulk trains. The total tonnage carried was 810,625 tons; of this the main traffics were oil to Worcester and Stourport, grain to Tewkesbury, timber to Worcester and Stourport, aluminium to Stourport, and wood-pulp, copper and zinc to Worcester.

Conclusion

THE interesting thing about the canal network of the Midlands described in this book and its companion is that most of it has proved so durable. Lines like the Trent & Mersey, Staffordshire & Worcestershire, Coventry and Oxford, have carried commercial traffic for nearly two hundred years; for longer, that is to say, than any significant railway line or most turnpike roads. And even now, though the commercial value of the smaller ones may be ending, they are finding new ways to usefulness.

*Canals and Navigations in the Midlands by Type of Waterway**

Date	*Ship Canal*	*Broad Canal*	*Narrow Canal*	*Tub-boat or Small Canal*	*River Nav.*	*Total*
	miles	*miles*	*miles*	*miles*	*miles*	*miles*
1760	—	—	—	—	249½	249½
1770	—	16½	37¾	6½	249½	310¼
1780	—	86½	276⅜	8½	258¾	630⅛
1790	—	86½	342¼	10¾	258¾	698¼
1800	—	312	493½	44¼	262½	1,112¼
1810	½	373⅛	576⅛	44¼	240¾	1,234¾
1820	½	351⅜	710¾	37⅞	240¾	1,341¼
1830	—	355⅛	717⅛	36	240¾	1,349
1840	—	355¼	822½	21½	240¾	1,440
1850	—	355¾	820¼	21½	240¾	1,438¼

* The canals and navigations included are those listed in Appendix I of this and its companion, *The Canals of the East Midlands*, that fall within the range of dates quoted. For classification purposes a ship canal is a canal that admitted sea-going ships; a broad canal one with locks at least 12 ft wide; a narrow canal one with locks less than 12 ft wide; and a tub-boat or small canal one taking boats carrying a few tons each. See my *British Canals*, 2nd ed., 1959, pp. 55–6, for a fuller description. For some branches I have had to conjecture the dates. Readers may like to compare these figures with those given in *The Canals of Southern England* and *The Canals of South Wales and the Border*.

Until the success of the locomotive railway, we can see in the figures given the quick expansion of the canal system in mileage and carrying facilities to cope with the needs of industry for the carriage of raw materials and finished goods, and to some extent those of agriculture also: not only the building of main lines, but the proliferation of branches to works and mines, or of tramroads where a branch was impracticable or too expensive.

There was a moment when it seemed that railways might take the passengers and light goods, and canals the bulky and heavy traffics. But speed, larger units of organization, the ability of the companies to carry goods themselves, collection and delivery services, and the spreading of overheads over both passengers and goods, were among the advantages the railways had.

Some canal companies saw quickly enough the danger from railways—more quickly than some railway companies, anxious for a smooth passage of their bill through Parliament and no rate cutting afterwards, saw how little they really had to fear from the smaller waterways. So the quick sales; for instance, the Cromford, Ashby and Macclesfield. Some railways tried to have second thoughts, but were not allowed to cancel their agreements by the Stratford, Nottingham or Grantham companies. A few small concerns were closed down—like the Oakham or the Newport Pagnell —but most continued, to develop in dissimilar ways.

The Shropshire Union, at first an independent attempt at some form of rail-canal integration, was soon leased by the L.N.W.R. and then discouraged from long-haul traffic to and from other canals, though welcome to develop within its own system certain specialized trades which supplemented those of the railway, and, in so doing, to build up the trade of Ellesmere Port. The Birmingham Canal Navigations, having the same master, developed similarly: discouragement of transfer traffic to other canals and intensive use of its own network, both for loads carried all the way by water, and for those transhipped to and from rail in the specialized interchange basins. The Trent & Mersey, owned by the smaller North Staffordshire Railway, developed in an opposite way, as a means by which the railway company could carry long-haul traffic to and from Liverpool, Runcorn, the Mersey and Manchester in one direction and the Trent in the other, so much so that in 1875 the independent Weaver trustees opened the Anderton lift to develop interchange traffic with it.

On other waterways, such as the Nottingham, Cromford and

CONCLUSION 293

Ashby, railway ownership led at first to some neglect, and later to more. But this influence was always harmful to the future of water transport because it kept the canals as they were, and hindered the negotiation of through tolls, amalgamation and modernization.

As the century moved on we see the inability of the independent canal lines, however hard they tried, to maintain, let alone to increase, their share of an expanding market. The Warwick and Grand Junction route, well-organized, powerful, with some ability to raise new money, a single carrying business and the enterprise to run power-driven craft, did best. The Leicester line, a sufferer from too many small companies managing too little canal, much worse. But the result was the same in the end.

The waterways reacted in two ways to their critical situation. One was to build up sources of income ancillary to tolls, from the sale of water to other canal companies, public authorities and industry; the development of property or interest derived from the proceeds of selling it; in the case of the Regent's from the use of their dock; and a little from fishing and pleasure boat licences. By the end of the century some companies, the Leicester, Grand Junction and Coventry among them, derived a third to a half of their revenue from such sources.

The other was the reduction of compensation tolls, modernization and, sometimes, amalgamation. The Staffs & Worcs saw the value of improving the Severn, and put much money behind it. The Shropshire Union sought amalgamation and introduced (though temporarily) steam-hauled barge trains. In the nineties the Grand Junction bought the old Grand Union and the Union, and built the Foxton inclined plane in a gallant effort to open a broad waterway to revive the waterborne coal trade from Derbyshire to London. In the present century the enterprise of the Trent Navigation Co and the city of Nottingham transformed the River Trent.

Finally, these lines of development were brought together in the later Grand Union: amalgamation, modernization and diversification. Diversification was successful, amalgamation helped: but a great effort to rebuild narrow-boat carrying only demonstrated its limitations.

Meanwhile the twentieth century had brought the motor lorry, far more than the railway the enemy of the smaller canals. For both railway and canal were alike in this, that much of their traffic had to begin and end its journey by road. When it became possible to carry all the way by lorry, without transfer of cargo, the older ways had to seek new methods, or to succumb.

Date	Ship Canal	Broad Canal	Narrow Canal	Tub-boat or Small Canal	River Nav.	Total
	miles	miles	miles	miles	miles	miles
1900	—	334	835⅜	8	152	1,329⅜
1947	—	253¾	646¾	—	135	1,035½

The lorry caused the canal network to contract, by the abandonment of rural or less useful industrial canals, such as much of the Shropshire Union, the Grantham, and the Droitwich. Yet much remained in existence. The bigger waterways still have a future as large-scale carriers of goods. Many of the smaller, those that run quietly through the countryside, see a new life opening in cruising, fishing, and the pleasure of those that walk beside them. Others, still useful to the community, will end their days as channels for storing and moving water wherever it may be wanted.

Much might have been different. All the same, it is not a bad record.

This 'Conclusion' is repeated in *The Canals of the East Midlands*. Generalizations are risky at the best of times, but they would be riskier still were they to be made about only a part of the Midlands.

Author's Notes and Acknowledgements

It is impossible for me individually to acknowledge the assistance I have had in writing this book—those who have sent me material, or whom I have consulted, are numbered in hundreds. I thank them all.

It could not have been written at all without the willing and efficient help of the staff of British Transport Historical Records and of the House of Lords Record Office, and the co-operation of many librarians and archivists. Again, without the friendships that link the members of the Railway & Canal Historical Society, and the aid they give each other, it would have been much the poorer. My fellow-members have answered questions, read sections of the text, and sought information for me, willingly and generously.

I should especially like to thank Mr C. P. Weaver for reading a file of *Aris's Birmingham Gazette*, and for doing much special research on the Birmingham Canal Navigations, and the Black Country and Newdigate canals; Mrs Mary Thomas for also reading *Aris*; Major Whitehead for reading the *Derby Mercury*, Mr J. C. Gillham for reading *Berrows' Worcester Journal*, Josiah Wedgwood & Sons Ltd for access to the Wedgwood Collection, Mr P. Stevenson for showing me his extracts from the Nutbrook Canal records and Stanton & Staveley Ltd for permission to use them, Mr. C. R. Clinker for checking the references to railways in the text, and officials of the British Waterways Board, especially Mr W. L. Ives, Mr C. M. Marsh, Mr A. J. Brawn and Mr C. N. Hadlow, for answering questions.

I am most grateful for a grant towards the costs of research made by the Leverhulme trustees, and for the patient work of my secretary, Mrs. Ann Simpkins, in typing the text.

AUTHOR'S NOTES AND ACKNOWLEDGEMENTS

My thanks are due to the following for permission to reproduce photographs and other illustrations: Waterways Museum, Stoke Bruerne: Plates 2(b) and 11, Figs. 1, 8 and 17; British Transport Historical Records, Figs. 4, 13 and 18; British Transport Historical Relics, (photo: W. H. R. Godwin), Plate 1; British Waterways Board, Plates 3 and 13(a), Figs. 2 and 15; British Railways Board, London Midland Region, Plate 13(b); Mrs John R. Greene, Aqualate Hall, Staffs, and the Staffordshire County Record Office (photo: Bertram Sinkinson), Plate 2(a); The Trustees of the William Salt Library, Stafford, and Messrs Hand, Morgan and Owen (photo: Bertram Sinkinson), Plate 4; C. P. Weaver Esq., Plates 5, 6 and 7, Figs. 6, 7, 19 and 20; George Smallshire Esq., Plate 8(a); The Institution of Civil Engineers (photo: W. H. R. Godwin), Plate 9; E. A. Wilson Esq., Plates 10, 12 and 14, Fig. 11 and jacket picture; Josiah Wedgwood and Sons Ltd., Plate 15; P. A. Norton Esq., Plate 16(a), A. P. Voce Esq., Plate 16(b); R. J. Dean Esq., Fig. 3; J. M. Palmer Esq., Fig. 5; R. J. Dean Esq., for drawing Figs. 3, 4, 5, 11, 13 and 18.

Finally, no man can write in his spare time—as I did while most of this book was being drafted—unless he has the daily encouragement and support of his wife and the tolerance of his children. She and they have helped me more than words of mine can tell.

CHARLES HADFIELD

NOTES

Notes to Chapter I

1. For Erasmus Darwin, see R. E. Schofield, *The Lunar Society of Birmingham*, 1963, and D. King-Hele, *Erasmus Darwin*, 1963.
2. For Josiah Wedgwood, see E. Meteyard, *The Life of Josiah Wedgwood*, 1865, and R. E. Schofield, *The Lunar Society of Birmingham*, 1963.
3. A. L. Thomas, 'Geographical Aspects of the Development of Transport and Communications affecting the Pottery Industry of North Staffordshire during the Eighteenth Century', in *Collections for a History of Staffordshire*, ed. William Salt Archaeological Society, 1934. 1935, p. 101.
4. In 1770 a total of 164,194 pieces was sent from the Potteries. Ibid.
5. See Charles Hadfield, *British Canals*, 2nd ed., pp. 16-17.
6. *Reports of the late John Smeaton*, 1812, I, 15.
7. 10 Will III, *c.* 26.
8. *Reasons Humbly offer'd against the Bill for . . . making navigable the River Trent*, Wm. Salt Library, Stafford, M/743.
9. J. Phillips, *General History of Inland Navigation*, 1795, p. 186. See also *Supplement to a Pamphlet entitled 'Seasonable Considerations'* etc. April 1766. B.T. Hist. Recs. HRP 6/12. The lease for three lives cost £2,500 In addition, the lessees paid £4,000 to their predecessors for wharves, etc and invested another £4,000 in additional wharves, craft and improvements.
10. Petition in favour of the Trent & Mersey Canal, JHC.XXX, 720-1.
11. T. S. Ashton and J. Sykes, *The Coal Industry of the Eighteenth Century*, 1929, p. 231.
12. T. Nash, *Collections for the History of Worcestershire*, quo. T. S. Ashton, *Iron and Steel in the Industrial Revolution*, 1951, p. 243.
13. Ashton, *Iron and Steel*, p. 244.
14. T. S. Willan, 'The River Navigation and Trade of the Severn Valley, 1600-1750', *Economic History Review*, VIII.
15. *Aris's Birmingham Gazette*, 24 May 1762.
16. Ibid., 2 November, 28 December 1761.
17. 7 Geo I *c.* 10.
18. T. S. Willan, *The Navigation of the River Weaver in the Eighteenth Century*, 1951, for this and subsequent information.
19. 33 Geo II *c.* 49.
20. The history of the Weaver will be given in a forthcoming volume in this series by Charles Hadfield and Gordon Biddle, *The Canals of Northern England*.
21. Anon, *The History of Inland Navigations*, 2nd ed., 1769, pp 55-6, quoting from Sir Richard Whitworth's pamphlet, *The Advantages of Inland Navigation*, 1766, refers to a survey by Taylor of Manchester and Eyes of Liverpool of a canal from the Trent to the Mersey at the expense of Liverpool corporation. I can, however, find no evidence of this survey or of its support by the corporation.
22. *Derby Mercury*, 7 December 1758.
23. *Reports of the late John Smeaton*, I, 13-17. A map, with Smeaton's revisions, shows branches to Newcastle-under-Lyme and from near Fradley to Lichfield, with a branch off that to Tamworth, Staffs C.R.O. D.593/H/9/1.
24. Herbert Clegg, 'The Third Duke of Bridgewater's Canal Works in Manchester', *Trans. Lancs & Cheshire Antiq. Soc.*, LXV, 1955.

25. Hugh Malet, *The Canal Duke*, 1961, p. 104.
26. Letter from Josiah Wedgwood to Dr Erasmus Darwin, 3 April 1765, Wedgwood collection.
27. Letter from Josiah Wedgwood to Thomas Bentley, 7 October 1765.
28. Letter from Josiah Wedgwood at Burslem to John Wedgwood in London, 11 March 1765.
29. For their relations, see Neil McKendrick, 'Josiah Wedgwood and Thomas Bentley', *Trans. R. Hist. Soc.*, 5th Ser., Vol. 14, 1964.
30. R. S. Sayers, *Lloyds Bank in the History of English Banking*, 1957, p. 5.
31. Josiah Wedgwood to John Wedgwood, 3 April 1765, 'before breakfast'.
32. W. H. B. Court, *The Rise of the Midland Industries*, 1938.
33. Josiah Wedgwood, letter of 3 April 1765 already quoted.
34. Wedgwood collection.
35. Letter from Josiah Wedgwood to Dr Darwin, April 1765.
36. *Aris's Birmingham Gazette*, 29 April, 6 May 1765.
37. Josiah to John Wedgwood, 13 April 1765, Wedgwood collection.
38. For the part played by John Gilbert in the building of the Bridgewater Canal, see Hugh Malet, *The Canal Duke*.
39. Josiah Wedgwood to Dr Darwin, 15 April 1765.
40. Josiah Wedgwood to Dr Darwin, ND.
41. Josiah Wedgwood to Dr Darwin, ND. See *Aris's Birmingham Gazette*, 8 July 1765.
42. For Sir Richard Whitworth, see S. A. H. Burne, 'Parochial Documents', *Trans. N. Staffs. Field Club*, 1927-8, LXII.
43. J. Phillips, *General History of Inland Navigation*, 2nd ed., 1795, sets out in full the economic arguments for Whitworth's and Wedgwood's lines.
44. Josiah Wedgwood to Dr Darwin, 16 May 1765.
45. Ibid., May 1765.
46. Josiah Wedgwood to Dr Darwin, 5 June 1765.
47. John Sparrow to Dr Darwin, 24 June 1765.
48. Josiah Wedgwood to John Wedgwood, 6 July 1765.
49. Ibid., 29 July 1765.
50. Josiah Wedgwood to Thomas Bentley, November 1765.
51. Willan, *River Weaver*, p. 91.
52. Josiah Wedgwood to Dr Darwin, 16 May 1765.
53. Letter from George Heron to Sir Peter Warburton, quo. Willan, *River Weaver* p. 92.
54. Josiah Wedgwood to Thomas Bentley, 15 December 1765.
55. Josiah Wedgwood to Thomas Bentley, 12 December 1765.
56. Ibid.
57. Ibid., 15 December 1765.
58. Ibid., December 1765.
59. *Derby Mercury*, 17 January 1766.
60. Willan, *River Weaver*, p. 92.
61. 6 Geo III *c.* 96.
62. 28 April 1766.
63. See the description of this ceremony in Charles Hadfield, *British Canals*, 2nd ed. pp. 38-9.
64. 6 Geo III *c.* 17.
65. *Aris's Birmingham Gazette*, 24 March 1766.
66. 6 Geo III *c.* 97.

Notes to Chapter II

1. Josiah Wedgwood to Thomas Bentley, June 1766.
2. Ibid., 2 March 1767.
3. Ibid., 2 April 1767.

pages 30–36   NOTES   299

4. Josiah Wedgwood, perhaps to Thomas Bentley, probably September 1767.
5. Josiah Wedgwood to Thomas Bentley, 2 April 1767.
6. Ibid., July 1767.
7. *Aris's Birmingham Gazette*, 14 September 1767.
8. *Derby Mercury*, 20 April 1770.
9. *Aris's Birmingham Gazette*, 18, 25 November 1771.
10. Josiah Wedgwood to Thomas Bentley, 24 December 1767.
11. Ibid., 28 September 1772.
12. Josiah Wedgwood to Tarleton, November 1768.
13. Josiah Wedgwood to Thomas Bentley, 18 July 1766.
14. Ibid., 12 November 1768.
15. Liverpool Town Books, 23 November 1768.
16. Josiah Wedgwood to Thomas Bentley, July 1769.
17. Wedgwood Collection, Printed notice of 26 August 1769, 32/31000.
18. 10 Geo III *c*. 102.
19. *Derby Mercury*, 5 July 1771.
20. *Aris's Birmingham Gazette*, 19 October 1772.
21. Ibid., 17 April 1775.
22. Ibid., 9 October 1775.
23. *Glocester Journal*, 27 February 1775.
24. See 22.
25. Josiah Wedgwood to Thomas Bentley, 11 September 1774.
26. Ibid., 19 September 1774.
27. Rees, *Cyclopaedia*, 1819, art. 'Canal'.
28. Henshall settled at Longport after he had finished the Trent & Mersey and Chesterfield Canals. He did a little canal surveying in later years, but for most of the time until his death in 1817 he was in business at Longport with Mrs Brindley's second husband and their children, the Williamsons.
29. 15 Geo III *c*. 20.
30. A staircase of three at Lawton was rebuilt as four separate locks under an Act of 1809.
31. So Rees; de Salis gives 2,897; perhaps it was slightly lengthened when the second tunnel was built.
32. *A State of Facts respecting some Differences which have arisen betwixt His Grace the Duke of Bridgewater and The Proprietors of the Navigation from the Trent to the Mersey.* 1785 (Wedgwood Collection).
33. For inclined planes on canals, see Charles Hadfield's *British Canals*, 2nd ed., pp. 64–6.
34. Josiah Wedgwood to Thomas Bentley, 23 January 1773.
35. Ibid., 22 November 1773.
36. Ibid., 14 November 1775.
37. *Derby Mercury*, 14 November 1793.
38. 16 Geo III *c*. 32.
39. A letter of 9 January 1780 from Edward Bill to Edward Sneyd (Wm. Salt Library, Stafford, Sneyd papers) says that the tonnage on the branch from opening to 18 December 1779 was £896. Given that the quarterly tolls in 1783 were some £500, but on the other hand that the tramroad had had to be repaired, we can guess a date early in 1779.
40. This account of the tramroads is based on a paper, 'The Caldon Low Tramways', read to the Cheadle Historical Society by Dr J. R. Hollick on 24 March 1954.
41. As 39.
42. 23 Geo III *c*. 33.
43. John Phillips, *General History of Inland Navigation*, 1795, 2nd ed., p. 370.
44. Thomas Pennant, *The Journey from Chester to London*, pp. 55–6.
45. Shaw's 'Tour to the West of England', pp. 317–18, in *A General Collection of the best and most interesting Voyages and Travels*, by John Pinkerton, Vol. II, 1808.
46. Ibid.
47. Willan, *River Weaver*, pp. 115–16.

48. H. Holland, *A General View of the Agriculture of Cheshire*, 1813, p. 320.
49. Information from L. T. C. Rolt.
50. H. Thorpe, 'Lichfield: A Study of its Growth and Function', *Trans. Staffs Record Soc.*, 1951-2, 1954, p. 196.
51. *Derby Mercury*, 21 April 1780.
52. Ibid., 7 September 1770.
53. Josiah Wedgwood, *Some Considerations on the Expediency of the Proprietors of the Navigation from the Trent to the Mersey acting as Carriers upon the Canal*. ND (c. 1785) Wedgwood Collection.
54. A. C. Wood, 'The History of Trade and Transport on the River Trent', *Trans. Thoroton Soc.*, 1950, p. 35.
55. *Derby Mercury*, 23 August 1787.
56. *A State of Facts respecting some Differences which have arisen betwixt His Grace the Duke of Bridgewater and The Proprietors of the Navigation from the Trent to the Mersey*. By Order of the Committee, 24 and 25 February 1785. Wedgwood Collection.
57. Letter from R. Levitt to E. Sneyd, Wm. Salt Library, Stafford, HM 37/37.
58. Staffs & Worcs Canal Minute Book, 7 January 1779.
59. Notice, Wedgwood Collection, 32/24177.
60. 23 Geo III c. 33.
61. 15 Geo III c. 16.
62. Chester Canal Minute Book, 6 April 1780.
63. Trevor H. Ford, 'The Speedwell Mine in the 18th Century', *Derbyshire Countryside*, April-May 1960.
64. John Farey, *A General View of the Agriculture of Derbyshire*, I, 330.
65. For these underground canals, see Hugh Malet, *The Canal Duke*, 1961, and Frank Mullineux, 'The Duke of Bridgewater's Underground Canals at Worsley', *Trans. Lancs & Cheshire Antiq. Soc.*, vol. 71, 1961.
66. Much of the material for this account is taken from an article, 'The Canal System of East Shropshire and the Industries it served', by W. Howard Williams in the *Shropshire Magazine* for May 1954, or from information given by Mr Howard Williams.
67. Map of the Donnington Wood colliery, dated 1 August 1788, in the possession of the Lilleshall Co.
68. *Salopian Shreds and Patches*, vol. 7, reprinted with additions, 1885.
69. Agreement to transfer land, 23 July 1768, Lilleshall Co.
70. See Herbert Clegg, 'The Third Duke of Bridgewater's Canal Works in Manchester', *Trans. Lancs & Cheshire Ant. Soc.*, LXV, 1955.
71. See Charles Hadfield, *The Canals of Southern England*, 1955, p. 154-5.
72. This was the recollection of old Mrs Talbott, aged 95 in 1964, who remembered the plane working, and especially the boats splashing into the water at the bottom—the sort of thing a child would recall.
73. *Derby Mercury*, 1 March 1771.
74. JHC, 26 February 1771.
75. Josiah Wedgwood to Tarleton, November 1768, Wedgwood Collection.
76. Chester Canal Minute Book, 1 February 1772.
77. Ibid.
78. Ibid.
79. 12 Geo III c. 75.
80. *Aris's Birmingham Gazette*, 4 May 1772.
81. Chester Canal Minute Book, 10 July 1772.
82. Ibid., 19 February 1774.
83. *Annual Register*, 1775, p. 85.
84. 17 Geo III c. 67.
85. Chester Canal Minute Book, 20 January 1780.
86. Chester Canal Minute Book, 15 December 1781.
87. Ibid., 22 March 1782.
88. Ibid., 17 April 1789.
89. Ibid., 15 February 1790.

90. Ibid., 22 November 1790.
91. Ibid., 19 November 1779. See R. Willett, *Memoir of Hawarden Parish*, 1822; *Cheshire Sheaf*, 1943, No. 8325; 1815 survey plan in Flintshire C.R.O.
92. See N.L.W. MS 4877E (Pennant Papers, Vol. 1), Cledwyn Hughes, *The Western Marches of Wales*, 1953, p. 138, and A. H. Dodd, *The Industrial Revolution in North Wales*, pp. 101–2.
93. 28 Geo III *c*. 72.
94. See George Lloyd, 'The Flint Canal Company', *Journal of the Flintshire Historical Society*, 1962. Especially for Thomas Williams, see J. R. Harris, *The Copper King*, 1964.

Notes to Chapter III

1. *Aris's Birmingham Gazette*, 23 June 1766.
2. Staffs & Worcs Canal Committee Minute Book, 6 November 1770.
3. *Aris's Birmingham Gazette*, 1 April 1771.
4. T. Nash, *Collections for the History of Worcestershire*, 1781, II, 46.
5. Staffs & Worcs Canal Committee Minute Book, 28 May 1772.
6. Ibid., 25 July 1766.
7. Ibid., 18 August 1768.
8. 10 Geo III *c*. 103.
9. *Staffordshire Canal—A Hard Case!* (Birmingham Ref. Lib., 177408) *c*. 1790.
10. See Charles Hadfield, *British Canals*, 2nd ed., p. 45.
11. Stourbridge Canal Proprietors Minute Book, 2 January 1786.
12. Sharp papers, Hardwicke Court, Glos.
13. R. C. Gaut, *A History of Worcestershire Agriculture*, quoting from *Berrows Worcester Journal*, September 1775.
14. J. Randall, *The Severn Valley*, 1882, p. 428, quoting an earlier edition.
15. See Charles Hadfield, *The Canals of Southern England*, pp. 59–63.
16. *Aris's Birmingham Gazette*, 19 January 1782.
17. *Aris's Birmingham Gazette*, 27 January 1783.
18. See Charles Hadfield, *The Canals of Southern England*, pp. 65–7.
19. 'Navigator', *Observations on a 'Design for Improving the Navigation of the River Severn'*, 1788, Stoke on Trent P.L.
20. Staffs & Worcs Canal Committee Minute Book, 20 April 1784.
21. J. Randall, *History of Madeley*, 1880, p. 258.
22. J. Plymley, *General View of the Agriculture of Shropshire*, 1813, art. on 'Canals' by T. Telford, 1797, p. 287.
23. A. E. Richardson, *Robert Mylne*, 1955, p. 127.
24. 'Navigator', *Observations*.
25. R. A. Pelham, 'The Worcester & Birmingham Canal', *University of Birmingham Historical Journal*, 1955, Vol. 1, p. 65.
26. Papers, Staffs C.R.O., D260/M/E/430/30.
27. 23 Henry VIII *c*. 12.
28. T. S. Ashton, *Iron and Steel in the Industrial Revolution*, 1951, p. 242.
29. *Aris's Birmingham Gazette*, 2 November, 28 December 1761.
30. 12 Geo III *c*. 109.
31. Staffs & Worcs Canal Minute Book, 16 October 1777.
32. *Aris's Birmingham Gazette*, 30 March 1789.
33. A fuller account of the river navigation can be found in Charles Hadfield and John Norris, *Waterways to Stratford*, 1962.
34. 24 Geo II *c*. 39.
35. Oxford Canal Committee Minute Book, 17 January 1785.
36. See T. C. Cantrill and Marjory Wight, 'Yarranton's Works at Astley', *Trans. Worcs. Arch. Soc.*, 1929, vi, 92, and J. M. Palmer and M. I. Berrill, 'Andrew Yarranton and the navigation works at Astley', *Journal of the Railway and Canal Hist. Soc.*, May 1958, p. 41.

37. Car II, P.A.
38. Wm. Salt Library, Stafford, D.1788, Parcel 3, Bundle 8.
39. A. Yarranton, *England's Improvement by Sea and Land*, i, 66.
40. For the Stour schemes generally, see the collection of material in the William Salt Library, Stafford.
41. River Avon, *Orders in Council, etc.*, Tewkesbury, 1826.
42. R. C. Gaut, *History of Worcestershire Agriculture*, p. 114.
43. *Berrow's Worcester Journal*, 4 August 1825. See also ibid., 26 April 1810, 5 February and 30 April 1829.
44. Nash, *Worcestershire*, 1781, i, 306. Deed 484 (3), Droitwich Corporation records.
45. Ibid.
46. T. H. Willan, *Economic History Review*, 'The River Navigation and Trade of the Severn Valley', viii, 71.
47. Deed, 13 October 1673, Worcs. C R O.
48. Minute of Committee, 8 January 1846, Worcs C.R.O.
49. 8 Geo III *c.* 37.
50. Nash, *Worcestershire*, i, 306.
51. Droitwich Canal Minute Book, 4 March 1768.
52. Birmingham Canal Minute Book, 7 October 1768.
53. Memo, allegedly by Brindley, in Worcs C.R.O.
54. Worcs C.R.O.
55. A. Rees, *Cyclopaedia*, 1819, art. 'Canal'.
56. *Berrow's Worcester Journal*, 14 March 1771.
57. Droitwich Canal Minute Book, 3 March 1786.

Notes to Chapter IV

1. W. Hutton, *An History of Birmingham*, 2nd ed., 1783.
2. Preamble to the Birmingham Canal Minute Book.
3. Birmingham Canal Minute Book, 4 June 1767.
4. Ibid., 13 November 1767.
5. Ibid., 13 January 1768.
6. 8 Geo III *c.* 38.
7. Birmingham Canal Minute Book, 9 June 1768.
8. Ibid., 7 April 1769.
9. Ibid., 3 November 1769.
10. J. Cary, *Inland Navigation, or Select Plans* etc., 1795.
11. Ibid. for previous price. An advertisement of 5 February 1770 in *Aris* gives retail prices as 5d cwt at Friday Street coalyard, and 6d at Mr Baylis, Camphill.
12. *Aris's Birmingham Gazette*, 14 May 1770.
13. Birmingham Canal Minute Book, 20 October 1769.
14. Ibid., 10 November 1769.
15. Ibid., 15 November 1769.
16. *Aris's Birmingham Gazette*, 12 March 1770.
17. Ibid., 30 October 1769.
18. Letter to Lord Dartmouth, Staffs C.R.O. D.564/12/3.
19. Ibid., 21 September 1772.
20. Ibid., 5 October 1772, advertisement by Thomas Tonkys.
21. *Case of the Birmingham Canal Committee in Opposition to the Dudley Canal Extension Bill* (author's collection).
22. *Aris's Birmingham Gazette*, 24 December 1770.
23. Birmingham Canal Minute Book, 20 October 1769.
24. Sharp Papers, Hardwicke Court, Glos.
25. Hutton, *Birmingham*, 2nd ed., 1783.
26. Ibid., 6 August 1770.
27. Ibid., 29 October, 8 and 26 November, 10 and 17 December 1770, 17 January, 17 August and 2 September 1771.

28. Birmingham Canal Minute Book, 25 January 1782. See also *Case relative to the Navigable Canal intended to be made from the Coal Mines in the Parish of Wednesbury, and the Neighbourhood thereof, to Birmingham and to join the Coventry Canal at Fazeley* (author's collection).
29. *Aris's Birmingham Gazette*, 20 January 1783.
30. Oxford Canal Minute Book, 20 June 1782.
31. Hutton, *Birmingham*, 2nd ed , 1783.
32. 23 Geo III *c*. 92.
33. By 24 Geo III *c*. 4.
34. Cary, *Inland Navigation*, 1795.
35. Ibid.
36. H. Thorpe, 'Lichfield: a Study in its Growth and Function', *Trans. Staffs Rec. Soc.* 1951–2, 1954, p. 196.
37. *Aris's Birmingham Gazette*, 22 June 1789.
38. Letter of Thomas Sherratt to Oxford Canal Co., 2 November 1793, B.T. Hist. Recs.
39. *Glocester Journal*, 20 February 1775. A survey from Stourbridge to Stourton with branches to the mines on Pensnett Chase, was made by Whitworth in 1774; this was re-surveyed with an extension to Dudley in 1775 (both in Dudley P.L.)
40. Birmingham Canal Minute Book, 29 March 1776.
41. 16 Geo III *c*. 28.
42. D. R. Guttery, *From Broad-Glass to Cut Crystal*, 1956, p. 94.
43. *Aris's Birmingham Gazette*, 6 December 1779.
44. 22 Geo III *c*. 14.
45. A. Rees, *Cyclopaedia*, 1819, art. 'Canal'.
46. The arguments of the Staffs & Worcs are set out in William Jessop's pamphlet of January 1786, *River Severn*. (Staffs C.R.O. D 260/M/E/430/29).
47. *Aris's Birmingham Gazette*, 22 May 1786.
48. 16 Geo III *c*. 66.
49. *Aris's Birmingham Gazette*, 1 June 1778.
50. 25 Geo III *c*. 87.
51. Dudley Canal Proprietors' Minute Book, 5 September 1785.
52. *Aris's Birmingham Gazette*, 19 September 1785.
53. Dudley Canal Proprietors' Minute Book, 7 September 1789.
54. Dudley Canal Committee Minute Book, 14 May 1789.
55. Ibid., 13 September 1791.
56. *Aris's Birmingham Gazette*, 19 December 1791.

Notes to Chapter V

1. Birmingham Canal Minute Book, 25 September 1789
2. *Case of the Birmingham Canal Committee in Opposition to the Dudley Canal Extension Bill*, 1792.
3. Ibid.
4. Birmingham Canal Minute Book, 23 June 1793.
5. *Staffordshire Advertiser*, 6 July 1799.
6. Birmingham Canal Proprietors' Minute Book, 27 September 1793.
7. Ibid., 31 March 1815.
8. 55 Geo III *c*. 40.
9. Birmingham Canal Proprietors' Minute Book, 29 September 1815.
10. 9 & 10 Vic *c*. 269.
11. *Life of Thomas Telford*, ed. Rickman, 1838.
12. Joseph Parkes, *A Statement of the Claim of the Subscribers to the Birmingham and Liverpool Rail Road*, 2nd ed., 1825. Birmingham P.L.
13. *Aris's Birmingham Gazette*, 6 December 1824.
14. Birmingham Canal Proprietors' Minute Book, 28 September 1827.

15. Birmingham Canal Proprietors' Minute Book, 28 September 1827. It should be noted that the canal company was authorized to charge the same tolls on the shortened lines as on the original lengths: the economy to the user was in speed and convenience. See 46 Geo III c. 92, sect. i. Considerable exceptions were made by 5 Will IV c. 34, sect. cxxvii.
16. *British Almanac*, 1830.
17. Ibid.
18. Birmingham Canal Proprietors' Minute Book, 11 May 1838.
19. Ibid., 9 November 1838.
20. Ibid.
21. *Case in support of the Birmingham Canal Bill*, 1839. Birmingham Public Library 177408.
22. 2 & 3 Vic c. 61.
23. 3 Vic c. 24.
24. Birmingham Canal Proprietors' Minute Book, 27 March 1818.
25. 51 Geo III c. 105, sect. v.
26. Parkes, *A Statement*, op. cit.
27. Ibid.
28. *Case in Support of the Birmingham Canal Bill*, op. cit.
29. 5 Will IV c. 34.
30. Birmingham Canal Minute Book, 10 November 1837.
31. Coventry Canal Minute Book, 11 May 1824.
32. *Berrows' Worcester Journal*, 16 December 1824.
33. Coventry Canal Minute Book, 10 March 1825.
34. Birmingham Canal Proprietors' Minute Book, 9 November 1838; 14 May 1841.
35. Ibid., 13 November 1840.
36. Ibid., 5 March 1839.
37. 3 Vic c. 24.
38. *Wolverhampton Chronicle*, 10 August 1791. For this and some other information used in this account I am indebted to C. J. Gilson, 'The Wyrley and Essington Canal', a paper presented to the Lichfield Archaeological and Historical Society.
39. Preamble to 1792 Act.
40. 32 Geo III c. 81.
41. Wyrley & Essington Proprietors' Minute Book, 10 May 1792.
42. 34 Geo III c. 25.
43. Wyrley & Essington Canal Proprietors' Minute Book, 10 November 1794.
44. Ibid.
45. Ibid., 11 May 1795.
46. *Aris's Birmingham Gazette*, 15 May 1797.
47. E. J. Homeshaw, *The Corporation of the Borough and Foreign of Walsall*, 1960, p. 104.
48. *Staffordshire Advertiser*, 15 June 1799.
49. John Farey, *A General View of the Agriculture of Derbyshire*, III, pp. 455-6.
50. *Staffordshire Advertiser*, 8 September 1798.
51. H. Thorpe, 'Lichfield: A Study of its Growth and Function', *Trans. Staffs Record Soc.*, 1951-2, 1954, p. 197.
52. E. J. Homeshaw, *The Story of Bloxwich*, 1955, p. 124.
53. J. Cary, *Inland Navigation*, 1795, p. 48.
54. *Berrow's Worcester Journal*, 28 March 1822.
55. *Aris's Birmingham Gazette*, 5 November 1804.
56. Wyrley & Essington Canal Proprietors' Minute Book, 11 November 1822.
57. Ibid., 11 May 1829.
58. Ibid., 10 May 1830.
59. Ibid., 10 May 1838.

Notes to Chapter VI

1. Stourbridge Canal Committee Minute Book, 2 February 1792.

pages 101–118   NOTES   305

2. Stourbridge Canal Proprietors' Minute Book, 6 July 1807.
3. Stourbridge Canal Committee Minute Book, 16 October 1830.
4. Ibid., 2 April 1836.
5. *Prospectus* and *Plan*, 1836 (W.R. Deeds & Records, Stourbridge Extension Canal papers).
6. MS plan, W.R. Deeds & Records, loc. cit.
7. 7 Will IV *c*. 53.
8. The 1837 Act made curious provisions for this lock at the junction of the Stourbridge and the Extension canals. It was to be controlled by the company whose water was the higher, and, should the difference in level at any time exceed 6 in., then the company with the lower level should pay the other 3s for each 4,000 ft^3 that passed through the lock.
9. Dudley Canal Committee Minute Book, 1 September 1792.
10. 33 Geo III *c*. 121.
11. J.H.C. evidence on bill, 11 February 1793.
12. *Aris's Birmingham Gazette*, 29 April, 6, 13 May, 17 June 1793.
13. Dudley Canal Letter-book, letter to J. C. Jervoise.
14. *Aris's Birmingham Gazette*, 30 January 1797.
15. Dudley Canal Letter-book, 28 May 1798, letter from T. Brettell to William Hooper.
16. Dudley P.L.
17. Ibid.
18. Dudley Canal Committee Minute Book, 5 December 1797.
19. Dudley Canal Letter-book, T. Brettell to Samuel Leach, 24 November 1797.
20. Dudley Canal Proprietors' Minute Book, 6 September 1830.
21. Dudley Canal Committee Minute Book, 17 May 1836.
22. Dudley Canal Letter-book, 1 August 1805.
23. Dudley Canal Proprietors' Minute Book, 5 September 1842.
24. Dudley Canal Committee Minute Book, 17 January 1796.
25. Dudley Canal Letter-book, p. 61. 1802 or 1803.
26. Ibid., 24 August 1803.
27. Dudley Canal Committee Minute Book, 26 February 1839.

Notes to Chapter VII

1. *Annual Register*, 1800, p. 24.
2. *Hereford Journal*, 1 April 1801.
3. Ibid., 31 March 1802.
4. *Berrow's Worcester Journal*, 2 August 1804.
5. See H. W. Paar, *The Great Western Railway in Dean*, 1965.
6. See Charles Hadfield, *Canals of South Wales and the Border*, and H. W. Paar, *The Severn & Wye Railway*, 1963.
7. See Charles Hadfield, *The Canals of South Wales and the Border*.
8. *Glocester Journal*, 1 April, 13 May 1793.
9. See Charles Hadfield, *The Canals of Southern England*.
10. For Coalbrookdale, see A. Raistrick, *Dynasty of Ironfounders*, 1953.
11. C. Hulbert, *The History and Description of the County of Salop* (1837 ed.), p. 347.
12. Ibid., p. 348.
13. *Berrow's Worcester Journal*, 1 December 1808.
14. *Aris's Birmingham Gazette*, 26 November 1792, see also Charles Hadfield, *The Canals of Southern England*.
15. 1 August 1825.
16. Gloucester & Berkeley Canal Minute Book, 16 December 1840.
17. *Aris's Birmingham Gazette*, 25 July 1825.
18. *Derby Mercury*, 26 September 1827.
19. Hulbert, *Salop*, op. cit., p. 81.
20. T. C. Turberville, *Worcestershire in the Nineteenth Century*, 1852, p. 282.

U

21. *Hereford Journal*, 27 January, 24 February 1830. *Aris's Birmingham Gazette*, 5 April 1830.
22. *Hereford Journal*, 8 February 1832.
23. Worcester & Birmingham Canal Proprietors' Minute Book, 5 January 1836.
24. Staffs & Worcs Canal Minute Book, 16 February 1837.
25. Gloucester & Berkeley Canal Minute Book, 30 March 1837.
26. *Hereford Journal*, 18 November 1840.
27. *Berrow's Worcester Journal*, 10 December 1840.
28. Worcester & Birmingham Canal Proprietors' Minute Book, 6 July 1841.
29. Plymley, *Shropshire*, op. cit., p. 289.
30. H. M. Rathbone, *Letters of Richard Reynolds, with a Memoir of his Life*, 1852.
31. *Worcestershire*, 1799, p. 46.
32. *Aris's Birmingham Gazette*, 30 March 1789.
33. 39 Geo III *c.* 8.
34. *Staffordshire Advertiser*, 30 August 1800.
35. Staffs & Worcs Canal Minute Book, 28 February 1884, 2 April 1885.
36. *Berrow's Worcester Journal*, 4 April 1822.
37. Ibid., 6 January 1825 etc.
38. *Glocester Journal*, 31 August 1801.
39. Ibid., 28 September 1801.
40. Ibid., 5 July 1802.
41. 43 Geo III *c.* 129.
42. An advertisement in *Berrow's Worcester Journal* of 2 August 1804 implies that the path was open.
43. *Berrow's Worcester Journal*, 22 February 1810.
44. 49 Geo III *c.* 121.
45. *Berrow's Worcester Journal*, 4 June 1807.
46. 51 Geo III *c.* 148.
47. *Hereford Journal*, 3 March 1824.
48. Ibid., 18 October 1826.

Notes to Chapter VIII

1. Staffordshire & Worcestershire Canal Minute Book, 21 February 1811.
2. Ibid., 4 September 1828.
3. Ibid., 14 September 1832.
4. This particular drawback was reduced in 1820, when the Worcester & Birmingham agreed to raise its tolls proportionately.
5. *Berrow's Worcester Journal*, 17 November 1825.
6. *Staffordshire Advertiser*, 10 February, 8 September 1798.
7. See Kenneth Brown, 'Stafford's First Railway', *Railway Magazine*, November 1939, p. 333.
8. Staffs & Worcs Canal Committee Minute Book, 1 February 1816.
9. Ibid., 26 May 1825.
10. Ibid., 16 December 1835.
11. *Hereford Journal*, 17 June 1829. The *Agenoria* is now in the Railway Museum at York.
12. Wyrley & Essington Canal Proprietors' Minute Book, 6 July 1798.
13. Staffs & Worcs Canal Committee Minute Book, 16 April 1841.
14. E.g. *Aris's Birmingham Gazette*, 14 September 1801.
15. Droitwich Canal Minute Book, 26 November 1810.
16. Worcester & Birmingham Canal Proprietors' Minute Book, 4 July 1810.
17. Ibid., 2 January 1821.
18. Droitwich Canal Minute Book, 29 January 1821.
19. *Additional Reasons in favour of the Worcester and Birmingham Canal*, 1790, Birmingham Ref. Lib. 636062.

20. 31 Geo III c. 59. For the background to its passing see R. A. Pelham, 'The Worcester and Birmingham Canal', *Univ. of Birmingham Hist. Journal*, Vol. V, No. 1, 1935.
21. R. C. Gaut, *A History of Worcestershire Agriculture*, quoting from a newspaper.
22. Quoted in full in J. A. Langford, *A Century of Birmingham Life*, 1868, I, 366.
23. *Derby Mercury*, 12 July 1792.
24. Worcester & Birmingham Canal Committee Minute Book, 30 October 1796.
25. Worcester & Birmingham Canal Proprietors' Minute Book, 5 July 1796.
26. A. Rees, *Cyclopaedia*, 1819, art. 'Canal'.
27. *Hereford Journal*, 12 April 1797; for date see *Aris's Birmingham Gazette*, 3 April 1797.
28. Worcester & Birmingham Proprietors' Minute Book, 2 July 1799.
29. *Berrow's Worcester Journal*, 19 March 1807.
30. Ibid.
31. Ibid., 4 June 1807.
32. Ibid., 18 May 1808.
33. Ibid., 7 July 1808.
34. For the lift, see Edward Smith, *A description of the patent perpendicular lift erected on the Worcester & Birmingham Canal*, etc. 1810. Inst. of Civil Engs. Lib., Tracts 8vo, Vol. 5.
35. *Aris's Birmingham Gazette*, 11 February 1811.
36. In full in the Worcester & Birmingham Canal Committee Minute Book, 22 May 1811.
37. Worcester & Birmingham Canal Proprietors' Minute Book, 2 January 1816.
38. Staffs & Worcs Canal Minute Book, 10 April 1816.
39. Worcester & Birmingham Canal Proprietors' Minute Book, 6 January 1820.
40. Samuel Salt, *Statistics and Calculations essentially necessary to persons connected with Railway or Canals*, 1845.
41. Worcester & Birmingham Canal Proprietors' Minute Book, 3 January 1825.
42. *Glocester Journal*, 11 July 1825.
43. Ibid., 10 January 1825.
44. Ibid., 11 July 1825.
45. Plan of branch, B.M. 4 e 13/94.
46. *Berrow's Worcester Journal*, 26 August 1830.
47. Two fed the canal, Bittall Upper and Tardebigge, and five supplied the mill-owners on the Rea and the Arrow, Lifford, Wychall, Cofton, Harborne, and Bittall Lower.
48. *Berrow's Worcester Journal*, 14 October 1830.
49. Ibid., 21 October 1830.
50. Ibid.
51. Worcester & Birmingham Canal Proprietors' Minute Book, 6 July 1841.
52. For a more detailed account, see Charles Hadfield and John Norris, *Waterways to Stratford*, 1961.
53. For William James, see *Waterways to Stratford* and E. M. S. Paine, *The Two James's and the Two Stephensons*, 1861, reprinted 1961.
54. There were 15 shares, eight leasehold and seven freehold. He almost certainly bought the eight in 1813 from George Wigley Perrott, the owner of the Lower Avon. The seven had been advertised for sale in December 1806 on the death of the Rev W. W. Fitz-Thomas, descendant of Lord Windsor the former owner, and James may have bought them then. It is more likely, however, that they passed through intermediate hands.
55. 32 Geo III c. 83. Sarah Mumford was a Miller nominee. The Miller family, with various partners, kept a large interest in the canal till 1871.
56. *Glocester Journal*, 19 March 1798.
57. Coombe Hill Canal Minute Book, Glos. County Records.
58. *Aris's Birmingham Gazette*, 12 July 1802.
59. See Phillips, *Inland Navigation*, 5th ed., p. 594. The proposal was briefly revived in 1810, but dropped because of the cost, and again in 1822.

60. Counsel's brief of 1809 says 'full £6,000', but the minute book for 16 June 1870 says £5,055 15s. The £100 shares had a value of £101 2s 3¾d, which confirms this figure.
61. Counsel's brief on bill of 1809. Glos. County Records Office.
62. See H. W. Paar, *The Severn & Wye Railway*, 1963.
63. For the Bullo Pill line, see H. W. Paar, *The Great Western Railway in Dean*, 1965.
64. Counsel's brief.
65. John Hodgkinson's evidence on the bill, House of Lords Record Office.
66. 49 Geo III *c*. 23. For a description of the line, see B. Baxter, 'The Route of the Gloucester and Cheltenham Tramroad', *Railway Magazine*, February 1953. The Leckhampton–Cheltenham section was opened on 2 July 1810, and the Gloucester section on 4 June 1811.
67. *Glocester Journal*, 10 January 1825.

Notes to Chapter IX

1. *Eddowe's Salopian Journal*, 6 January 1798.
2. Unless otherwise acknowledged, this account is based on material provided by Mr W. Howard Williams, mainly in an article in the *Shropshire Magazine* for 1954, 'The Wombridge and Ketley Canals'.
3. For a general account, see A. Raistrick, *Dynasty of Ironfounders*, 1953.
4. See map by M. Lloyd, 1955, 'Sketch Map of Plateways and Canals in the Coalbrookdale District'.
5. See W. Howard Williams, 'The Wombridge and Ketley Canals', *Shropshire Magazine*, 1954.
6. J. Plymley, *General View of the Agriculture of Shropshire*, 1803.
7. See the description of the plane quoted from Plymley, op. cit., in my *British Canals*, 2nd ed., 1959, p. 65.
8. See D. H. Tew, 'Canal Lifts and Inclines', *Trans Newcomen Soc.*, XXVIII, 1951-2, p. 35, and W. A. McCutcheon, *The Canals of the North of Ireland*, 1965.
9. He probably had contacts with John Smeaton or William Jessop, both of whom were concerned with those on the Tyrone Navigation.
10. See Charles Hadfield, *The Canals of Southern England*, p. 56.
11. Ibid., p. 57.
12. John Farey, the author of the article on 'Canals' in Rees's *Cyclopaedia*, confuses the Wombridge and Ketley Canals. It seems that the reference in the text is to the Ketley.
13. Quo. Raistrick, *Ironfounders*, p. 189.
14. Staffordshire C.R.O., D.593/B/11/7.
15. Shropshire Canal Minute Book, 13 June 1788.
16. J. J. Hirsch, *Notice sur les Elevateurs*, etc., p. 11.
17. *Derby Mercury*, 21 June 1787; *Aris's Birmingham Gazette*, 25 June 1787.
18. In Plymley, *Shropshire*.
19. Shropshire Canal Minute Book, 12 and 13 June 1788.
20. This description is based on the interesting Birmingham School of Architecture 1964 thesis of R. L. Tonkinson, 'Inclined Planes on the Shropshire Canals'.
21. Raistrick, *Ironfounders*, p. 188.
22. Coalbrookdale Collection, Shropshire C.R.O.
23. J. Randall, *History of Madeley*, 1880, p. 94.
24. Herefordshire & Gloucestershire Canal Minute Book, 3 August 1829.
25. Plymley, *Shropshire*.
26. Ibid.
27. *Eddowe's Salopian Journal*, 3 December 1794.
28. 33 Geo III *c*. 113.
29. *Eddowe's Salopian Journal*, 16 November 1796.
30. S. Smiles, *Lives of the Engineers*, 1862, II, 346.
31. Shrewsbury Canal Minute Book, 6 July 1793.

32. Ibid., 12 February 1842.
33. *Eddowe's Salopian Journal.*
34. Ellesmere Canal report, 5 February 1800 (Shrewsbury P.L.).
35. Prospectus of the Stirling Canal, 13 December 1835.
36. Shrewsbury Canal Minute Book, 8 December 1838.
37. Shrewsbury Canal Minute Book, 14 October 1843. Letter dated 5 October.

Notes to Chapter X

1. Chester Canal Minute Book, 15 February 1790.
2. Joseph Turner, *Description of the Intended Canal from Shrewsbury to Chester and Liverpool*, etc., 1791. Birkenhead P.L.
3. Ellesmere Canal Proprietors' Minute Book, 7 November 1791.
4. Ibid., 21 August 1792.
5. *Report*, 1805, p. 21.
6. 33 Geo III c. 91.
7. Ellesmere Canal Committee Minute Book, 23 September 1793.
8. *Eddowe's Salopian Journal*, 29 July 1795.
9. *Nottingham Journal*, 27 February 1796.
10. Chester Canal Minute Book, 24 January 1797.
11. One is illustrated in Charles Hadfield, *British Canals*, 2nd ed., 1959, pp. 171-2.
12. Ellesmere Canal Committee Minute Book, 17 January 1794.
13. Ibid., 31 March 1794.
14. See Charles Hadfield, *British Canals*, 2nd ed., pp. 103-4.
15. Ellesmere Canal Committee Minute Book, 19 August 1795.
16. See the extract quoted in A. Gibb, *The Story of Telford*, 1935, p. 32.
17. *Life*, ed. John Rickman, 1838.
18. *Report*, 1806, p. 10.
19. Ibid.
20. 36 Geo III c. 96.
21. Patent of 18 March 1794. Earlier, in 1790, Duncombe had invented some form of counterbalanced lift, but does not seem to have followed it up (see *Aris's Birmingham Gazette*, 3 May 1790).
22. Ellesmere Canal Committee Minute Book, 4 December 1794.
23. *Aris's Birmingham Gazette*, 16 May 1796.
24. Samuel Egerton had died without heirs in 1780. He was succeeded by his sister, who took his name, and also died in the same year. Her son William Egerton is referred to.
25. Chester Canal Minute Book, 22 June 1795.
26. Ibid., 14 September 1795.
27. 44 Geo III c. 54.
28. *Eddowe's Salopian Journal*, 3 January 1810.
29. Ibid., 1 January 1806.
30. 53 Geo III c. 80.
31. *Eddowe's Salopian Journal*, 5 June 1816.
32. 7 & 8 Geo IV c. 102.
33. *Illustrated London News*, 23 September 1843, p. 210.
34. Ellesmere & Chester Canal Minute Book, 8 August 1844.
35. Birmingham Canal Proprietors' Minute Book, 26 March 1824.
36. Ellesmere & Chester Canal Committee Minute Book, 3 January 1825.
37. 7 Geo IV c. 95.
38. See F. C. Mather, 'The Duke of Bridgewater's Trustees and the Coming of the Railways', *Trans. R. Hist. Soc.*, 5th ser., XIV, 1964.
39. Sir John Rennie, *Autobiography*, 1875, pp. 243-4.
40. 7 & 8 Geo IV c. 2.
41. Birmingham & Liverpool Junction Canal Proprietors' Minute Book, 19 January 1832.

42. W. Cubitt, *A Second Report on the Financial State of the Birmingham and Liverpool Junction Canal*, 1836 (author's collection).
43. Birmingham & Liverpool Junction Canal Proprietors' Minute Book, 17 January 1839.
44. Article, 'Horsehay Iron Works', written 1876, Shropshire C.R.O.
45. Birmingham & Liverpool Junction Canal Report, 23 February 1843.
46. Birmingham & Liverpool Junction Canal Proprietors' Minute Book, 2 August 1844.
47. Ellesmere & Chester Canal Minute Book, 12 June 1845.
48. Staffs & Worcs Canal Committee Minute Book, 7 December 1843.
49. Information from Mr F. C. Mather, Southampton University, who is working on a history of the Bridgewater trustees, 1830–72.
50. Ellesmere Canal Minute Book, 25 October 1792.
51. 34 Geo III *c*. 39.
52. See Charles Hadfield, *The Canals of South Wales and the Border*, p. 192.
53. *Case of the Montgomeryshire Canal Co . . . in respect of the proposed tax on inland navigation*, Shrewsbury, 1797. Inst. Civil Engineers Lib., Tracts 8vo, Vol. 98.
54. Montgomeryshire Canal Committee Minute Book, 3 July 1797.
55. T. Martyn, 'An Account of a Tour of Wales', 1801, N.L.W. 1340 C.
56. W. Pugh, *To the Proprietors of the Western Branch of the Montgomeryshire Canal*, 1834, Inst. Civil Engs. Lib., Tracts 8vo, Vol. 66.
57. *Eddowe's Salopian Journal*, 7 September 1814.
58. 55 Geo III *c*. 83.
59. Montgomeryshire Canal (E.B.) Committee Minute Book, 6 July 1818.
60. Letter of 24 August 1823, Glansevern Correspondence, N.L.W., No. 2332, Group 1.
61. Ibid., Letter No. 12,499 of 12 September 1832.
62. 4 Will IV *c*. 20.
63. Letter of 7 June 1835, Glansevern Correspondence, N.L.W., No. 2143.

Notes to Chapter XI

1. *Derby Mercury*, 27 October 1796.
2. *Case of the Company of Proprietors of the Navigation from the Trent to the Mersey* on the bill. B.T. Hist. Recs. HRP/6/36.
3. 37 Geo III *c*. 36.
4. It is still possible to trace much of the old line.
5. 37 Geo III *c*. 81
6. *Staffordshire Advertiser*, 14 September 1811.
7. W. Parson and T. Bradshaw, *Staffs General and Commercial Directory* for 1818, Part 2.
8. 42 Geo III *c*. 25.
9. See John Farey, *A General View of the Agriculture of Derbyshire*, Vol. III for a description of the line.
10. 1 Will IV *c*. 55.
11. For their courses, see Thomas Hargreaves's map of the Staffordshire Potteries and Newcastle of 1832, in the Stoke-on-Trent P.L. For distances and levels, see *Lengths and Levels to Bradshaw's Maps*, 1833.
12. John Ward, *The Borough of Stoke-upon-Trent*, 1863, p. 159.
13. *Derby Mercury*, 6 November 1800.
14. Regent's Canal Proprietors' Minute Book, 27 March 1816.
15. Bridgewater Collection, Shrewsbury P.L.
16. Ibid.
17. 4 Geo IV *c*. 87.
18. Staffordshire C.R.O. Deposited plans Nos 42 and 44.
19. So de Salis, 1928 ed., p. 12, but on p. 195 he says 2,919.
20. De Salis, *A Chronology of Inland Navigation*, 1897.

pages 204-224   NOTES   311

21. 8 Geo IV c. 81.
22. *Aris's Birmingham Gazette*, 11 April 1825.
23. Ibid., 22 October 1838.
24. 35 Geo III c. 87.
25. Statement to the Board of Trade, 1864, Newcastle Canal papers.
26. Chester Canal Minute Book, 6 April 1780.
27. 'The intended Newcastle Junction Canal and Railed-Ways', in the possession of Knight & Sons, solicitors, Newcastle, together with the Minute Book and a collection of papers about the canal.
28. 38 Geo III c. 29.
29. Preamble.
30. *Staffordshire Advertiser*, 13 July 1799.
31. Newcastle-under-Lyme Junction Canal Minute Book, 9 December 1831.
32. *Aris's Birmingham Gazette*, 2 December 1765.
33. Peak Forest Canal Committee Minute Book, 21 December 1795.
34. *Derby Mercury*, 18 February 1796.
35. See Deposited Plan No. 50 in the Staffs C.R.O.
36. Ibid., 20 October 1824.
37. Peak Forest Canal Committee Minute Book, 19 November 1824.
38. *Derby Mercury*, 6 April 1825.
39. 7 Geo IV c. 30.
40. *Derby Mercury*, 16, 23 November 1831.
41. Peak Forest Canal Committee Minute Book, 7 April 1831.
42. Ibid., 19 June 1838.
43. Called the Manchester & Birmingham Junction.
44. The Oxford Canal had been shortened, the section forming part of the London-Manchester route from $34\frac{7}{8}$ miles to $23\frac{3}{4}$ miles, but the toll applicable to the former mileage was payable. Therefore the Oxford charge was $1\frac{1}{2}$d on the nominal, 2d on the actual mileage.
45. See Peak Forest Canal Committee Minute Book, 30 January, 27 March 1839.
46. Peak Forest Canal Committee Minute Book, 21, 22 May 1840.

Notes to Chapter XII

1. Borough Surveyor's Office, Newcastle-under-Lyme.
2. Macclesfield Canal Proprietors' Minute Book, 17 July 1845.
3. Macclesfield Canal Committee Minute Book, 17 July 1845.
4. Ibid.
5. Ibid., 18 March 1846.
6. 9 & 10 Vic c. 266.
7. 9 & 10 Vic c. 279.
8. Manchester, Sheffield & Lincolnshire Railway Directors Minute Book, 13 December 1847.
9. Plan in author's collection. See Peak Forest Canal Committee Minute Book, 5 September, 22 November, 12 December 1838. Macclesfield Canal Committee Minute Book, 31 May 1837, 17 October, 7 December 1838, 18 January 1839.
10. North Staffordshire Railway Report, 23 September 1846.
11. 9 & 10 Vic c. 85.
12. It is shown on plan No. 14 at the Derbyshire C.R.O.
13. North Staffordshire Railway Report, 1 July 1847.
14. Worcester & Birmingham Canal Committee Minute Book, 11 February, 19 May 1848.
15. F. C. Mather, 'The Duke of Bridgewater's Trustees and the Coming of the Railways', *Trans R. Hist. Soc.*, 5th Ser., Vol. 14, 1964.
16. 10 & 11 Vic c. 108, clause 38.
17. North Staffordshire Railway Report, 28 January 1856.

18. This account is taken from Appendix No. 22, by W. Burchell, to the *Report* of the Select Committee on Canals, 1883.
19. North Staffordshire Railway Report, February 1862.
20. Ibid., 6 February 1874.
21. Ibid., 1 February 1875.
22. 54 & 55 Vic *c*. 34.
23. North Staffordshire Railway Report, 10 August 1894.

Notes to Chapter XIII

1. Ellesmere & Chester Canal Minute Book, 12 June 1845.
2. Ibid.
3. Staffs & Worcs Canal Minute Book, 4 September 1845.
4. Shropshire Union Railways & Canal Committee Book, 4 July 1845.
5. 9 & 10 Vic *cc*. 322, 323, 324.
6. See H. Scrivenor, *The Railways of the United Kingdom statistically considered*, 1849.
7. Printed Notice, 6 December 1846.
8. Printed Report, 6 December 1846.
9. 10 & 11 Vic *c*. 121.
10. Printed Report of the L.N.W.R. accountant upon the S.U. figures, B.T. Hist. Recs.
11. Report, 25 September 1851.
12. Shropshire Union Railways & Canal Executive Committee Minute Book, 26 September 1856.
13. Ibid., 28 January 1858.
14. Ibid.
15. R. L. Tonkinson, *Inclined Planes on the Shropshire Canals*, 1964 thesis, Birmingham School of Architecture.
16. Newspaper cutting, B.T. Hist. Recs., RAC/1/367.
17. It was not the first. In August 1839 the Forth & Clyde Canal company, experimenting with fast passenger craft, had laid track for a locomotive and tender, which is said to have hauled a boat round two curves at $17\frac{3}{4}$ m.p.h.
18. For the Glyn Valley Tramway, see D. L. Davies, *The Glyn Valley Tramway*, 1962.
19. North Staffordshire Railway Canal Traffic Committee Book, 10 May 1870.
20. 25 & 26 Vic *c*. 98.
21. For an account of closing the gap, see Bosdin Leech, *History of the Manchester Ship Canal*, 1907, ii, 110–12.
22. B.T. Hist. Recs., RAC/1/368.
23. Shropshire Union Railways & Canal Executive Committee Minute Book, 14 October 1903.
24. See Charles Hadfield, *British Canals*, 2nd ed., 1959, pp. 231–3.
25. Notice of 1 June 1921, RAC/1/369.
26. *L.M.S. Railway Magazine*, II, May 1925.

Notes to Chapter XIV

1. 7 Vic *c*. 11.
2. *Derby Mercury*, 9 August 1843.
3. Dudley Canal Minute Book, 29 November 1845.
4. 9 & 10 Vic *c*. 269.
5. 9 & 10 Vic *c*. 244.
6. House of Commons Select Committee on O.W.W.R. bill, 28 May 1846.
7. Oxford, Worcester & Wolverhampton Railway Report, 21 February 1855.
8. Ibid., 28 August 1855.
9. Ibid., 26 February 1856.
10. 17 & 18 Vic *c*. 112.

11. 18 & 19 Vic c. 121.
12. *Berrow's Worcester Journal*, 5 January 1856.
13. See Charles Hadfield, *The Canals of Southern England*, p. 99.
14. B.C.N. Proprietors' Minute Book, 30 October 1857.
15. Ibid., 27 February 1856.
16. Stourbridge Canal Proprietors' Minute Book, 2 November 1852.
17. Ibid., 3 October 1854.
18. O.W.W.R. Report of Shareholders' Committee of Investigation, 1856.
19. Stourbridge Extension Canal Proprietors' Minute Book, 22 July 1845.
20. 9 & 10 Vic c. 278.
21. Stourbridge Extension Canal Committee Minute Book, 24 February 1847.
22. For the Stratford & Moreton Tramway, see Charles Hadfield and John Norris, *Waterways to Stratford*, 1962.

Notes to Chapter XV

1. For a full account of the Stratford Canal, the Upper and the Lower Avon, and the Stratford & Moreton Tramway, see Charles Hadfield and John Norris, *Waterways to Stratford*, 1962. For a note on the later history of the Stratford Canal, see *The Canals of the East Midlands*.
2. Worcester & Birmingham Canal Proprietors' Minute Book, 7 January 1845.
3. Ibid., 6 July 1847.
4. Worcester & Birmingham Committee Minute Book, 11 February 1848.
5. 15 Vic c. 22.
6. Worcester & Birmingham Canal Proprietors' Minute Book, 6 January 1852.
7. Ibid., 4 January 1853.
8. 8 & 9 Vic c. 42.
9. Gloucester & Berkeley Canal Report, 31 March 1858.
10. Worcester & Birmingham Canal Proprietors' Minute Book, 3 January 1865.
11. 37 & 38 Vic c. 181.
12. Report of Sharpness New Docks Co., 4 May 1881.
13. H. R. Hodgkinson, 'Notes on the History of Midland Waterways', *Birm. Arch. Soc. Trans*, XXXIX, 1914.
14. Staffs & Worcs Canal Committee Minute Book, 12 December 1844.
15. Ibid., 30 December 1844.
16. Ibid., 4 September 1845.
17. Ibid., 1 April 1847.
18. Staffs & Worcs Canal Committee Minute Book, 1 November 1850.
19. Ibid., 4 July 1867.
20. Ibid., 5 May 1881.
21. J. Randall, *The Severn Valley*, 1882, p. 428.
22. For the Thames & Severn Canal, see Charles Hadfield, *The Canals of Southern England*.
23. Staffs & Worcs Canal Committee Minute Book, 1 December 1881.
24. Report, Glos. C.R.O.
25. 39 Vic c. 30.
26. Severn Commission Minute Book, 24 May 1843.
27. Worcester & Birmingham Canal Proprietors' Minute Book, 2 January 1844.
28. Severn Commission Minute Book, 9 September 1845.
29. *Hereford Journal*, 18 August 1847.
30. Severn Commission Minute Book, 13 September 1852.
31. 16 Vic c. 47.
32. Staffordshire & Worcestershire Canal Committee Minute Book, 2 November 1854.
33. Ibid., 3 September 1862.
34. For these, see Charles Hadfield, *The Canals of Southern England*.
35. Severn Commission Assembly Minute Book, 10 August 1914.

APPENDIX I

Summary of Facts about the Canals and Navigations of the West Midlands

A. *Rivers Successfully Made Navigable*

River	Date of Act under which Work was begun	Date Wholly Opened	Approx. Cost at Opening	Terminal Points
Avon (Lower)	1636[1]	1639	£20,000[2]	R. Severn, Tewkesbury–Evesham Bridge
Avon (Upper)	1636[1]	1639	£20,000[2]	Evesham Bridge–Stratford-upon-Avon
Dick Brook	None	c. 1653		R. Severn–Yarranton's Forge
Severn	1842	Always navigable	£180,000[5]	Gladder Brook above Stourport–entrance lock of Gloucester & Berkeley Canal[6]
(towing paths)	1772 1799	1800	£2,000	Bewdley Bridge–Meadow wharf, Coalbrookdale
	1803	c. 1804		Bewdley Bridge–Diglis
	1809	1809	£5,000	Meadow wharf, Coalbrookdale–Shrewsbury
	1811	c. 1812	£10,000	Diglis–Lower Parting

[1] Letters patent.
[2] Upper and Lower Avon together.
[3] And, until recently, two watergates.
[4] And one watergate.

SUMMARY OF FACTS ABOUT THE CANALS

Length	Greatest Number of Locks	Size of Boats Taken	Date of Disuse for Commercial Traffic (N.B. 'used' means in 1947)	Date of Abandonment	Whether bought by Railway and Present Ownership
28¼ miles	7[3]	70 ft by 14 ft 6 in.	Used		Lower Avon Navigation Trust
17½ miles	11[4]	c. 58 ft by 11 ft 6 in.	1875		Bought on behalf of O.W.W.R., 1859. Now Upper Avon Navigation Trust
¾ mile	2 flash-locks				
42⅝ miles later 43½ miles	7 (1 narrow)	Stourport–Worcester 87 ft by 15 ft 6 in. Worcester–Gloucester 135 ft by 22 ft Gloucester–Lower Parting, 87 ft by 15 ft 6 in. Maisemore lock 73 ft by 7 ft 3 in.	Used[7]		B.W.B.
24 miles			1884		
16¾ miles			c. 1906		
23¼ miles			1885		
30 miles			c. 1912		

[5] Under the 1842 Act. Expenditure was £300,000 up to 1905.
[6] Extended downwards for ¾ mile to Lower Parting under 1869 Act.
[7] Except Gloucester–Lower Parting, disused 1924, and Maisemore lock, disused early 1920s.

B. Rivers with Uncompleted Navigation Works

River	Date of Act under which Work was begun	Money Spent	Terminal Points Authorized	Length on which Work was done
Salwarpe	1662	c. £8,000	R. Severn–Droitwich	
Stour	1662	c. £1,300[1]	R. Severn–Stourbridge	Kidderminster–Stourbridge

[1] This figure probably represents Yarranton's own charge, and not the cost of labour and materials.

Greatest Number of Locks	Size of Boats Taken	Date of Abandonment of Works	Later Events
5 out of 6 said to have been built		c. 1675	Replaced by Droitwich Canal
12 locks and 4 half-locks built	16 tons	c. 1670	Replaced by Staffs & Worcs and Stourbridge Canals

APPENDIX I

C. *Canals, the Main Lines of which were completed as Authorized*

Canal	Date of Act under which Work was begun	Date wholly Opened	Approx. Cost at Opening	Terminal Points	Branches Built
Birmingham	1768	1772	£112,000[1]	Birmingham–Staffs & Worcs C., Aldersley	
		1772		Newhall	
		1812		Gibson's	
		1789–90		Birmingham Heath Engine	
		1769		Wednesbury	
				Izon	
				Union	
		1799		Walsall	
		1833		Haines	
				Dank's	
		1805		Ocker Hill Tunnel	
		1800		Gospel Oak	
		1812–13		Monway	
				Bilston	
		1803		Willenhall	
		1830		Anson	
		1843		Bentley	
		1845		Neachells	
		1841		Walsall Locks	
		1826		Ridgacre	
		1828		Dartmouth	
		1828		Halford	
		1831		Jesson	
		1837		Titford	
		1858		Causeway Green	
				Houghton (Chemical Arm) (private)	
				Oldbury Loop Bypass South Jn./North Jn.	
		c. 1778		Lord Ward's (private)[4]	
		c. 1805		Tipton Green locks	
		1809		Toll End locks	
		1774		Ocker Hill	
		1818		Bradley	
		1849		Bradley locks	

[1] Including Wednesbury and Newhall branches.
[2] Increased to 30, 1784–7, by addition of one to Wolverhampton flight; decreased to 24 from 1787 onwards by the lowering of the summit at Smethwick.

SUMMARY OF FACTS ABOUT THE CANALS

Length	Greatest Number of Locks	Size of Boats Taken	Date of Disuse for Commercial Traffic (N.B. 'used' means in 1947)	Date of Abandonment	Whether bought by Railway and Present Ownership
⅜ miles	29[2]	71 ft 6 in. by 7 ft 1 in.	Part used		Leased by L.N.W.R., 1846. B.W.B.
mile	2		1901	1901/1948	
mile	1		c. 1920		
mile	None				
mile	None				
miles	3		Used	1954/60[3]	
mile	None		Used	1954[3]	
mile	None			1954/65	
miles	8		Used		
mile	None				
mile	None			1954/60	
mile	None		Used		
mile	None			1954	
mile	None			1957[3]	
mile	None		c. 1922	1953	
mile	None		c. 1922	1953	
miles	None			1956/61	
miles	10		Used	1961[3]	
mile	None			1953	
mile	8		Used		
mile	None		Used		
mile	None			1947[3]	
mile	None			1947[3]	
mile	None			1954	
miles	6		Used	1960[3]	
mile	None			1954/9/60[3]	
mile	None				
mile	None			1957/60	
mile	None				
mile	3			1960	
miles	7		Used 1960	1955	
mile	None			1955/9/61	
mile	None			1961	
mile	9				

[3] Part not abandoned.
[4] Before Dudley tunnel built.

Canal	*Date of Act under which Work was begun*	*Date wholly Opened*	*Approx. Cost at Opening*	*Terminal Points*	*Branches Built*
		1789 1799 1844 1838–48 1836 1850 *c.* 1829		Birmingham & Fazeley Digbeth Tame valley Parker Union (Roway) Gower Dunkirk Dixon Horseley Colliery	
	Shortened line. Total length 15⅝ miles. This was made up of new canal as follows: Old Turn Jn.–Ladywood Jn. ¼ mile Icknield Sq. Jn.–Cape Arm Jn. 1¼ miles Smethwick Jn.–Bromford Jn. 2⅜ miles Izon's Turn S. end–Tipton Factory Jn. 2⅞ miles Bloomfield Jn.–Deepfields Jn. 1⅜ miles 8⅛ miles with old canal improved to new canal standard as follows: Broad St. Bridge–Old Turn Jn. ⅛ mile Ladywood Jn.–Icknield Sq. Jn. ⅜ mile Cape Arm Jn.–Smethwick Jn. ⅝ mile Bromford Jn.–Izon's Turn S. end ½ mile Tipton Factory Jn.–Bloomfield Jn. ¼ mile 1⅞ miles and old canal which was improved over the years as follows: Old Wharf–Broad St. Bridge ¼ mile Deepfields Jn.–Aldersley Jn. 5⅜ miles 5⅝ miles				
Birmingham & Liverpool Junction	1826	1835	£800,000	Staffs & Worcs C., Autherley–Ellesmere & Chester C., Nantwich	
		1835			Norbury–Shrewsbury C., Wappenshall. Humber Arm from above

[1] To Whittington Brook.
[2] Wappenshall–Newport.
[3] Newport–Norbury.

Length	*Greatest Number of Locks*	*Size of Boats Taken*	*Date of Disuse for Commercial Traffic* (N.B. *'used' means in* 1947)	*Date of Abandonment*	*Whether bought by Railway and Present Ownership*
20¾ miles[1]	38		Used		
1 mile	6		Used		
8½ miles	13		Used		
⅛ mile	None		c. 1936	1953	
¼ mile	None			1955	
½ mile	3		Used		
⅛ mile	None			1953	
¾ mile	None			1954–65	
⅛ mile	None				
39½ miles	28 & 1 stop-lock	72 ft by 6 ft 11 in.	Used		Absorbed by Ellesmere & Chester C. 1845; part of Shropshire Union 1846; leased by L.N.W.R. 1847; to L.M.S.R. 1922.
10½ miles	23	72 ft by 6 ft 11 in.	1939[2]		
			1944[3]	1944	B.W.B.
¾ mile	None	72 ft by 6 ft 11 in.		1944	

APPENDIX I

Canal	Date of Act under which Work was begun	Date wholly Opened	Approx. Cost at Opening	Terminal Points	Branches Built
Coombe Hill	1792	c. 1796	£5,000	R. Severn–Coombe Hill	
Donnington Wood	None	c. 1768		Donnington Wood–Pave Lane	Hugh's Bridge–Colliers End
Droitwich	1768	1771	£23,500	R. Severn, Hawford–Droitwich	
Droitwich Junction	1852	1853	c. £28,000	Worcs & B'ham C.–Droitwich C.	
Dudley	1776 1785 1793	1779 1792 c. 1840 1798 1858 1803 1858	£9,700 c. £50,000 c. £140,000	Stourbridge C., Black Delph–Park Head Park Head–B'ham C.–Dudley Jn. Blower's Green Jn.–Worcs & B'ham C., Selly Oak	Pensnett (private) Grazebrook Two Lock line Withymoor Bumblehole Netherton Tunnel

¹ Before the inclined plane there was a shaft and tunnel lift.
² Later 8.
³ Including a portion of tunnel and canal built earlier; see text for details.
⁴ Later 4.
⁵ Part not abandoned.

SUMMARY OF FACTS ABOUT THE CANALS

Length	Greatest Number of Locks	Size of Boats Taken	Date of Disuse for Commercial Traffic (N.B. 'used' means in 1947)	Date of Abandonment	Whether bought by Railway and Present Ownership
2¾ miles	2	probably 64 ft by 14 ft 6 in.	1876	1876	
5½ miles	None	19 ft 8 in. by 6 ft 4 in.	1890–1904		Built by Earl Gower & Co. Later owned by Lilleshall Co.
2 miles	inc. plane and 7 locks[1]	19 ft 8 in. by 6 ft 4 in.	c. 1879		
6¾ miles	8	64 ft by 14 ft 6 in. lengthened 1854 to 71 ft 6 in. by 14 ft 6 in.	1916	1939	Leased by Sharpness New Docks Co., 1874. Now owned by Wychavan District Council, and leased to Droitwich Canals Trust
1¾ miles	7	71 ft 6 in. by 7 ft 1 in.	1928	1939	Leased by Sharpness New Docks Co. Now various owners.
2¼ miles	9[2]	71 ft 6 in. by 7 ft 1 in.	Used		B.W.B.
2⅜ miles[3]	5[4]		Used		
1¼ miles	None		1940s		
⅛ mile	None			1953	
10⅞ miles	None		1917	1953[5]	
⅜ mile	2		1909	1954	
¼ mile	None			1960	
½ mile	None		Used	1955[5]	
2⅜ miles					

APPENDIX I

Canal	Date of Act under which Work was begun	Date wholly Opened	Approx. Cost at Opening	Terminal Points	Branches Built
Glynne's, Sir John	None	1768		Bretton–Saltney	
Gresley's, Sir Nigel	1775	c. 1776		Newcastle-under-Lyme–Apedale collieries	
Ketley	None	1788		Oakengates–Ketley[1]	
Macclesfield	1826	1831	£320,000	T. & M. C., Hall Green–Peak Forest C., Marple	High Lane
Montgomeryshire (Western Branch)	1815	1819–21	£53,400	Montgomeryshire C. (E.B.)–Newtown	
Newcastle-under-Lyme	1795	c. 1800	£10,500	T. & M. C., Stoke–Newcastle-under-Lyme	
Newcastle-under-Lyme Junction	1798		£5,150	Newcastle, Stubbs Walk–Gresley's C., Newcastle	
Shrewsbury	1793	1796	£65,000–£70,000	Shrewsbury–Wombridge C.[2]	
Shropshire	1788	1792	£47,500	Donnington Wood C.–Coalport	Coalbrookdale

[1] Later joined Shropshire Canal.
[2] Rather over a mile of the Wombridge Canal was bought, and a junction then made between it and the Donnington Wood Canal.
[3] Excluding the purchased portion.
[4] As on Shropshire and Donnington Wood Canals.
[5] Shrewsbury basin.
[6] Longdon–Shrewsbury.

SUMMARY OF FACTS ABOUT THE CANALS

Length	Greatest Number of Locks	Size of Boats Taken	Date of Disuse for Commercial Traffic (N.B. 'used' means in 1947)	Date of Abandonment	Whether bought by Railway and Present Ownership
c. 1 mile	None		1780s		Built by Sir John Glynne
3 miles	None		c. 1857		Built by Sir Nigel Gresley
1½ miles	1 & 1 inc. plane	20 ft by 6 ft 4 in.	c. 1816		Built by William and Richard Reynolds
26¼ miles ¼ mile	12 & 1 stop-lock	70 ft by 7 ft	Used		Bought by Sheffield Ashton & M'ter Rly. 1846. To L.N.E.R. B.W.B.
7⅞ miles	6	73 ft 9 in. by 6 ft 11 in.	1936	1944	Bought by Shropshire Union, 1850. To L.M.S.R. B.W.B.
4 miles	None	72 ft by 7 ft		1921 1935	Leased to North Staffs Rly. 1863
1⅛ miles			c. 1851		Part sold to North Staffs Rly. 1851
17 miles[3]	11 & 1 inc. plane	Tub-boats[4] & 81 ft 5 in. by 6 ft 4 in.	1921[5] 1936[6] 1939[7]	1931[8] 1944[9]	Part of Shropshire Union, 1846. To L.M.S.R. B.W.B.
7¾ miles 2¾ miles	3 inc. plane	20 ft by 6 ft 4 in.	1858[10] c. 1894[11], 1913 c. 1801[12] 1858	1857[10] 1913 1944 1857	

[7] Longdon–Wappenshall.
[8] Donnington Wood—bottom of Trench inclined plane.
[9] Rest of canal.
[10] Bottom of Wrockwardine Wood plane to bottom of Windmill plane, and branches.
[11] Blist's Hill–Coalport.
[12] Horsehay–Coalbrookdale.

APPENDIX I

Canal	Date of Act under which Work was begun	Date wholly Opened	Approx Cost at Opening	Terminal Points	Branches Built
Staffordshire & Worcestershire	1766	1772 1841 1816	c. £100,000	R. Severn, Stourport –T. & M. C., Great Haywood	Hatherton Pratt's lock & Stour Stafford
Stourbridge	1776	1779	£38,000	Staffs & Worcs C., Stourton–Black Delph	Stourbridge Fens
Stourbridge Extension	1837	1840	£49,000	Stourbridge C., Brockmoor–Oak Farm	Bromley Sandhills
Trent & Mersey	1766	1777	£300,000[2]	Bridgewater C., Preston Brook–R. Trent, Derwent Mouth	
	1776 1797	c. 1779 1802			Caldon Leek
	1797	1811			Uttoxeter
	1827	1831			Hall Green
	1827	1833			Wardle
	1797	1805 bef. 1809			Bond End[7] Burslem Foxley (private)

[1] Including two barge locks at Stourport. There are also four narrow locks there.
[2] Main line.
[3] Seven are wide. There were originally 74; one was added at Lawton in the early nineteenth century.

Length	*Greatest Number of Locks*	*Size of Boats Taken*	*Date of Disuse for Commercial Traffic (N.B. 'used' means in* 1947)	*Date of Abandonment*	*Whether bought by Railway and Present Ownership*
$46\frac{1}{8}$ miles	43[1]	72 ft by 7 ft	Used		B.W.B.
$3\frac{1}{2}$ miles	8		c. 1949		
$1\frac{1}{4}$ miles	1		c. 1949		
1 mile	1		Early 1920s		
$5\frac{1}{8}$ miles	20	70 ft by 7 ft	1941		B.W.B.
$1\frac{1}{4}$ miles	None				
$\frac{3}{4}$ mile	None			1935/60	
2 miles	1 stop-lock	72 ft by 7 ft		1935 1960 (part)	Bought by O.W.W.R. 1846. To G.W.R. B.W.B.
$\frac{3}{8}$ mile	None				
$\frac{5}{8}$ mile	None				
$93\frac{3}{8}$ miles	75[3] & 1 stop-lock	Preston Brook–Middlewich orig. 74 ft by 14 ft 3 in.[4] Middlewich–Burton 72 ft by 7 ft Burton–Derwent M. 76 ft by 13 ft 6 in.			Bought by North Staffs Rly. 1846. To L.M.S.R. B.W.B.
$17\frac{1}{2}$ miles[5]	16[6]		Part used		
$2\frac{3}{4}$ miles	None	72 ft by 7 ft	1939	1944	
$13\frac{1}{4}$ miles	17	72 ft by 7 ft	c. 1847	1847	
$1\frac{1}{2}$ miles	None	72 ft by 7 ft	Used		
$\frac{1}{16}$ mile	1	72 ft by 7 ft	Used		
$\frac{3}{8}$ mile	None	72 ft by 7 ft			
$\frac{5}{8}$ mile	1	72 ft by 7 ft	c. 1934		

[4] The length Preston Brook–Middlewich was built for barges but, being used only by narrow boats, narrow structures were later built. In 1894 it was partially re-widened between Anderton and Middlewich, and later again narrowed when the Croxton aqueduct was built.

[5] $17\frac{1}{4}$ miles as built. Extended $\frac{1}{4}$ mile in 1783.

[6] Later 17; Caldon Place lock was added.

[7] See R. Trent (Burton) in *The Canals of the East Midlands*.

APPENDIX I

Canal	Date of Act under which Work was begun	Date wholly Opened	Approx. Cost at Opening	Terminal Points	Branches Built
Wombridge	None	c. 1788	£1,640	Wombridge–Donnington Wood	
Worcester & Birmingham	1791	1815	£610,000	B'ham C., Worcester Bar–R. Severn, Worcester	
		1836			Bittall[3]
Wyrley & Essington	1792	c. 1795	c. £25,000	B'ham C., Horseley Fields–Wyrley	
		c. 1798			Short Heath
		c. 1798			Birchills
		1857			Essington
	1794	1797	c. £75,000	Birchills Jn.–Coventry C., Huddlesford	Wyrley Bank
		1800			Lord Hay's
		1863[5]			Cannock Extension
		1888			Norton Springs
		1860			Churchbridge locks
		1800			Daw End
		1847			Rushall
		1850			Anglesey

[1] Rather over one mile bought by Shrewsbury Canal.
[2] Two barge locks, Diglis basin to R. Severn.
[3] Navigable feeder
[4] Abandoned from Ogley to Huddlesford.
[5] Open to the point of junction with Churchbridge locks by c. 1858.
[6] 4¼ miles from Watling Street bridge to Hednesford basins was abandoned in 1963.
[7] The Daw End branch is still open from Catshill Junction to Longwood Junction, 5⅜ miles. A further 260 yd to Squash Lane bridge was abandoned in 1954. Beyond that is a further 352 yd of canal to Hay Head.

Length	*Greatest Number of Locks*	*Size of Boats Taken*	*Date of Disuse for Commercial Traffic (N.B. 'used' means in 1947)*	*Date of Abandonment*	*Whether bought by Railway and Present Ownership*
1¾ miles[1]	None	Probably 19 ft 8 in. by 6 ft 4 in.	*c.* 1904		Built by William Reynolds
30 miles	58	71 ft 6 in. by 7 ft 76 ft by 18 ft 6 in.[2]	Used		Bought by Sharpness New Docks Co., 1874. B.W.B.
½ mile	None				
8½ miles	5	71 ft 6 in. by 7 ft 1 in.	Used		B.W.B.
⅛ mile	None		1909		
2⅛ miles	None		Used		
¾ mile	4				
1½ miles				1954	
15½ miles	30		Used[4]	1954[4]	
1¼ miles	None			1930, 1954	
5⅝ miles			Used	1963[6]	
⅛ mile	None				
⅝ mile	13			1955	
5⅝ miles	None		Used[7]		
2⅞ miles	9		Used		
1½ miles	None		Used		

D. Canals, the Main Lines of which were not Completed

Canal	Date of Act under which Work was begun	Date Opened	Approx. Cost at Opening	Authorized Terminal Points	Terminal Points as Built
Chester	1772	1779	£71,000	R. Dee, Chester–Middlewich	R. Dee, Chester–Nantwich
Ellesmere (later Ellesmere & Chester)	1793		£500,000	Ellesmere Port–Chester–Ruabon–Shrewsbury	
		1795			Ellesmere Port–Chester
		1805			Pontcysyllte–Weston
		1833			
		1805			
		1796			
		1808–11			
		c. 1806			
		1804			
		1808			
		c. 1820–30			
Montgomery-shire	1794	1797	£71,100	Porthywaen–Newtown	Ellesmere C., Carreghofa–Garthmyl[4]
		1797			

[1] Except R. Dee section, disused c. 1932–4.
[2] Both narrow and barge locks at Ellesmere Port. The lowest originally gave access to the R. Mersey, later to the Manchester Ship Canal.

Branches Built	*Length*	*Greatest Number of Locks*	*Size of Boats Taken*	*Date of Disuse for Commercial Traffic ('used' means in 1947)*	*Date of Abandonment*	*Whether bought by Railway, and Present Ownership*
	19¼ miles	16 & sea-lock	74 ft 11 in. by 14 ft 3 in.	Used[1]		Amal. with Ellesmere C. 1813. Part of S.U., 1846. To L.M.S.R. B.W.B.
						Amal. with Chester C. 1813. Part of S.U., 1846. To L.M.S.R. B.W.B.
	8¾ miles	3[2]	74 ft 1 in. by 14 ft 3 in.	Used		
	17¾ miles	6	72 ft 6 in. by 6 ft 10 in.	1917[3] 1937		
Middlewich	9¾ miles	3	72 ft 6 in. by 6 ft 10 in.	Used		
Hurleston (Chester C.)–Frankton	29 miles	19	72 ft 6 in. by 6 ft 10 in.	1939	1944	
Frankton–Carreghofa (Montgomerysh. C.)	11 miles	3	72 ft 6 in. by 6 ft 10 in.	1936	1944	
Whitchurch	1 mile	None	72 ft 6 in. by 6 ft 10 in.	1936–8	1944	
Prees (Quina Brook)	3¾ miles	None	72 ft 6 in. by 6 ft 10 in.	1938–9	1944	
Ellesmere	¼ mile	None	72 ft 6 in. by 6 ft 10 in.	1939	1944	
Llantisilio (nav. feeder)	5¾ miles	None	72 ft 6 in. by 6 ft 10 in.	1937	1944	
Plas Kynaston (private)	*c.* ⅝ mile	None	72 ft 6 in. by 6 ft 10 in.	*c.* 1914		
	16¼ miles	13	73 ft 9 in. by 6 ft 11 in.	1936	1944	Bought by S.U. 1847. To L.M.S.R. B.W.B.
Guilsfield	2¼ miles	None			1944	

[3] Between Hordley wharf and Weston. Rest 1937.
[4] The section Garthmyl–Newtown was later built by the Montgomeryshire Canal Western Branch) (q.v.), the original company becoming the Eastern Branch.

E. *Canals Partly Built but not Opened*
   None.

F. *Canals Authorized but not Begun*
   1788   *Flint Coal Canal* from Greenfield to the River Dee, with a branch to Pentre.

APPENDIX II

Principal Engineering Works

A. *Inclined Planes*

Canal	Name of Plane	Vertical Rise	Dates Working	Notes
Ketley	Ketley	73 ft	1788–c. 1816	Self-balancing, double-track, boats carried in cradles
Shropshire	Wrockwardine Wood	120 ft	1791–1858	Double-track, boats carried in cradles, worked by steam engine
	Windmill	126 ft	1791–1858	Double-track, boats carried in cradles, worked by steam engine
	The Hay	207 ft	1792–c. 1894	Double-track, boats carried in cradles, worked by steam engine
Donnington Wood	Hugh's Bridge (Lilleshall)	42 ft 8 in	c. 1794–c. 1879	Probably double-track, boats carried in cradles, worked by steam engine. See text
Shrewsbury	Trench	75 ft	1797–1921	Double-track, boats carried on cradles, worked by steam engine

B. Lifts

Canal	Name of Lift	Vertical Rise	Dates Working	Notes
Donnington Wood	Hugh's Bridge	42 ft 8 in.	[1]–c. 1794	Tunnel to bottom of vertical shaft. Crane to lift goods to higher level
Ellesmere	Site unknown, probably near Ruabon	Not known	Trials 1796	A float in a well of water raised or lowered a tank carrying a boat
Worcester & Birmingham	Tardebigge	12 ft	Trials 1808– c. 1813	A boat floated in a tank suspended by chains from carrying wheels, and balanced by an equivalent weight of bricks. Motive power manual

C. Tunnels over 500 yards

Canal	Tunnel	Length
Dudley Canal	Lappal	3,795 yd
Dudley Canal	Dudley	3,172 yd
Birmingham Canal Navigations	Netherton	3,027 yd
Trent & Mersey Canal	Harecastle (new)	2,926 yd
Trent & Mersey Canal	Harecastle (old)	2,880 yd
Worcester & Birmingham Canal	West Hill	2,726 yd
Trent & Mersey Canal	Preston Brook	1,239 yd
Shrewsbury Canal	Berwick	970 yd
Worcester & Birmingham Canal	Shortwood	613 yd
Eardington Forge Canal	Eardington	c. 600 yd
Worcester & Birmingham Canal	Tardebigge	580 yd
Trent & Mersey Canal	Barnton	572 yd
Dudley Canal	Gosty Hill	557 yd

[1] Opening date unknown.

PRINCIPAL ENGINEERING WORKS

D. *Outstanding Aqueducts*

Birmingham Canal Navigations	Steward (Spon Lane) (473 ft level over 453 ft)
	Salford (Tame)
	Telford (engine branch over 453 ft level at Smethwick)
Birmingham & Liverpool Junction Canal	Stretton (A5)
Ellesmere Canal	Chirk
Ellesmere Canal	Pontcysyllte
Macclesfield Canal	Dane
Montgomeryshire Canal	Vyrnwy
Montgomeryshire Canal	Berriew (Rhiw)
Shrewsbury Canal	Longdon (Tern)
Staffordshire & Worcestershire Canal	Great Haywood (Trent)
Staffordshire & Worcestershire Canal	Sow
Trent & Mersey Canal	Dove
Trent & Mersey Canal	Trent
Trent & Mersey Canal	Denford (Leek branch over Caldon branch)

INDEX

The principal references to canals and river navigations are indicated in bold type

Acrefair, 176
Acton, 31-2
Admiralty, The, 284
Afon-eitha, 176, 239, 243
Agricultural produce, carried on canals, etc., 47, 53. *See also* Cheese, Corn, Flour, Fruit, Malt, Meal, Wool
Aire & Calder Navigation, 16
Alcester, 140, 144
Aldersley, 49 n., 50, 64, 68, 75-6, 88, 104, 115, 128-9, 131, 135, 256-7, 280
Alrewas, 33
Alton, 201
Altrincham, 19, 187, 212, 221
Aluminium, carried on canals, etc., 290
Alvechurch, 140
Anderton, 35-7, 226, 229, 244, 292. *See also* Lift
Anderton Co., carriers, 202, 245
Anglesey branch, 254-5, 261, 328-9
Anglesey, Marquess of, 261
Anker River, 71
Anson branch, 99, 254-5, 318-9
Anson (Mr. & Lord), 19, 26, 51
Apedale, 40, 208-9, 217-8
Aqueducts, canal, 130-2; Berriew, 190, 192, 335; Chirk, 170-1, 173, 176, 192, 335; Dane (Macclesfield), 335; Dane (T & M), 33; Denford, 200, 335; Dove, 32, 335; Gowy (Chester), 44; Great Haywood (S & W), 335; Holmes, 162, 172; Leasowes (Dudley), 108; Longdon-on-Tern, 160-2, 171-2, 242, 335; Mersey (project), 24, 26, 31; Pontcysyllte, 168, 170-4, 176-8, 181, 192-3, 235, 335; Salford, 335; Sow (S & W), 335; Steward (Spon Lane), 335; Stour, 74; Stretton, 335; Tean, 210; Telford (Smethwick), 335; Trent (T & M), 33, 335; Wolverton, 47; Vrynwy, 190, 192, 195, 335
Arkwright, Richard, 211
Arley, 288
Arlingham, 117, 126
Armitage, 32
*A*1, steamboat, 289
Appleby & Co., carriers, 202
Ashbourne, 201

Ashby-de-la-Zouch Canal, 197-8, 292-3
Ashleworth, 117, 126
Ashted, 88-90, 256-7
Ashton-under-Lyne Canal, 213, 220
Ashwood, 132, 280
Aston (B'ham), 88-9, 256-7
Aston (Salop), 167, 170
Atalanta, steamboat, 289
Atcham, 22, 126
Atherstone, 70
Athlete, steam-tug, 279
Audlem, 186
Autherley, 49, 64, 131, 163, 167, 181, 183, 185-6, 188, 232, 235, 245, 251, 256-7
Avon, Lower, Navigation, 17, **56**, 58, 115, 137-8, 145-6, **147, 269-70**, 274 n., 284, 314-5
Avon, Lower, Navigation Trust, 138, 270
Avon, Upper, Navigation, 17, **56**, 58, 109, 115, 142, 145, **146-7**, 184, **269-70**, 314-5

Bache, Samuel, carrier, 202
Baker, promoter, 60
Baker, John, clerk of works, 49
Bala, 178
Baldwyn family, promoters, 59
Ballard, Stephen, canal clerk, 159
Ball's Hill branch, 254-5
Banks, and canal coys, 102, 142
Baptist End, 107
Barbridge, 167, 181, 204, 232
Bark, carried on canals, etc., 192
Barnton, 32, 35-6, 228
Barrow Hill, 105
Bate, Edward, carrier, 205
Bawtry, 16
Beck, George, carrier, 250
Beechey, Capt., engineer, 284
Beeston (Cheshire), 44-5, 179, 206, 236
Belan, 192
Belvide, *see* Reservoirs
Bentley Canal, 99, 252, 256-7, 261, 318-9
Bentley, Thomas, promoter, 20, 22, 24, 29, 31, 33
Bentley, William, promoter, 65, 69

337

INDEX

Berkeley, 117
Berry, Henry, engineer, 19
Bersham, 47, 166-8, 174, 178
Berwick tunnel, *see* Tunnel
Berwyn, 242
Bevere, 283
Bewdley, 15, 17-18, 28, 53, 55, 106, 124, 133, 280, 286, 288
Bewdley-Coalbrookdale Horse Towing Path, *see* Severn H.T.P.
Bidder, G. P., engineer, 224
Bignall End, 208
Bill, John and Robert, quarry lessees, etc., 33, 38
Bilston, 64, 68, 75 n.
Bilston branch, 254-5, 318-9
Birchills, 84, 95, 98
Birchills branch, 95-7, 254-6, 328-9
Birkenhead, 231, 240, 245
Birkenhead Railway, 170, 235-6
Birmingham, *passim*
Birmingham & Bristol Channel Improved Navigation, 274 n.
Birmingham & Bristol Railway project, 146
Birmingham Canal, 49 n., 50-1, 60, **63-73**, 74, 76-7, **83-94**, 96, 98-9, 104-8, 112-13, 129, 131, 136-9, 142, 166-7, 169, 181, 183-4, 186-7, 213, 232, 241, **252-64**, 265, 271, 276-7, 279-80, 292, 318-21, 334-5
Birmingham Canal Navigations, *see* Birmingham Canal
Birmingham & Derby Junction Railway, 93
Birmingham, Dudley & Wolverhampton Junction Railway project, 88
Birmingham & Fazeley Canal, 70-2, 74, 83-4, 89, 95-5, 197, 320-1
Birmingham & Gloucester Railway, 104, 146, 232, 270-1
Birmingham Heath branch, 254-5, 318-9
Birmingham-Liverpool Railway project (1824), 86. 72-3, 185, 205, 276
Birmingham & Liverpool Junction Canal, 49 n., 86, 88, 98, 125-6, 130-1, 150, 161, 163-4, 166-7, 181-2, **183-9**, 192, 197, 204-5, 212, 221, 231-3, 239, 266, 276-7, 320-1, 335
Birmingham & Liverpool Ship Canal project, 226, 245
Birmingham, Walsall & L'pool Junction Canal project, 93
Birmingham & Warwick Junction Canal, 89
Birmingham West Suburban Railway, 273-4

Birmingham, W'ton & Stour Valley Railway, 258
Bishton, William, towing contractor, 188, 240
Bittall arm, 143, 146, 328-9
Black Delph, 73, 76, 256-7, 260-1
Blackpark, 243
Blisworth, 116
Blist's Hill, 238
Bloomfield, 68, 85-8, 104, 241, 256-7
Blower's Green, 256-7, 260, 263
Bloxwich, 94-5, 97
Board of Trade, 251, 264, 271-2
Boatage services, 241, 249
Boddington, R., engineer, 270
Bordesley, 89, 112
Bosley, 212
Boulton, Matthew, 20, 26, 51, 64, 77
Boulton & Watt, 70, 154
Bounties, payment of, 102, 142
Bourneville, 276
Bouverie, P. P., committeeman, 184, 213
Brades locks, 256-7
Bradford, Henry, engineer, 19
Bradley, 256-7, 264
Bradley branch, 85, 254-7, 318-9
Bradley-Fazeley Canal project, 89, 94
Brassey, Thomas, contractor, 273
Brassworks, 69
Braunston, 51, 197-8
Breedon, 33
Brentford, 53
Brettell, Thomas, canal clerk, 108
Bretton, 47
Brewin, Thomas, superintendent, 111-14, 184
Bricks, carried on canals, etc., 70, 75, 97, 100, 103, 206, 267
Brickworks, 116, 239
Bridgnorth, 15, 17-18, 22, 53, 55, 124-5, 288
Bridgewater Canal, 19, 21-2, 24, 26, 31-2, 38, 41, 44, 67, 129, 181, 184, 188, 205, 212-3, 221-5, 229, 235, 243-5, 280
Bridgewater, Duke of, 19-21, 23-4, 26-7, 31, 38, 40, 42-4, 179, 205
Bridgewater, Earl of, 179
Brierley Hill, 76
Brierly Hill (Salop), 154, 157
Brimscombe Port, 117
Brindley, James, engineer, 19-21, 24, 26-32, 41, 44, 49, 60-1, 63-5, 69, 88, 197
Brindley, John, 27
Bristol, 15, 17-18, 53, 62, 115, 117-8, 128-9, 135-7, 142, 145, 274, 280
Bristol, Earl of, promoter, 58-9

INDEX

Bristol Rail Road Co., 144
Bristol & Severn Canal project, 117, 137 n.
British Railways, 249
British Transport Commission (B.W.), 251
British Waterways Board, 138, 249, 266
Broadwaters, 71–2, 85, 95
Brockmoor, 102–5
Bromley, 102, 267
Bromley branch, 105, 326–7
Bromsgrove, 75, 140
Broseley, 17–18, 66
Broughton Hackett, 144
Broughton, John, canal manager, 269
Brown & Son, carriers, 118
Brownhills, 95
Brunner Mond works, 229
Brymbo, 166, 236. *See also* Ffrwd branch
Buck, George, engineer, 194–5
Bude Canal, 152
Building materials carried on canals, etc., 35, 178, 187, 192, 206. *See also* Bricks, Lime, Slates, Timber
Buildwas Bridge, 171 n.
Bull, John, surveyor, 77
Bullo Pill, 116, 149, 288
Bumblehole, 113, 260
Bumblehole branch, 254–5, 322–3
Bunbury, 44–5
Burgedin, 189, 192
Burslem, 15, 20, 26–7, 198, 201, 235
Burslem branch, 202, 326–7
Burton-on-Trent, 16–17, 32–3, 97, 110, 198, 201, 211, 223, 226
Burton Boat Co., 17, 20, 110
Burton Navigation, *see* Trent (Burton) Navigation
Bushbury, 253, 258

Cadbury Bros., 290
Cadbury, George, 274
Caldon branch, 34, 39, 198–202, 210, 230, 326–7
Caldon Low, 33, 38, 181, 201, 206, 225, 229
Cambrian Railways, 238
Camp Hill, 146
Canal Boats Acts, 247
Canal Clauses Act (1845), 272
Canal digging machine, 49
Canal mania, 84, 106, 117, 138, 168
Cannock, 70, 89–90, 93, 96–7, 256–7, 260–1, 263–4, 276, 279, 281
Cannock Extension branch, 254–5, 260–3, 279, 328–9
Cape Arm, 68
Capital, of canals, etc., 27–9, 31–2, 43–4, 48, 50, 60–1, 65, 68, 73–4, 76, 90, 95–6, 107, 109, 138, 140, 142, 148, 153, 169, 177, 184, 190, 194, 206, 208–9, 265, 283
Cardiff, 117, 288–9
Carreghofa, 170, 190, 192, 196, 250
Carrying, by canal, etc. coys., 36–9, 44, 66–7, 115, 117 n., 182, 188, 202–3, 205, 220, 223, 225, 228, 235–6, 239–41, 244–5, 247–8, 270, 277–8, 293
Carrying concerns, 36–8, 44, 112, 115–18, 122, 125, 128–9, 140, 142, 163, 182, 202, 205, 213, 221, 223, 240–1, 244–5, 247, 249–50, 260, 278, 290
Cartwright, Thomas, engineer, 138–40
Castlefield, 19, 41
Castle Mill, 76–80
Causeway Green branch, 254–5, 318-9
Cavendish Bridge, 15 n., 51
Cavendish Bridge Boat Co., 36
Ceiriog River, 170–1, 243
Chapman, William, engineer, 185
Cheadle (Staffs), 198, 201
Cheap Trains Act, 272
Cheddleton, 34, 200, 230
Cheese, carried on canals, etc., 15, 18, 42
Cheltenham, 54, 116, 147–9, 270–1, 281–2
Chemical Arm (Houghton), 254–5, 318–9
Chepstow, 117
Cheslyn Hay, 132, 279
Chester, 15, 30, 42–4, 47, 166–70, 174, 176, 178, 181–2, 184, 198, 206, 233–6, 241, 249, 251
Chester & Birkenhead Railway, 235
Chester Canal, 30, 40, 42–5, 163, 166–9, 176–9, 181, 198, 204, 206, 330–1
Chester & Crewe Railway, 232, 234
Chester & Holyhead Railway, 234
Chester & Liverpool Lighterage Co., 249–50
Chesterfield, 211
Chirk, 170, 173, 178–9, 181, 238, 242. *See also* Aqueduct *and* Tunnel
Chocolate crumb, carried on canals, etc., 276
Church Eaton, 185
Churchbridge, 132, 256–7, 279–80, 328–9
Churnet River, 34, 201
Churnet Valley Railway, 221, 223
City of Worcester, steamboat, 284
Clay, carried on canals, etc., 75, 100, 103, 230. *See also* Pottery clay
Clegram, W. B., engineer, 286
Clive, Lord, 181, 184, 192, 234. *See also* Powis, Earl of

340 INDEX

Clowes, Josiah, engineer, 44, 79, 108, 138, 160–3, 171
Clywd, Vale of, Canal project, 47
Coal, carried by coasting trade, 247; by road transport, 102, 136, 140, 159–60, 165, 190, 192, 264, 271; on canals, etc., 15, 17–19, 33, 35, 39–41, 44, 47, 51, 53–4, 58–61, 63, 65–7, 69–70, 74–6, 83–5, 88–9, 92, 94–7, 102–4, 107–9, 112–4, 118, 121, 128–9, 134–7, 140, 142, 145–9, 151, 159–60, 163–4, 169, 173, 176, 178, 186–7, 193, 195, 204–6, 208, 212, 217, 220, 230, 236, 238–9, 241–2, 247, 250, 262, 264, 266–8, 270–1, 277, 280–1, 286, 289; on tramroads, 102, 104–5, 132, 135, 149, 157, 176, 229, 240; sold by canal, etc., coys., 66, 69–70, 74, 96, 100, 113, 206, 208
Coal mines, navigation levels in, 21, 41, 150
Coalbrookdale (and Coy), 53–4, 115–6, 124–5, 129, 150–4, 157, 159, 162–3, 187, 236, 280, 287
Coalbrookdale branch, 41, 153–4, 157–9, 187, 237, 324–5
Coalport, 102, 116, 124, 129, 150, 152, 154, 157–8, 237–8
Coasting trade, 15–16, 129–30, 183, 213–4, 247, 285, 288–9
Cockrell, Joseph, canal owner, 282
Cofton, 142
Coleshill agreement (1782), 71
Colwich, 26 n., 221
Commercial Canal project, 177, 198, 200, 206
Commissioners, appointed under Canal etc. Acts, 16, 19, 23, 50–1, 54, 69, 107, 121, 134
Compton, 49, 280
Congleton, 210–11
Connah's Quay, 48
Consall, 34
Cookley, 49
Coombe Hill Canal, 115, 144, **147–9**, 270, 277, **281–2**, 322–3
Copestake, Henry, quarry lessee, 33
Copper mines, 47
Copper, carried on canals, etc., 290
Corbyn's Hall, 104–5
Corn, carried by road transport, 140; on canals, etc., 16, 18, 35, 39, 94, 112, 121, 140, 202, 220, 223, 245, 247, 250–1, 289–90
Coseley, 85, 88, 256–7, 260
Cotton, carried on canals, etc., 220
Cotton mills, 47, 211
Countess of Bridgewater, The, steamboat, 179

Coventry, 169
Coventry Canal, 30, 39, 70–2, 86, 89, 92–4, 97, 184, 197–8, 204, 213, 229, 291, 293
Cressy, 249
Crewe, 221, 232–4
Crewe & Worcester Railway, 232
Crewe works, 239, 241
Crickheath, 190, 235
Cromford Canal, 197, 202, 204, 292
Cromford & High Peak Railway, 204, 211–12, 221
Crompton Samuel, 26
Crosley, William, engineer, 138, 142, 211
Cubitt, William, engineer, 121–2, 183, 186, 196, 233, 283–4
Cuirassier, steamboat, 278
Curdworth, 256–7
Curr, John, engineer, 157

Dadford, John, engineer, 189–90
Dadford, Thomas, sen., engineer, 49, 51, 75, 77, 190, 192
Dadford, Thomas, jun., engineer, 74, 189–90
Dane River, 33
Danks Branch, 89, 254–5, 318–9
Danks & Co., carriers, 112, 278
Darbys, the, ironmasters, 116, 153
Darby, Samuel, treasurer, 153
Darlaston, 85
Darley, 40
Dartmouth branch, 254–5, 318–9
Darwin, Dr. Erasmus, 15, 19–21, 29, 64
Davies, Arthur, surveyor, 170
Davies, Joseph, carrier, 244
Davies, William, contractor, 173
Daw End branch, 95, 97–9, 254–5, 263, 328–9
Dawley, 187
Dean, Forest of, 17, 116, 118–9, 129, 146, 149, 288
Dee River, 15, 42–4, 47, 167–71, 174, 176–8, 181, 198, 236, 251
Deepfields, 68, 85–8, 256–7
Denford, 200
Denson, Thomas, engineer, 169, 179
Derby, 16, 26, 31, 93, 97, 168
Derby Canal, 162, 172, 201, 229
Derwent Mouth, 15 n., 29–30, 32, 197, 229
Derwent River, 16, 31 n.
Devey, carrier, 278
Dick Brook, **56–8**, 314–5
Digbeth, 55, 85, 115
Digbeth branch, 84, 254–5, 320–1
Diglis, 54–5, 62, 75, 122, 124–5, 142–3, 283, 287, 290

Dilhorne, 198
Dividend guarantees, 75, 100-1, 107, 133-4, 137-8, 222, 225-6, 253, 265, 271
Dividend limitation, 54, 64, 190
Dividends, on canal etc. shares, 39, 50, 61, 68, 75, 83, 90-1, 98, 100, 109-10, 125, 127-8, 133, 135, 143, 145, 158, 160, 163, 179, 185, 188, 192-5, 203-4, 209-10, 212, 217-19, 222, 240, 248, 252-3, 260-2, 264-6, 270, 272-3, 277, 281, 287-8
Dixon branch, 254-5, 320-1
Donnington Wood, 40-1, 116, 150-1, 154, 157, 159-60, 173, 185, 232, 250-1
Donnington Wood Canal, **40-1, 150,** 151, 153, 155, 185, **238,** 322-3, 333-4
Dove River, 32, 198
Downing, Francis, mine-agent, 109
Drawbacks, on tolls, 112, 129, 135, 143, 149
Droitwich, 17-18, 59-62, 129, 133, 135, 140, 143, 264, 271-2
Droitwich Canal, **60-2,** 75, 115, 122, **133-5,** 138, 140, 143, 145, **270-6,** 283-4, 294, 322-3
Droitwich Junction Canal, 143, **270-6,** 322-3
Dudley, 18, 53, 55, 73, 75, 105, 107, 109, 112, 114, 253, 258, 264
Dudley Canal, 50, 53, 73-4, **75-80,** 93-5, 98, 100-2, 104-5, **106-14,** 129, 135-8, 142-3, 184, **253,** 260-1, 263-5, 276, 322-3, 334
Dudley family, 142
Dudley, Lord, 51, 54, 73, 75-7, 79-80, 86, 103-6, 109, 113, 132. *See also* Ward, Lord
Dudley Port, 87, 258
Dudley tunnel, *see* Tunnel
Duke's Cut, 54
Duncombe, John, engineer, 167-70
Dunhampstead, 143-4
Dunkirk branch, 254-5, 320-1
Dutens, engineer, 152

Eardington Forge Canal, **62**
Earthenware, *see* Pottery
Eastham, 239, 245
Easton, Alexander, engineer, 185, 188
Edgbaston, 143
Edgmond, 185
Egerton, Samuel, 44-5, 167
Egerton, William, 177
Electric power stations, using canal coal, 264, 281
Electric traction on canals, 228
Ellesmere, 167, 168 n., 232

Ellesmere branch, 166, 177, 250-1, 330-1
Ellesmere Canal, 45, 161-3, 166, **167-79,** 189-90, 192, 195-6, 330-1, 334-5
Ellesmere & Chester Canal, 164, 166-7, **179-83,** 184-5, 188-9, 192, 196, 204, 212, 221, 231-3, 276, 330-1
Ellesmere, Lord, 224
Ellesmere Port, 166-7, 169-70, 179, 181-4, 188, 231-2, 235, 239-40, 242, 244-5, 247, 249-51, 292
Elliott, George, contractor, 273
Endon, 34, 200, 210, 230
Engine Branch, 254-5, 318-9
Enterprize, steamboat, 285
Erewash Canal, 225
Essington, 84, 97
Essington branch, 94-7, 254-5, 328-9
Estates, income from, 266, 293
Etruria, 34, 201-2, 217
Evesham, 18, 56, 140, 145-7, 269-70
Exchequer Bill Loan Commissioners, 186-7, 189, 194-5
Eyton, 161, 242
Eyton, Thomas, treasurer, 161, 171

Family boats, 247-8
Farey, John, author, 40-1, 96-7
Farmer's Bridge, 54, 68, 71, 84, 88-9, 112, 256-7
Fazeley, 70-2, 86, 92, 197
Fellows, Joshua, carrier, 278
Felspar, carried on canals, etc., 230
Fens branch, 73, 102
Fens Hall, 176 n.
Ffrwd branch, 174, 176
Firebrick works, 265
Fishing, in canals, 293-4
Fladbury, 56, 147
Flint Coal Canal, **47-8,** 332
Flint-stones, carried by coasting trade, 15; by road transport, 15; on canals, etc., 39, 206, 247
Flotheridge, 132
Flour, carried on canals, etc., 39, 212, 223
Fly-boats, 86, 116, 128, 130, 142, 196, 235, 247
Foley family, 73, 75, 85
Ford Green, 201
Fosbrooke, Leonard, navigation lessee, 16
Fossdyke, 16
Foster, James, ironmaster, 105
Foster, John, promoter, 73
Fowler, William, engineer, 103-5
Foxley, 230
Foxley Canal, 201, 326-7
Fradley, 70, 197-8, 229
Framilode, 53, 115, 117, 126

342   INDEX

Frampton-on-Severn, 117
France, 278
Frankton, 166, 168, 170, 173, 176 n.,
    177–9, 250–1
Freeth, John, canal clerk, 184
Frodsham Bridge, 18, 20, 22
Froghall, 34, 200–1, 223, 229–30
Frost, James, contractor, 105
Frost, Robert, engineer, 132
Fruit, carried on canals, etc., 18, 136

Gad's Green, 79, 101, 256–7
Gailey, 49
Gainsborough, 15–16, 223
Galton, Samuel, promoter, 64
Galton, S. T., committeeman, 184
Garbett, Samuel, promoter, 20, 29, 64,
    67, 69–70
Garthmyl, 166, 190, 192, 194
Gibbons & Co., colliery owners, 102–3,
    105
Gibson's branch, 254–5, 318–9
Gilbert, John, 19, 21, 24, 26, 29, 33, 38,
    40, 67, 160
Gilbert, Thomas, 21, 26–7, 29, 33, 38,
    40, 153, 160
Glassware, carried on canals, etc., 53, 75,
    100
Glassworks, 74, 265
Gledrid, 243
Gloucester, 17–18, 53–4, 58, 73, 115–122,
    125–7, 135, 144–5, 147–9, 274, 278–9,
    282–6, 288–90
Gloucester & Berkeley Ship Canal, 116–
    120, 122, 126, 144, 148–9, 265, 272–
    274 n., 282, 286. *See also* Sharpness
    New Docks Co.
Gloucester & Worcester Horse Towing
    Path Co., 120, 126–7, 286–7, 314–5
Glynne's, Sir John, Canal, **46**–7, 324–5
Gnosall, 131, 185–6
Golden Hill, 235
Gornal Wood, 104, 130
Goscote, 97
Gospel Oak branch, 254–5, 318–9
Gosty Hill, *see* Tunnels
Gower branch, 254–5, 320–1
Gower, Earl, 19–21, 24, 26–7, 40–1. *See
    also* Stafford, Marquess of, *and* Sutherland, Duke of
Grain, *see* Corn
Grand Connection Railway project, 104
Grand Junction Canal, 47, 84, 116, 140,
    145, 184, 197–8, 202, 213, 224, 272,
    293
Grand Junction Railway, 93, 104, 186–7,
    205, 212, 221–3, 232, 234, 252–3, 276
Grand Union Canal (new), 293

Grand Union Canal (old), 184, 202, 293
Grantham Canal, 292, 294
Grazebrook branch, 254–5, 322–3
Greatbridge, 241
Great Central Railway, 220 n.
Great Haywood, 22, 28, 36, 49, 51, 129–
    30, 229
Great Western Railway, 223, 237–8, 243,
    249, 258, 263, 265, 267, 269, 283, 286,
    288
Great Wyrley, 97, 132
Greaves, John, & Son, carriers, 112
Green, James (B'ham), engineer, 74
Green, James (Exeter), engineer, 104–5
Green, Thomas, agent, 108, 111
Greenfield, 47–8
Gresley, Sir Nigel, 40, 198, 206
Gresley, Sir Nigel B., 40, 206, 208
Gresley, Sir Roger, 209
Gresley's, Sir Nigel, Canal, **40**, 198, 206–
    10, **217**–8, 324–5
Grindley Brook, 178
Grissell & Peto, contractors, 283
Groceries, carried by road transport, 15;
    on canals, etc., 15, 39, 121
Guide Bridge, 220
Guilsfield branch, 189–90, 192, 250, 330–
    1
Gunnery, John, engineer, 79
Gwersyllt, 174

Hadley, 161, 238
Haines branch, 254–5, 318–9
Halesowen, 107–8, 113, 273
Halesfield, 238
Halford branch, 254–5, 318–9
Hall Green branch, 204, 210, 212, 221,
    229, 326–7
Hanbury, 143, 271–2
Hanley, 20, 34, 201–2
Harborne, 273
Harecastle, 20, 22, 24, 27, 29–33, 35, 39,
    51, 111, 184, 197–8, 203, 210, 219,
    221, 226
Hay, The, 152–4, 157–8, 162, 238
Hatherton branch, 132–3, 279–81
Hatherton, Lord, chairman, 122, 132,
    280
Hawarden Canal, *see* Glynne's, Sir John
Hawford, 60–1
Hawkes, Abiathar, treasurer, 75, 199
Hay Head, 95, 98
Hay Head branch, 90, 95, 97
Hayne, navigation lessee, 16
Hazeldine, William, ironmaster, 125,
    173, 176, 190
Hazelhurst, 200
Heart of Oak, trow, 117

INDEX

Heathcote, Robert E., canal-owner, 209, 217-8
Heathcote, Sir John E., coalowner, 208
Heathcote's Canal, *see* Gresley's, Sir Nigel
Hednesford, 260, 263
Hempstones, 19, 26-7
Henshall, Hugh, engineer, 22, 27-8, 31-2
Henshall, Hugh, & Co., carriers, 36-8, 202, 223
Herbert's Park, 256-7
Hereford, 116
Herefordshire & Gloucestershire Canal, 116, 120, 283, 286
High Lane branch, 324-5
High Offley, 185
High Peak Canal project, 202
Hill, Richard, quarry lessee, 33, 38
Hill, Thomas, banker, 102
Hinksford, 103-5, 132
Hockley Coal & Boat Co., 113
Hodgkinson, Samuel, surveyor, 103
Holt, 168, 174
Holt (Severn), 283
Holywell, 47
Homer & Co., colliery owners, 102
Homfray, Francis, sen. and jun., 74, 102
Homfray, Thomas, 102
Hooper, Thomas, treasurer, 138-9
Hooton & Helsby railway line, 239, 247
Hopwood, 139
Hordern, James, promoter, 95, 97
Hordley, 170, 173, 250
Horninglow, 32, 198
Horsehay (and Coy), 151, 154, 157, 159, 187, 236
Horseley Colliery branch, 320-1
Horseley Fields, 84, 94, 97, 256-7
Horton, Daniel, coalmaster, 103
Houghton (Chemical) branch, 254-5, 318-9
Huddlesford, 84, 95-6, 256-7, 263
Hudson, canal manager, 269
Hugh's Bridge, 41, 238, 322-3
Hull, 15-16, 20, 38, 202, 223
Humber Arm, 185, 239, 242, 250-1, 320-1
Humber River, 262
Hunt, Charles H., solicitor, 106
Hunt, Rowland, chairman, 168
Hunt, Thomas, solicitor, 106
Hurleston, 166, 178, 250-1

Icknield Port Road Line, 68
Idle River, 16
Imports, carried on canals, etc., 17-18, 53

Inclined planes, canal, 154-5, 158, 209, 262; Combe Hay, 41; Hugh's Bridge, 41, 238, 333; Ketley, 151-4, 333; The Hay, 153-4, 157-9, 162, 238, 333; Trench, 151, 160, 162-4, 239, 251, 333; Windmill, 153-4, 157, 162, 237, 333; Worsley, 41, 158; Wrockwardine Wood, 153-5, 237-8, 333; tramroad or railway, 132, 152, 157, 159, 201, 229, 244
Inland Waterways Association, 270
Interchange facilities, *see* Railway-canal interchange facilities
Ireland, 44, 152, 278
Iron, carried by coasting trade, 129, 214, 247; by road transport, 15, 17, 181, 187; by tramroads, 157, 181; on canals, etc., 15, 17, 39, 59, 70, 75, 100, 102, 112, 129, 157, 159, 163, 178, 181-2, 186-7, 206, 212, 214, 235, 242, 244-5, 247, 251, 260, 266-8, 280, 289
Ironbridge, 116, 124, 232, 282
Iron lock-gates, 179, 195
Iron manufactures, carried by road transport, 18; on canals, etc., 15, 18, 51, 75
Iron-ore and ironstone, carried by coasting trade, 247; on canals, etc., 73, 75, 92, 94, 100, 151, 157, 205-6, 235, 242, 247, 266-7
Ironside, steamboat, 278
Ironworks, 17-18, 41, 53, 56, 59, 92, 97, 100-1, 104, 116, 150-4, 157, 162, 166, 201, 206, 208, 217, 235, 238, 243, 258, 263, 265, 267, 280
Izon branch, 254-5, 318-9
Izon Old Turn, 254-5

Jacobs, H., surveyor, 144
James, William, promoter, 146-7
Jebb, G. R., engineer, 242-3, 245
Jesson branch, 254-5, 318-9
Jessop, Josias, engineer, 185, 193-4
Jessop, William, engineer, 47, 54, 71, 77, 141, 153, 162-3, 168-72, 174, 176-7, 179, 192, 198
Jiggers Bank, 159

Keeling, G. W., engineer, 282
Kemberton, 238
Ketley, 44, 116, 150-4, 157, 160, 162, 333
Ketley Canal, 151-2, 153-5, 324-5, 333
Kidderminster, 49, 51, 55, 58, 75, 130, 249, 265
Kidsgrove, 226
King's Mills, 16-17
King's Norton, 139, 142-3, 273, 274 n.

Kingswinford, 102–3, 105, 132, 267
Kingswood, 83–4, 112, 272. *See also* Lapworth
Kinnersly, Thomas, coalowner, 208–9
Knighton, *see* Reservoirs
Knipersley, *see* Reservoirs
Knutsford, 24, 221
Kynaston, Col. John, *see* Powell

Lancaster Canal, 211
Land carriage, *see* Road Transport
Langley (Salop), 154
Lappal tunnel, *see* Tunnels
Lapworth, 115. *See also* Kingswood
Lawton, 22, 203, 210
Lawton, John, engineer, 43
Lays Junction, 73
Lead, carried on canals, etc., 15, 40
Lead mines and works, 40, 47
Lechlade, 21, 53
Leckhampton, 148
Ledbury, 116
Lee, Thomas E., canal solicitor, 130, 183–4
Leek, 33, 200, 210, 229–30
Leek branch, 33, 200, 210, 230, 326–7
Lees, Abraham, engineer, 74, 77
Leggers, 112, 197
Leicester, 168, 204, 211
Leicester line of canal, 293
Leominster Canal, 190
Lichfield, 20, 29, 36, 63, 70, 72, 95, 97
Lifford, 274 n.
Lifts, canal, 174, 176; Anderton, 226, 244, 292; Hugh's Bridge, 334; Ruabon, 174, 334; Tardebigge, 140–2, 334
Lightmoor, 237
Lilleshall (and Coy), 40–1, 150, 152–3, 159–60, 185, 237–9, 242, 251
Lime, carried on canals, etc., 27, 33, 39, 41, 92, 108, 113, 131, 163, 173, 178, 186–7, 192–3, 212, 241
Limekilns, 34, 105, 173, 178, 181, 192, 206, 208
Limestone, carried by road transport, 76, 190, 196; on canals, etc., 27, 33–4, 39, 41, 70, 73, 75–6, 79, 92, 94, 97, 100, 110–11, 113, 157, 163, 170, 173, 178, 181, 186–7, 192–3, 195–6, 200, 203–4, 206, 212, 223, 225, 230, 235, 241–2, 262; on tramroads, 34, 144, 157, 192, 229
Limeworks, 33, 41, 95, 98, 150, 168, 173, 238
Lincoln, 16, 223
Lincomb, 283, 289
Little Eaton, 201
Littleworth, 260

Liverpool, 15, 19–21, 23–4, 26, 31, 33, 36, 42, 44, 47, 86, 92–3, 129, 142, 167, 170, 178–9, 181–3, 185–8, 197, 202, 204–5, 222–3, 235–6, 239–40, 244–5, 247, 249, 262, 280, 292
Liverpool & Manchester Railway, 184, 195, 205
Llanfynydd, 174
Llangollen, 167, 178, 238
Llangollen branch, 166, 178, 242, 250, 330–1
Llanthony (Gloucester), 286, 288, 290
Llantisilio, 178, 242, 251
Llanymynech, 166–7, 170, 173, 178, 181, 189, 192
Llanymynech branch, 166, 168, 176, 189–90, 192, 235, 250, 330–1
Lloyd, Rev. E. R., promoter, 167
Lloyd, Sampson II, 17, 20
Llwynenion, 239
Loch, James, agent, 184, 232
Locks, 203, 230, 271–2, 275; Ashted, 88–9, 256–7; Aston, 88–9, 256–7; Beeston, 45, 179; Bentley, 256–7; Black Delph, 76, 256–7, 260–1; Blower's Green, 256–7, 261; Brades, 256–7; Bradley, 254–7, 318–9; Churchbridge, 132, 254–7, 279–80, 328–9; Curdworth, 256–7; Ellesmere Port, 169, 182–3; Essington, 94–6, 254–5; Farmer's Bridge, 88–9, 256–7; Frankton, 173; Gibson's, 256–7; Hazelhurst, 200; Minworth, 256–7; Ogley, 256–7, 261; Oldbury, 256–7, 264; Park Head, 76, 256–7; Perry Barr, 256–7; Radford, 130; Riders Green, 70, 72, 256–7; Rushall, 256–7; Smethwick, 70, 72, 88, 256–7; Sneyd, 94, 254–7; Spon Lane, 70, 254–7; Stanley, 34, 200; Stockton, 34, 200; Stourport, 49, 281; Stourton, 73, 103; Tardebigge, 140, 142–3; Thurlwood, 230; Tipton, 87, 256–7; Tipton Green, 88, 254–7, 318–9; Toll End, 88, 256–7, 318–9; Walsall, 99, 254–7, 262, 318–9; Wolverhampton, 64, 68, 256–7, 263, 279; Wordsley, 73, 103, 265–6. *See* Iron lock-gates
Locomotive towing, 241–2
Lodge Farm, 114, 256–7, 263–4
London, 16, 29–30, 53, 58, 60, 69, 83, 97, 102, 107, 109, 112, 115–6, 129, 131, 148, 178 n., 196, 203–4, 206, 212–4, 223, 274
London & Birmingham Canal project, 131
London & Birmingham Junction Canal project, 185

INDEX

London & Birmingham Railway, 86, 92–3, 186, 196, 223, 232, 234, 252–3, 258
London, Midland & Scottish Railway, 230, 249–51
London & North Western Railway, 224, 226, 232–42, 248–50, 252, 258, 260–3, 265, 271, 292
Longdon-on-Tern, 160–1, 171, 242, 251
Longport, 36, 202
Longton, 201–2
Lord Hay's branch, 95, 97, 254–5, 260, 263, 328–9
Loughborough Navigation, 225
Lowdon, John, engineer, 154–5
Lower Avon, *see* Avon
Lower Avon Navigation Trust, 270
Lower Lode (Severn), 126
Lower Mitton, 49
Lubstree wharf, 185, 239, 251
Ludlow, 58
Lydney, 149
Lydney Canal, 116

Mabson, John, canal lessee, 142, 144
McClean, J. R., contractor, 273
Macclesfield, 24, 27, 200, 210–2, 219, 221
Macclesfield Canal, 186–7, 197, 204–5, **210–14**, **219–20**, 221, 229, 292, 324–5, 335
Madeley (Salop), 66, 124, 153–4, 236–7, 251
Madeley (Staffs), 22, 24, 222
Maesbury, 249–50
Maisemore, 117, 286, 290
Malt, carried on canals, etc., 205, 212, 223
Manchester, 18–19, 21, 23–4, 32, 36, 38, 41, 53, 55, 142, 167, 181–2, 185–7, 197, 203–6, 210–3, 220–1, 223, 234, 280, 292
Manchester & Birmingham Junction Canal project, 187, 212–3, 221
Manchester & Birmingham Railway, 219, 224, 232, 234
Manchester & Salford Junction Canal, 224 n.
Manchester, Sheffield & Lincs Railway, 220 n.
Manchester Ship Canal, 226, 245, 247, 249, 278 n., 280
Manure, carried on canals, etc., 27, 35, 92, 131, 187. *See also* Lime
Market Drayton, 150, 177, 232
Marple, 200, 210–2, 220
Marston (T & M), 230
Marten, H. J., engineer, 280
Meal, carried on canals, etc., 39

Merchant Shipping Act (1914), 249
Meredith, John, canal clerk, 65
Merionethshire Canal project, 178 n.
Mersey River, 15, 18–19, 24, 26, 31, 42, 166–70, 178, 182–4, 186, 198, 205–6, 221–2, 228, 235–6, 239, 244–5, 247–9, 292
Mersey Carrying Co., 240
Mersey & Irwell Navigation, 224 n.
Mersey, Weaver & Northwich Carrying Co., 245
Mersey, Weaver & Ship Canal Carrying Co., 245
Mid & S.E. Cheshire Water Board, 251
Middleport, 202
Middlewich, 22, 31–3, 35–6, 42–4, 167, 181, 187, 204, 212, 226, 232, 245
Middlewich–Altrincham Canal project, *see* Manchester & B'ham Junc. Canal
Middlewich branch, 181–2, 185, 204, 221, 235–7, 239, 241, 244, 330–1
Midland Railway, 263, 271, 273, 274 n., 280
Minworth, 256–7
Mills, on navigable rivers, 16, 59, 192
Mills, Samuel, committeeman, 184
Milton, 230
Milton, Thomas, lessee, 147
Moat, 256–7
Moat Colliery Co., 130
Molineux, C. H., committeeman, 184
Molineux, George, promoter, 95
Monmouthshire Canal, 119, 122
Montgomery, 190
Montgomeryshire Canal, 166, 170, 178, 184, **189–96**, 238, 242, **250**, 335; Eastern Branch, 166, 181, 193–6, 232–3, 330–1; Western Branch, 166, 193–6, 232–3, 324–5
Monway branch, 254–5, 318–9
Moon, engineer, 44
Moorcroft Junction, 85
Morris, Thomas, engineer, 44
Mount Manisty, 239
Muxton, 238
Mylne, Robert, engineer, 54–5

Nantwich, 22, 42, 44, 130, 163, 167, 170, 181, 184–6, 198, 206, 232, 235
Navigation Levels, 21, 40, 150, 152–3
Neachells branch, 254–5, 318–9
Neptune, trow, 118
Netherlands, 19
Netherpool, *see* Ellesmere Port
Netherton, 84, 106–7, 111–2, 322–3. *See also* Tunnels
Newark, 223
Newbold-on-Avon, 260

346 INDEX

Newcastle-under-Lyme, 20, 23, 27, 40, 206, 208, 210, 217–9
Newcastle-under-Lyme Canal, **206–10, 217–19**, 225, 324–5
Newcastle-under-Lyme Junction Canal, 198, **206–10, 217–8**, 324–5
Newhall, 64, 66, 68, 71, 254–5, 318–9
New Marton, 173, 242
Newport (Mon.), 117, 120, 122
Newport (Salop), 41, 116, 164, 184, 232, 251
Newport branch, 125, 150, 161, 163–4, 185–7, 239, 250–1, 320–1
Newtown, 166, 189, 192–6, 231–2, 234, 238, 250–1
Norbury (Cheshire), 210
Norbury (Salop), 185
North Staffordshire Conference, 245
North Staffordshire Railway, 217–226, 229, 232, 236, 243–5, 292
North Staffordshire Railway & Canal Carrying Co., 223, 270
Northampton, 168
Northgate (Chester), 43
Northwich, 19, 24, 32, 35–6, 42, 210
Norton (B.C.N.), 201, 254–5, 260, 328–9
Norton Bridge, 221, 232–3
Norton Priory, 32
Nottingham, 16, 197, 204, 211–2, 293
Nottingham Canal, 292

Oak Farm, 104–6, 267
Oakamoor, 201
Oakengates, 151–2, 154, 159, 237
Ocker Hill, 256–7
Ocker Hill (and Tunnel) branch, 65, 68, 70, 254–5, 318–9
Offenham, 270
Ogley, 256–7, 261, 263
Oil, carried on canals, etc., 290
Old Park works, 157
Old Wharf branch, 254–5
Oldbury (Glos), 117
Oldbury (Worcs), 64, 84, 88, 106–7, 113, 256–7
Oldbury Loop Canal, 254–5, 318–9
Oldknow, Samuel, shareholder, 211
Oozell's Street branch, 68, 254–5
Oswestry, 167, 190, 232, 236, 238
Oswestry, Ellesmere & Whitchurch Railway, 238
Oswestry & Newtown Railway, 238
Otherton, 93
Oulton, William, carrier, 240
Outram, Benjamin, engineer, 139, 162, 172, 200, 210
Overton, 167
Owen, William Mostyn, promoter, 167
Oxford, 54, 83, 136, 197–8, 213
Oxford Canal, 30, 49, 54, 70–1, 103, 138, 145, 197, 202, 260, 276, 291
Oxford, Worcester & Wolverhampton Railway, 253, 258, 264–7, 269, 271–2, 283, 286
Oxley, 267

Paget, Lord, *see* Uxbridge, Earl of
Park Head, 76, 113, 256–7, 260
Parker branch, 254–5, 320–1
Partridge Nest, 208
Partridge, William, carrier, 278
Passenger carrying on canals, etc., 44–5, 118, 140, 169–70, 179, 188, 219, 242, 249, 252, 290
Pave Lane, 40, 150
Peak Forest Canal, 200, 202, 204, 210–4, 219–21
Peates, millers, 249–50
Pelsall, 95, 260
Penk River, 130
Penkridge, 49, 93, 97
Pensnett Canal, **105**, 254–5, **263**, 322–3
Pensnett Chase, 73–4, 76
Pensnett Railway, 132
Peoploe, Dr. Samuel, 43
Perrotts, Avon Navigation owners, 56, 137, 147
Perry, James, promoter, 28, 50, 53
Perry Barr, 89–90, 93, 256–7
Perry Well, 256–7
Pershore, 270
Phillipps, Douglas, railway manager, 226, 228
Pickering, Exuperius, inventor, etc., 174; jun., 176
Pickfords, carriers, 118, 130, 142, 213, 221
Pidcock, John, promoter, 74
Pinkerton, John, contractor, 72, 77
Pitchcroft, 41
Pitt, William, engineer, 96
Planes, *see* Inclined Planes
Plas Kynaston, 166, 174, 176
Plas Kynaston Canal, **175–6, 243**, 330–1
Plas Madoc, 176
Pleasure boating, 23, 51, 220, 251, 266, 270, 280–1, 290, 293–4
Plymouth, Earl of, promoter, 59
Pontcysyllte, *see* Aqueduct, Tramroad
Pool Dam (Newcastle), 217–9
Pool Quay, 192, 238
Poor, The, affected by canals, 64, 85, 201–2
Port Vale, 202
Porthywaen, 189–90, 192
Potter, James, engineer, 203

INDEX 347

Potteries, The, 15 et seq., 44, 53, 186, 198, 201-2, 205, 212, 221-2, 226, 228, 230, 236, 241, 244-5, 247
Potteries Railway, 217
Pottery, carried by coasting trade, 15; by road transport, 15; on canals, etc., 15-16, 35-6, 39, 42, 53, 75, 205-6, 222, 225, 244, 247
Pottery clay and stone, carried by coasting trade, 15; by road transport, 15; on canals, etc., 15, 36, 39, 100, 205-6, 225, 244-5, 247
Pottery works, 15, 27, 158, 198
Potts, Charles, solicitor, 167
Powell, Col. J. Kynaston, promoter, 167
Powick Bridge, 59
Powis, Earl of, 167, 184, 192, 196, 232, 234, 236. See also Clive, Lord
Pownall, Robert, engineer, 22
Poynton, 210
Pratt, Isaac, committeeman, 77, 79, 100, 138
Prees branch, 166, 177, 250, 330-1
Preesgwyn, 243
Preston (Salop), 126
Preston Brook, 26-7, 31-3, 86, 204, 212-13, 221-2, 226, 228-9, 244
Priddey, John, engineer, 60-1
Proof House, 256-7
Pugh, David, landowner, 195
Pugh, William, shareholder, 194-5
Pulford, 168, 174

Quarries, 33-4, 38, 41, 76, 79-80, 95, 97-8, 110, 144, 148, 166, 170, 174, 176, 181, 189-90, 192, 196, 201, 225, 229
Quina Brook, 166, 177-8

Raby, Alexander, 113
Radford, 130
Railway-canal interchange facilities, 222, 236, 241, 258, 260, 263, 265, 279, 292
Railway & Canal Traffic Act (1888), 228, 244, 262, 265, 280, 289
Railway Commissioners, 224, 269
Railways Act (1921), 250
Railways, Horse, see Tramroads
Randal, inventor, 30
Rastrick, J. U., engineer, 103-5, 132
Rathbone family, 152-3
Rating of canals, 144
Redditch, 140, 270, 272
Regent's Canal, 203, 293
Registration (Barges) Act (1795), 117
Rennie, John, engineer, 141, 174, 201, 203
Rennie, Sir John, engineer, 185

Reservoirs, 33, 54, 77, 131, 140, 142, 174; Belvide, 186-7; Bittall, 146; Bunbury, 44-5; Cannock, 70, 96, 256-7, 261, 263-4; Cofton, 142; Gad's Green, 79, 101, 256-7; King's Norton, 142; Knighton, 186; Knipersley, 203; Lodge Farm, 114, 256-7, 263-4; Pensnett Chase, 73-4, 76, 105; Smethwick, 70, 90; Sneyd, 96, 256-7, 263-4; Rotton Park, 70, 87, 256-7, 263-4; Rudyard, 200, 210; Titford, 70, 256-7, 264
Reynolds, family, 153
Reynolds, Joseph, ironmaster, 152, 160
Reynolds, Richard, ironmaster, 44, 124, 150-2
Reynolds, William, ironmaster, 151-4, 160-4, 171 n.
Rhiw River, 190, 192
Rhodes, engineer, 119
Rhos, 243
Ricardo, J. L., railway chairman, 220, 224-5
Richardson, William, engineer, 105
Rickford, William, committeeman, 184
Riders Green, 70-2, 256-7
Ridgacre branch, 254-5, 318-9
Roads, 27, 31, 33, 36, 92, 159, 187, 190, 196, 291
Road transport, 15, 18, 31, 38, 44, 63, 72, 102-3, 130, 134-6, 140, 143, 147-8, 159-60, 165, 173, 181, 192, 205, 250, 264, 266, 271, 293-4
Roberts, Charles, mine agent, 109, 208
Roberts, W. A., solicitor, 106-7, 133-4
Rocester, 201
Rode Heath, 230
Roebuck, John, manufacturer, 20
Rolt, L. T. C., author, 186, 249
Rope (or chain) haulage of boats, 228, 284
Rotton Park, 70, 87, 256-7, 263-4
Rotton Park loop, 254-5
Rowland, Edward, inventor, 174
Rowley Regis, 88, 107
Royal Commission on Canals, 228-9, 262, 274, 289
Ruabon, 166-8, 173-4, 176, 178, 181, 235-6, 238
Rudyard, see Reservoirs
Rufford, Francis (Belbroughton), 266
Rufford, Francis (Prescot), 105, 266 n.
Rugeley, 33
Runcorn, 23-4, 26-7, 31-2, 42, 44, 93, 205, 244, 292
Runcorn & Weston Canal, 224 n.
Rushall Canal, 89, 99, 252, 256-7, 261, 328-9

348 INDEX

Sabrina, steam tug, 118
St. Columb Canal, 152
St. Helen's Canal, 23
Sale Moor, 19
Salford Bridge, 89, 256-7
Salt, carried by road transport, 15, 18, 271; on canals, etc., 15, 18-19, 31, 35, 39, 42, 60, 121, 135, 143, 145, 204, **223**, 232, 244, 270-1, 284, 289
Salt duties, 135, 145
Salt works (and Coys), 17-18, 36, 44-5, 59-60, 122, 135, 144, 230, 272, 275
Saltersford, 19, 22, 32, 228
Saltney, 47, 236
Saltney Canal, *see* Glynne's, Sir John, Canal
Salwarpe, 61
Salwarpe River, **59-60**, 61, 272, 316-7
Sand, carried on canals, etc., 92, 114, 250, 267, 279, 289
Sandbach, 31, 229
Sandhills branch, 104-5, 326-7
Sandys, William, engineer, 56, 58
Sankey Brook, *see* St. Helen's Canal
Saxon's Lode, 121
Say, William, promoter, 56
Scotland, 214
Sedgley, 104
Selly Oak, 83, 101-2, 106-7, 111, 113, 129, 137, 139, 143, 256-7
Severn Barrage, 290
Severn Bridge, 288
Severn & Canal Carrying Co., 278, 281, 289
Severn Carrying Co., 290
Severn Commission, 115, 122, 124, 146, 278, 280-90
Severn Horse Towing Path Co. (Bewdley-Coalbrookdale), 55, 124-5, 287, 314-5
Severn Horse Towing Path Extension Co. (Bewdley-Worcester), 125, 280, 286, 314-5
Severn Improvement Association, 122
Severn Improvement Co., 120-2
Severn Navigation Co., 119, 121
Severn River, 15, **17-18**, 21-2, 24, 26, 28, 49, 51, **53-5**, 56, 58, 60, 67, 73-4, 79, 83-4, 102-4, 107, 109, 112, **115-27**, 128-9, 135, 137-8, 141-8, 151-3, 157, 159-60, 166, 187, 194, 232, 262, 269, 271-2, 276-81, **282-90**, 293, 314-5
Severn Valley Railway, 287
Severn & Wye tramroad, *see* Tramroad
Shaftesbury, Lord, 132, 144
Shardlow, 15 n., 36, 51, 226
Sharp, James, 51, 69
Sharpness, 117, 286, 288

Sharpness New Docks, etc. Co., 137, 274-5, 278, 280, 282, 288
Sheffield, 211
Sheffield, Ashton & Manchester Railway, 220
Shelmore, 186
Sherratt, Thomas, carrier, 140
Sheriff, James, surveyor, 106
Shelton, 202
Shobnall, 198
Short Heath branch, 254-5, 328-9
Shortwood tunnel, *see* Tunnels
Shotton, 48, 251
Shrewsbury, 17, 22, 28, 54, 124-5, 150, 159-60, 162-8, 173-4, 176, 178, 185-6, 196, 231-4, 236, 238, 242, 250-3, 287-8
Shrewsbury & Birmingham Railway, 223, 233, 237, 252-3
Shrewsbury Canal, 126, 151, 153 n., **159-65**, 171-2, 184-5, **232-3**, 238, 242, **250-1**, 324-5, 333-5
Shrewsbury & Chester Railway, 236
Shrewsbury-Coalbrookdale Horse Towing Path Co., 125-6, 287-8, 314-5
Shrewsbury, Earl of, 33, 59
Shrewsbury & Trent Valley Railway, 232-3
Shrewsbury, Wolverhampton, etc. Railway, 234, 252
Shropshire Canal, 41, 116, **152-9**, 160, 162, 164, 187, 232, **233**, **237-8**, **250-1**, 324-5, 333
Shropshire Union Railway, 233-4, 238, 242
Shropshire Union Railways & Canal Co., 167, 189, 192, 196, 226, 229, **231-51**, 277, 279-80, 292-4
Shugborough, 30, 51
Shut End, 103-4
Shutt End Railway, 103-5, 132
Silk mills, 211
Silverdale, 208, 217, 219
Silverdale & Newcastle Railway, 217-8
Simcock, Samuel, engineer, 28, 49, 65, 69
Simpson, John, contractor, 173, 190
Skey, Robert, canal manager, 237, 239
Skey, Samuel, canal manager, 188
Slag, carried on canals, etc., 262
Slates, carried on canals, etc., 35, 70, 121, 192, 204; on tramroads, 242-3
Small, Dr. William, promoter, 64
Smallbridge, 202
Smeaton, John, engineer, 16, 19-20, 26, 72
Smethwick, 64-5, 68, 70, 72, 83, 87-8, 90, 253, 256-7

INDEX 349

Smyth, Thomas, promoter, 58-9
Snape, John, surveyor, 77, 106, 138
Snedshill, 153-4, 237
Sneyd, 84, 94, 96-7, 254-7, 263-4
Sneyd, Edward, committeeman, 29
Sneyd, Ralph, ironmaster, 217-8
Soho branch, 254-5
Somers, Lord, 134
Somersetshire Coal Canal, 41
South Staffordshire Mine Drainage Commissioners, 263-4
South Staffordshire Railway, 279
Southall Bank (Salop), 153, 155
Sow River, 130
Sowerby, Edward, canal-owner, 282
Sparrow, John, canal clerk, 23, 27
Speedwell Level, 40
Spelter works, 243
Spon Lane, 70, 241, 254-7
Spooner, Isaac, sen., 106; jun., 142
Stafford, 22, 93, 130, 226, 232-4
Stafford branch, 130, 280
Stafford, Marquess of, 41, 130, 150, 153, 160, 184-5
Stafford's, Marquess of, Canal, *see* Donnington Wood Canal
Staffordshire Potteries Railway project, 221
Staffordshire & Worcestershire Canal, **28**, 38, **49-55**, 58, 63-5, 67-8, 73-6, 85-6, 92-3, 95, 97-8, 102-5, 107, 112, 115, 119, 121-2, 124-5, **128-33**, 135-6, 142, 163, 166-7, 181, 183-6, 188, 204, 213, 221, 229, 231, 241, 270, **276-81**, 282-3, 285-8, 291, 293, 326-7, 335
Staffordshire & Worcestershire Canal Society, 266
Stamford, Earl of, 33, 73
Stanford-on-Teme, 59
Stanhope, Lord, 203
Stanley, 34, 200, 230
Stanlow, 251
Stansty, 174
Steamboats and tugs, 118, 167, 183, 188, 212, 219, 226, 231, 240-1, 247, 249, 274, 278-9, 284-6, 289
Steam engines, 70, 77, 89-90, 108, 112, 114, 143, 154-5, 157, 162, 169, 194
Stephenson, George, engineer, 209
Stephenson, Robert, engineer, 196, 232-3
Stewponey, 51
Stirchley, 154
Stockport, 24, 27, 210
Stockton, 34, 200
Stoke-on-Trent, 15, 19-20, 31, 34, 200-2, 206, 217, 219-20, 226, 230
Stoke Works, 135, 145, 270-1

Stone, 30, 35, 150, 213, 221, 232
Stone, carried by road transport, 192; on canals, etc., 27, 33, 41, 60, 66, 70, 92, 114, 187, 192, 204, 220, 241, 243; on tramroads, 243
Stony Stratford, 168
Stour (Worcs) River, 18, **58**, 59, 74, 280, 316-7
Stourbridge, 18, 53-5, 58, 73-4, 101, 104, 112, 115, 129, 135, 264-5, 280
Stourbridge Canal, 51, 53, 58, 62, **73-5**, 76-7, 83, **100-3**, 104-7, 113-15, 122, 129, 137-8, 142, 184, 241, 264-6, 267, 276-7, 326-7
Stourbridge Extension Canal, 100, 102, **103-6**, 132, 264-5, **266-8**, 326-7
Stourbridge, W'ton & B'ham Junction Canal project, 104, 106, 111
Stourbridge-Worcester Canal project, 54, 62, 75, 133, 138
Stourport, 28 n., 38, 49-55, 74-5, 100, 102, 115-7, 119, 121-2, 124, 128, 135, 140, 142, 249, 253, 269, 279, 281-2, 285, 288-90
Stourton, 49, 73, 75, 103, 105, 256-7
Stow Heath, 256-7
Stratford-upon-Avon, 56, 73, 112, 146-7, 269
Stratford-upon-Avon Canal, 83, 106, 108-9, 112-14, 138-9, 142-3, 145-7, 184, 266, 269, 272, 292
Stratford & Moreton Tramway, 109, 114, 267
Streethay, 72
Stretford, 19
Strickland, A. A. de L., canal-owner, 282
Stroud, 53, 115, 117
Stroudwater Navigation, 53, 115, 117, 126, 280
Subsidence, 111, 237-8, 260, 263, 272
Sunday work, 128
Sutherland, Duke of, 41, 163, 232, 239, 251
Sutherland's, Duke of, Canal, *see* Donnington Wood Canal
Sutton Coldfield, 95
Sutton wharf (Severn), 159
Swarkestone, 229
Sweden, 17

Tame River, 19, 71, 89, 96
Tame Valley Canal, 89, 94, 99, 187, 252, 261, 320-1
Tamworth, 19-20, 63, 71, 96
Tar, carried on canals, etc., 251
'Tar Tunnel', 152-3
Tardebigge, 134-5, 139-44, 272, 274
Tattenhall, 166

Taylor, John, banker, 20
Taylor, Joseph, engineer, 44
Tean River, 201
Telford, Thomas, engineer, 36, 86-7, 118, 154, 157, 160-2, 169-72, 174, 179, 182-6, 203, 211
Teme River, 58-9
Tettenhall-Autherley Canal project, 131, 186
Tewkesbury, 17-18, 53, 56, 117-18, 121, 135, 145, 147-8, 269, 271, 284-5, 287, 290
Tewkesbury-Cheltenham Canal project, 116, 148
Tewkesbury-Winchcombe Canal project, 116
Textiles, carried on canals, etc., 18, 53, 212
Thames & Medway Canal, 260
Thames River, 21, 30, 53, 74, 115, 136, 197
Thames & Severn Canal, 53-4, 74, 79, 115-7, 137 n., 280, 288
Thurlwood, 230
Tilstock Park, 177-8
Timber, carried by road transport, 192; on canals, etc., 15, 39, 53, 59, 66, 70, 121, 178, 182, 192, 195, 204, 223, 250, 289-90
Timmins, Benjamin, engineer, 108
Tinplate works, 265
Tipton, 64, 68, 76, 79, 87-9, 110, 112-3, 241, 254-8, 264
Titford, 70, 88, 90, 256-7, 264
Titford branch, 254-5, 261, 318-9
Tirley, 117
Titton Brook, 28
Toll End, 88, 256-7
Toll End branch, 254-5
Tolls, compensation, 76, 79, 83-6, 131-3, 136, 146, 181, 184-6, 204, 213, 221, 236, 244, 277, 293
Tolls, through, 280, 289, 293
Tomes, John, committeeman, 184
Towing, 16, 18, 67, 118, 183, 188, 226, 228, 240, 247, 278. *See also* Electric traction, Locomotive towing, Rope haulage, Steam tugs
Towing paths, 18-19, 22, 54-6, 59, 86-7, 117, 124-7, 134, 143, 163, 203, 226, 260, 286-8, 314-5
Townshend, Benjamin, engineer, 105
Traders (N.S.) Carrying Co., 244
Tramroads, horse, 134, 139, 151, 193, 208, 258; Anderton, 36; Ashby Canal, 33; Blisworth, 115; Bullo Pill, 116, 149; Caldon, 34, 201, 229; Cheadle, 201; Cheslyn Hay, 132-3, 279; Coalbrookdale area, 153, 157, 159; Donnington Wood-Severn, 153, 159; Dudley Canal Extension area, 114; Ellesmere Port, 239-40, 247; Foxley, 201; Gloucester & Cheltenham, 148-9; Glyn Valley, 243; Himbleton, 144; Littleworth, 260; Llanymynech, 192; Madeley area, 154; Pontcysyllte, 176, 181, 239, 242-3; Porthywaen, 190; Severn & Wye, 116, 135, 149; Shutt End, 103, 132; Stafford, 130; Stoke-on-Trent, 201-2; Stour River, 58; Stourbridge Canal, 102-3, 105; Stratford & Moreton, 109, 114; Tardebigge, 144; Wyrley Bank, 97
Trench, 160-1, 164. *See also* Inclined planes
Trent (Burton) Navigation, 15-17, 20, 38, 197-8
Trent Canal project, 197
Trent & Mersey Canal, 15, 19-39, 40, 42-5, 49-50, 60, 63, 70-2, 93-4, 150, 167, 181, 184-6, 197-206, 208, 210-3, 217-20, 221-30, 236, 276-7, 280, 291-2, 326-7, 334-5
Trent River, 15-17, 19, 22-4, 27, 31 n., 32-3, 38, 54, 71, 77, 197-8, 204, 226, 229, 292-3
Trent Valley Railway, 221, 223, 232
Trentham, 219
Trevalyn, 168
Trevor, 166, 176, 178, 181, 235
Trows, 18, 53, 117-8, 282, 284
Trubshaw, Charles, engineer, 218
Trye, C. B., committeeman, 148
Tub-boats, 33, 40, 58, 116, 151 *et seq.*, 187, 241
Tunnels, canal, 65, 75, 104, 107, 168-9, 198; Alton, 201; Armitage, 32; Ashted, 256-7; Barnton, 32-3, 228, 334; Berwick, 160, 163-4, 334; Blisworth, 116; Brettell Lane, 73; Brewin's, 114, 261; Chirk, 168, 173, 243; Cookley, 49; Coseley, 88, 256-7, 260; Cowley, 186; Curdworth, 256-7; Dudley, 74-80, 83, 100, 104-6, 110-12, 128, 135-7, 256-7, 262-3, 334; Dudley & Ward's, Lord, 76-8; Dunhampstead, 143-4; Edgbaston, 143; Ellesmere, 177; Froghall, 34; Gosty Hill, 107, 256-7, 334; Harecastle (old), 20, 24, 27, 29-32, 35, 51, 111, 197, 203, 334; Harecastle (new), 184, 203, 226, 228, 334; Ketley, 151; Lappal, 106-9, 111-13, 115, 128, 256-7, 263, 334; Leek, 200; Netherton, 106, 113, 254-7, 260-1, 263, 322-3, 334; Newbold, 260; Oakengates, 154; Ocker Hill, 254-5, 318-9; Preston

Brook, 31, 33, 228, 334; Saltersford, 32-3, 228; Shortwood, 140, 143, 274, 334; Snedshill, 154, 237; Stirchley, 154; Stourton, 49; Strood, 260; Tardebigge, 139-41, 143, 274, 334; West Hill, 139, 143, 274, 334; Whitehouses, 173. *See also* 'Tar Tunnel'.
Tunnels and Shafts, Castlefield, 41; Coalbrookdale, 41, 157; Hugh's Bridge, 41, 334
Turner, Joseph, engineer, 167
Turner, William, engineer, 168-70
Two Lock line, 254-7, 260-1, 263, 322-3
Tyrley, 186
Tyrone Canal, 152

Underhill, William, engineer, 108
Union branch, 254-5, 318-9.
Union (Roway) branch, 254-5, 320-1
Upper Avon, *see* Avon
Upper Lode (Severn), 285, 287, 289
Upton, 17-18, 55, 119, 122, 126, 283-5
Upton Snodsbury, 144
Uttoxeter, 198, 200-1, 221
Uttoxeter branch, 200-1, 223, 326-7
Uxbridge, Earl of, 16-17, 47

Varley, James, contractor, 170, 172
Vernon, Henry, coalowner, 95, 97, 132
Vron, 168, 173
Vyrnwy River, 190, 192

Walker, James, engineer, 282, 284
Walsall, 70-1, 85, 93-9, 253-4, 318-9
Walsall Canal project, 85
Walsall-Fradley Canal project, 70
Wappenshall, 160-1, 164, 185, 187, 235-6
Ward, Lord, 258, 260
Ward's, Lord, branch, 76-9, 254-5, 318-9
Wardle branch, 181, 204, 213, 221, 229, 236, 244, 326-7
Warehouses, 16-17, 33, 36, 53, 112, 143, 148, 154, 181-3, 188, 201-3, 224, 235, 239, 245, 247, 281
Warrington, 93, 186
Warwick, 70
Warwick & Birmingham Canal, 83-6, 88-9, 92, 94, 103, 109, 112, 184, 276
Warwick line of canal, 89, 213, 293
Warwick & Napton Canal, 83, 103, 184, 276
Water, sale by canal coys, etc., 98, 131, 187, 220, 251, 266, 279, 290, 293-4
Water, supplies to canals, etc., 16, 20, 33, 45, 54, 70, 83-4, 90, 94, 96, 101, 131-2, 137, 140-1, 143, 150, 153, 169, 177-8,

184, 187, 194, 200, 203, 252, 263-6, 277, 279
Waterhouses, 229
Watt, James, sen., engineer, 76-7, 154
Watt, James, jun., 77, 184
Weaver River, 15, 18-20, 21 n., 22-4, 26-7, 31-2, 35-6, 38, 42, 226, 229, 243-4, 280, 292
Weaver Carrying Co., 244
Webb, Francis W., engineer, 241
Wedgwood family, 21-2, 208
Wedgwood, Godfrey, 244
Wedgwood, Josiah, 15, 19-24, 26-7, 29-33, 38, 64
Wednesbury, 65, 70, 88-9, 99
Wednesbury branch, 64-5, 68, 71, 318-9
Wellington, 116, 177, 232-3, 236
Wellington & Severn Junction Railway, 236
Welshpool, 17, 166, 189-90, 192, 232, 238, 284, 288
Wem, 167, 178, 232, 242
Wepre, 47-8
West Birmingham Railway & Canal Co., 273
West Bromwich, 262
West Hill tunnel, *see* Tunnels
West Midland Railway, 267, 269, 273
Weston, Samuel, engineer, 43-4
Weston branch, 176, 178, 242, 250
Weston Lullingfields, 163, 166, 168, 173-4
Wheelock, 44
Wheelock River, 230
Whieldon, Sampson, quarry lessee, 33
Whitby Wharf (Locks), *see* Ellesmere Port
Whitchurch, 166-8, 176 n., 177-8, 232
Whitchurch branch, 166, 169, 177-8 250, 330-1
Whittington Brook, 92, 256-7
Whitworth, Sir Richard, 22, 24, 26-9, 150
Whitworth, Robert, engineer, 53, 65, 73-4, 79, 108, 198
Whixall Moss, 177
Wilden ironworks, 280
Wilden Ferry, 15-17, 19-20, 22, 26-7
Wilkinson, John, ironmaster, 47, 98, 153-4, 160 171 n.
Wilkinson, Joseph, promoter, 65
Willenhall, 93-4
Willenhall branch, 254-5, 318-9
Williams, Alfred Leader, 278
Williams, Edward Leader, engineer, 122, 278, 284, 286
Williams, Sir Edward Leader, engineer, 278 n.

INDEX

Williams, Henry, engineer, 154–5, 164
Williams, John, engineer, 194
Willington, 15, 222
Willmore Bridge, 41
Wilson, John, contractor, 185
Wilson, W., contractor, 185
Winchcombe, 116–7
Windmill, *see* Inclined Planes
Windmill End, 107, 114
Windsor, Baroness, 272
Windsor, Lord, 56, 58–60
Winsford, 15, 18, 22, 24, 35, 226
Wirral line, 168–70, 176–8, 182, 198, 236
Witham River, 16
Withymoor branch, 114, 254–5, 322–3
Witton Bridge, 18, 24, 36
Witton Brook, 18–19, 24
Wolseley Bridge, 26, 28, 51
Wolverhampton, 28, 41, 49–51, 55, 63–4, 68, 75, 84–6, 88, 90, 93–7, 104, 107, 116, 226, 231–5, 249, 252–3, 256–8, 263, 267, 274, 279–80
Wolverton, 47
Wombridge, Canal, **151**, 153 n., 160, 328–9
Woodhouse, John, engineer, 138, 140–2
Wood-pulp, carried on canals, etc., 290
Woofferton, 190
Wool, carried on canals, etc., 18
Worcester, 17–18, 22, 51, 54–6, 58, 61–2, 73, 75, 83, 101–2, 104, 115, 117–22, 124–6, 129, 135–6, 138–40, 142–4, 160, 231–4, 269–70, 274, 276, 278, 283, 287–90

Worcester Bar, 85–6, 89, 113, 137, 139, 142, 146, 253, 256–7
Worcester & Birmingham Canal, 75, 77, 83–6, 88–9, 92, 100–1, 106–7, 109, 112–5, 118–22, 124, 128–9, 133–4, **135–46**, 147, 149, 184, 223, 253, 265, 269, **270–76**, 278, 281–3, 285, 288, 328–9, 334
Worcester & Gloucester Union Canal project, 118, 144
Wordsley, 73. *See also* Locks
Worleston, 241
Worsley, 19, 21, 40–1
Worthington & Gilbert, carriers, 38
Wren's Nest branch, 78–9
Wrexham, 168, 174, 178, 236, 243
Wribbenhall, 17, 53
Wrinehill, 24
Wrockwardine Wood, 151–5, 237
Wyrley Bank, 84, 132, 260
Wyrley Bank branch, 93–4, 96–7, 254–5, 260–1, 263, 328–9
Wyrley & Essington Canal, 70, 84, 86, 89, 91, 93, **94–9**, 111, 131–2, 184, 187, 252, 260, 263, 328–9

Yarranton, Andrew, engineer, 55–6, 58–9
Yarranton, Robert, engineer, 58
Young, George, surveyor, 54, 160

Zinc, carried on canals, etc., 290